GATH'S LITERARY WORK AND FOLK

AND OTHER

SELECTED WRITINGS

OF

GEORGE ALFRED TOWNSEND

JERRY SHIELDS

GATH'S LITERARY WORK AND FOLK
and Other Selected Writings of George Alfred Townsend

by Jerry Shields

Copyright ©1996
Delaware Heritage Press

All rights reserved.

No part of this publication may be reproduced or transmitted in any form or by any means, electronic or mechanical, including photocopy, recording, or any information storage and retrieval system, without permission in writing from the publisher.

A DELAWARE HERITAGE PRESS BOOK

First Printing, April 1996

ISBN: 0-924117-06-0

Library of Congress Catalog Card Number: 96-83177

The Delaware Heritage Commission
Carvel State Office Building
820 North French Street, 4th Floor
Wilmington, DE 19801

ACKNOWLEDGEMENTS

Many people have been helpful as this project has advanced, and I would like to express my appreciation to all of them. First, to Executive Director Deborah Haskell and the Publication Committee—Richard Carter, Dan Griffith and Reba Hollingsworth—of the Delaware Heritage Commission. Also to Lynda Cook of DHC for her help on typing and formatting. Thanks also to the McKinstry Committe for helping fund the project.

To John P. Reid, friend indeed, who got me involved in the first place, and to Ruthanna Hindes, Gath's first real biographer, who pointed me to the Maryland Archives. To Dr. John Munroe, who has been a steady source of inspiration and encouragement for my delvings into Delaware's history. And to Leon deValinger, Jr., former State Archivist, whom I often call upon when needing help with a hard question. To Dr. Howard Row, who gave my transposition of Gath's literary memoir a first reading and offered valuable suggestions. To Casey O'Connor and Steve Newton at the PDQ desk of the Delaware Division of Libraries, who've retrieved many a dusty fact for me when I've needed it.

To staff members of the Maryland Archives, Delaware Archives, Historical Society of Delaware, Wilmington Institute Free Library, University of Delaware Library (especially Rebecca Johnson Melvin and John Hoffman), Dover Public Library (with very special thanks to Interlibrary Loan Desk staffer Peggy Prouse, for her aid in recovering works I thought I'd never find), Don Rydgren, curator of the Goodstay Center's Lincoln Collection, and other research facilities where I've gone in search of information.

To George Rhodes, a descendant of Gath's wife Bessie, for supplying me with copies of Gath's letters. To park rangers at Maryland's Gathland State Park.

And finally to my wife Jane, who has made it possible for me to take the time to do this.

Portrait of George Alfred Townsend in the collection of the *Historical Society of Delaware* painted when Townsend was about 40 years old. *Original portrait photographed by Steven N. Shields, 1995.*

GEORGE ALFRED TOWNSEND

who writes under the famous *nom de plume*, "Gath," is corpulent both in face and abdomen, and wears a fine specimen nose of the *genus* Wellington or Roman, has a low but broad forehead, a big head, a large mouth, and a double chin, and looks as if he knew what to do with a good dinner before letting it spoil. He seems about 45, without being gray, has a fondness for Panama hats and white vests in summer, and his clothes look as if they had been thrown on with a pitchfork. He is known everywhere in the newspaper world and before the American people. His style of writing is brilliant—corruscating and epigrammatic—remarkable not for poetical numbers and sentiments or rounded corners, but for sudden turns and happy hits, particularly characteristic of nobody but "Gath," and for quick transitions in description or assertion from what the reader expects to something the reader does not expect, but always very "pat." He is a ready and pleasant conversationalist, with a faculty of "drawing men out"; and, though he may say sharp things of a man today, he treats him tomorrow as if he had not skinned him the day before. He made his reputation as a correspondent during the war, and if there is anything for which, in his political writings, Mr. Townsend is particularly famous[,] it is the absolute accuracy of all his statements! He has written letters from Europe to the New York *Tribune*, contributed to the magazines and "written a book," or several of them, and some poems. He is now connected with the Cincinnati *Enquirer*. He is devoid of politics, but is a sort of a journalistic statesman.

Anonymous Contemporary of GATH

Dedication

To Ruthanna Hindes,

    who first broke trail and pointed out the way.

TABLE OF CONTENTS

Introduction
George Alfred Townsend: A Sketch of His Life 1
    by Jerry Shields.

GATH's Literary Work and Folk 49
    Previously unpublished memoir of Townsend
    written in his later years with extensive annotation
    by Jerry Shields.

Other Selected Writings by George Alfred Townsend
Two Days of Battle 117
    The Californian, c. 1865.
An American War Correspondent in England 129
    Harper's New Monthly Magazine, 1863.
The Life, Crime and Capture of J. Wilkes Booth 145
    Dick & Fitzgerald, Publishers, 1865.
The Life and Battles of Garibaldi 189
    American News Company, New York, 1867.
The Real Life of Abraham Lincoln: A Talk with Mr. Herndon 227
    New York: Publication Office, Bible House, 1867.
The Mormon Trials at Salt Lake City 241
    New York: American News Co., 1871.
John M. Clayton of Delaware 275
    Enquirer, New York. April 28, 1880.
    Enquirer, Washington. April 12, 1882.
Recollections and Reflections 313
    Lippincott's Monthly Magazine, November, 1886.
An Interviewer Interviewed: A Talk with GATH 325
    Lippincott's Monthly Magazine, November, 1891.
Hearing My Requiem 339
    Lippincott's Monthly Magazine, October, 1892.
Monticello and Its Preservation 349
    Gibson Bros, Washington, D.C., 1902.
Credits 374

INTRODUCTION

This book, while part of a long-term effort to gain greater recognition for Delaware writers and their works, had its genesis three years ago when John P. Reid, editor-publisher of *Collecting Delaware Books*, asked if I would write something on a lower-Delaware author for his newsletter.

I chose George Alfred Townsend since his book *The Entailed Hat* is probably the best-known novel ever written about the Delmarva Peninsula. I knew little else about "Gath," as he called himself, except that he had been born in Georgetown and won fame as a newspaper writer in Victorian times. But I was curious to learn more, and doing an article for John's newsletter seemed a good way to become better acquainted with his life and writings.

Little did I realize where the project would take me. As I compiled a bibliography of his published works, I realized three things: (1) he had written a great deal more than I'd realized, (2) several of his writings had never gotten into print, and (3) of the ones which had, nearly all are now rare and hard to find.

It was puzzling that a writer so famous in his own time could be so little-known in ours. But I summarized what I found into a brief biographical sketch and catalogued the books and pamphlets he was known to have written. Knowing my catalogue was incomplete, I called it a checklist rather than a bibliography, hoping to add to it later.

The article I produced, instead of satisfying my curiosity about Gath, only intensified it, since I now felt that much more remained to be done. This was heightened further when John Reid put me in contact with Ruthanna Hindes, who had written and published her master's thesis on Townsend half a century ago.

Ruthanna whetted my appetite by telling me that a cache of Townsend's papers now reposes at the Maryland Archives in Annapolis, and that, when she was working on her thesis, Gath's grandson, who then owned them, allowed her only limited access to these documents. A first trip to the Archives convinced me that much more of this Delaware writer's work than is presently known should be brought to light.

One item which early caught my attention was a manuscript titled "Gath's Literary Work and Folk," which Townsend, then old and sick, had penned shortly before his death. This had never been published, or even typed, as far as I know, and it presented a golden opportunity to get the great columnist's own thoughts about his literary output.

Contacting the Delaware Heritage Commission, I proposed transposing this work from Gath's handwriting, which fortunately is not difficult to read, to type, then annotating it to illuminate the many references made therein to various people, books, events, etc. The Commission agreed to help underwrite this work and publish it when finished.

Soon after, one member of the Commission who had a deep interest in Townsend suggested that, if a new book about him was to be done, it might as well include a representative sampling of his writings. This idea fit well with my own wish to revive Gath's writings and reputation, so I searched for other of his short works to put in.

What is contained here, then, is an expanded biographical sketch of Townsend (not complete enough to be properly called a biography), followed by "Gath's Literary Work and Folk" with my notes, plus a sampling of his works as a journalist and literary writer.

As a journalist, Townsend was a pioneer in the true sense of that word. He was one of the first and best war correspondents, going to the Civil War as a young man of 21 carrying a pen instead of a sword or gun. At the war's end, he made an early and major contribution to investigative journalism by reporting extensively on Lincoln's assassination and Booth's conspiracy.

Later he moved into political correspondence, writing from Washington for newspapers around the country. He became so famous at this that, around the turn of the century, a Cincinnati tobacco company marketed a "Gath" cigar, announcing it was naming this product "in honor of George Alfred Townsend, Esq. ... the greatest of living correspondents."

This announcement also called Gath "a versatile writer and author," which in fact he was. Over the years he had produced numerous poems, plays, short stories and novels in addition to his newspaper correspondence. His novel *The Entailed Hat* has served to keep his memory alive while most of his other writings, undeservedly, sank into obscurity.

As I was working to explicate "Gath's Literary Work and Folk" by providing notes for the many references to people and events mentioned therein, I was also retrieving other examples of Townsend's writings to include in this book. Several were exceptionally hard to find and obtain copies of, making me realize the truth of his own statement that interest in historical matters largely dies after a generation or two.

Gath's reputation today, faint though it is, has survived better than those of most Delaware writers. A broad effort should be made to rescue, preserve, disseminate, read and appreciate many of the works these persons created while they can still be found. A number are both quite rare and very fragile. If neglected, they will soon disappear entirely.

The selection of Gath's writings which follows the biographical sketch and annotated memoir has been chronologically arranged to offer examples encompassing a forty-year period of his career, 1862-1902. While he was writing both earlier and later than this, the samples are drawn from what may be considered his most productive years.

"Two Days of Battle" was written when he was a green young war correspondent not long out of high school. "An American War Correspondent in England" was done as a magazine piece soon after his return from Europe in 1864. "The Life, Crime and Capture of John Wilkes Booth" appeared as a series of newspaper articles even as the last events of Booth's conspiracy were playing themselves out.

A pair of newspaper-length biographies, "The Life and Battles of Garibaldi" and "The Real Life of Abraham Lincoln," feature two of Townsend's chief heroes from this period. Garibaldi was fighting to free Italy from French domination, Lincoln had been martyred after leading the struggle to preserve the union of states and rid the nation of slavery. To write the latter work, Townsend became one of the first Lincoln biographers to contact and interview the dead President's former law partner William Herndon.

An interest in the Utah Mormons as another oppressed people led to composition of "The Mormon Trials at Salt Lake City." A boyhood memory of attending a Newark speech by Delaware Senator John M. Clayton, plus fresh knowledge of how this former lawyer had earlier prosecuted the Patty Cannon gang of murderers and kidnappers inspired Gath to write a newspaper biography of Clayton.

Several reminiscences from near the end of his career follow. His "Recollections and Reflections" provides insights into his early and later days as a newspaperman. In "An Interviewer Interviewed," he tells how he became a writer in his teens. "Hearing My Requiem" recounts a close call he had while researching a newspaper series, "The Swamp Outlaws," later reprinted in softcover.

"Monticello and its Preservation after Jefferson's Death" reflects Townsend's love of visiting historic houses in order to "realize" their former occupants or see how later generations have treated their memories.

If there is a common theme in these works, and in his writings as a whole, it is Gath's concern that the ideals embodied in the United States Constitution and the minds of the founding fathers be carried out to the fullest extent possible. Townsend's own brand of patriotism was far more complex and better informed than those of most Americans then or now. In his work and in much of his spare time as well, he was constantly educating himself about various aspects of the country's history and political system.

He strongly believed, always, that the government should work fairly, for the good of all. Ever quick to jump in on the side of an underdog, yet too tolerant and empathetic to be rabidly partisan, Gath often let his political feelings dictate the tone and subject matter of his writings. He hated few things more than to see youthful idealism erode and go sour.

Two of his chief villains, if they can be called that, were Dr. Thomas Cooper and U.S. Supreme Court Chief Justice Roger Taney. Both were strong supporters of the Southern stand on slavery prior to the Civil War. What Townsend couldn't forgive them for, however, is that both, earlier in their lives, had taken vocal positions *against* slavery. In turning their coats as older men, they had betrayed their own ideals in his eyes.

He was too perceptive of human frailty to idealize his heroes very much. Everyone had weaknesses, he knew, and he tried to portray his characters as real people, not stereotypes, when writing either fact or fiction. He was also consistent in seeking reasons for why people behave as they do, which added depth and dimension to his portrayals. He was a realist in an increasingly sentimental age, a complex rather than a simple moralist.

Lacking a university education, he possessed more intellectual curiosity than many of his contemporaries who did. If this put him at a disadvantage, it was one which affected his style more than his substance. But his writing style, largely self-taught, I have found to be nearly always lively, vivid and immediate.

That is a judgment, though, which readers should make for themselves, and it is toward this end that the above-mentioned examples of his writings are included. I shall only add in conclusion that these examples are but a tiny fraction of Gath's works which need resurrecting. The book you hold is a small step in that direction.

About the Author:

Jerry Shields holds an AB and MA in Journalism from the University of North Carolina and a MA and a Ph.D in English from Duke University. An educator for many years and a Dover resident since 1972, he is co-author (with William Hoffman) of **Doctors on the New Frontier** *(Macmillan, 1981) and author of the* **Invisible Billionaire Daniel Ludwig** *(Houghton Mifflin, 1986). In addition to numerous periodical articles on a variety of other topics, he writes and speaks frequently about Delaware history and literature.*

The Reverend Stephen Townsend, a Methodist Preacher,
and his wife Mary Milbourne.
Courtesy of the University of Delaware Library, Newark, Delaware.

GEORGE ALFRED TOWNSEND: A SKETCH OF HIS LIFE

THE EARLY YEARS

That the man later known as "Gath" got his first glimpse of the world in Georgetown, Sussex County, Delaware, was due to his father's occupation. The Reverend Stephen Townsend, raised a Quaker, had converted to Methodism as a young man, becoming a minister of that faith in 1834. Being a Methodist preacher meant moving periodically, since John Wesley, the denomination's chief founder, had decreed decades earlier that its pastors serve a given community for no more than three years. Stephen Townsend was completing an appointment in the Georgetown area when, on January 30, 1841, a son was born to his wife Mary and christened George Alfred.

Alfred, as they usually called him, was the fourth child born to the couple. The first two, Julia Ann Wesley and George Edwin, had not survived infancy. A third, Stephen Emory, born December, 1835, did thrive, and was past five when Alfred came.

The house the Townsends were inhabiting was a modest two-story frame dwelling near the circle marking Georgetown's center and passing by the Sussex County Courthouse. An earlier courthouse had stood on the site when the county seat was moved there in the early 1790s from Lewes (vulnerable to attacks by water and not centrally located) to the middle of the county. Land being bought for that purpose, a new courthouse and jail were soon erected, giving Georgetown its genesis. Few of those early buildings still stand, and the house the Townsends lived in at the time of Alfred's birth was torn down around 1885.

They had not remained there long. At the annual Methodist Conference that year, Stephen Townsend had been appointed to a circuit near Salisbury, Maryland, so, when Alfred was three months old, the family packed its belongings into a wagon and headed south. After a year in Salisbury, it was back to the First State, this time to Delaware City. Three years would be spent there, toward the end of which another son was born and christened Ralph Milbourne Townsend (Milbourne being his mother's maiden name).

In 1845, the family moved again, to Port Deposit, Maryland, near the head of Chesapeake Bay. After a year there, the Reverend Townsend was appointed to a circuit further upriver at Columbia, Pennsylvania. The next year, he was transferred to Marcus Hook just north of the Pennsylvania-Delaware border. Two years later, the family was moved back down the Peninsula to Chestertown, Maryland.

It was here, during 1849 or '50, that Alfred received his first formal schooling. He was now eight or nine. Having received the rudiments from his mother, and raised under the strict discipline of his father, he seems to have taken to school work rather readily. Attending Chestertown's Washington College, which accepted young as well as older students, and rooming part of the time at the home of a Senator Vickers, the boy proved an apt pupil, well-behaved, hard-working, eager to please.

In 1851, when he was ten, his father was appointed to a circuit at Newark, Delaware. The family moved again, and older brother Stephen Emory (called "Emory" by acquaintances) entered Delaware College while Alfred was placed in the adjunct Academy built in 1841 as a school for younger boys. While Alfred continued diligent in his studies, Emory did not. During the fall term of 1852 he was suspended, then expelled from the college for getting drunk and setting off firecrackers. This was a major embarrassment to the family. The expulsion of a Methodist minister's son for drinking and misbehavior set neighborhood tongues a-wagging, and the Reverend Stephen Townsend must have been mortified at having to face his congregation the Sunday morning after the news was out. As for Alfred, he probably felt even more pressure to be a good son as a way of compensating for his older brother's transgressions.

While a pupil at the Newark Academy, Alfred became increasingly aware of the sectional and political issues dividing the country. Two of the most powerful men in Congress—Henry Clay and Daniel Webster—died during that time after being unable to settle the question of whether to expand slavery to those Western territories then becoming states. Alfred also attended a speech by Delaware's own Senator John Middleton Clayton, an abolitionist who years earlier, as a Dover lawyer, had successfully prosecuted kidnappers and murderers of freed slaves, including members of the Patty Cannon gang. At Newark, Clayton spoke "for education and against Negrophobia."

Around this time, Alfred's father bought and read the first novel he had allowed to sit on the shelf with his religious books—Harriet Beecher Stowe's *Uncle Tom's Cabin*. Alfred read it also and was moved by it, writing later that this had a profound influence in shaping his own views about slavery.

Not yet in his teens, Alfred in Newark was starting to form his own values and wondering what to do with his life. Perhaps his older brother's disgrace made him superconscious of his own responsibilities, but he was maturing faster than most boys his age, and with this maturity came ambition.

Newark Academy.
"Gath" studied here when his father was appointed to a Methodist circuit at Newark, Delaware.
Courtesy of Delaware State Archives.

Once when he was eleven, he visited a nearby city (probably Wilmington) and saw at a market a woman selling books and water-color illustrations. This was an epiphany; he immediately bought some of her books and a box of water-colors and set about becoming an artist. Over the next three years, he copied hundreds of other people's drawings, then began sketching and painting from life. His friends and relatives, seeing the energy he was putting into this hobby, thought him destined for a career in art. But this would soon change.

In 1853, his father was reassigned once more, this time to a circuit in a suburb of Philadelphia, and the family moved again. It would be the last long move the Townsends would make as a household. The family would live successively at South Penn, Cohocksink and Kensington. Congregations were a bit more affluent here, and greater cultural opportunities could be found.

During nineteen years in the Methodist itinerancy, the Reverend Townsend had been assigned mostly to small churches in out-of-the-way communities, where congregations were usually so hard-pressed financially that he had often worked as a carpenter to supplement his meager income from church offerings. Habits of thrift, though, had enabled him to save enough money to buy several farms on the peninsula during his sojourn there, one of them in an area of Eastern Shore Maryland where during the 17th Century an early settler, Augustine Herman, had agreed to map the country for the Calvert proprietors in exchange for a tract of land he called Bohemia Manor.

Another of Stephen Townsend's landholdings was near the tiny crossroads community of Kenton, Delaware. When his three sons were on vacation from school during the summers, they could usually be found working on one of their father's farms. Thus Alfred, although the family was living in southeastern Pennsylvania during much of the late 1840s and '50s, did not entirely lose touch with the peninsula of his birth and early years—a region which would play a significant role later in his life.

For the present, he and other family members were adapting to a more urban environment than they were accustomed to. Mary Milbourne Townsend was the most relieved at living in the new setting. For more than two decades she had worn herself out moving from one small community to another with her husband and, as the family grew, with three active sons who also made demands on her waning strength and health. Each year at conference time she had hoped against hope that the Reverend Townsend would be assigned to one of the larger, more prosperous circuits where his salary would be sufficient to allow the family a few of the luxuries the smaller churches did not offer. And each year for many seasons she had paled in silent disappointment as the plums had gone to other pastors while her husband was either reassigned to the poor churches he was already serving or moved to another circuit as bad or worse. Now, however, his long years of service had led to assignment in an area where prospects were somewhat brighter. But this had been a long time coming. While he was still energetic and ambitious at age 45, she, six years older than her husband, was tired and frail.

Once the family was settled near Philadelphia, Alfred was put in Fox Chase School, where his preparatory studies were on a par with those he had received at Chestertown and Newark. It was during these years of 1854-55 that he gravitated from drawing to writing. While he does not say precisely what caused the change, undoubtedly his writing urge sprang from his eagerness to read whatever he could find that engaged his imagination at this time. He particularly liked patriotic and historical fiction.

Alfred soon found employment as "a boy of all work in a city store," using part of his earnings to buy inexpensive editions of popular novels. He was also perusing whatever newspapers he could lay hands on. Reading these story papers and novels kindled a desire to produce works of the same sort. At age thirteen, he made up his mind to be a writer—an ambition he would never forsake.

In 1856, after two years of study at Fox Chase, he was ready to move on to Philadelphia's Central High School, highly regarded as a center of learning. Central offered instruction equivalent to many colleges, even granting a bachelor of arts degree to those who completed four years of course work successfully. His father's city church was then in the Philadelphia suburb of Kensington where the family was living. To attend Central, Alfred had to walk four miles each way.

HERCULES THE BOY

In his diary, fifteen-year-old George Alfred Townsend would write: "Saturday, February 9, 1856. The most important day in my life. Admitted to the Central High School today about 1 o'clock. Average 75.5."

Whether this average was one he'd brought from Fox Chase or the result of his first day's efforts at Central is not clear, but his recording of it is noteworthy, as is his remarking how significant he felt his admission to the High School was at this point in his life. Two months later, another diary entry states, "Tuesday, April 8. Got a cipher [zero] in history, the result of too much attention to foreign matter [extracurricular reading, presumably]. Average in writing, 100, surpassing last month by 3. Clear gain."

Many entries in Alfred's diary are useful primarily because they reveal a boy who was uncommonly eager and anxious to succeed. But they also show a youth who, while he initially desired to do, and *did* do, well in most subjects, came to focus increasingly on writing superbly while letting other areas slide.

Not all entries in Alfred's diary were about schoolwork. One dated May 1 [1856] reads: "Today as I was taking off my overcoat at the High School, [classmates] Leaver and Stevens told me that a private in Walker's Army named Townsend had been killed. As Emory was there at last account, I thought it must be him and shed tears. Mother thinks otherwise."

Emory Townsend, after his expulsion from Delaware College, had left Delaware in disgrace to pursue a military career. At some point he had allied himself with adventurer William Walker, who was then known as a "filibuster." While that word today calls to mind obstructionist activities in Congress to block legislation, its earlier meaning, derived from the old Dutch *vrijbuit* ("free booty"), meant "pirate" or "freebooter." The French and Spanish versions of the Dutch term, being rendered respectively as "filibustier" and "filibustero," had come into English as "filibuster." Today we might call General Walker a "mercenary," "hired gun" or "soldier of fortune."

When civil war broke out between two political factions in Nicaragua during 1855, one side recruited Walker from California, where he had taken refuge in 1853 after an unsuccessful attempt to wrest Baja California away from Mexico. Walker's backers included certain slaveholding interests in the U. S. which had helped foment the earlier war with Mexico and wanted to see slavery extended into Latin America.

In September, 1855, at the head of a force of 110 men, Walker captured the capital city of Nicaragua and installed a new government with himself as generalissimo. By year's end he had raised an army of 1400 troops. In February of 1856, to oust these "foreign invaders," the neighboring country of Costa Rica declared war on Walker's regime. During subsequent fighting, Emory Townsend was killed on April 9. Years later, Walker was captured and turned over to Honduran authorities, by whom he was court-martialed, then put before a firing squad and shot on September 12, 1860.

Alfred, as it turned out, had been right about his brother's death. A later diary entry, dated July 31 [1856], reads: "Received the painful intelligence today that my brother Stephen Emory Townsend was really killed at the battle of Rivas, April 9th, fought between the American and Nicaraguan forces on one side and the Costa Ricans under Baron Bulow on the other side. General Walker commanded the Nicaraguan army in which my brother was a soldier. He was a noble boy, generous, frank, brave, ambitious and intelligent[;] he commanded the admiration and envy of all. Unfortunately he was led into a career of [words illegible] by some students of Delaware College and has ever been a source of trouble and anxiety to my father.... I intend to write a memoir of him which will be found in my manuscript."

It must have been painful for Alfred, if he was at all aware of the politics at that time, to know his brother had died fighting for the cause of promoting slavery in Latin America. Whether he carried out his intent to write a memoir of Emory is not presently known.

In any case, he had numerous writing opportunities. Central High policy required a theme a week from each student, and Alfred was highly enough motivated to go well beyond the minimum. A diary entry for May 3, 1856, notes: "Bought a quire of foolscap and commenced writing a book. I shall compose it first and then write it."

Why this eagerness to write? He may have been doing it for attention and praise. Having found something at which he could excel, Alfred stood out in competition with his fellow students, winning recognition not only from his instructors and peers but, as his articles were published in city newspapers, from the general public as well. He was also eager to bring home good grades to his father, whose approval he sought and needed.

The Reverend Stephen Townsend was no slack scholar himself. Not long after coming to Philadelphia, he obtained a medical degree and set up a practice to supplement his activities as a minister. Before the end of his life, he would pursue further graduate studies and earn a Doctorate of Philosophy degree. Alfred appears always to have been in awe of his father and desirous of living up to the paternal example and expectations.

But there was a strong sense of personal ambition as well. Alfred as a boy revealed often that he felt destined for greatness in his chosen field of endeavor. Moreover, he continued to demonstrate the drive and desire to do whatever it took to get him there. Self-conscious and insecure in many ways, he became assertive and confident with a pen in his hand, and amazingly prescient about the tools he would need to gain fame as a writer.

As a freshman at Central in 1856, he was honing his skills before presenting his writings to a larger audience. In his sophomore year, the budding author began to bloom. Among his papers at the Maryland Archives is a scrapbook titled *Miscellanies 1857-58*. Inside, he wrote: "My First Published Articles," then pasted into this scrapbook a series of clippings, mostly from newspapers, revealing much of what he was writing during his sophomore and junior years. The sum of these pieces is so impressive both as to quantity and quality that it is difficult to imagine finding a college student now capable of doing equivalent work.

Whether he or his teachers knew it at the time, he was getting exactly the kind of education needed. Having settled on writing as a career, and possessing an uncanny awareness of what he would later write about, he had the good sense at this age to slight those subjects he didn't need to know about in order to concentrate on those he *would* need.

His leisure hours were often spent in similar pursuits. While his peers were idling away their weekends and holidays in games and pastimes, Alfred was using these times to enhance his knowledge of local and regional history. He frequently hiked to neighboring communities to see "battle-fields like Brandywine, Valley Forge, Germantown, and Red Bank," taking along a detailed history book for reference. In these outings, the boy was getting a sense of place and terrain at sites where these Revolutionary War battles had occurred. Putting these elements together with what he was reading in source-books, he relived the scenes of conflict in his mind with a vividness most visitors to the sites could not approach.

Later he would often employ the word "realize" to describe the process he was experiencing. To Townsend, "realizing" an event meant accumulating and reading whatever relevant written materials he could find about it, then going on-site and visualizing in his well-informed imagination what it must have been like at the moment of its happening. The next step was to transfer his visual images into clear, evocative poetry or prose.

He could scarce have anticipated—or could he?—that, five years hence, as a 21-year-old war correspondent, he would be reporting grisly scenes of the most horrific war in the nation's history—watching it happen before his eyes and drawing on knowledge gleaned from his walks around Revolutionary battle-fields to make the Civil War so real and vivid for his readers.

Perhaps he *did* know, at some level of consciousness, what lay ahead for himself and his country. The unsettled conflict over slavery had been going on for such a long time that it was not unlikely, sooner or later, the matter would have to be settled through bloodshed, pitting section against section—even brother against brother—if no acceptable compromise could be found.

How well Alfred could predict the future at this time is hard to say, but many writings in his high school scrapbook reveal that he was thinking about problems facing the nation with a maturity remarkable in a 16-year-old boy.

Other writings of this period, though, show him experiencing many of the same concerns most adolescents have. Several of his articles and poems are thinly disguised autobiography, some hardly even disguised. He was taking a hard, critical look at himself, and being astonishingly candid about what he saw. One essay, titled "The Trials of a Timid Man," begins:

"I am a strange fellow. I don't know what I was created for, unless it was to write poetry and spin long stories; for I have inherited 'all the ills that flesh is heir to,' as well as a great many which are not necessarily to the good of flesh. For instance, I have a large, warrior-looking body, prominent bones, big feet and a tragic aspect, united with an exceedingly nervous constitution, a very small proportion of genuine 'pluck,' a most singular bashfulness, and a disastrously unwary tongue. Ambition is my ruling passion. My thirst for fame has never been surpassed."

Concern about his lack of "pluck" is a subject he would frequently broach at this age. In his literary memoir he tells of writing and delivering a poem titled "The Pleasures of Timidity" at the high school and winning a prize for his effort. As his later adventures during the war would amply demonstrate, he certainly did not lack personal courage of the sort that made him willing to expose himself to imminent danger in order to be an eyewitness at battle scenes. On the other hand, he did not like to fight, and seems to have avoided those childhood confrontations which lead to fisticuffs. Growing up with an older brother might have been a factor in this. So might being raised by a strict disciplinarian father.

In one poem extant from this period, titled "Perversion of Scripture," Alfred discusses the "spare the rod and spoil the child" adage and complains about boys getting whipped by their fathers. One can infer from reading these verses that Alfred felt he and his brothers had been treated more harshly than they deserved by their patriarchal parent. We can also wonder if Emory's rebellious behavior was rooted in his reaction to such discipline.

Alfred, in another poem written about this time, expresses regret at not having a sister to grow up with. Had there been a girl child in the family, he muses, he might have had someone in whom he could have confided and found more compatible than his two brothers. He would not be the first nor the last male writer to recognize both a masculine and a feminine side in his nature, each having its own needs. But his self-proclaimed bashfulness made him something of a loner, spending much of his spare time writing or taking long hikes alone rather than indulging in more social pursuits.

Most writers, however, write to be read, else they would simply think their ideas rather than putting them in tangible form. So Alfred, in his second year at Central, made a point of becoming connected with the student newspaper, *The High School Journal*. By remarkable coincidence, the editor of that publication was a boy with whom he shared two names. George Nathaniel Townsend was an upperclassman who, so far as Alfred was aware, had no traceable blood relationship to him. Soon, the masthead of the *HSJ* was showing the paper to be basically a two-student operation: G. N. Townsend was editor while G. A. Townsend was editorial correspondent. It would remain that way until October, 1858, when Nathaniel would step down and

Alfred would assume the editor's chair. Meantime, both boys were busy contributors to the pages of their ambitious publication.

Alfred often signed his articles and poems with the *nom de plume* "Gealto," comprised of the first two letters of each of his three names. He may have used other pen-names as well, for some of the works signed "Eagle Eye" and other nicknames are written in a style resembling his own. Other works preserved in his scrapbook are signed with his full name.

Profitable time could be spent analyzing all of the articles Alfred got into print during his high school years. While most were for the *High School Journal*, some appeared in a student publication called the *Welcome Visitor* and others in the Sunday supplement of the Philadelphia *Dispatch*. Several of these early pieces are alluded to in Townsend's memoir written more than half a century later, indicating that he had neither forgotten these juvenile writings nor was inclined to scorn them.

In one article, "The Colored People of this City," Alfred took it upon himself to inform his fellow Philadelphians that blacks, given equal opportunities, might prove they were not inferior to whites in intellect or ambition. This was not mere philosophical rambling; to bolster his case, he found and interviewed a number of city blacks who had "made good" and established respectable reputations in the community. While acknowledging that many of the 20,000 or so free blacks living in the city were poor, this was not, he felt, due to stupidity or laziness. Rather, he argued, they lacked education and decent job opportunities.

He also scolded Philadelphia for being the only large Northern city to forbid blacks from riding on public transportation. Read now, this article shows not only how far this 17-year-old youth's social consciousness had progressed to that point, but also how mature his research and writing skills had become.

Another *Sunday Dispatch* article, "An Itinerant Clergy, as Exemplified in the Methodist Episcopal Church," displays Alfred's sophisticated grasp of an issue being much debated in that denomination. It was, of course, a subject he was familiar with after growing up in the household of an itinerant minister. In "The Preacher's Son," a prize-winning story he wrote for the *High School Journal*, he continued analyzing how Methodism had affected his own life.

A short novel, *The Two Students: A Story of College Life* was also autobiographical and apparently difficult to write. After serialization in the *HSJ* it was clipped by Alfred and pasted in his scrapbook with the handwritten notation: "Thank Heaven it is Concluded!"

Alfred's literary endeavors during his high school years were not confined to print. Starting in 1858, he began giving talks on a variety of subjects both for school-connected events and public occasions. Several lectures were presented at his father's church, but chiefly about literary topics. He was reading the Romantic poets at this time, and giving public performances of essays he had written on Byron, Shelley and other poets. He was also conquering his adolescent shyness and developing more confidence, along with some local reputation as a speaker. That most of his talks were well-received attests to his maturing abilities.

A telling assessment, however, was given of his performance skills by a reviewer covering a Central High School declamation and composition contest he had entered: "Mr. Townsend's poem was a well written and elaborate view of the life and fortune of the poet. His style of writing is far superior to the general run of young men and we cannot see why he was not placed among the writers of the evening. In speaking he does well, but has not the advantage of a strong voice. He will make his mark as a writer, rather than a speaker."

As he approached graduation day in February of 1860, Alfred could look back upon the truly prodigious amount of work he had accomplished in his four years at Central. While he had not excelled academically in all areas of study, this was by choice. He had accomplished his goal of being the school's outstanding writer during his years of attendance. This had taken brains, energy and perseverance, and he had passed all the tests he had set for himself. In essence, he had served out an apprenticeship of sorts, being driven more by his own ambition than by what any schoolteacher was asking or expecting from him. His chief masters were not those who stood over him in classes at Central High. They were the authors of those books, poems, essays, plays, newspaper and magazine articles he had read, seeking to absorb, then emulate, then surpass what these predecessors had written.

He had practiced writing in all of the recognized literary genre: novel, short story, drama, poetry and essay. He had become adept at turning out verses in regular meter and rhyme in much the same way he had learned to draw—by copying existing models until he became proficient at form, then launching into his own experiments and practicing tirelessly. One of his stories in the *HSJ* had been about a boy who could not stop speaking in rhyme although ordered by his elders to do so. It was obviously autobiographical.

Many years later, when he had become a rich and successful writer, Townsend, inscribing for his daughter a copy of a book he had authored decades before, wrote on its flyleaf the following verse:

This book I wrote at 28 and thought it only light and flip
And did not know, till now, too late, our best is in apprenticeship;
That while we learn, we so enjoy, as, when we're learned, we never can;
The feats of Hercules, the boy, he never matched when he was man.

NEWSPAPER DAYS

On January 30, 1860, Alfred celebrated his 19th birthday. In two weeks he was scheduled to graduate from Central High with a Bachelor of Arts degree. What was to happen after that he didn't know. He had hoped for a career in literature or journalism, but thought his prospects dim. Only a handful of people in America were making a living from literary writing, and as for journalism, he felt himself still too timid to go after stories aggressively. But a former student at Central had been following his writings with interest and was in a position to offer him a job on one of the city's daily papers.

The newspaper in question was the Philadelphia *Inquirer*. The individual offering the job was an employee named Child not much older than himself. The starting salary—six dollars a week—was not bad in a profession where the top men in the field were earning $20 a week.

After his initial elation and surprise at getting a job the moment he graduated, Alfred soon found his situation less than ideal. For one thing, after working his way up to a degree of fame and prestige at Central, he was now at the bottom of the ladder again—a shy, green boy among older, more experienced newsmen. The capacity he had formed for hard work, however, soon kicked in, and he set about to impress those around him with his diligence and skills. Impress them he did, but not in the way he'd intended. His writing was so professional that the other reporters felt he must be copying from other sources, while his tendency to put his own impressions into his articles rankled the editorial writers, who insinuated that he should stick to facts and leave opinion-expressing to them.

As a writer, Townsend never would make a sharp distinction between "fact" and "opinion." What he saw as an observer, being filtered through his own mind and value system, came out as interpretation, not flat, photographic verisimilitude. Much of the appeal of his style lay in his personal slant on what he was experiencing, and to take his own thoughts and impressions from his written accounts of people and events would be equivalent to removing the flavors from food.

As matters turned out, Alfred was soon assigned to writing editorials, which is usually considered a promotion in the newspaper world. But to him it was somewhat suffocating to be closeted with other editors whose stock in trade was opinion—men who, in his view, thought more highly of their own opinions than was merited. To put some life back into his own writing, Alfred abandoned the editorial desk and returned to the streets as a reporter.

What he *really* wanted to do at this time was literary work, but he was realistic enough to recognize that his prospects for making a living from such efforts were slim. If he was to be stuck in journalism, he wanted to be a "special correspondent," with the freedom to go out and write about events of wider interest. But the newspaper he worked for tended to focus mainly on local news and was unwilling to underwrite expenses for the kind of free-lancing he had in mind. Alfred was not at this point financially secure enough to go out on his own as a free-lance, pay his own way, and recover his expenses through sales of his articles. For the time being, he was stuck in Philadelphia, writing stories in which, for the most part, he had little interest.

Where travel was concerned, he had done better while still in high school, when he could at least use his weekends and holidays to get out of the city's confines. Still, as Philadelphia was a major metropolitan center, a few interesting stories did happen downtown that he could cover. One of these was the first visit by an embassy from Japan to the United States during 1860. Commodore Matthew Perry in 1854 had made the first official overture to open diplomatic and trade relations between the U. S. and the Japanese government. Treaties had been signed as a result, and now the Japanese were returning the courtesy call and getting a first glimpse of the West. When the embassy visited Philadelphia, Alfred was sent down to report the event.

He also covered, soon after, an official visit made to the city by Queen Victoria's oldest son and heir-apparent, Edward, Lord Renfrew. Born in 1841, he was no older than Alfred. Four decades later, after his mother's death in 1901, he would be King Edward VII, ruling monarch of the British Empire.

The most important news event of 1860, however, was the Presidential election campaign pitting Republican Abraham Lincoln against Northern Democrat Stephen A. Douglas, Southern Democrat John C. Breckinridge and Constitutional Union Party nominee John Bell. The country was badly split over slavery, the tariff and other issues, and political feelings were running high.

Even the nominating process had been hotly contested. New York's William H. Seward had gone to the Republican convention in Chicago as the front-runner, but with Lincoln not far behind on the strength of his showing in a series of 1858 debates against Stephen A. Douglas (when both were seeking a Senate seat from Illinois). The Lincoln-Douglas debates, carried in many newspapers around the nation, had brought to a focus most of the main issues of the slavery controversy, and, while Douglas had won the election, many Republicans felt Lincoln had won the debate and were willing to back him for the nation's highest office.

Alfred's employer, the Philadelphia *Inquirer*, was owned by the prosperous Harding family of that city. During the early 1830s, entrepreneur Jesper Harding, having become rich publishing Bibles, had bought the *Pennsylvania Inquirer*, a struggling, Democratic-leaning paper supporting then-President Andrew Jackson. Making it Republican and business-friendly, he had also made it pay. In 1859 control had been turned over to his son William, who had changed its name to reflect its city of origin in 1860, about the time Alfred was hired.

William's two sons were actually running the newspaper, and one of them, George, had been a patent attorney in a civil suit involving reaper patents a few years earlier—a case in which he and fellow lawyer Edwin M. Stanton had essentially snubbed another member of the defense team—their Illinois attorney-of-record Abraham Lincoln—in winning the case. The Hardings' support for the Presidency had gone to John McLean, a U. S. Supreme Court Justice who had written a strong dissent in the Dred Scott case, taking issue with Chief Justice Roger Taney's opinion that blacks were by nature inferior beings who could not exist on an equal basis with whites.

Alfred believed the *Inquirer*'s publishers were inclining toward McLean largely because he was related to George Harding's wife. He also felt they were out of touch with Lincoln's popularity among mainstream Republican voters in the North and West. He would recall in his literary memoir that, when Lincoln was nominated on the third ballot with the support of nearly all except Seward's supporters, the Hardings, caught in the embarrassing spot of knowing next to nothing about him, could not put together a decent story announcing his triumph at the convention.

The Democrats, meanwhile, were hopelessly split. Weeks before the Republicans gathered in Chicago to nominate Lincoln, party Democrats had met in Charleston, South Carolina, to nominate—nobody. After 57 ballots, no candidate could get the 202 votes necessary to win, and the convention adjourned, vowing to meet at Baltimore in June to try again. There, after Northern Democrats held sway and nominated Stephen A. Douglas, Southern members of the party bolted and met later to nominate John C. Breckinridge of Kentucky as an "Independent Democratic" candidate. A few days after this, the Southern Democratic Party was formed, and its delegates also picked Breckinridge to run as its standard-bearer.

Douglas had been unable to keep Southern Democrats tied to his candidacy. Although he favored slavery, he also favored the Union, and many Southerners, once Lincoln was named the Republican nominee and seemed likely to win, believed that, if he *did* win, Southern states would have to secede in order to protect the right to hold slaves. They could not embrace Douglas as their candidate when he was committed to preserving the Union.

Other voters and political figures who could not support the candidates nominated by the Republicans or the various Democratic conventions broke away to form the Constitutional Union Party and nominate John Bell of Tennessee to run for President.

As the campaign progressed, Alfred reported on some of the candidates. First he met and interviewed Douglas, whom he found sitting in a hotel room, boots and coat off, feet propped on a table-top, with a decanter (probably containing brandy, Alfred thought) sitting beside him. He found the Northern Democratic candidate worried, bitter and disappointed that the debates in Illinois two years earlier had brought the obscure Lincoln so much fame and support that he was likely to win the Presidency.

Though only 19, Alfred was intuitive enough to perceive deep meaning in events he was covering. Sent to Trenton when Lincoln was campaigning north of Philadelphia, he noticed that, when the Republican asserted in a speech that a tough stance might be necessary against the slave-holding states, the New Jersey crowd applauded wildly. At that point, Alfred said later, "I realized that the North was ready for war and rather desired it."

In the election Lincoln won a plurality of the popular vote, receiving more than 1,866,000 to Douglas's 1,375,000, while Breckinridge got 848,000 and Bell 590,000. The Republican also garnered nearly 60 per cent of electoral votes, winning in 18 of the 33 states. Due to the sectional nature of the vote, Breckinridge carried eleven states and Bell three, with Douglas prevailing in only one state, Missouri.

With the votes in and Lincoln looming as President-elect, South Carolina seceded from the Union on December 20, 1860, nullifying its ratification of the federal Constitution some seventy years earlier. In January and February of '61, Mississippi, Florida, Alabama, Georgia, Louisiana and Texas would follow South Carolina out, to be joined in April, May and June by Virginia, Arkansas, North Carolina and Tennessee. The die was cast; the Union was broken and four years, plus an enormous amount of bloodshed and property destruction, would be required to put it back together.

During the early months of 1861, the nation's future looked grim indeed. Young George Alfred Townsend's future, on the other hand, brightened somewhat when a rival newspaper, the Philadelphia *Press,* offered to hire him away from the *Inquirer* and make him its city editor. The *Press* had been founded in 1857 by Pennsylvania newspaperman John Wien Forney, a longtime Buchanan supporter disappointed by not getting a patronage job after his candidate was elected President in 1856. Forney and the *Press* were more acerbic and innovative than the conservative *Inquirer*, which suited Alfred fine. The pay was also better, and Forney liked him enough that, after a few months in the city editor's chair, Alfred was named dramatic editor as well, replacing a far more experienced journalist at the job.

Being the *Press*'s dramatic editor didn't add much to his salary but gave him free passes to the city's theaters and a chance to become more familiar with plays and with Philadelphia's literary and artistic life. As a reviewer, he got to meet and talk with a number of prominent actors, including the renowned E. L. Davenport and young John Wilkes Booth, son of one famous thespian and brother of another.

Alfred's own creative impulses were so stimulated that he found time to write a play of his own, *The Bohemians, or Life in a Newspaper*, a satirical comedy reflecting the vicissitudes of his own professional life. Whether it was ever performed is not now known, but, as published by the Marlow Dramatic Club of Philadelphia, it constituted the first of his substantive literary works to reach print after the periodical articles of his high school days. Decades later, he would call it a "raw play," but he would also put it first in his personal list of published literary works.

When not busy with newspaper work, Alfred continued to write verses, and was elated when war poems of his, after appearing in the *Press*, were reprinted in *The Rebellion Record,* a nationally-circulating periodical carrying poetry and prose pieces from both Northern and Southern supporters. Some famous American poets, among them John Greenleaf Whittier, William Cullen Bryant and Dr. Oliver Wendell Holmes, along with scores of lesser lights, were being published in the *Record*. Alfred was so delighted to hear that one of his own poems, "Roanoke," had been read at a public lecture by Dr. Holmes that he went to Boston to call upon the distinguished author in person.

Dominating Alfred's life at this period was a conviction that he was destined for something far beyond a career on a Philadelphia daily newspaper. He had high literary ambitions, believing enough in his own talents to feel that, if he could find time, masterpieces would come pouring out of his fertile mind and pen. As it was, he had to earn enough on a regular basis to meet his expenses, which were enlarging as he acquired tastes much above those he had experienced as an itinerant minister's son and farm boy.

These needs and wants kept him tied to daily newspaper work, but he was not content. Normally, advancement in the journalistic field comes through moving from reporter to editor and possibly even publisher. But this was not what he wanted. What Alfred was best at, and what he chiefly yearned to do, was writing. His forte was creating, not managing other people's efforts. Moreover, he wanted to write about those subjects which interested *him*, not the average Philadelphia newspaper reader. Philadelphia was a large city, but it was a distant second to New York where journalism and book publishing were concerned. Once past his 21st birthday, he felt it was time to move on.

Industrious to a fault, he had been picking up odd jobs to supplement his earnings at the *Press*. One of these involved reporting Philadelphia-area news for the New York *Herald*, which boasted a national circulation. So he leaped at the chance when that paper offered him the opportunity to go to the war as a special correspondent and send back dispatches from the front.

OFF TO THE WAR

Soon he was on his way to Washington to pick up his authorization from the Union's new Secretary of War, Edwin M. Stanton. He was also issued a horse by the federal government, and was soon riding this decrepit mount across the Potomac on his way south. He did not get far, though, before contracting a fever which sent him back to Washington to recuperate.

Recovering, he was reassigned, this time to the Army of the Potomac under General McClellan, which was then making its way down the Chesapeake to the tip of the Virginia Peninsula near Norfolk with orders to move up that neck of land between the James and York Rivers and launch an attack on the Confederate capital of Richmond. General McDowell with another army was coming down by land from Alexandria via Fredericksburg, and the plan was to attack Richmond from two directions and capture it, thereby, it was hoped, ending the war, which had been going on nearly a year.

Things went well for a while. McClellan advanced cautiously up the Peninsula and laid siege to Yorktown, which the Confederates evacuated in early May before much damage was done. A more spirited engagement followed on May 29 at Seven Pines and Fairoaks, where the Rebels drove Union forces back briefly before being pushed back themselves. Alfred at the scene wrote accounts to send back for the edification of *Herald* readers.

After defeating the Confederates at Williamsburg, McClellan's army moved northwest to the Chickahominy River area, a swampy land infested with mosquitos. Many troops, and Alfred as well, became ill with what was termed "Chickahominy fever," a typhus-like ailment which killed some men and incapacitated thousands of others. Close to Richmond, McClellan's momentum, often criticized for being too lethargic even when victorious, bogged down. Between June 26 and July 1, 1862, the so-called "Seven-Days Battle," and particularly the Battle of Malvern Hills, ended the Union advance and sent McClellan and his men back down the Peninsula in retreat.

Alfred chronicled these days and battles for the *Herald* in a graphic, personal style which led readers to feel they were on the scene themselves. Focusing as much on enlisted men as officers, and on civilians as much as military personnel, his accounts gave a balanced, realistic feel to his reporting. He also included himself as an eyewitness and participant, enabling those who were reading these accounts to identify with him and his experiences.

Once McClellan's drive was blunted and repulsed, the scene of combat turned elsewhere. On July 12, Alfred was reassigned to an army commanded by General John Pope, who had just been reassigned himself from Missouri to northern Virginia. In the subsequent campaign to drive the Confederates out of the Virginia mountains, Alfred reported the events in his vivid, personal style.

A hard battle fought at Cedar Mountain on August 9 was written up by the young man for the *Herald*. Pope's forces emerged more or less victorious in that engagement, but would suffer a severe defeat weeks later at the Battle of Second Bull Run. By that time, however, Alfred, more seriously ill with "Chickahominy fever," had left the army and would soon set sail for England where he hoped to recuperate and perhaps find opportunities to gain a measure of fame as a journalistic or literary writer.

ADVENTURES ABROAD

On October 1, 1862, Alfred landed in Liverpool with a little cash and a lot of ambition. On the passage over, he had made friends with a young man named Hipp, who, once Alfred revealed that he had once made a bit of money and reputation giving talks in Philadelphia, suggested a partnership: Alfred would lecture in England about his Civil War experiences; Hipp would act as his agent/manager, handling all business arrangements.

For a few weeks, the two youths followed through with this plan. Townsend gave talks and Hipp managed the details. But instead of getting rich, they found their combined assets trickling away. Many people in that part of England were more sympathetic to the Confederate than the Union side, and Alfred was not attracting large enough audiences to pay for living expenses and hall rentals. Faced with this sobering fact, they decided to part company, with Hipp going to Ireland and Alfred heading for London.

Some of his adventures in London Alfred later related in chapters of his 1866 book *Campaigns of a Non-Combatant*. While there he was able to sell articles to two prominent British literary magazines, *Chambers's Journal* (having arrived with a letter of introduction from an American contact to publisher Robert Chambers, who befriended him) and *The Cornhill*

Magazine, to which he sold two war-related pieces, "Campaigning with General Pope" and "Richmond and Washington during the War."

After nine months in England, most of it spent living in a northern suburb of London, Alfred had adequately recovered from his typhus-like symptoms. He had also largely exhausted the hope of supporting himself handsomely as a literary writer or journalist. The war information he had left America with in the summer of '62 was now old news, and, while he could sell enough stories to periodicals on other subjects to keep a roof over his head and food on the table, this was not what he wanted.

He had tried writing a novel called *The War Correspondent* based on his Virginia adventures, but could find no publisher for it. He parceled out chapters of it to the periodical press, but with only partial success. His restless nature was telling him to move on again, and the European continent was beckoning just across the English Channel.

Now 22, Alfred had spent the years of his youth working hard. After committing himself to becoming a writer, he had devoted most of his energies toward accomplishing that goal. It seems to have occurred to him at this time that he was due for some enjoyment. He had long been fascinated with the concept of "Bohemianism"—the life of the artist. He had worked on a farm in the Old Bohemia section of Eastern Shore Maryland. He had written a play about newspaper writers like himself and titled it *"The Bohemians."* But he had never had much of a chance to experience the life of a Bohemian in fact. Now there was time at last to do so. And where better to do it than in Europe?

In the summer of 1863, George Alfred Townsend bade good-bye to England and sailed across the channel to France. He was looking for romance—love even—and whatever else the Continent might offer in the way of literary success to a young American writer. He would stay there about a year, writing stories and poems about his experiences which he would not publish until seventeen years later. He would also apparently fall in love.

The poem "Little Grisette" and the story "Married Abroad," as published in his 1880 book *Bohemian Days*, survive from this period of his life. Both speak wistfully of an *affair de coeur* which he seems to have looked back upon as a fond memory mingled with feelings of guilt and regret. The Grisette of the poem is probably also the Suzette of the story—a French girl with whom the young American artist falls in love and lives with before the relationship breaks apart and he departs for Italy. It is hard to read "Little Grisette" and "Married Abroad" without believing them autobiographical.

After a year on the Continent, Alfred decided to return to America. His reasons for doing so are not clear, though he seems to have convinced himself by now that Europe offered fewer opportunities for a successful writing career than did his native land. The 1866 book he published about his experiences during the war years, *Campaigns of a Non-Combatant,* contained one chapter about his time in England and another about a sojourn of several months in Italy. No mention at all was made of his stay in France. Only in *Bohemian Days,* published 14 years after *Campaigns,* would he include writings from his months in Paris.

BACK TO THE WAR

In mid-1864, after being abroad for nearly two years, Alfred returned to New York where he worked for a time as literary editor for a metropolitan daily. He still harbored hopes of being able to live off his income as a literary writer, but could not sell enough creative work to periodicals to do so. He did manage to place in the January, 1865, issue of *Harper's New Monthly Magazine* one article, "An American War Correspondent in England" (later included as a chapter in *Campaigns*), but it soon became apparent that, if he wanted the degree of independence he had earlier sought and gained from the routine of daily newspaper work, he would have to become a special correspondent again and go back to the war.

So off he went, down through New Jersey, Philadelphia and Washington on his way to the battlefields of Virginia. At the latter city he paused briefly to reflect on whether it would ever again be the whole nation's capital and, if so, what kinds of facilities it would need to build in order to serve the Reunited States with dignity and efficiency.

March, 1865, found him with General Sheridan's army as it pressed on toward Richmond. Much had happened since he had left as a victim of Chickahominy fever in August of '62. At that time the outcome of the war had been much in doubt, with Pope's defeat at Second Bull Run and other Confederate victories still to come. But the Rebels, after carrying their offensive up through western Maryland and into Pennsylvania, had suffered a critical defeat at Gettysburg during the first three days of July, 1863. From that point, the tide had turned. Lincoln had finally found a general, Ulysses S. Grant, both willing and able to use the North's superiority in men and munitions to overwhelm the Confederate forces, though at great cost. By the time Alfred Townsend arrived at the war again, it was almost over except for some mopping-up operations remaining to be done.

One can almost believe it was destiny which sent Alfred back to the war so that he might make a name for himself. He was the only experienced correspondent on hand when Sheridan fought and decisively defeated a large Confederate force in the Battle of Five Forks, captured a crucial road junction

Lieutenant General Ulysses S. Grant as a Civil War officer. Engraving circa 1880.
Courtesy of University of Delaware Library, Newark, Delaware.

and forced the Rebels to evacuate Richmond and Petersburg. Being on the spot, Alfred received a detailed account of the battle directly from Sheridan's own mouth, wrote a lively, comprehensive story from it, then got the news to New York before any other writer was aware of the event. This gave Alfred a "scoop" his fellow correspondents could only envy.

Making a name for himself was now possible in a way it had not been earlier in the conflict. His previous letters and dispatches to the New York *Herald* had all been published anonymously, as had those of every correspondent to that and other papers. While these "specials" had gotten paid for doing the work and taking the risks, the glory had belonged to the newspapers, not to themselves. But, by the time he returned to the front, Alfred recalled later, "the government had compelled the newspapers to print their correspondents' names, so that in a few weeks I had the reputation I should have had in 1862. There began my bias for the government, as better than any of the institutions which berate it."

Sheridan's April 1 victory at Five Forks helped set in motion a chain of events which would bring a quick end to the war. The remains of Lee's army, exhausted and starving, left Richmond the following day and retreated westward, but got no further than Appomattox Court House, where they surrendered a week later. Within a short time, the remaining Rebel forces would surrender as well and Confederate President Jefferson Davis would be captured in Georgia.

Alfred, after moving into Richmond with Sheridan's forces, took a room at the Spotswood Hotel with his good friend and fellow "special" Jerome B. Stillson and from that headquarters they reported to the New York *World* on the desolate condition of this former Confederate capital and stronghold. In the South, misery and destruction were the rule, though there was also a sense of relief that the long, bitter struggle was finally over.

In the North, there was immediate jubilation—but not for long. On the evening of April 14—five days after Lee's surrender at Appomattox—Union President Abraham Lincoln, while attending a play at Ford's Theater in Washington, was shot by an assassin and died the next day.

On hearing of the shooting, Townsend and Stillson moved quickly to get a train to Washington in order to cover the story for the *World*. Stillson did much of the leg work and early fact-gathering, interviewing numerous people. It had been learned that the murder of Lincoln was not a single act but part of a conspiracy which also had as its aim the slaying of other federal officials, including Secretary of State William Seward. Attacked in his sickbed by another of the conspirators, Seward was stabbed and wounded but would recover. Lincoln, with a bullet in his brain, had not.

Lincoln's assailant had been seen by many in the audience as he leapt from the Presidential box onto the stage after the shooting and made his escape on a waiting horse. Several had recognized him as actor John Wilkes Booth. Alfred had known Booth since his stint as drama editor for the Philadelphia *Press* four years earlier, and had chatted briefly with him only a few weeks before the shooting when he had stopped over in Washington on his way to join Sheridan's army. He was thus in a unique position to write about this assassin who was still being sought after escaping with an accomplice through southern Maryland on his way to Virginia.

By the time Booth was caught and killed at Garrett's farm below the Potomac, Townsend had already compiled considerable information about him from a variety of sources. These included several police detectives he had known as a newspaperman in New York, who were willing to confide to him inside information about the case other reporters did not have. He was even made a special deputy sheriff for a time, which gave him access to documents and other data most civilians were not allowed to see. Alfred would write later that he felt he had come to know more details of the Booth conspiracy than any person in the country. He had good reasons for saying so.

The initial result of his efforts was a series of letters on the conspiracy to the *World*, which, carrying his byline, added to the fame already created by his recent reporting of the war. These, without his knowledge or permission, were opportunistically collected once completed and published as a paperbound pamphlet selling for a quarter. When he learned of this, Alfred confronted the publisher and demanded recompense. He ended by signing away his rights for $300 in cash.

Later results of his research on Booth would include a magazine article and a novel. Standing in the rotunda of the Capitol where Lincoln's body was lying in state, Townsend had struck up a conversation with one of the late President's personal secretaries, John Hay, who would soon become a good friend. Alfred had made a vow at the time to write a novel some day about the assassination and its perpetrators. This promise would not be kept for two decades, but during the early 1880s, while taking brief breaks from column-writing, Townsend would begin researching an aspect of the murder he felt every other writer on the subject had missed. He'd come to feel it was connected somehow with John Brown's 1859 raid on the federal arsenal at Harper's Ferry, Virginia.

Booth, he'd learned, had been present as a young Virginia military school cadet when marines under Col. Robert E. Lee stormed the arsenal and captured Brown and his remaining fellow raiders. So had another cadet, a friend of Booth's named John Yates Beall. While Alfred was working as a newspaperman in New York during early 1865, Beall had been hanged as a Confederate spy who had gone to Canada, hijacked a ship and attacked Union installations. Townsend, after attending Beall's hanging and writing an account of it for a newspaper, developed a theory that perhaps Booth, in addition to his Southern sympathies, had developed a personal hatred toward Lincoln for not pardoning Beall when an appeal was made for him to do so.

During the 1880s, while researching a novel that would link Brown's raid to Booth's conspiracy, Alfred made a point of retracing Booth's known movements around the time of the assassination. In doing so, he discovered an individual in southern Maryland, one Thomas Jones, who admitted to hiding and feeding Booth for a week after the shooting and to helping him cross the Potomac. Until then, Booth's whereabouts for that week had remained a mystery for nearly twenty years. Townsend sold the story to a magazine and had the satisfaction of knowing he had gotten another scoop—many years after the fact.

The novel he would write about the conspiracy, however—*Katy of Catoctin* —would do little to enhance his reputation as a literary man, being too cluttered with excess fictional baggage to allow his tale to flow swiftly and easily. But in 1865 *Katy* was far into the future, Lincoln and Booth just dead.

POSTWAR SUCCESS

His recent war correspondence and writings about the Booth conspiracy put Alfred in great demand as a lecturer. Public speaking, along with music and drama, were popular forms of entertainment in the 1860s, even during the war. Almost every town of any size, except in the ruined South, boasted an auditorium where residents could assemble to observe the latest show or lecturer passing through.

Alfred was well prepared. As a high school student he had conquered his bashfulness by forcing himself to stand in front of a crowd and speak.. This had come easier with practice, and now the fame, money and opportunities he had sought three years earlier in Liverpool were being thrust upon him in America. He would soon be traveling from town to town, city to city, giving talks to receptive audiences across the country and continuing to build the national reputation he had long been seeking.

Meantime, he would take another brief turn at editorship. Charles G. Halpine, a good friend from the war, had asked him to help start a newspaper, the New York *Citizen*, to crusade against corruption in city government. As a Union staff officer, Halpine had risen to the rank of general while finding time to write a newspaper humor column laced with satire and current-events commentary under the pen-name "Private Miles O'Reilly." Alfred would dedicate his *Campaigns of a Non-Combatant* to Halpine in the latter guise, but, finding his friend's excessive drinking a problem and not liking editorial work much anyway, he soon left the *Citizen*, which did not continue past Halpine's death in 1868.

He was also pursuing a romance—a Philadelphia woman, Bessie Evans Rhodes. Bessie's father was a well-to-do merchant from Manchester, England. Her mother was a Vandegrift descended from one of the earliest Dutch families on the Delaware. Her grandmother Evans numbered among her kin Mary Ann Evans, better known to the world as novelist George Eliot. Elsewhere in Bessie's ancestry was a tie to Benjamin Franklin.

While in Europe, Alfred had been corresponding with Bessie (whom he seems to have represented as "Lizzie"—the cause of Suzette's jealousy—in his novellette "Married Abroad"), and he had wasted little time in paying her a visit when he returned to America in June, 1864. But it was one of those on-again-off-again courtships in which Bessie kept him dangling awhile before deciding to say yes. At one point her brother Tom, taking pity on Alfred, advised him not to marry her. The advice was not taken, and, having finally gotten her consent, Alfred prepared to abandon his carefree bachelor days for a life of wedded bliss. He and Bessie were married December 21, 1865, at St. Philip's Episcopal Church in Philadelphia, with 2,000 guests attending.

During the first year of their marriage, he was on the road lecturing so much they scarcely had time to see one another. What the protagonist of "Married Abroad," Ralph Flare, had told Suzette was true of Alfred as well. He was essentially married to his work and any relationship with a woman had to come second to that. His letters to her at this period indicate that she was complaining frequently about his absence and her loneliness. A lecture tour early in 1866 took him to the Midwest, and, as that ended, the Austrian-Prussian War in Europe brought a demand for his services overseas as a special correspondent again. On this venture abroad, Bessie went with him, but it was not to be much of a honeymoon. While she stayed in French hotels, he traveled to German cities where the fighting was.

Bessie had become pregnant within a month after their marriage, and in October, 1866, their first child—a daughter, Genevieve Madelaine—was born in Paris. Over the next few years they would have three more children, but only Genevieve—the apple of her father's eye—and George Alfred, Jr., would live past childhood.

During 1867 Alfred completed another lecture tour and made a third trip to Europe to cover the opening of the Paris Exhibition. Once lecture demands tailed off, he decided to settle at Washington in order to write political correspondence for newspapers around the country from the seat of the federal government. Even as a boy, Alfred had displayed an uncommon curiosity about the nation and its history. After roaming around Europe long enough to get a sense of how national governments there worked or failed to work, he was curious to learn how America's government compared to these.

Having just witnessed first-hand the tragic struggle which occurred once a previously united governmental system had broken apart over irreconcilable differences, Alfred had to wonder whether a "nation conceived in liberty and dedicated to the proposition that all men are created equal" (as Lincoln had phrased it at Gettysburg) was really an achievable concept and, further, "whether that nation or any nation so conceived and so dedicated can long endure."

When he was curious about something, Alfred's practice was to read as much as he could, then go to the spot and see what more he could learn about it on-site. He had become knowledgeable about military strategy from visiting Revolutionary War battlefields. Now he intended to learn about government by watching its inside workings on a day-to-day basis and sharing his insights with readers. He came at first as a skeptic, having seen for himself the greed and corruption which had been so manifest in war-time Washington. But, as he became more acquainted with post-war activities in the nation's capital, he would also develop a broader understanding of the political process and a greater tolerance for the results it produced.

Over the next seven years, Alfred would become one of the nation's premier political correspondents, as he had earlier been one of the Union's best war correspondents. Through press contacts made in cities where he had lectured since the war, he had no difficulty finding newspapers willing to pay him by the word for regular correspondence. He soon had so much column-work committed, in fact, that he could not keep up with it writing longhand and had to hire stenographers to whom he could dictate his daily output.

He later estimated that he had produced no less than 4,000 words a day (about 16 typed, double-spaced pages) in political correspondence for various newspapers over a span of several decades—at least 50 million words by his own count. These, if collected into books, might constitute between 400 and 500 thick volumes filling a goodly number of library shelves. Nearly all of these writings, however, were ephemeral—found only in newspapers and magazines rather than books. Most are still recoverable, if anyone were willing to sift through existing copies of the periodicals he wrote for to locate and copy those articles identifiable as his work.

These would certainly be enlightening to historians, biographers, political scientists and other scholars able to benefit from candid, honest, informed accounts by a self-trained, well-placed observer—one whose main purpose was to tell the truth about those contemporary men and events making news of national importance in the post-Civil War era.

With all the column work he had committed to do, Alfred was still trying to find time for what he called his literary writing. Separating literature from journalism is not always easy, since the one often overlaps the other. Articles written for newspapers are sometimes reprinted in books and pamphlets, thereby becoming less ephemeral. But are they more "literary" in book form?

"Literary" may mean "written in one of the literary genre," that is, in the form of a novel, novellete (to use the spelling of Alfred's day), short story, poem or essay. Many essays may be considered journalism if they appear in a newspaper, or as literature if they are published in book or pamphlet form or in a literary magazine. If printed in both forms, they may be called both literary and journalistic simultaneously. Drawing a clear line, then, between Townsend's literary and his journalistic writings is difficult, but he did make the distinction himself, listing his various works to one category or the other.

In 1867, two biographical essays Alfred wrote were published both as newspaper correspondence and as separate publications. Early in the year, an article he wrote after interviewing William Herndon, called "Mr. Lincoln and his Law Partner," was also printed separately as a pamphlet with the grandiose title *The Real Abraham Lincoln*.

Anyone approaching this work under the misconception that it contained the last word about the Great Emancipator would be sorely disappointed. Yet, for all its brevity, it offered insights about Lincoln which could be found nowhere else—thoughts which were typical Townsend, shedding a fresh glimpse of light on some facet of this Illinois country lawyer who had become the nation's leader during its years of crisis. One such comment was Alfred's remark that Lincoln acquired most of his education about the world through reading newspapers, not books—a fact nearly as true of the writer as it was of his subject, and explanatory of many elements in the lives of both men.

Another of Alfred's telling observations was that Lincoln, during his years as President, largely ignored and distanced himself from the widespread graft and other forms of corruption happening in and around Washington in order to stay focused on holding the Union together and winning the war. But, while Lincoln himself, Townsend felt, was personally honest, many people in his administration were not, and it was too much to expect of any one man that he could keep the entire government clean and free from scandal in a time of such grave national upheaval.

Later in the year Townsend turned another series of newspaper letters into a small biography of Giuseppe Garibaldi, the Italian patriot and guerilla leader who had fought many years to free his country from French control and unite it as a nation. At various times Garibaldi had been forced to flee his native land, living for a time in Brazil, later on Staten Island, New York, before returning to resume his political and military activities in Italy.

Alfred looked upon Garibaldi as an heroic revolutionary figure and a man his fellow Americans should know more about. While he was making money—sometimes a lot of it—writing about such subjects, he was also aiming to fulfill his larger purpose of educating the American public about people and matters he felt were important enough to demand their attention. Like several of the Founding Fathers, he felt that a democracy could only run effectively if the electorate was adequately educated and informed, and he often saw himself as a kind of history teacher, doing what he could to make sure this goal was realized—first by informing himself, then by informing others, about significant issues of present and previous times.

In 1869, Alfred would publish the fruits of his labors in his first "big" book—a 650-plus page work titled *The New World Compared with the Old*—in which he attempted to analyze the differences between the governments and public institutions of the United States and those of several European nations. This was an ambitious effort for a young man of 28 lacking a scholarly education, but it was well-received, selling over 80,000 copies—more than any of his later books would.

Compared to most of his writings, *The New World Compared with the Old* seems rather dry now, but it was well-researched and painstakingly executed, endeavoring to put between the covers of one volume all Alfred had learned and theorized about government to that point in time. Published by the subscription house of S. M. Betts, it added measurably both to his reputation as a serious student of politics and to the money he was making as a widely-read newspaper correspondent.

This money also enabled him to have published a collection of some of the better poems he had written up to this time. He had started writing verses in high school and never stopped. Even as a war correspondent he had occasionally taken time from his prose descriptions of the conflict to scribble a few lines in poetic form. It brought a bit of order to the chaos around him.

THE LITERARY MAN

While he earned his living mostly from newspapers, Alfred was also acutely conscious that his writings in that medium were ephemeral and not likely to carry his work and reputation far into the future. Such immortality as writers can gain comes mainly, he knew, through literary writings preserved in books, and it was perhaps his fondest hope at this point to be remembered as a poet long after his reputation as a journalist had been forgotten.

It was toward this end that he prepared *Poems*—containing what would later be called "the most deliberate of his work in verse"—for publication in 1870. This work of 160 pages was dedicated to "Father, Brother, and the memory of Mother." Alfred's mother had died in 1868 at age 66, leaving her husband and their two remaining sons, Alfred and his younger brother Ralph, as immediate survivors. Ralph Milbourne Townsend, carrying his mother's maiden name but following his father's example, had obtained a medical degree and set up a practice. He had also allied with a wealthy family, marrying Ida Hollingsworth, daughter of a partner in the prominent Wilmington, Delaware, shipbuilding firm Harlan & Hollingsworth.

Alfred's book of *Poems* carried the imprint of a publishing firm named Rhodes & Ralph—an obscure company with no reputation in the trade. It may have been a venture put together primarily for the purpose of publishing this particular volume of verse. Was it only coincidence that one of the partners—Rhodes—carried the surname as Alfred's in-laws, while the other—Ralph—shared that name with his own younger brother? "But," someone may object, "Ralph is the *first* name of Alfred's brother, while surely it is the *last* name of Rhodes' publishing partner."

Not necessarily. If Alfred wanted to self-publish this literary work of his, or have it published as a joint venture between, say, his brother Ralph and his brother-in-law (and good friend) Thomas Rhodes, he might well disguise this somewhat embarrassing fact. What poet, after all, wants to admit publicly that he cannot find anyone but himself or family members who like his verses well enough to publish them? To hide this, the poet might contrive to have such a work come out under the imprint of a company which, as far as most people would know, had no apparent family connection. Brother Ralph Townsend, of course, could not use his own last name without betraying that connection. But his first name? Certainly.

The guess here, until evidence surfaces to disprove it, is that Rhodes & Ralph was a family venture through which Alfred self-published his poems without giving the impression of doing so. It was not, after all, a major hoax, only a small deception letting Alfred save face while getting his verses before the public—a few of them, anyway, since *Poems* was printed in an edition of only 300 copies. But he could now boast that he was truly a published poet.

Later in 1870 he also brought out, through the subscription house of S. M. Betts, a humorous novel titled *Lost Abroad*. In the introduction, he claims to have conceived of and started this work on a previous trips to Europe, which may be so. But its contents and timing make the book seem an obvious attempt to capitalize on the popularity of Mark Twain's *The Innocents Abroad,* published the previous year. Its reception, however, was a good deal less enthusiastic, and its scarcity today suggests it sold few copies.

While he could be funny on occasion, humor wasn't Townsend's forte. Many writers of the time, with varying degrees of success, were writing political satire for the newspapers. Several of the best, including Twain (Samuel Langhorne Clemens) and "Orpheus C. Kerr" (Robert Henry Newell) were among Alfred's friends and acquaintances. But, lacking the gift of wit the cleverest of these comic writers enjoyed, he wrote better when he stayed in his own vein and did not try to emulate the humorists.

He also worked better alone than with other people. He and Charles Halpine ("Private Miles O'Reilly") had been good friends but didn't mesh well in tandem. Soon after leaving Halpine's employ at the *Citizen*, he had tried to team up and do political writing with another former war correspondent, William Swinton, but that hadn't worked out either. Swinton had gone to California in 1869 to teach English and later published textbooks which would make him wealthy and famous.

In 1871, Alfred made yet another foray into partnership and editorial work, joining with Ohio-born Donn Piatt to found the Washington weekly *Capitol*, centering on political news. Much as he liked and respected Piatt—he would name a son born December 23 of that year after him—Townsend left this paper as well after a short time and went back to writing on his own. Piatt stayed on for nine more years, making the *Capitol* one of the most influential U. S. newspapers of the decade and setting a high standard for integrity and political astuteness.

After leaving the *Capitol*, Townsend in September of '71 gave the commencement address to the graduating class of Delaware College in Newark, where he and his family had resided two decades earlier. His talk took the form of a lengthy poem about the institution, for which he had done considerable research to augment his boyhood memories. This effort, combined with a recent visit to Chestertown, had begun to rekindle his interest in the peninsula where he had spent his earliest years.

But he soon headed west to Utah where he would cover the trials of several Mormon leaders being prosecuted by the federal government. Actually the charges had been brought by the federal court for the territory, and the sitting judge was known for being intensely anti-Mormon. As a Central High student, Alfred had come to sympathize with the Mormons, whose revolt of 1856-57 had inspired him to write a blank-verse drama, "The Enthusiast."

In 1871 he still retained these sympathies. Covering the trials, he portrayed the Mormons, including Brigham Young, in a favorable light. While he expressed his personal disbelief in the religion, strongly advised its leaders to abandon their practice and defense of polygamy, and considered founder Joseph Smith a fraud, Alfred felt that, on the whole, Young and the Utah Mormons had done a remarkable job in colonizing the desert and creating prosperous, essentially law-abiding communities in an otherwise "wild West."

He also compared the disciplines of the Mormon Church with those of the Methodist system he'd been raised in and did not find them wanting. If anything, he viewed the Methodist hierarchy as less republican and more autocratic. In correspondence written for Eastern newspapers (republished in pamphlet form as *The Mormon Trials at Salt Lake City*), he used the comparison to air old grievances against those Methodist conferences where "my father was ordered off, by government as absolute as Brigham Young's, to live two years in some swampy part of the earth for such a salary as could be picked up—marriage fees and presents of sausage and sparerib about Christmas thrown in."

BACK TO DELAWARE

Yet, while he retained bitter memories of the hardships his family had endured in the Methodist itinerancy, he also recalled pleasant times from his peninsular childhood. In 1872, to rest from the hurly-burly of Washington and the daily pressures of writing about politics, he took steamer trips down the eastern and western shores of that irregular-shaped strip of land separating Delaware and Chesapeake Bays.

The northern part of the region now known as "Delmarva" is about equally divided by the north-south boundary line run in the mid-1760s by English surveyors Charles Mason and Jeremiah Dixon to settle an ancient boundary dispute between the Penn and Calvert proprietaries. East of this line is the state of Delaware, west of it is upper Eastern Shore Maryland. Below Delaware, lower Eastern Shore Maryland extends from the Chesapeake to the Atlantic. Further south are two Virginia counties set apart from the rest of that state by the waters of the Chesapeake.

Cruising down the shores of his native region, Alfred stopped at several of its chief ports of call to renew old acquaintances, make new ones and gather bits of historical and current information. From these he would compose an article—"The Chesapeake Peninsula," for the March, 1872 issue of *Scribner's Magazine*— which may have been the first attempt to write about this area as a self-contained geographic entity.

Alfred's peninsula article, focusing only upon a few shore communities, was not meant to be comprehensive. But, taken together with his Delaware

College commencement poem, it marked the beginning of his renewed interest in the history, character, and literary possibilities of his native region.

Scribner's Magazine at this period was helping to set the pattern for a new trend in American literature. Known as "local color writing," it aimed at healing the wounds of sectional enmity which had culminated in the Civil War and Reconstruction. Local color writing of a sort had existed before the war, but the regional traits it detailed were often used as the bases for cruel humor, with North and South lampooning one another's peculiarities

Post-bellum local color writers, on the other hand, were looking at regional characteristics with a fond, romantic eye, and often with nostalgia. Some went so far as to portray slavery as a benevolent practice in which masters and slaves were almost equally content.

The fact that Americans in most of the country were now willing to read and accept at face value these romanticized accounts of regional life was a sign of forgiveness for the injuries done by and to both sides in the bitter struggle. Suddenly there was an appetite for stories and articles about localities, and Townsend, when writing about the area of his own early memories, would add pieces to the mosaic of local color literature becoming popular in the early 1870s.

While he continued to supply newspapers with daily correspondence out of Washington, many of these letters as well began to focus on local color, looking at the Capital City's past as well as its present. Many of these essays he collected into a 750-page book, *Washington Outside and Inside*, which Betts and Co. would publish in 1873. This was the first book in which he would sign himself "Gath"—a pseudonym he'd recently adopted for his newspaper columns—rather than George Alfred Townsend.

This name, he explained to readers, was comprised of his three initials plus the letter H, which gave a softer, more pleasant sound than "GAT." It was also the name of a Philistine city mentioned in the Bible, there being a verse reading, "Tell it not in Gath." He had experimented with *noms de plume* before, but this one would stick and become famous around the nation as more newspapers signed on for his correspondence.

With these successes came misfortunes in his personal life. In mid-March of 1873, his four-and-a-half-month-old daughter Ella, born December 1 of the previous year, died. Around the same time, the country's financial news turned bad, triggering the Panic of '73, a downturn which caught many people, including Gath, by surprise and left them poorer. The following year, he concluded he would have to give up his literary ambitions and go back to New York, where he knew he could find additional newspaper work.

Why Alfred returned to New York in 1874 is not clear from his own accounts. In one place he states that, having learned about the nation's politics, he now wanted to know how its financial system operated, and New York was the best place to study that. Elsewhere he says he'd become satiated with Washington and yearned for a change of scene. Other evidence indicates he'd lost so much money in the Panic that he needed more regular income than the Capital could provide. Perhaps all of these factors played a part.

In any case, after seven years of Washington life, he moved his family to a dwelling on 34th Street in mid-Manhattan, which would remain his principal home for years to come. Later he would start commuting back to Washington by train on a regular basis and eventually buy another house there. The trip was an easy one of five or six hours each way, and he could write or dictate as he rode. When he had made his first trip down by rail in 1861, only one train per day ran on the single set of tracks from New York to Washington, taking a long day to make the journey. The war, if it had done nothing else positive, had significantly increased the nation's rail capacity and efficiency.

Early in 1874, a son was born to Alfred and Bessie, somewhat easing the loss of infant daughter Ella the previous March. During the following March, however, three-year-old Donn Piatt Townsend succumbed to illness. Having produced four children in eight years, the Townsend household was down to two: Genevieve, approaching nine years, and baby George Alfred, Jr. Both would grow to adulthood, marry and have children of their own.

In New York, Alfred used what time he could spare from newspaper work to visiting the homes and haunts of the state's prominent historical figures, often turning what he learned about these men into articles for the periodical press. Exploring history in the area surrounding wherever he happened to be had long been his favorite form of recreation. Far from being an idle pursuit, it added dimensions to his writing which other newspaper columnists, more focused on the immediate present, often lacked.

He still felt drawn, though, back to his home peninsula, and in 1876, he made a more leisurely journey to the region than he'd had time for in '72. Boarding a steamer in Baltimore, he cruised down the Chesapeake again, this time to the Pocomoke River of Maryland's Eastern Shore. At the river's mouth, the stern-wheeler turned inland and paddled far upstream.

Here was the country where his parents and several generations of ancestors had been born. Many had lived out their lives without ever leaving the region. Alfred, who had spent much time tracing other people's roots, now felt impelled to trace his own. He wanted to get a sense of the land where those earlier Townsends and Milbournes had lived and died. In ways it was a search for his own identity as well, and for him the quest soon became an

A political rally held in Georgetown, Delaware, c. 1900.
Courtesy of the Purnell Collection, Delaware State Archives.

obsession. He sensed there were wonderful, mysterious stories—some in dusty courthouse records, others to be found only in the memories of certain elderly inhabitants of that flat country. It was as if they had long been waiting for him to come back and discover them.

Leaving the steamer at Pocomoke City, he explored the surrounding area, poking into old courthouse ledgers, talking to people, taking copious notes of what he was finding. Then he made his way north to Georgetown, Delaware—his first trip back, perhaps, since he'd left it as an infant—where he visited General Alfred Torbert, a former Union officer who had served with distinction in western Virginia and, after the war, as a diplomat. (Following the general's death in 1880, he would write a detailed account of Torbert's life and career for the *Army-Navy Journal*.) Before leaving Georgetown, Alfred also made inquiries about General John Dagworthy, who had commanded Sussex County militia units during the American Revolution.

His '76 peninsula excursion—made during the Centennial year when patriotic feelings were running high—convinced Alfred that, as time allowed, he would return whenever he could to gather more local facts and legends. He wanted to write these down, mainly to preserve them, but also with the idea of becoming the peninsula's chief historian and story-teller. No one else, he thought, was as equipped to do this as himself, and he took on the task with a sense of mission.

Eighteen hundred seventy-seven brought another loss to the family: his younger brother, Dr. Ralph Milbourne Townsend, died at the age of 32. Now only Alfred and his father were left of the family which, thirty-odd years earlier, had periodically packed its belongings into a wagon and moved up and down the peninsula.

He had come a long way since then. In New York and in Washington he was quite the man about town, a social being who did not let his heavy work schedule keep him from enjoying the fruits of his labors and the company of men he liked. Such notables, most as busy and prominent as himself, often furnished him with grist for his writing mill. On occasion they could be generous toward his literary ambitions as well.

On an April evening in 1879, Alfred met for dinner with ten friends at the Gilsey House in Manhattan. After the meal, which had included the appropriate wines and spirits, conviviality reigned. They were taking turns entertaining one another and Alfred, either from impulse or request, pulled from his pocket the poem "Little Grisette" he had written to commemorate a lost love in Paris. When he read it aloud, his fellow diners were so moved that, when someone suggested they pledge money to publish some of his literary writings in book form, each promised $100 toward the venture.

With this unexpected $1,000 to spur him, Alfred soon pulled together 27 literary works—14 poems and 13 stories—into a book, *Tales of the Chesapeake,* to be published by the American News Company. This work, put into the hands of reviewers, booksellers and influential acquaintances, received a warm welcome. Several fellow writers, including such friendly spirits as Mark Twain, Orpheus C. Kerr, E. C. Stedman and Dr. Oliver Wendell Holmes—and even "The President of the United States," Rutherford B. Hayes—wrote complimentary letters from which blurbs could be extracted to promote later printings.

With the favorable reception given *Tales,* Gath felt he had finally arrived at the point of being accepted as a literary man as well as a journalist. Not one to rest on his laurels, he immediately put together another book, *Bohemian Days,* interspersing four poems, including "Little Grisette," with three short novels. But whereas all of the works in *Tales* were set in the Chesapeake region (including Delaware and tidewater Maryland), nearly all the pieces in *Bohemian Days* took place in Europe during the 1860s. The one exception, a novellete called "The Deaf Man of Kensington," harked back to his earlier days in suburban Philadelphia.

Bohemian Days was originally to be called *Naughty Paris* but someone, feeling this title too daring, substituted the tamer one. *Tales* having appeared early in 1880 and *Bohemian Days* in July of that year, a second series of *Tales of the Chesapeake,* uniform with the first, was advertised to be brought out in November, but was never published. Something apparently got in the way of this projected work and stopped its progress. This something may have been *The Entailed Hat.*

THE ENTAILED HAT

Many writers will confirm that, when they open the closet door to their creative processes, they are not at all sure what will spring out. Sometimes a work takes control of the writer rather than vice-versa. If this happens, it's often best if the writer just puts down what comes to mind, goes along for the ride, and waits to see where it will all end. This is what Townsend did.

The process started in Snow Hill, where he found in the Worcester County Court House the will of a maternal ancestors. Alfred, reading through the document, was astounded to find that in 1800 this individual had bequeathed to a son "my best hat ... and no more of my estate." This odd bequest acted on Gath's imagination. He wondered what the family situation could have been to cause a father to leave his son nothing but a hat. Was there anything special about this hat? Surely such strange matter could become a story.

He started this tale of a hat by creating in his mind an image of the man who had worn it. This individual would have lived most of this life in the 18th Century. But the hat itself might be much older—might even have passed down from father to son through several generations. This possibility opened new vistas. Alfred had been researching peninsula history off and on for nearly a decade, probing all the way back to the earliest settlements. He imagined the hat being as old as these, and it became for him a device for linking together many seemingly unrelated events and people.

As he pursued this line of thinking, he found his story running away from him, leading him toward relatively unexplored areas of peninsular history. While researching at Chincoteague, he ran across old tales recalling the once-notorious Patty Cannon. He had first heard about Patty at his mother's knee—had been told she was leader of a gang of murderers and kidnappers who, in the early years of the 19th Century, abducted many free Negroes and sold them to slave-traders from the deep South.

The gang had flourished from around 1808—when Congress, freed from a 21-year waiting period imposed by the Constitution, passed a law forbidding the importation of any more slaves from abroad—to the early 1820s, when several members were charged with crimes and one was tried and convicted. Patty herself had been arrested in 1829 and indicted for murder. She was awaiting trial in Georgetown, Delaware, when she cheated the hangman by poisoning herself.

The Patty Cannon story was still familiar on the peninsula, being passed down, mostly by word of mouth and with many embellishments, for more than half a century. Having come across it again, Alfred found it too interesting to ignore. He decided to incorporate elements of it into his entailed hat story. Once he did, his tale rapidly outgrew short-story or novellete length, becoming a novel-sized manuscript of several hundred pages—so long that he had to cut much of it out before a publisher would accept it.

The Entailed Hat was published by Harper & Brothers in 1884. Though offered as historical fiction, it contained so much fact and local legend—some of it previously obscure—that it became a kind of peninsula classic and has remained popular in the region ever since, particularly among collectors and lovers of area history. More than anything else he had written or would write, this book assured Townsend some of the literary immortality he'd long sought.

While writing *The Entailed Hat,* Gath had also been busy with other projects. In 1881—the year his father died—his *Poetical Addresses* was published, presenting five occasional poems he had written and delivered during the past decade. Though falling short of great poetry, these works are nonetheless worth reading, if only for the historical research they contain.

When asked to deliver such addresses on notable occasions, Alfred always took them seriously and put much work into them. In one, he lamented the fact that his own periodical writings, and those of other journalists, were destined to be "unindexed and unfound"—ignored and unread by future generations.

Around 1882, Gath made another trip to England, where he spent time researching Oliver Cromwell, another historical figure who had long fascinated him. Cromwell, after his death in 1658, had long been the victim of royalist attacks upon his reputation. But Scotsman Thomas Carlyle, some two centuries later, had written a well-documented life of the Protector which succeeded so far in turning public opinion around that Cromwell, in Victorian times, was being revered as an honest statesman and military hero.

Alfred, after reading Carlyle's work, had come to view Cromwell as an important ancestor of America's republican form of government. While the government he had established in England was soon overturned by the Restoration, it had planted the seeds of the constitutional monarchy which would evolve later. It had also provided a model for the United States Presidency, Alfred felt, and he wanted to point this out to his fellow Americans. His play "President Cromwell" was published in a small edition during 1884 but, as the actor who had intended to perform the title role was drowned off Australia, the play was never performed. It remains unknown, being one of a dozen dramatic writings by Townsend to share that fate.

Also in 1884, after finishing *The Entailed Hat*, the tireless Townsend began researching another novel—this to fulfill a promise made to John Hay in 1865 that he would someday write a book about the Lincoln assassination plot. To research this work, he retraced Booth's movements as nearly as he could, both at Harper's Ferry in 1859 and later, when the actor fled south into Maryland and Virginia after shooting the President.

GAPLAND

Gath's travels on the trail of Booth, besides providing him with fresh information and new perspectives, also accomplished two other important things. The first was to bring him, on the road from Harper's Ferry, Virginia, to Frederick in western Maryland, past South Mountain where the Battle of Crampton's Gap had been fought during the Civil War. Noting the beauty of the place and being aware of its recent historic associations, Alfred fell in love with it at once. He felt it was a spot where he would like to spend as much of his life as he could afford to, and soon made arrangements to buy a hundred acres of land at the site. Over the next decade he would erect there a complex of houses, most of them architecturally impressive, for himself, his wife, his

Newspaper Photograph of Memorial to Civil War Correspondents
at "Gapland," Townsend's Estate.
Courtesy of University of Delaware Library, Newark, Delaware.

children, and guests. Once these were built, he would add a large monument to memorialize his fellow war correspondents and himself.

The second important discovery he made was Thomas Jones who, once Gath found him, admitted that it was he, Jones, who had sheltered and fed Booth during the week he had hidden out on the Maryland side of the Potomac after shooting Lincoln and before crossing the river. He and a few neighbors had kept this secret for nearly twenty years before Townsend, tracking Booth's movements and asking questions, uncovered it.

While researching his novel about the Booth conspiracy—a book he would title *Katy of Catoctin* and see to publication by D. Appleton in 1886—Townsend was putting together a new collection of shorter pieces as a sequel to *Tales of the Chesapeake* and *Bohemian Days*. These stories, referred to by him as *Tales of Gapland* and *Tales of Upper Maryland* were apparently never published in book form, though evidence in Gath's papers at the Maryland Archives suggests some may have been printed as pamphlets or in periodicals. When *Katy of Catoctin* appeared as a book, most reviewers did not take kindly to it. Coming on the heels of *The Entailed Hat* and *Tales of the Chesapeake*, *Katy* set Gath's reputation as a literary man back somewhat.

Still, his reputation as a journalist remained secure, as an autobiographical article in the November, 1886, issue of *Lippincott's Magazine* showed, allowing him to ramble informatively about his quarter-century as a newspaper correspondent. This and his long involvement in Washington politics would win him a plum of sorts. For the 1888 election, he was asked to write the campaign biography of Levi P. Morton, Republican candidate for the Vice-Presidency of the United States. The biography of the Presidential candidate, Benjamin Harrison, was being written by former Union General Lew Wallace, author of the best-selling 1880 novel *Ben Hur*.

The request to do Morton's book was both an honor and an indication of how well thought of Gath was by the hierarchy of the party which had been in power (with the exception of Grover Cleveland's victory in '84) since Lincoln's first election in 1860. It wasn't that he was highly partisan; he had earned a reputation for being balanced and fair as a political columnist, and of refusing to hold grudges, often praising an office-holder for a particular deed or vote after roasting him for a previous one. But, having taken sides decades before as an abolitionist and Union supporter, he had long been identified as partial to the Republicans, to the point where one prominent Democratic editor in these partisan times had referred to him as "the hired poet of the Ring." Certainly he had made friends in political circles, the large majority being Republicans who were the majority party in power in Congress during most of his years as a writer. The fact that the Republicans recaptured the White House in 1888 did not hurt Gath's standing with them at all.

With *Katy* done and the '88 election past, Townsend started a new novel. Ever attracted to revolutionary individuals, he had become interested in Dr. Joseph Priestley, an English scientist best remembered for discovering the element oxygen, but also a political and religious activist. Going against the prevailing views of his country, Priestley had been a vocal supporter of both the American and French revolutions, making himself so unpopular in England that an angry mob had wrecked his laboratory and library. He emigrated to America in 1794, where he would introduce Unitarianism to his adopted country and spend the remaining decade of his life.

Priestley was a conspicuous figure in Philadelphia during Washington's first term as President before moving to more permanent quarters in central Pennsylvania. Gath, in researching Priestley, was also learning more about the politics of that critical period when the new government was struggling to get established and the differing views of Alexander Hamilton and Thomas Jefferson were striving to take it in opposite directions.

Alfred was dismayed by how little Americans, even historians, of his own time seemed to know or care about these important men and matters. Washington, Jefferson and Hamilton were still famous and familiar figures, but mostly in a superficial way. Parson Weems' made-up story about the admirable boy who cut down his father's cherry tree and refused to lie about it was far more familiar to Americans of Gath's day than were Washington's real accomplishments as President.

Always looking for the "insider" angle—the key element others had missed—Townsend dug deeply into the early Federalist period. Among other things he discovered that, when Priestley came to America to live, he was accompanied by a strange little man, Dr. Thomas Cooper, who was a disciple of the famous chemist, but also, Gath came to believe, a parasitic hanger-on who would eventually betray Priestley's revolutionary ideals and sow the first seeds of South Carolina's secessionist movement. Cooper, Alfred found, had gone to Charleston during the late 1820s, where he concocted legal arguments for nullification. South Carolina, using these arguments, would later assert its right to nullify its 1788 ratification of the federal Constitution and break away from the union of states.

As South Carolina's withdrawal from the Union in December, 1860, led to the formation of the Confederacy and the onset of the Civil War, Gath wondered whether Cooper's following Priestley to America and his subsequent activities in South Carolina might have been the trigger for the war.

In trying to write the story of Priestley and Cooper and the early Federalist government at Philadelphia into a novel, Townsend repeated the mistake he had made with *Katy*—he got so many threads going at once that he could not tie them all into a neat, book-sized package.

"Man's reach should exceed his grasp," Townsend's contemporary Robert Browning would write, "or what's a heaven for?" But the gap between Alfred's reach and his grasp forced him to make major cuts in his manuscript in order to reduce it to a suitable length for publishing.

Money was certainly a factor. A "rich friend," as Townsend described him, had offered to underwrite the costs of this book after Alfred successfully tracked Cooper to Charleston. But when the manuscript grew to the point where it far exceeded what could be asked of his friend's generosity, Gath went to his summer residence at Crampton's Gap and cut hundreds of pages from what he'd written—a process so painful he compared it to opening his veins and letting his lifeblood flow out.

The resulting book—*Mrs. Reynolds and Hamilton*—largely omitted the Priestley and Cooper materials, focusing instead on Alexander Hamilton, whom Gath portrayed as a heroic figure wronged by the machinations of Jefferson. Published during 1890 in a small, paperbound edition, the work was a pale shadow of what Alfred had intended it to be. Like *Katy*, it did little to advance his reputation as a literary writer.

GATH'S CONTRIBUTIONS

His journalistic career had reached the point where he was coming to be regarded as a pioneer—an old-timer, as it were—in the field of news correspondence. As the subject of "An Interviewer Interviewed" for the November, 1891 issue of *Lippincott's Magazine,* he was asked if he had, as some were saying, actually *invented* the technique of the interview. Gath replied that he had not—that he had merely used it often and helped popularize it once he overcame his embarrassment about asking people personal questions.

The fact that this question was asked of him only emphasizes Gath's point that people tend to forget history quickly. He was now nearing the end of a successful journalistic career and was already a legend about whom myths had grown up. He had also won a reputation as a literary writer in some circles, though far better known as a columnist.

His best poetry, according to critics, had been done in his youth, while his fiction after 1884 received little attention. Still, at age 50, he continued to write. The habits and discipline of more than 30 years were hard to shake. In

1892, Lippincott published his short piece *Columbus in Love* first in its magazine, then as an offprint. In 1893, a novel called *Cuckoo* was completed but not published. The manuscript has not been discovered.

By 1897 he had produced another series of short works, probably in the same format as *Tales of the Chesapeake*, titled *Tales of Washington City*. These were not published either, and seem to have disappeared.

During the early-to-mid-1890s, Gath was spending a large part of his earnings turning his mountain retreat into what some would call a "baronial estate," erecting more and grander buildings on the site and furnishing them partly with antiques and art objects acquired in his travels abroad. He had also accumulated a working library of some 5,000 volumes, some of these books quite rare. To make sure his and his family's bodily remains would be properly secured after their deaths, he designed and supervised the building of a mausoleum at "Gapland," as he now called his estate. Over the mausoleum entrance was a marble slab engraved with the words: "Good Night, Gath."

Having finished these various buildings for personal use, Alfred decided one more thing was needed—a large monument to the correspondents, artists and photographers of the Civil War, he, of course, being one. After designing a version of what he thought this monument should look like, he launched a subscription drive among friends and acquaintances, receiving $5,000 in pledges from such individuals as Thomas Edison, J. Pierpont Morgan, John Wanamaker, Chauncey Depew, Joseph Pulitzer and others.

With the money collected, and employing native stone for the most part, he soon had constructed at Gapland a 40 by 50 foot structure to commemorate those men who had reported the great war to the American public in words and pictures. As the first monument ever made, so far as is known, to honor those who inform the people through the medium of newspapers, it would be officially opened and dedicated on October 16, 1896, by Governor Lloyd Lowndes of Maryland.

During 1897 and '98 Gath, by his own account, wrote two more novels about notable Marylanders. One, *Talbot's Hawks*, was based on the Maryland adventures of Colonel George Talbot, a cousin of the Calverts who came over from Ireland in the 1680s to settle and guard the northern sector of the royal land grant made to Lord Baltimore. A colorful, soldierly leader, Talbot reacted to the feuds going on between Protestant and Catholic forces in England and the colonies by stabbing a royal customs collector to death. Fleeing prosecution, he hid out in a cave on a bank of the Susquehanna, sustaining himself, legend claims, with meat brought by his trained falcons.

Gath's other novel, *The Taneys*, stemmed from another piece of historical research he had done—this based on a long-simmering grudge. In 1856, U. S.

Supreme Court Chief Justice Roger Taney, in the majority opinion for the landmark Dred Scott decision, had ruled that Scott, a Negro slave, had no right to freedom despite the fact that his white master had brought him to live in a state where slavery had been outlawed. Taney's ruling, at this highest level of the American judicial system, had given additional legitimacy to the institution of slavery when it was under heavy attack in the North. Most galling to Alfred (then a high school student) was the insulting language Taney had used to characterize blacks as little better than animals and unworthy of the rights and privileges the law accorded to white people.

To rebut Taney's widely-publicized decision, Alfred at the time had written a Philadelphia newspaper article on "The Colored People of this City." Nearly three decades later, while researching *Katy* and following Booth's trail down Western-shore Maryland, Alfred had been told by the defense attorney for two of the conspirators that Justice Taney's father had murdered a man and escaped capture, being aided by his son during his fugitive years.

This episode, though known to some in the region, had never surfaced in the national press to damage the younger Taney's public career or reputation. Gath, after ascertaining its truth, determined to write a novel dragging the Taney skeleton out of the closet and revealing the Chief Justice who had written the Dred Scott decision as no model of propriety himself.

In 1899, with money left over from the War Correspondents' Memorial subscription funds, Townsend brought out in book form a collection of his verses titled *Poems of Men and Events*. In its preface, he wrote that he had originally planned to include all of his poetry worthy of being published, but, to keep costs down, had decided to omit most poems extant in previous books. He limited the number of copies to 500, many reserved for subscribers.

After *Poems of Men and Events* appeared, Gath received some belated critical recognition for his poetry. Montgomery Schuyler, a highly respected writer, featured Alfred as the subject of a May, 1900, *North American Review* article, "A Neglected American Poet," praising him not as a great American poet but as a representative one who was well worth reading.

While Schuyler's assessment of him as a poet fell somewhere between adulation and faint praise, Alfred was glad to receive it. He was not unaware of his shortcomings as a poet, but this had never stopped him from trying. He had failed to write the sort of poems which become immortal through inclusion in textbooks, but he had produced a number of verses able to stand comparison with those of individuals who had achieved reputations as poets. Of the huge amount of verse written during Victorian times, the vast majority was mediocre or worse. If Townsend's poems did not earn him a place among the chief bards of his day, they were well enough received to give him a wide reputation as a popular occasional poet.

In 1902, he was asked to help commemorate the 131st anniversary of Old Drawyer's Presbyterian Church just north of Odessa, Delaware. This was also the 60th anniversary of an 1842 address by a minister of that church, Reverend George Foot. On researching the church's history for the poem he would write and deliver, Townsend learned that Foot's speech, printed soon after he gave it, was the earliest known attempt at a comprehensive history of Delaware. He was also pleased when his own poetical address on that anniversary occasion was printed as a pamphlet shortly after he delivered it.

Rev. George Foot

The same year, he visited Charlottesville, Virginia, spending a night at Jefferson's former home, Monticello, as the guest of its current owner, a Mr. Levy. His host was descended from a naval officer of that name who had bought the place soon after Jefferson's death and saved it from ruin. Gath, in *Mrs. Reynolds and Hamilton*, had treated Jefferson badly as the opponent of the book's hero Hamilton. No trace of that rancor exists in *Monticello and its Preservation Since Jefferson's Death*, published as a small book after Townsend had visited the site and written his impressions of it.

On May 30, 1903, Alfred's wife, Bessie, died after years of declining health. Theirs had not been a very close marriage even in the early years, as his writings and travels left him little time for family life. Even at Gapland, where he had finally begun to settle down, he and Bessie lived mostly apart in the separate houses he had built to protect his privacy.

Gath was invited in 1904 to address the Columbia Historical Society of Washington, D. C. Allowed to choose his topic, he decided to explode the myth that many early houses and other colonial American buildings had been constructed of bricks brought over from England. In earlier research, he himself had been duped into believing this legend certain historians held to be so. But, after taking a closer look at the evidence, he found the legend evaporating and soon concluded that early colonists nearly always made their own bricks near their homesites, using local clay. He said as much to the Columbia Historical Society, which printed his remarks in its journal, and felt good about his role in replacing an erroneous legend with verifiable facts.

Following Bessie's death, Alfred was now spending much of his time at his South Mountain estate. He continued to write steadily, producing over the next several years a series of plays and several novels, none of which was ever published. One novel was about Major John Andre, the British officer who helped Benedict Arnold change sides during the Revolution. Andre had been hanged as a spy, but later generations of Americans had come to regard him as more of a romantic figure than a villain. Historians recalled gratefully that Andre had drawn the only surviving sketch of Dover's famous beauty Mary Vining, paramour of General "Mad Anthony" Wayne.

LATER YEARS

For most of the nation's newspaper readers, Gath was becoming a fading memory, a relic of the past. But he was not entirely forgotten, particularly in the states of his birth and current residence. In 1909 Delaware officials asked him to write a poem for the 300th anniversary of Henry Hudson's discovery of Cape Henlopen. That same year, two of his poems and a short prose piece were included in an anthology, *Maryland in Prose and Poetry*.

By now he was ailing physically, plagued with diabetes. Never careful about his health, he had always tended to eat and drink too much, fueling his prodigious output with prodigious intake. Growing older, he lived a sedentary life among his books.

He was also suffering from lack of funds, not having saved enough money when earnings were high to support a long retirement. With his newspapering days over, income was scarce and outgo frequent. His medical bills were increasing rapidly, and maintaining Gapland was becoming a problem.

In 1911, soon after his 70th birthday, an old friend, Wilmington textile industrialist Samuel Bancroft, Jr., made him a proposal. If Gath would pull together all of the Delaware and Eastern Shore poems he had written over the years, Bancroft would see that they were published as a book. Proceeds from its sale could help defray Townsend's expenses.

Alfred was grateful for the offer, which he accepted, but could not supply copies of his peninsula poems very quickly, since his worsening diabetic condition was causing him to spend much of his time in hospitals. He had trouble finding several of his early poems and never did come up with a copy of "Caesar Rodney's Fourth of July" in time to include it in the book.

When *Poems of the Delaware Peninsula* finally went to press in 1913, Gath's reputation was so obscure that only a few copies were sold. Prior to this, he had been forced to sell his beloved collections of books and autographs in order to keep his bills paid.

Shortly before his peninsula book came from the printers, Alfred set himself one more writing task. Now nearly 72, he had left a long paper trail behind him—journals, scrapbooks, letters and autobiographical essays on various aspects of his career in addition to his journalistic and literary writings, published and unpublished. But he wanted to take a final look back over what he called his "literary work and folk," summarizing these for himself and posterity.

What emerged was some forty pages of manuscript in his own hand attempting to "separate my literary from my news life," as he wrote, "and reassemble the authors and composers I have known." He started the memoir under the title "My Literary Work and Folk," then crossed out "My" and wrote in "Gath's." The narrative, though seeming to ramble, follows a generally chronological order with some backtracking. Much of its value stems from the insights it provides into Townsend's literary productions and, toward its end, his political associations as well.

How long it took him to complete his literary memoir is not known, but he lived just over a year and three months after starting it. At the time of his death on April 15, 1914, he was staying with daughter Genevieve and her husband Edmond F. Bonaventure in New York City. During the 1880s Genevieve had married a man only three years younger than her father but, as Gath's son-in-law, Bonaventure had published under his own imprint several of Townsend's literary writings.

After her father's death, Genevieve had him interred in the Townsend family plot at Philadelphia rather than in the mausoleum he had built at Gapland. His grave would be "marked by a marble column surmounted by a bronze bust" according to a contemporary account. Following her husband's death in 1918, Genevieve sold off the Gapland estate. The buildings Gath had so proudly designed and supervised the construction of would, after some years of neglect, crumble in decay. Only the War Correspondents' Memorial would survive more or less intact.

But Townsend's reputation, though dimmed, would not be entirely extinguished. In 1922, the lengthy obituary article he had written in 1880 about General Alfred Torbert was reprinted in pamphlet form by the Historical Society of Delaware. Some years after this, the Gapland property Genevieve had sold was purchased by the state of Maryland and converted into Gathland State Park.

Temple University graduate student Ruthanna Hindes in 1946 wrote her master's thesis on *George Alfred Townsend: One of Delaware's Outstanding Writers* and published it as a book soon after. In 1950, Lida Mayo republished all of the war correspondence chapters in Townsend's *Campaigns of a Non-Combatant* under the title *Rustics in Rebellion*. Issued by the University of North Carolina Press, this book helped introduce a new generation of readers to Townsend's Civil War writings. The same year, an article on him appeared in *The Goldfish Bowl*, newsletter of the National Press Club.

In 1952, University of Delaware English Professor Augustus H. Able III, a specialist in Delaware literature, took it upon himself to savage Townsend's ambitions as a literary writer in a graduate lecture printed in *Delaware Notes*. The tenor of Able's attack was that literature needed to be protected from upstarts like Townsend who lacked the talent to qualify as a true literary artist. Despite this harsh opinion, Gath's *The Entailed Hat* has continued to be sought and read by knowledgeable Delaware book collectors and others.

Maryland Governor Millard Tawes and other admirers of Gath made a serious and heroic effort to boost what Townsend had done. Their plan, unveiled in 1962, was to construct at Gathland State Park, next to Alfred's War Correspondents' Memorial, a National Newspaper Hall of Fame, honoring the best and most respected members of all the journalistic writing fraternity who had kept America's readers informed down through the centuries. This concept got as far as an architect's drawing and a dedication ceremony at the site, but unfortunately did not move to completion, possibly for lack of financial support. Had it been realized, the project would no doubt have done much to promote Townsend's reputation as a journalistic pioneer.

A few of Gath's literary creations were anthologized in a 1974 anthology of Maryland writing titled *Shoremen*, and in 1987 his 1872 essay on "The Chesapeake Peninsula" was reprinted in an anthology featuring peninsular writers. His reputation has thus been kept alive to some extent, but chiefly as a minor writer of local color fact and fiction.

Although some of his published works, including *The Entailed Hat*, have been republished in modern times, most are hard to find even in reprint, which shows at least that there is a demand for them, limited though it may be. In his day, however, he was a giant, familiar to most American newspaper readers and a friend to many of the leading men of his era. The fact that many of his later literary writings have never been published or even typed is a matter that could be remedied, and the recovery of much of his journalistic output is a task more easily accomplished in our present age of computers and scanners than it would have been earlier.

Gath wanted his fellow Americans to learn the lessons a broad knowledge of history can teach. He had spent much of his life and energy trying to realize this goal. It would be a shame, after all his work, not to take advantage of it.

GATH'S LITERARY WORK AND FOLK
Jan 8, 1913

CHAPTER I. THE BLIND GUIDE

Chiefly to have a task at the brink of my seventy-second year, I try to separate my literary from my news life and reassemble the authors and composers I have known.

How I became a *belles lettres* boy I barely know. Perhaps some parental crossing made the concussion, but I started before I was twelve years old to draw and paint and earlier felt the ecstacy of color, varnish and pictorial action. Our parsonage library had no vivid books except my mother's works of John Bunyan,[1] which were more of a puzzle to me than a delight. In country towns I read fragments of borrowed books in hay mows or under the school desk, particularly Smollett's *Roderick Random*.[2] Sometimes a pirate book with colored pictures would be found in the parlor of a parishioner. My reverend father bought *Uncle Tom's Cabin* when it appeared and guided by his laugh I read it and was confirmed in a mutinous bias against the slavery around me.

When we moved to the rustic environs of Philadelphia the Boston periodicals with patriotic novelletes[3] and *Native American Excitations*[4]

---

[1] John Bunyan (1628-1688), an English Puritan preacher during Cromwell's Protectorate, authored the allegorical *Pilgrim's Progress* (1678, 1684) as well as a 1682 book, *Holy War*, and his autobiographical *Grace Abounding to the Chief of Sinners*. *Pilgrim's Progress*, written in a simple style, was enormously popular, going through numerous editions, some lavishly illustrated. Mark Twain wrote in *Huckleberry Finn* that virtually every home in America possessed a Bible and a copy of *Pilgrim's Progress* even if no other books were in the household.

[2] *Roderick Random* by Tobias Smollett (1721-1771), an autobiographical novel published in 1748, enjoyed immediate success and is still read as one of the best works of fiction from the 18th Century.

[3] Following the end of the War of 1812, a so-called "third war with England," also called the "Paper War," was fought using words instead of military weapons. In New England especially, patriotic feeling ran high and literary men began a movement to establish a distinctly American literature which could avoid imitation and stand apart from British models by drawing from native materials. The *North*

took my small pocket money, often obtained by planting corn and potatoes. I heard the son of a church member speak admiringly of *The Scarlet Letter,* which I did not read for years.

Becoming a boy of all work in a city store I read some novels cheaply published, such as George Lippard's *Quaker City.*[5] Later, a pamphlet story against the Volunteer Fire Department by Henry Watson[6] controversially affected me.

I went to a grammar school and quickly passed up into four years at the High School by which time I wrote verses and delivered a poem called *The Pleasure of Timidity*[7] and gained a prize for public composition.

American Review (founded 1815) and similar Boston periodicals carried on this literary war in their magazines for decades, particularly after British critic Sydney Smith, in an 1820 issue of the prestigious *Edinburgh Review,* posed the provocative and sneering question, "In the four corners of the globe, who reads an American book?" Stung by this insult, which contained more than a grain of truth, many writers tried consciously to create literary works which could compete successfully with British ones in the world market. The Boston periodicals Gath speaks of, and which he was reading as a boy, were serializing, in the 1840s and '50s, many of these "patriotic novelletes" mentioned here. [His spelling of the latter word, while later superseded by "novelette," was standard for that time.]

[4] Presumably a patriotic literary periodical of the period.

[5] George Lippard (1822-1854) was an appropriate role model for the young Townsend. Becoming a reporter on the Philadelphia newspaper *Spirit of the Times* at age nineteen, he was an idealistic crusader by nature—a tireless defender of the underdog and a reformer who often exposed corruption by the wealthy in his news stories and literary works. In both his journalistic writings and his novels and plays Lippard antipated the muckraking writers of a later era. His novel *The Monks of Monk Hall* (1844), about the late-night orgies of a number of "respectable" Philadelphians, caused an instant sensation and was widely read. After its title was changed in 1845 to *The Quaker City,* the book went through numerous editions.

[6] Henry Clay Watson (1831-1867), a young Philadelphia reporter and author of popular histories. His most famous work, *Campfires of the Revolution,* was published in 1850 before he was twenty. His entry in the *Dictionary of American Biography* says that "Although his books are no longer read, they were forerunners of the Nineteenth Century type of literature that aimed to present the facts of history in interesting form as a means of popularizing knowledge."

[7] No copy of this poem has yet been found in Townsend's scrapbooks at the Maryland Archives or elsewhere, but an essay titled "The Trials of a Timid Man" done by him for the Philadelphia *Sunday Dispatch* during 1857-58 seems revealingly autobiographical though written to amuse.

> **LECTURE**
> BY
> **GEORGE A. TOWNSEND,**
> BEFORE THE
> **Bryant Literary Institute,**
> Monday Evening, December 27th 1858,
> **SPRING GARDEN ASSEMBLY ROOM,**
> SUBJECT—" George Gordon Byron,"
> **TICKETS 25 Cents.**

Here I joined a household club of five members called *The Quill*, which stimulated production. At that time I first read Shakspere and immediately wrote a rationale of *Macbeth*.

I took a leading part in forming debating societies and in public speaking. Some magazine articles on the Mormons as persecuted affected me to commence a blank verse play called *The Enthusiast*.[8] I wrote for literary and Sunday newspapers.[9] My whole mind was filled with conceptions and experiments in verse and prose. In some way I owned Sabine's *American Loyalists*[10] and started a debate as to whether they were wrong or right. I delivered lectures on Lord Byron's works[11] in a public hall and in my father's city church.

---

[8] This early play is another "lost work."
[9] In the Townsend Collection at the Maryland State Archives in Annapolis is a "Scrapbook of articles written for the *High School Journal*, Philadelphia, and other newspapers, 1857-1858." One such newspaper was the Philadelphia *Sunday Dispatch*, Many other clippings are from *The Welcome Visitor and Young Man's Advocate*, which he edited and may have founded. See George Alfred Townsend Collection, G684, Item 6.
[10] Massachusetts writer Lorenzo Sabine (1803-1877) published his *The American Loyalists, or Biographical Sketches of Adherents to the British Crown in the War of the Revolution* in 1847. He later served as a Whig Congressman in the U. S. House.
[11] George Gordon, Lord Byron (1788-1824), wrote the sort of romantic, iconoclastic poetry that appealed to the young Townsend.

A book fell into my hands called *A Boy's Dream of Geology*,[12] which turned my doubts in that direction. I read Shelley[13] with more zest than comprehension and ran chances to get books from the subscription libraries. My school tasks went under, for promiscuous reading. I walked to Revolutionary battlefields with Lossing's *Camp Fires*,[14] attacked the itinerant system of Wesley's preachers, advocated Lay Delegation in the Conferences[15] and otherwise was nettlesome and mettlesome from some law of my nature.

My father studied medicine and mixed medication with miracles. The secular life was at work in the parsonage.

When I graduated at Nineteen my school endeavors had recommended me to a daily newspaper, else I might have become a preacher of some kind. I went with a newspaper with the same challenge of affairs about me and a certain literary scorn of the

---

[12] *The Fossil Spirit: A Boy's Dream of Geology* by John Mill (1815-1881) was published in London circa 1850. An 1854 American edition, published in New York by Evans & Dickerson, was probably the one Alfred read. The findings of geology, as presented by Charles Lyell and others during the early and middle years of the 19th Century, were casting doubt on the literal truth of the Biblical account of Creation, and would lead Darwin, bolstered by his own observations as ship's naturalist aboard the *H.M.S. Beagle*, to start forming his own theories about the origins of species and of man.

[13] Percy Bysshe Shelley (1792-1822), like Byron a talented romantic poet who wrote iconoclastic verse, was an outspoken atheist and a rebel against all authority. While attending Central High, Townsend was elected president of the school's Shelley Club.

[14] Townsend seems here to have confused historian Benson J. Lossing's *A Pictorial Field-Book of the Revolution* (two volumes, copyrighted 1850, published in 1851 and 1852) with Henry C. Watson's *Campfires of the Revolution* (see note 6) published in 1850. In an 1891 *Lippincott's Monthly* article "An Interviewer Inteviewed," he stated that Lossing's *Field Book* was the work he took on outings to Revolutionary battlefields.

[15] A major dispute had arisen in the Methodist Church during the 1840s over whether laymen could attend the annual conferences and have a vote. Denial of voting power to the laity led to a breach, with those calling themselves Methodist Episcopal Protestants pulling away to form their own churches. The schism would not be healed until 1938. Young Alfred, in advocating lay delegations at the conferences, was staying true to form and upholding the rights of the underdog against authoritarian rule.

commercialisms and cowardice of the political press.[16] It never did occur to me to become owner of a newspaper; that field I explored for excursions and history.

Yet I was precipitated into great events, like the Japanese Embassy's first visit,[17] the Prince of Wales in America,[18] Lincoln's election, Secession, Civil War. These subjects belong to my news diary, though often interlaced with Letters.

I had much more mental than physical temerity,[19] hated to run my face to fires and celebrations and constantly hoped to resume the literary occupation.

Philadelphia had been a focus of abortive literature but was declining. George H. Boker,[20] a fair poet, Henry B. Hirst,[21] a good

---

[16] While taking up journalism as a way of making a living, Townsend frequently stated his wish that he could earn enough as a literary writer to give up reporting. His bitterness at having to grind at the mill of the daily press sometimes expressed itself in carpings at the compromises such work entailed. The distorting influence of business and politics on news writing was a bone of complaint which Alfred gnawed often.

[17] Following the 1854 expedition of Commodore Matthew Perry to Japan and trade treaties signed between Japan and the U.S. during 1857-58, Japan in 1860 sent its first embassy ever to the United States. Townsend, as a young reporter in Philadelphia, covered the embassy's visit to that city.

[18] In 1860, when Queen Victoria's eldest son Edward (later Prince of Wales but then "Lord Renfrew") made an official visit to the United States, Townsend was assigned to cover his appearance in Philadelphia. Edward, born in 1841, was then nineteen (the same age as Townsend). He would become King Edward VII after his mother's death in 1901.

[19] A biographical sketch of Townsend appearing in the *Breakwater Light* newspaper of Lewes on September 9, 1876 (the year of the Centennial, when Gath was 35), said of him: "He has confidence only with his pen in hand, when he is indifferent and invincible to public opinion or to power."

[20] According to *The Reader's Enclopedia of American Literature* (1962 edition), George Henry Boker (1823-1890) was a Philadelphia-born "poet, playwright [who] wrote many plays in verse, but only *Francesca da Rimini*... (1856) won much critical success.... In Philadelphia he helped to edit *Lippincott's Magazine*, and did much to encourage young writers and to restore the city to literary eminence."

[21] *The Reader's Encyclopedia* identifies Henry Beck Hirst (1817-1874) as a "lawyer, newspaperman, poet [who] was one of the few male writers who have assumed the name of a woman ['Anna Maria Hirst'] as a pseudonym; .... His first work, *The Book of Caged Birds* (1843) gave hints to bird lovers and contained a few poems. *Endymion* (1848) was an imitation of Keats; a year later he published *The*

poet but a vagrant drunkard, Paul Sinding,[22] a Swedish historian come to mind, as well as Madame de Marguerittes,[23] a cockney French translator. I had the free entry to the theatres and saw, under the stock system, the round of classical plays with a prepossession for poetical melodrama. The best actor was E. L. Davenport,[24] with a face protean for all noble parts.

I saw what facilities a newspaper publisher had for being the town villain and wrote a raw play called *The Bohemians, or Life in a Newspaper*.[25] I also challenged slavery with a depiction of the more prosperous free Negroes in Philadelphia.[26]

Penance of Roland. He was for a time a friend of Poe, but offended him by writing a parody of *The Haunted Palace*. In later years Hirst became an absinthe addict and [subsequently] died in an asylum for the insane; at this time [before his death] he began claiming the authorship of Poe's *The Raven*."

[22] Paul Christian Sinding (1812-1887) was a Danish-(not Swedish-)American historian of the period. See O. J. Falnes, "Paul Christian Sinding, an Early Scandinavian-American Historian" in *American-Scandinavian Review*, March, 1960, pp. 53-58.

[23] London-born Julie de Marguerittes (1814-1866) made a reputation as an opera singer, appearing in successful productions of Rossini's *La Gazza Ladra* in New York and Philadelphia. After retiring from the stage she became drama critic for the Philadelphia *Sunday Transcript*, also writing books on European subjects for American readers.

[24] Boston-born Edward Loomis Davenport (1816-1877), after making his acting debut in 1836, became one of the nation's ablest tragedians. Glenn Hughes, in *The Story of the Theatre* (New York: Samuel French, 1928), says that, "next to Edwin Booth," Davenport "was considered the best American Hamlet of the nineteenth century" (p. 333).

[25] *The Bohemians* was described by Ruthanna Hindes, in her *George Alfred Townsend: One of Delaware's Outstanding Writers* (Wilmington: Hambleton Printing & Publishing Co., 1946), as "His first attempt, and was unsuccessful." She added "To date no copies are available." During my research for the present work, several copies were located in U. S. libraries. It was published in 1861 by the Marlow Dramatic Club in Philadelphia. Whether it was also performed then is not now known.

[26] Townsend's article "The Colored People of this City," unsigned, was published in a Philadelphia newspaper (probably the *Sunday Dispatch*, but not identified in his scrapbook), during 1858 or soon after.

My war poems got in the *Rebellion Record*[27] and Doctor Oliver Wendell Holmes[28] recited one, *Roanoke*,[29] in a lecture on the War Literature. I called on Dr. Holmes in Boston at his office. Colonel Forney[30] made me dramatic Editor in place of Mr. Shelton Mackenzie[31]

---

[27] *The Rebellion Record* (1861-1868), a notable periodical of the Civil War era, was edited by Frank Moore. It strove to be objective and provided a historical and literary forum for writers on all sides of the issue to air their views and get works published. William Cullen Bryant, John Greenleaf Whittier, Oliver Wendell Holmes, along with many poets and prose writers of lesser fame, were contributors. One of Townsend's war poems, "The Volunteer's Wife," run earlier in the Philadelphia *Press*, was reprinted in the *Rebellion Record* (pp. 64-65) during late 1861, being followed by a poem of George H. Boker, mentioned in Gath's memoir as a "fair poet" (see Note 20 above).

[28] Dr. Oliver Wendell Holmes (1809-1894) was a man of many parts and talents. A physician by training and practice, he was also noted as a leading poet, wit and essayist of his era. A Boston Brahmin of independent mind, he was a staunch, vocal and prominent critic of slavery. Townsend obviously felt pleased and proud to have one of his own poems recited in a lecture by a man he so greatly admired, so much so that he felt emboldened to seek out Dr. Holmes in Boston and pay him a personal visit. In 1880, after reading Townsend's *Tales of the Chesapeake*, Holmes sent him a letter praising the book.

[29] *Roanoke*, a poem of 96 lines, was written early in 1862 by Townsend soon after a joint Army-Navy operation under Union naval officer Louis M. Goldsborough and General Ambrose Burnside attacked and defeated a Confederate garrison on Roanoke Island, North Carolina, in February, 1862. Townsend's verses linking Sir Walter Raleigh's 1585 "Lost Colony" with the recent Union victory at this site were later included on pages 81-84 of his book *Poems* (1870).

[30] Newspaperman John Wien Forney (1817-1881) had founded the Philadelphia *Press* in 1857 after failing to receive a patronage job in the administration of President James Buchanan, whose candidacy he had long and ardently supported. The *Press* was often critical of the Buchanan administration, reflecting its editor's disappointment. But Forney would later serve as Clerk of the U. S. House, still later as Secretary of the Senate, meanwhile continuing to publish both the *Press* and the Washington *Daily Morning Chronicle*. During 1861, he hired young George Alfred Townsend away from the Philadelphia *Inquirer* to become city editor of the *Press*. Within a short time, Forney named Townsend as the paper's dramatic editor as well, allowing him more exposure to the theater, where he would make the acquaintance of John Wilkes Booth and be inspired to write *The Bohemians*.

[31] Robert Shelton Mackenzie (1809-1881), Irish-born British journalist who came to New York in 1852 and to Philadelphia in 1857 where, upon the establishment of the Philadelphia *Press* that year, he was named its literary and foreign editor and dramatic critic. His sketch in the *Dictionary of American Biography* states, "This position he retained for over twenty years," but there is no reason to doubt

Important operations in war and government[32] two years. I wrote papers there for the *Cornhill Magazine*[33] and *Chambers' Journal*.[34]

When I returned in 1864 I became a literary Editor in New York City[35] till another digression into the news carried me a second time into War Correspondence. I married and then had to depend on newspapers for support, but I made a strong effort while lecturing over the country to compose a novel,[36] the daily compulsions breaking up

---

Townsend's statement that he replaced Mackenzie for a while as drama critic for the *Press*.

[32] These "important operations" included Townsend's adventures as a Union war correspondent for the *New York Herald* covering the Peninsula and other campaigns during 1862. A detailed account of these is in *Campaigns of a Non-Combatant* (1866).

[33] *The Cornhill Magazine,* founded at London in January, 1860, was published by Smith, Elder & Co. William Makepeace Thackeray, author of *Vanity Fair* and one of Victorian England's leading literary figures, served as its first editor until March, 1862. Later that year Townsend submitted his American Civil War articles. The first of these, "Richmond and Washington during the War," appeared on pages 93-102 of *The Cornhill*'s December, 1862, issue. The second, "Campaigning with General Pope," occupied pages 758-770 of the January, 1863, issue. Chapter 21 of Townsend's 1866 book *Campaigns of a Non-Combatant* is also titled "Campaigning with General Pope," but the texts are quite different. In his *Cornhill* article (unsigned, as was his prior piece), Townsend portrayed Pope as "Vain, imprudent, and not proverbially truthful...." No such description appears in *Campaigns,* published under his own name.

[34] At the beginning of *Tales of the Chesapeake,* Gath writes that "Of the following pieces, two, 'Kidnapped' and 'Dominion over the Fish,' have been previously published in *Chambers's Journal,* London." *Chambers's Journal of Popular Literature, Science, and Arts,* conducted by brothers William and Robert Chambers, was published in London and Edinburgh during the mid-19th Century. A Philadelphia edition was put out by Lippincott, Grambo & Company.

[35] Townsend, when he returned from Europe in 1864, became a writer and editor on the New York *World,* for which he had been writing special correspondence while abroad.

[36] Townsend relates in the preface of *Lost Abroad* that in 1864 he had first started trying to write a humorous book about his European travels, employing the device of a fictional narrator, while sailing home from France. As it is unlikely he would have considered that work a novel, this may have been his initial attempt at long fiction.

Political Cartoon, circa 1880, featuring "Gath" loading the musket. *Courtesy of Maryland State Archives.*

the continuity. In 1865 I joined Charles G. Halpine[37] publishing the *New York Citizen*[38] and fought the Tweed ring[39] to the last, while Halpine extricated the registership for himself and died of prosperity.

I became aware of the fatuity of mixing Letters with newspapers and projected a joint correspondence with William Swinton[40] at Washington. He went off to publish school books; I saw him, later, selling premium gold at the Capitol for Wall Street, and there he died on one of his Scotch aberrations.

I took up Washington correspondence in 1867 and speedily attracted newspaper employers and for a few years had a good income and exhausting work, till in 1874, the financial panic drove me back to New York for several years, to again lose my literary dreams in dogged

---

[37] Charles Graham Halpine (1829-1868), Irish-born American newspaperman who, having attained a reputation as a humorist before the Civil War, enlisted as a Union officer, served as chief-of-staff to General David Hunter, commander of the Department of the South, and rose to the rank of Brigadier General before retiring from the army in July, 1864. [For his wartime relations with Admiral Du Pont, see John D. Hayes (ed.), *Samuel Francis Du Pont: A Selection from his Civil War Letters* (Ithaca: Cornell University Press, 1969).] During the war, Halpine, using a pseudonym, wrote newspaper correspondence for Northern papers. Many of these pieces were reprinted in *The Life and Adventures, Songs, Services and Speeches of Private Miles O'Reilly* (1864). As a token of his regard for Halpine, Townsend in 1866 dedicated his *Campaigns of a Non-Combatant* to "Private Miles O'Reilly."

[38] When Halpine, after retiring from the army, started the New York *Citizen* newspaper as an instrument to fight the corrupt Tweed Ring then dominating New York City politics, he hired Townsend as its editor.

[39] William Marcy Tweed (1823-1878), headed a political "ring" in New York City which swindled taxpayers of millions of dollars. Working mainly out of the city's administration building, Tammany Hall, Tweed and his cronies survived charges of corruption for years before being brought to justice. Political cartoonist Thomas Nast, drawing for *Harper's Weekly* magazine, built a reputation attacking Tweed and the "Tammany Tiger." In 1873, Tweed was convicted of fraud and died in jail five years later.

[40] William Swinton (1833-1892), born in Scotland, taught school in New York City before going into newspaper work. He covered the Civil War as a New York *Times* correspondent. From 1869 to 1874 he taught English at the University of California, but quit after a disagreement with administration officials and began writing textbooks. With public education on the rise, his *Readers* became standard texts in many of the nation's elementary schools. Townsend, who knew Swinton as a fellow war correspondent, planned a working partnership with him after Halpine's death, but this did not materialize.

journalism. I then returned to Washington and resumed political letter-writing to the present time.

In 1869 I published *The New World Compared with the Old*,[41] a subscription compilation which earned me about $3500. Also a small book of Poems[42] and a romaunt called *Lost Abroad*.[43]

The incompatibility of Authorship and newspaper contributions almost wore me out. I had attained the age of forty and never realized a careful book. One night some roystering public men at a hotel[44] had me recite a poem, *Little Grisette*,[45] long ago composed and [,] under the inspiration of poetry and perhaps, spoil, they passed around a paper and subscribed $1000 to publish my pieces. I collected my fugitive stories into *Tales of the Chesapeake*,[46] printed them myself, and apparently put my foot for the first time on the sill of Literary Authorship. Godkin, in *The Nation*,[47] previously my Thersites,[48]

---

[41] *The New World Compared with the Old: A Description of the American Government, Institutions, and Enterprises, and of Those of our Great Rivals at the Present Time, Particularly England and France*, published in Hartford by S. M. Betts & Company, was an ambitious 663-page book written to set forth Townsend's thoughts and researches concerning how the government of his own country measured up against those of European countries he had studied.

[42] In 1870 Townsend had published, apparently at his own expense, his first book of *Poems* (Washington, D. C.: Rhodes & Ralph).

[43] *Lost Abroad* (Hartford: S. M. Betts & Company, 1870) is a 594-page effort at writing a humorous travel book. In the preface Townsend remarks that he had begun writing this book about his European travels in 1864.

[44] Gath's dedication of his *Bohemian Days* (1880) which he originally intended to title *Naughty Paris*, reads: "To ten friends at dinner, Gilsey House, New York, April 21, 1879; who made this publication a promise and an obligation."

[45] *Little Grisette*, a poignant poem about lost love, had appeared in *Poems* (1870) and was probably written during Townsend's sojourn in Paris during 1863-64.

[46] The $1,000 subscribed by his friends enabled Townsend to publish *Tales of the Chesapeake* (New York: American News Company, 1880) and win wider recognition as a literary writer than he had previously been able to do. A third edition of this work contains praises (included to boost sales) from such worthies as Mark Twain, Henry Wadsworth Longfellow, Oliver Wendell Holmes, E. C. Stedman, "the President of the United States" (presumably Rutherford B. Hayes) and others, showing that Gath was indeed running in heady company at this time.

[47] Edwin Lawrence Godkin (1831-1902) was a correspondent during the Civil War for the London *Daily News*. In 1865, he helped found and was first editor of *The Nation*. To keep it going, Godkin made *The Nation* the weekly edition of the

praised the book. From its encouragement I printed myself *Bohemian Days*, which lacked a publisher's impetus.

It was literally "to take up arms against a sea of troubles" to compose a novel, amidst distracting newspaper work, of not less than 5000 words every day, but with the desperate intent to recover my lost youth I sat down to *The Entailed Hat* in 1881 and wrested it from my marrow and bones. It was properly published and had no evil treatment except from a disconsolate refugee newspaper editor. It still circulates, though published nearly thirty years.

Now the revived hopes of Authorship militated against my profitable newspaper avocation. I wrote two more novels under the same slavery, *Katy of Catoctin*[49] and *Mrs. Reynolds and Hamilton*.[50] The former went through one edition when the publishers failed, from ultra[-]commercialism. A friend[51] gave me a thousand dollars to publish the second book, of which the news dealers stole the returns.

This second book had been first named *Dr. Priestley, or the Federalists*. I recall General Lew Wallace[52] asking me who Dr. Priestley was, after I thought I had told him minutely.

New York *Evening Post* during his tenure at the newspaper, from which he retired in 1900.

[48] Thersites, mentioned in *The Iliad*, is identified as "an ugly, abusive Greek soldier killed by Achilles [also a Greek] in the Trojan War." Godkin, possessed of a keen intellect and unquestioned integrity, was known for being a tough but fair critic. He had apparently been hard on some of Gath's previous writings, but liked *Tales of the Chesapeake*.

[49] Published by D. Appleton & Company in 1886. In this novel, written with the encouragement of John Hay and others and to fulfill a vow he had made in 1865, Townsend attempted to show a causal connection between John Brown's raid in 1859 and the assassination of Lincoln by Booth six years later.

[50] Published in New York by E. F. Bonaventure in 1890. As E. F. Bonaventure was Townsend's son-in-law, married to his only daughter Genevieve, this was a family-connected firm. The money underwriting its publication came from Gath's friend John G. Moore, but was apparently not sufficient for publishing the original work in its entirety.

[51] Probably John Godfrey Moore, to whom *Mrs. Reynolds and Hamilton* is dedicated.

[52] General Lew Wallace (1827-1905), while distinguished as a Union officer during the Civil War and an elected and appointed government official afterward, is now best remembered as the author of *Ben Hur: A Tale of the Christ* which sold millions of copies in his own time and millions more since.

This book I went to my country place of Gapland[53] alone in the dead of winter, lighted the fire in the semi-stable called Askelon[54] and cut it down like opening my veins, leaving an episode instead of the story. This was done to come within the expense. John Hay[55] took a long, friendly interest in this book and commended its portrait of Washington, which he thought a dangerous experiment.

Among my High School mates were two who came to some career as writers. Joel Cooke by the accident of a law office relation to a stockholder of the *London Times* became American correspondent of that paper, and financial reporter of the *Philadelphia Ledger*, and died rich, a member of Congress.

Another amateur writer, Albert Lancaster, had instant, catchy talent in verse. He drifted to the New York Sunday papers and almost disappeared there, figured slightly in dramatic production, and, as I afterward found, starved to death though of good example.

I may cite Mark Twain as a censor of writing life. When he was married at Elmira I was consulted about his character and habits by Washington city friends of the bride. I replied that he stood highest on the press and the Lyceum, and queried the mercantile family's non-importance in the public world.

"What is your business?" asked the [bride's] parent of Mark. "Writer, lecturer." "That is no business. Go buy a newspaper: that is a business." They bought him an interest in a Buffalo newspaper, the beginning of his stable life.

So, I unhesitatingly say to any young man with the writing propensity: be a promoter and not merely an employee! If you desire to be an author, get money first, so as not to be dependent on mercurial situations.

---

[53] Townsend's country home in Maryland between Harper's Ferry and Boonsboro.
[54] Askelon was the first and simpest of the buildings Gath erected on his Gapland estate starting in 1884.
[55] John Milton Hay (1838-1905), Lincoln's personal secretary and a valued friend of Townsend's, had a varied career in politics and journalism as well as being a literary writer and biographer.

Chapter II. Letters in News

When I was twenty four years old Mr. Lincoln's murder I heard of in burning Richmond City[56] and at Washington. I found Detective Police from everywhere, stimulated by the rewards, many of whom knew me in my police reporting days,[57] and they gave me advance information. My Booth letters to the New York *World* were collected in a pamphlet[58] which I saw before each member of the Military Court and found it quickly circulated at the Baltimore and Philadelphia news companies. When I called on the publisher he began the usual process of bluffing the author, so I sold for $300 a copyright good for the rest of my life.

But this historic crime held my interest a long time, partly through its inception in Maryland whence my people came. Missing links in the chain caused me to explore the Potomac peninsula and I found the spy who had fed and expedited Booth[59] and bought his narrative which I published in the *Century Magazine;* its efficacy is acknowledged in Nicolay and Hay's *Life of Lincoln*.[60] I probably possessed more details

---

[56] Townsend was in Richmond covering the war when he heard of Lincoln's being shot. Rushing to Washington, he initially used notes and interviews gathered by Jerome Stillson to write some of the earliest news reports of the assassination plot and the flight of Booth.

[57] In the Townsend Collection at the Maryland Archives is a document (Number 86 in the collection list and dated June 15, 1865) appointing Townsend as a Special Deputy Sheriff in New York. This probably aided his research on Booth, giving him access to materials only police officers could see.

[58] *The Life, Crime and Capture of John Wilkes Booth,* compiled from his New York *World* letters, had been published in pamphlet form by Dick & Fitzgerald in 1865, apparently without Townsend's permission. It was selling for a quarter a copy retail.

[59] He is referring to Thomas A. Jones, who (as detailed in Gath's April, 1884 *Century Illustrated Monthly Magazine* article, "How Wilkes Booth Crossed the Potomac") had abetted Lincoln's assassin for a week by hiding and feeding him while he was being sought by federal troops. Booth's whereabouts during that April 1865 week had been a mystery for nearly two decades until Gath's digging uncovered Jones and reported his story.

[60] On page 308, Volume 10, of John G. Nicolay and John Hay's *Abraham Lincoln: A History* is this statement: "After parting with Dr. Mudd, he [Booth] and Herold went to the residence of Samuel Cox...." The footnote for this statement reads, "What Booth and Herold were about during the week between the 15th and

of the President's murder than any person of my time and they persuaded me to combine John Brown's raid and Booth's cabal, as cause and result, in the historical novel *Katy of Catoctin*. With equal avidity I hunted down the actors in John Brown's raid. One day I found the brother of John Y. Beall,[61] whom I had seen hanged on Governor's [I]sland[62] and described it to the effect of beginning a career on that paper; Beall was Booth's intimate at Brown's raid and some reason exists for Mr. Lincoln's death following his refusal to pardon Beall.[63] Allstadt,[64] a prisoner of Brown in the Engine House,

the 22nd of April was not brought out upon the trial of the conspirators, but George Alfred Townsend, while making the extensive and careful studies for his historical novel, 'Katy of Catoctin,' reconstructed the entire itinerary of the assassin, and published an admirably clear account of it in 'The Century Magazine' for April, 1884." [This article is referred to in Note 59 above.]

[61] John Yates Beall (1833?-1865) was born to a wealthy Virginia family and educated at the University of Virginia. Beall was present at Harper's Ferry with Virginia militia when John Brown was captured. Commissioned a Confederate Army captain at the outbreak of the war, he served under "Stonewall" Jackson, later receiving a commission as acting master in the Confederate Navy. In September, 1864, as head of a Confederate raiding party, he went to Canada in civilian dress, boarded an unarmed steamer bound for Detroit, and, with some 25 other raiders, hijacked the ship, robbed the purser, threw part of the cargo overboard, then ran down another steamer, robbing and scuttling it. Landing the hijacked ship, Beall and his men then tried to derail and rob a train running between Buffalo and Dunkirk by placing obstacles on the track. When this failed, the group escaped to Canada. Arrested three months later, Beall was extradited, tried, convicted and hanged as a spy.

[62] When Beall was hanged at Governor's Island, New York on February 25, 1865, Townsend witnessed the execution and wrote about it for a New York newspaper.

[63] Gath, having learned that Beall and Wilkes Booth had been friends before the war, and that both had been present at Harper's ferry when John Brown was captured and executed, surmised that much of Booth's animosity toward Lincoln might have sprung from the fact that the President, when Beall was sentenced to die, had been asked (on grounds that Beall was acting under orders as a Confederate officer rather than as a spy) to commute the sentence but refused to do so. In 1864, Booth had written in a letter to his brother-in-law, "When I aided in the capture and execution of John Brown, I was proud of my little share in the transaction, for I deemed it my duty and [believed] that I was helping our common country perform an act of justice. But what was a crime in poor John Brown is now considered (by themselves) as the greatest-only virtue of the whole Republican party. Strange transmigration! Vice to become a *virtue* because *more* indulge in it." [Cf. Jules

minutely gave me the vivid occurrences there. Reading Miss Gibson's *Pennsylvania Dutch*[65] I became interested in the Dunkers,[66] whom I visited at Ephrata[67] and at Snow Hill,[68] in Penna. I drove from Hagerstown to Frederick city to discover a Dunker meeting house for my story. Judge Frederick Stone of lower Maryland,[69] counsel for Mrs. Surratt and David Herold[70] (to protect some important constituents) gave me less assistance than I gave myself. Jones, the go-between, guided me over the points of Booth's hiding. I went up the Rappahannock River and over Booth's route from Port Royal to Garrett's farm.[71] My novel was much called for after its publication

---

Abels, *Man on Fire: John Brown and the Cause of Liberty* (N.Y.: Macmillan, 1976), p. 384.

[64] John H. Allstadt was a farmer living near Harper's Ferry when several of Brown's fellow raiders, seeking local slaveholders to hold as hostages, took him and his son, along with six of their slaves, to confine at the Armory. Another hostage so taken was Col. Lewis Washington, grand-nephew of the nation's first President. Later Allstadt, Col. Washington and others would testify at Brown's trial that they had been protected and treated courteously during their captivity.

[65] Gath's memory is slightly faulty here. The book he refers to is obviously Mrs. Phebe Gibbons' (not Gibson's) *"Pennsylvania Dutch" and Other Essays* (Philadelphia: Lippincott, 1872).

[66] *The Reader's Encyclopedia* (1948 edition) defines Dunkers as "A religious sect akin to the Baptists, founded in Germany in 1708 by Alexander Mack. In 1719 a party of them emigrated to Pennsylvania. They follow Bible teaching as closely as possible and adhere to the simplicity of the primitive Church. They practice immersion, hence the name."

[67] Ephrata, a town north-northeast of Lancaster, is well-known for its Cloister, the religious community founded there in the early 1800s.

[68] As no community called Snow Hill shows up on present-day maps of Pennsylvania or in old gazetteers, we may assume that Gath is here referring to a Dunker settlement in Snow Hill, Maryland, though the syntax is confusing.

[69] Frederick Stone, born 1820 in Charles County, Maryland and educated at St. John's College in Annapolis, was admitted to the bar in 1841. Following the assassination of President Lincoln, he was named defense attorney for Dr. Samuel Mudd, accused of being an accomplice of John Wilkes Booth. Stone also assisted in the defense of David Herold, one of Booth's co-conspirators, later serving two terms in Congress before being appointed a judge.

[70] Mrs. Mary Surratt, a Washington boarding house proprietress, and David Herold, a former druggist's clerk, were tried as co-conspirators with Booth in the assassination plot. Both were convicted and hanged.

[71] Richard H. Garrett, a farmer near Port Royal, Virginia, owned the barn in which Booth was found hiding and shot to death.

ceased. Local constituencies in slave states are slow to find the book store. I wasted much literary demonstration on local themes in non-reading states. During those years the natural history of the romance reader became altered by the prosperity following the war. Information was unpopular and sensuous femininity ruled the publications.

However, my pursuit of materials was its own reward, and no doubt gave a literary finish to my newspaper letters, particularly in summarizing character.

Pennsylvania nearly equally disappointed me as a reading field. Some of the incongruous elements in that state seem to resent literary men and endeavor. Bayard Taylor[72] at a breakfast I gave him with Hay and Whitelaw Reid,[73] told how Philadelphia hissed his portrait in a lecture galaxy and he never made a mistake like his Pennsylvania novels which necessarily dealt with commonplace, substance people. The domination there of snarling Dutch newspapers[74] is fatal to books. The book reader requires an elevation of motive and artistic perseverence which are obnoxious to the printers of commonplace.

I put Pennsylvania with confidence as a wide state rather barren in books of romance. Judge Iredell's *Letters*,[75] published just before the Civil War, gave a vivid hint of the political society in Philadelphia in Washington's administration, leading features being the Bingham

---

[72] Bayard Taylor (1825-1878) was a well-known journalist, travel-writer and poet of the period. Hailing from Kennett Square, Pennsylvania, a short distance from the site of the Battle of the Brandywine and also from northern Delaware, he and Townsend had much in common as friends.

[73] Whitelaw Reid (1832-1912), one of Gath's fellow Civil War correspondents, became editor of the New York *Tribune* (1882-1905), later served as U. S. ambassador to Britain until his death.

[74] Gath is probably referring to Pennsylvania German ("Deutsch") newspapers, which he considered as provincial and having little interest in literary or intellectual matters.

[75] James Iredell (1751-1799), born in Lewes, England, came to America at age 18, became a lawyer in North Carolina, later served on the Supreme Courts of that state and, following appointment in 1790, of the United States. On the latter court, his opinion in *Chisholm v. Georgia*, says an encyclopaedia biography of him, "contains the germs of all the later doctrines of state rights." Justice Iredell's *Life and Correspondence* (N. Y.: Griffin J. McRee, 1857) offered an inside perspective of Philadelphia political life during the Federalist period of Washington's Presidency.

household[76] and Dr. Joseph Priestley,[77] discoverer of oxygen gas, and also Alexander Hamilton[78] who administered the Treasury and put down the Whiskey Insurrection there.[79] Probably the living people no longer considered those historic days. I gained at least an understanding of those affairs from my ardor to stand upon their sites. Graydon's *Memoirs*[80] a little piloted me. I went alone with some

---

[76] "In 1790," writes Horace Mather Lippincott in *Early Philadelphia: Its People, Life and Progress* (Phila.: J. B. Lippincott & Co., 1917; p. 40), "the rich William Bingham built his 'Mansion House' at Third and Spruce Streets, about which he placed Lombardy poplars, the first seen in the city. He had a high board fence about his grounds to conceal their beauty and keep the vulgar gaze from his lavish entertainments."

[77] Dr. Joseph Priestley (1733-1804), an English clergyman, philosopher and chemist, among other things, possesses what one biographer has called a "versatile and energetic mind." While contributing to many fields of learning, Priestley is best remembered today as the discoverer of oxygen. He was also a controversial figure, not afraid to express unpopular opinions. His religious views were complex. An avowed materialist, he nonetheless professed belief in redemption through Christ. France thought him a Christian while England considered him an atheist. A believer in freedom, he supported both the American and French Revolutions, his latter views so enraging some neighbors in Birmingham that they wrecked his house, including his library and scientific equipment. After this, he moved to America, settling in Northumberland, Pennsylvania, where a son was living. He is credited with founding the first Unitarian church in America, which John Adams and Thomas Jefferson both attended, during his stay in Philadelphia.

[78] Alexander Hamilton (1757-1804), after serving as Washington's aide-de-camp in wartime, was his chief advisor and Secretary of State during his Presidency. Perhaps the chief proponent of the Federalist form of government, Hamilton admired the English system of government and inclined toward a monarchy for the U. S., which led to a growing rift between himself and such liberal republicans as Jefferson and Madison. He was killed by Aaron Burr in a duel toward the end of Jefferson's first term as President.

[79] The Whiskey Insurrection took place in Western Pennsylvania during 1794 to protest an excise tax put on domestic distilled liquors three years earlier. This tax having been proposed by U. S. Secretary of State Alexander Hamilton, the insurrection was put down by armed forces under his command. This episode illustrated the growing hostility between Hamilton and Jefferson as members of Washington's cabinet. Jefferson would later resign, oversee the formation of the Democratic-Republican Party, and win the Presidency in the election of 1800.

[80] Alexander Graydon (1752-1818) published his *Memoirs of a Life, Chiefly Passed in Pennsylvania, within the Last Sixty Years; with Occasional Remarks upon*

temerity and at my own expense to out of the way places such as down the Monongahela River over one hundred miles and stops, by steamboat, to realize Albert Gallatin[81] at his farm by New Geneva. Everybody called him Gal*lan*tine, so perfectly had Jefferson's Secretary of the Treasury become erased. At Carlisle, where I addressed the literary societies and presented Bosler Hall to Dickinson's College,[82] I saw, as at Bedford, the camps of the Army of 1794,[83] drove from Brownsville to Little Washington, and went to Northumberland to visit Priestley's home and grave.

My second visit to Northumberland (where Priestley lived for years) was made from New York and I arrived in the early morning and before registering at the small hotel made my way into Priestley's great deserted house down by the river flats and was pacing and measuring the rooms, to fix the philosopher as in life, when a great crack, or settlement, went through the edifice, reminding me that I had left no clue to myself, was worth several hundred dollars in money and ornaments, and could be knocked on the head and buried in the cellar.

There, too, was confusion, boding no good to literary revival, as to whether I hunted Priestley's doctor son or the old chemical doctor.[84] Yet not long before[,] England and America had here blended

---

the General Occurrences, Character and Spirit of that Eventful Period (Harrisburg: John Wyeth, 1811), recounting his adventures as a Revolutionary War officer.

[81] Albert Gallatin (1761-1849) appears briefly as a character in Gath's *Mrs. Reynolds and Hamilton*. Born and raised in Switzerland, he came to America at age 19 to help in the Revolution after turning down a commission as a Hessian officer under the British. After the war he settled at New Geneva (named for his native city), Pennsylvania in 1783, where he and three partners built the first glass-making operation west of the Alleghenies. A leader in the Whiskey Insurrection, he became successful as a financier, later serving in Jefferson's and Madison's cabinets as Secretary of the Treasury.

[82] Dickinson College, founded at Carlisle, Pa., by Philadelphia physician and Revolutionary war figure Dr. Benjamin West, was named for his friend John Dickinson, Delaware-raised "Penman of the Revolution."

[83] The Army of 1794 was evidently the military force which under Secretary of State Hamilton put down the Whiskey Insurrection.

[84] Priestley's son, also named Joseph, had become a local physician of some reputation, so, when Townsend came to Northumberland and began asking older local inhabitants if they remembered Dr. Joseph Priestley, several responded by relating their memories of the younger man, making Gath's research more difficult.

telegraphy and salute to the banished chemist on the hundredth anniversary of oxygen's discovery.[85]

All the notices of Doctor Priestley in all the books said that he was the father in law of Doctor Thomas Cooper,[86] who came to America with his son. They had no relationship. Cooper was an injurious parasite of Priestley and embroiled him rather more than he could have embroiled himself, though he was frequently hunting a controversy, as with Edward Gibbon.[87] English Cooper was a principal author of

---

[85] In 1874, to celebrate the 100th anniversary of Priestley's discovery of oxygen, British and American scientists and other interested parties arranged a joint celebration, part of which featured telegraphed messages between the two countries. A new attempt was being made the same year at laying a transcontinental underwater telegraph cable, this one linking northern Ireland to the northeastern United States via Nova Scotia.

[86] Dr. Thomas Cooper (1759-1839), born in England and educated at Oxford, is referred to now in most sources as a "friend" or "associate" of Priestley but not as his son-in-law, as Townsend indicates the books of his own time did. In his youth he was an ardent sympathizer with the American and French revolutionary movements and an outspoken opponent of slavery. But, disgusted with the excesses of the Revolution in France, and having made himself unpopular in his native country, Cooper moved to America in 1794 with Priestley, settling near him at Northumberland, Pennsylvania. Cooper mainly followed Priestley as a disciple or protege during these years, embracing both Unitarianism and Jeffersonian Democratic-Republicanism when the latter was rising to oppose Federalism. After Jefferson's election as President, Cooper served as a Luzerne County, Pa. commissioner from 1801 to 1804, then as a state judge until 1811, when he and other judges came under fire from Democrats who perceived them as being too conservative. Lacking political backing from either party and charged with arbitrary conduct in office, Cooper was removed from the judiciary. He soon returned to teaching, first at Dickinson College, then at the University of Pennsylvania. In 1819 Jefferson recruited him to teach at the new University of Virginia, but, when local clergy objected to Cooper's Unitarian views, had to withdraw the appointment. Cooper then became a professor of economics at South Carolina College (later the state university) where he began to defend both the Southern position on the tariff and the slavery that he had denounced decades earlier. To further these interests, he developed a legal argument that individual states possessed the power to nullify their ratifying of the federal Constitution.

[87] Edward Gibbon (1737-1794) was author of *The Decline and Fall of the Roman Empire,* universally conceded to be the best work of history in the English language. The reference to Priestley's hunting a quarrel with Gibbon shows Gath's awareness that Priestley, a Unitarian who accepted revealed religion, had attacked Gibbon in *History of Corruptions of Christianity* as an unbeliever. Gibbon, in response,

nullification[88] in South Carolina and a ruffian judge in Pennsylvania,[89] rejected by both political parties. Yet when I corrected the author of a university book on that relationship he expressed great surprise and smothered the correction. Cooper had disappeared from the North. I pursued him to Columbia, South Carolina where nobody had apparently ever heard of him. The next day I went over the graveyards' walls and discovered his monument and found his plaster bust in one of the secret society lodge rooms at the College. This so tickled my rich travelling companion[90] that he published my book.

In some localities, or jurisdictions, the lesson of their local history appears not to survive two generations. There is a want of ideals in American daily life and the cause is the ubiquitous daily small newspaper which monotonizes the morning and afternoon with its locust whirr and unimportance and sheds its wing and dies. When Dr. Rush[91] banned newspapers from his endowed library as "bundles of

---

"declined the challenge in a polite letter, exhorting my opponent to enlighten the World by his philosophical discoveries...." (Edward Gibbon, *Memoirs of my Life* [edited by Georges Bonnard; New York: Funk & Wagnalls, 1969), p. 171].

[88] Townsend, in analyzing root causes of the Civil War, points out that Cooper, who had attacked slavery while in England, later became one of its staunchest defenders in America. A sketch in the *Dictionary of American Biography* says of Cooper: "Valuing union too little because he loved liberty too well, he was one of the first to sow the seeds of secession." The liberty Cooper espoused, however, obviously did not extend to black slaves. He did not live long enough to see South Carolina follow his reasoning to become the first state to secede from the Union and ignite the Civil War. But Townsend, having uncovered Cooper's seminal role in creating legal arguments for dissolving the Union in order to preserve slavery, wanted to reveal his apostasy for the nation to contemplate.

[89] See Note 86.

[90] Evidently John G. (for Godfrey) Moore of New York, to whom *Mrs. Reynolds and Hamilton* (originally titled *Dr. Priestley and the Federalists*) was dedicated. The book was published by Gath's son-in-law, E. F. Bonaventure, but Moore was paying to have it printed. The fact that it had to be so cut down, however, suggests that Townsend had written a much longer book than Moore's donation could pay for publishing in full.

[91] Probably Dr. James Rush, one of the sons of Dr. Benjamin Rush (1745-1813), Revolutionary-era patriot, physician, essayist, etc., and a principal founder of Dickinson College. Dr. James Rush was a distinguished physician and author in his own right, though he had a reputation as an eccentric. When he died in 1869, provisions had been made in his will for the establishment of the Ridgway Library (his wife Phoebe having been one of the New Jersey Ridgways) in Philadelphia.

unimportant trifles," I resented it, for all we who write them assume newspapers to be solely right. Yet, at my present age, I read old Shakspere after the day's newspapers are done, with gratitude that no small scribes disturbed his personality and abstract occupation.

Long after I published *Mrs. Reynolds and Hamilton*, I took solace at Bath Abbey Church, England, reading the burial tablet of William Bingham, the senator banker.[92]

At Warrington between Manchester and Liverpool, where Priestley had been a schoolteacher[,] I inquired of a policeman for his probable schoolhouse. The man had never heard of him but was manifestly pleased to aid a literary inquiry and set me to wondering if we are any better than other nations for forgetting historical reverence.

I must tell a story of John Sherman, Secretary of the Treasury[93] so long and well. Being at his house one Sunday, we discussed Alexander Hamilton, whom Mr. Sherman said had organized the Treasury and its bookkeeping as they still ran after a hundred years. "I'll tell you where

---

Several provisions of the will, including the one banning newspapers, were controversial and some led to litigation. The library, completed in 1877, was a major boon for researchers, but it was not in any true sense a "public" library, which many Philadelphians resented. Townsend, being familiar with the controversies surrounding the library as a young journalist, had initially resented the low esteem in which the benefactor had evidently held newspapers, but in his older years, he became, as he says here, more tolerant of Dr. Rush's distaste for "news."

[92] See Note 76. Bingham, buried at Bath Abbey, appears as a character in Gath's *Mrs. Reynolds and Hamilton*.

[93] John Sherman (1823-1900), brother of Union General William Tecumseh Sherman, was first elected to Congress from Ohio in 1854, then moved to the Senate in 1861, where he served as finance committee chairman until 1877, when he was appointed Secretary of the Treasury by President Rutherford B. Hayes. After Hayes left office after one term, Sherman was re-elected to the Senate, later (1897-98) serving as McKinley's Secretary of State. Contrary to the impression Townsend leaves, Sherman served only four years as Secretary of the Treasury (1877-1881), but chaired the Senate Finance Committee for many years, which is probably the cause of Gath's confusion. He was a favorite-son candidate for President in the election of 1888, losing to Benjamin Harrison. He is best remembered now as author of the Sherman Anti-Trust Act, aimed at promoting competition by breaking up monopolistic trusts.

President Rutherford B. Hayes as a Union army general.

you can find it all," said the author of *Specie Payments*;[94] "there is a book giving Hamilton's life and work. Get that!" "What book can it be?" "I forget who wrote it. But it's all there!" "You don't mean *The Rivals*, by Jerry Clemens?"[95] "No." "Or Margaret Moncrieff?"[96] "No, no." "You don't mean *Mrs. Reynolds and Hamilton?*" "Why, that's it." "I wrote that book." "Indeed? That's Hamilton exactly." Long after I published my book[,] at a possibly better interval, came *The Conqueror*[97] on the subject of Hamilton by a woman, so was my novel of Lincoln long after followed by *The Crisis* by Churchill.[98]

Possibly to be a newspaper participant is a bar to loftier letters and their recognition. Press men do not exploit a rival. Newspaper stories advertise each other.

CHAPTER III. LITERARY OUTINGS

The foregoing chapter inspires the idea that the United States is interesting to explore if we have studied its history as closely as that of Europe. Particularly does exploration for literary creation enliven and heroize the jagged news life. Knowledge and news favorably react on

---

[94] Gath is probably referring to "Species Resumption and Refunding of National Debt," an address given in the House by Sherman during the second session of the 46th Congress (1880-81) and printed as *House Executive Document Number 9*.

[95] Jeremiah Clemens (1814-1865) was elected to the U. S. Senate from Alabama in 1849, but his support for Millard Fillmore (who assumed the Presidency upon the death of Zachary Taylor) was so unpopular among his constituents that he retired from office and turned to writing fiction. *The Rivals*, an 1860 novel about Hamilton and Burr, is considered his best work.

[96] Margaret Moncrieffe Coghlan's *Memoirs of Mrs. Coghlan (Daughter of the Late Major Moncrieffe), Written by Herself and Dedicated to the British Nation; Being Interspersed with Anecdotes of the Late American and Present French War, with Remarks Moral and Political* was first published in London by John Lane in 1794. She is portrayed in Gath's *Mrs. Reynolds and Hamilton* as a girl of nearly 14 seduced and made pregnant by 20-year-old Aaron Burr, who then lied to Washington, telling him she was a precocious spy who should be immediately sent back to England.

[97] This biographical novel about Hamilton by Gertrude Atherton (1857-1948) was first published in 1902.

[98] American novelist Winston Churchill (1871-1947), not to be confused with the British statesman of the same name, published this Civil War novel in 1901.

each other; either, without the other, is like traveling on one leg, or on legs without a head. Frequently the news is barren without books.

For instance, when Lincoln was nominated President the publishing sons of an old newspaper publisher[99] had no biography of Lincoln, then a stark new Eastern quantity. This was the more remarkable as one of them, George Harding, had tried the Reaper case[100] with Edwin M. Stanton and Lincoln. Both regarded him as a slouch quantity, their mere attorney of Illinois record, and would not use his brief, though his fee in that case let him pursue Douglas with debate.[101] The two Harding brothers insisted that Justice John McLean[102] would be

---

[99] The newspaper referred to is the *Inquirer* of Philadelphia. Begun in 1829 as the *Pennsylvania Inquirer,* a Democratic organ supporting President Andrew Jackson, it did not thrive, and was bought by Bible-publisher Jesper Harding, who cut its Democratic ties, made it more business-friendly, and soon had it prospering. In 1859, control passed to Jesper's son William, and in 1860 its name was changed to the *Philadelphia Inquirer.*

[100] The "Reaper case" was a patent-infringement suit brought by Cyrus McCormick, inventor of the McCormick Reaper, against John H. Manny and associates, makers of a rival reaper in Rockford, Illinois. Manny's lawyers included George Harding, a Philadelphia patent attorney and a grandson (not a son) of Jesper Harding, publisher of the *Philadelphia Inquirer,* and Edwin M. Stanton (later Lincoln's Secretary of War). Lincoln was also retained on the advice of Elihu Washburne as Manny's attorney of record in Illinois, as being licensed to practice in Manny's home state. The trial was held, however, in Cincinnati, Ohio, and Lincoln, while attending, did not participate, being snubbed, some say, by the "high-powered" team of Harding and Stanton. Though ignored, Lincoln stayed on and listened to the arguments, telling friends he had learned much by doing so.

[101] While Lincoln was given no active part in the *McCormick v. Manny* trial, his retainer fee enabled him to run against Illinois' Democratic Senator Stephen A. Douglas in the 1858 elections. The seven Lincoln-Douglas debates during the campaign, reported extensively in the national press, helped focus the debate over the slavery issue as nothing else had previously. Douglas, not opposed to slavery, *was* opposed to secession. His stance in the debates, while it won him the Senatorial election against Lincoln, cost him the support of the South, and quite possibly the Presidency, in 1860. Lincoln, while losing to Douglas in 1858, was so elevated by his strong showing in the debate that he was able to win the nomination of the Republican Party and be elected President in 1860.

[102] New Jersey-born John McLean (1785-1861) spent a distinguished career in government, much of it in Ohio. While serving as an Associate Justice of the U. S. Supreme Court, he wrote a dissenting opinion taking issue with Chief Justice Taney and the majority in the famous Dred Scott case by stating his view that slavery had its origins mainly in power and was unjust, being sustained only by local laws in

nominated, and he was, I think, a connection of Harding's wife. When the evening news came in of Lincoln's nomination I was started out to find something about the lucky nominee. "Where shall I go?" "Go up the the Atheneum Library."[103] Of course, nothing was there. All they knew of Lincoln was that Elihu Washburne[104] told them, when they needed an Illinois lawyer of record, that as lawyer Arnold[105] was on the other side they might make use of a man, Lincoln. This name they found in a lawyers' Directory. They had not acuteness enough to appreciate him afterward. They had been thick with the greatest man to be in history and despised him as a rustic westerner. Spite of their scorn, the noble "Sucker"[106] offered them both important offices. At that time Lincoln's debates with Douglas had been published by Howells[107] and Howard, to both of whom he gave consulates. For want

---

certain parts of the United States. In 1848, McLean was a nominee for President at the Free Soil Party Convention. In the Republican Party conventions of 1856 and 1860 he received a number of votes as well. But the Hardings, like many others, had underestimated Lincoln's popularity and McLean lost.

[103] The Atheneum Library was at Sixth and Adelphi Streets in Philadelphia.

[104] Elihu Benjamin Washburne (1816-1887), born in Maine, attended Harvard Law School, then moved to Illinois, where he became a close friend of Ulysses S. Grant. Elected to Congress in 1852, he chaired the House Commerce Committee for a decade. Grant, elected President in 1868, named him Secretary of State, but Washburne resigned after less than a week in office, pleading ill health. He was then appointed minister to France, playing a key role there during the Austrian-Prussian War (covered by Townsend as a special correspondent for the New York *World*). After distinguished service in France, Washburne returned home in 1877. In the 1880 Election, his name was mentioned for the Republican Presidential nomination, but he refused to run. His later years were spent writing, lecturing and collecting books. Gath valued Washburne's friendship highly.

[105] Probably Isaac Newton Arnold (1815-1884), born in New York, admitted to the Illinois bar in 1835, appointed city clerk of Chicago in 1837. A prominent lawyer in Illinois at the time of the Reaper Trial, Arnold later wrote a life of Lincoln.

[106] In referring to Lincoln as the noble "Sucker" and putting the latter word in quotation marks, Gath may be using a word applied to him by either Harding or Stanton during the 1860 campaign or earlier. In those times the word "sucker" was already in use to mean "a gullible person, one easily duped," and Stanton's contempt for him during this period is a matter of record. Despite this, Lincoln, not being a man to hold grudges, chose Stanton as his Secretary of War in 1862 and offered George Harding an ambassadorship.

[107] William Dean Howells (1837-1920), later to become one of America's best-loved and most influential literary men, wrote and edited with J. L. Hayes (Howells

of a book the *Philadelphia Inquirer* had scant story next day of Abraham Lincoln. Nor had he friends in Pennsylvania except the Memnon of Union literary men, Cameron[108] and the politicians who opposed Seward[109] as too spiritual for Pennsylvanians. Lincoln was not as much scholar as Seward, but had tougher fibre.

My literary hopes, if not important in works, saved me from common associations and habits on the press. I explored the Wissa-

---

doing Lincoln and Hayes doing Hamlin) the 1860 campaign biographies *Lives and Speeches of Abraham Lincoln and Hannibal Hamlin*. For his work, Howells was rewarded by being named U.S. Consul at Venice. Gath is evidently mistaken here in using the name Howard instead of Hayes. As far as is known, no edition of the Lincoln-Douglas debates was published separately by Howells and anyone named Howard. Howells did include speeches from the Lincoln-Douglas debates in his campaign biography of Lincoln.

[108] Simon Cameron (1799-1889) of Pennsylvania, who, after years as a newspaper editor in Doylestown and Harrisburg, was elected a U.S. Senator. At the Republican convention of 1860 he was nominated for the Presidency. On the first ballot he received 50 and a half votes, placing him third behind William H. Seward (with 173 and a half) and Lincoln (with 102) in a field of thirteen. Cameron's name was then withdrawn and his supporters switched their votes to Lincoln, helping him carry the day against Seward and win the nomination. After being elected President, Lincoln appointed Cameron as his first Secretary of War. Gath's reference to him as the "Memnon of Union literary men" suggests Cameron had a powerful voice in the Republican Party. The original Memnon, in Homer's *Iliad*, was an Ethiopian king killed by Achilles but made immortal by Zeus. In Roman times, Memnon became mistakenly identified with the 47-foot-tall statue of another ancient African king, Amenophis (or Amen-hotep) III of Egypt. This statue was alleged to "speak," or to make a noise at intervals, which some hearers compared to the twanging of a harp-string or the striking of a piece of brass. Scholars since have speculated that a person concealed inside the statue could have caused the erroneously named Memnon-statue to sound off periodically. Others think it might have been a natural result stemming from a peculiarity in the statue's construction.

[109] William H. Seward (1801-1872), after making a reputation as an eloquent abolitionist attorney and election to the U. S. Senate from New York, was front-runner for the Republican Presidential nomination in 1860, but, after leading on the first ballot, could garner little additional support from backers of other candidates, most of whom swung to Lincoln on the strength of his showing in the 1858 debates with Democrat Stephen A. Douglas. After winning the election, Lincoln appointed Seward as Secretary of State, and in that position, he achieved his own immortality of sorts by negotiating the purchase of Alaska from Russia in 1867—a move that, being widely opposed at the time by many Americans, became known as "Seward's Folly."

hickon Creek[110] and wrote its legends in the newspaper. Greater war news abetted poems, not compensated for but companions of the fantasy. I almost knew Watson's *Annals*[111] by heart. Having had short childhood and no sisters, my sources of nature lay back in the Delaware Peninsula, and lay moist like its marshes till I began to explore it at middle age, partly to find out myself.

The court records my parents knew nothing about were all the time there. The preface to *The Entailed Hat* shows that I conjectured that story from the record at Snow Hill: "I leave to my son Ralph my best hat and no more of my estate."[112] That item had more influence than great news to me till I realized the old hat on the queer man.

I was much facilitated in those days by free Press passes on the railroads, which gave a helping hand to Letters. By their courtesy I went into the old peninsula to find where I came from and, if possible, why. With commendable ambition in genealogy the slave states were long behind New England in family certainty. My father's people had

---

[110] Wissahickon Creek runs through North Philadelphia's Fairmount Park before emptying into the Schuylkill River.

[111] John Fanning Watson (1779-1860) had written at least one draft of his *Annals of Philadelphia* by 1823, but its publication by Carey & Hart in 1830 was the first of many printings, later ones containing additions and revisions by the author.

[112] The passage Gath referred to here bears quoting (with clarifications) at some length: "... the heart [Gath's own] began to turn, as in first love, or vagrancy almost as sweet, to the little lowly region where his short childhood was lived, and where the unknown generations of his people darkened the sand—the peninsula between the Chesapeake and the Delaware [Bays].

"Far down this peninsula lies the old town of Snow Hill [Maryland], on the border of Virginia; there the pilgrim [Gath himself] entered the [Worcester County] court-house [Snow Hill being the county seat], and asked to see an early book of wills, and in it he turned to the name of a maternal ancestor, of whom grand tales had been told him by an aged relative. His breath was almost taken away by finding the following provisions [to his ancestor's will], dated February 12, 1800:

"'I give and bequeath to my son, Ralph Milbourn, MY BEST HAT, TO HIM AND HIS ASSIGNEES FOREVER [Gath's emphasis], and no more of my estate.' .....

"Everywhere he [the pilgrim, Gath himself] went[,] the Entailed Hat seemed, to the stranger in the land of his forefathers, to appear in the vistas, as if some odd, reverend, avoided being was wearing it down the defiles of time.... [T]his being took both sexes and different characters, as the author weighed the probabilities of its existence. At last he began to know it, and started to portray it in a little tale."

not moved since 1670,[113] yet were lost in conjecture till, after my father died, I discovered them in the Maryland Archives, published by the bequest of Harrison Everett.[114] Most Maryland history up to that time was a compound of romance and assertion, each author trying to prove his seat, or religion, to be the only credible one.

Into that old strand of my story and estuary I went alone with a fervid heart. It had few books. The far end of it looped with Accomac, Virginia. I explored Rehoboth,[115] where was the first Presbyterian ministry,[116] and crossed to Chincoteague Island and rediscovered Patty Cannon.[117] Places far away and preserved in their antiquity relieve the mind from the busy world, its small episodes and profitless problems. The prejudices I portrayed were not those of the more refined people there. Yet my *Entailed Hat* became the principal, if not the only novel there, and brought pilgrims back to see their heritage. One of the last

---

[113] The Townsends who were Gath's paternal ancestors had apparently inhabited the Worcester County area of Eastern Shore Maryland starting around 1670. In the "Preface" to Townsend's last published book, *Poems of the Delaware Peninsula*, his anonymous patron (Samuel Bancroft, Jr.) refers to "the region of his fathers, where his male ancestry was revealed, in 1686, as interpreters for the Eastern Shore Indians before Lord Baltimore's Council at St. Mary's."

[114] While Harrison Everett has not yet been identified, it is known that the Alfred and his parents had been friends with a family named Everett while residing in Chestertown.

[115] Rehobeth (the current standard spelling), Maryland, lies southwest of Pocomoke City. It should not to be confused with Rehoboth (Beach), Delaware. In the past both spellings have been used for both places. The word, Hebrew in origin, means "room for more."

[116] Rehobeth Presbyterian Church in Somerset County, Maryland, was begun in 1706 by the Rev. Francis Mackemie, considered the founder of Presbyterianism in America.

[117] Gath tells in his "Introduction" to *The Entailed Hat* that he first heard stories of the legendary exploits of kidnapper/murderer Patty Cannon and her gang at his mother's knee. How he came across other stories of Patty in Chincoteague, many miles from where she lived and operated on the Maryland-Delaware border west of Seaford, is not presently clear but her son-in-law Joe Johnson is known to have shanghaied free blacks from Philadelphia, Baltimore and other mid-Atlantic ports, and the gang's reputation apparently extended the length of the Peninsula and further. In *The Entailed Hat*, we first meet Patty's son-in-law and partner in crime Joe Johnson in Princess Anne, Maryland, where he is supposedly engaged in a kidnapping-for-hire project.

THE TOWNSEND FAMILY TREE

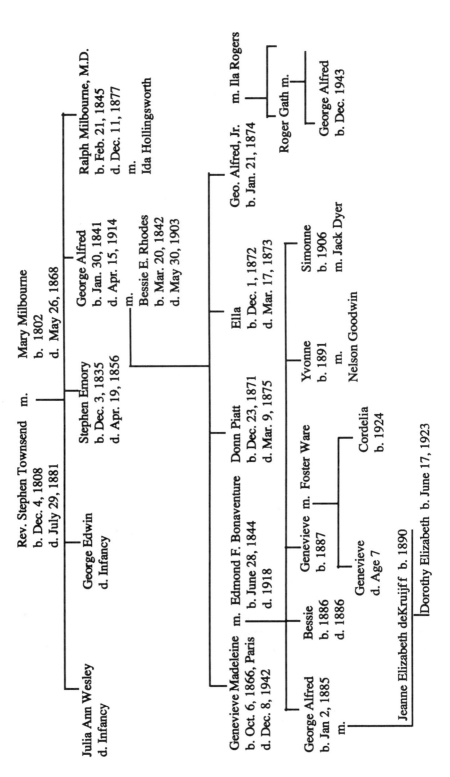

trips I made, years after the publication, was up the Sassafras River[118] from Baltimore, when I met a gentle couple on the steamboat, to whom I was unknown, and as I queried the old traditions, the lady mentioned my name, in full, as having restored their life. I felt that authorship had some rewards beyond shekels.

The best help I had in these peninsular forays was from a book on the early Methodist societies by Rev. John Lednum,[119] a local preacher my father had often sent me to get for our pulpit. To a secular perception the churches are repositories of biography, like the tombstones in old graveyards. A sermon delivered by Rev. George Foot [120] on Drawyers Church[121] was long the main history of Delaware

---

[118] The Sassafras, dividing the counties of Cecil and Kent in Maryland on the northeast side of Chesapeake Bay, runs through part of the old Bohemia Manor tract once owned by Augustine Herman.

[119] The Reverend John Lednum (1797-1863), born near Bridgeville, Delaware, entered the Methodist itinerancy in 1823, a dozen years before Townsend's father, who afterward came to regard him as a mentor and friend. In 1859 Lednum completed and published *A History of the Rise of Methodism in America* at Philadelphia, dying there four years later.

[120] The Reverend George Foot (1800-1867), while serving as minister at Drawyer's Presbyterian Church near Odessa, delivered there on May 10, 1842, *An Address, Embracing the Early History of Delaware, and the Settlement of its Boundaries, and of the Drawyers Congregation, with All the Churches Since Organized on its Original Territory.* This 68-page essay, printed at the office of the Christian Observer in Philadelphia the same year, is acknowledged as the earliest published history of Delaware.

[121] Drawyer's Presbyterian Church, now known as " Old Drawyer's," was founded on the bank of Drawyer's Creek, for which it is named, in 1711. How the creek got the name was long a matter of conjecture. Gath, thinking it must be a derivitive of "drawer," meaning one who draws ale from a keg, wrote in 1902 poem (see Note 122):
And Drawyer's Creek took name, as I opine
From one whose tavern drew new ale and wine.
A later researcher, attorney Joshua Clayton of Elkton, Md., after digging into the matter during 1934, concluded that (a) the first use of the name was on a map drawn by Augustine Herman, founder of Bohemia Manor, and (b) an early settler (probably of Swedish descent) named Anders Dreijer had owned a mill and land along the creek as early as 1656 and was the likely source of the name. Dreijer's Creek, according to Clayton, was rendered as "Drawyer's Creek" on the map Herman drew for the Calverts of Maryland during the 1660s.

State. In time I made the annual address in poetry there,[122] which his literary example had set on foot. This teeming country affords to not many a shrine of origin. The greatest of our Literature, possibly, is the copious local history which is supported by the self-esteem of a posterity. Large cities devour their rudiments, yet, perhaps, free the adult mind from too narrow limits to undertake broad history.

After I had published *Katy of Catoctin*, the Chief Justice of Canada (William?) Strong came to Washington on a commission of Award and had the landlord of the Arlington Hotel to invite me to meet him. Wondering what for, I found the Judge had read *Katy of Catoctin*, of which a scene was at St. Catharine's, Canada, which I visited to realize it. I found he knew the novel better than I did who wrote it, and I took him over the scenes, as he had a government carriage. He said he considered Washington the seat of the most interesting history and romance in the world. I did not say to him what I thought that its literary treatment was least appreciated by its own public men.

At Washington my frequent equal in literary mindedness was Samuel Tyler,[123] author of the *Life of Chief Justice Taney*,[124] of whom he was a townsman, worshipper and pro-slavery friend. Tyler was a man of the happy Southern manner and respect, much out of time with his views, but interesting even if agreeably egotistical upon the subject of a compendium of philosophy he had written, which Lady Amberley[125] and Sir William Hamilton[126] had praised. We often took

---

[122] To celebrate the 191st anniversary of the founding of Drawyer's, as well as the 60th anniversary of Foot's address (see note 200), Townsend read a long memorial poem he had written for the occasion, in which he gave a summarized history of early Delaware and the Church in verse. See *Poem by George Alfred Townsend Read at Drawyer's Presbyterian Church, New Castle County, Delaware, June 1st, 1902* (Wilmington: Printed for the Society of Friends of Old Drawyer's From *Every Evening*, 1902).

[123] Maryland-born Samuel Tyler, born 1809, after admission to the bar of his native state, settled at Frederick City and became known as a writer of philosophical and literary articles and books. His *A Discourse on the Baconian Philosophy* (1844) was followed in 1848 by his *Burns as a Poet and as a Man*. Tyler's *The Progress of Philosophy in the Past and in the Future* (1859) had a second issue in 1868.

[124] Tyler's biography of Justice Taney appeared in 1872. Townsend apparently found him an amiable, entertaining companion even if he did not share some of Tyler's views.

[125] Lady Amberley was the wife of Viscount Amberley who died in 1876.

our tipple together at Mrs. Whitney's tavern on Capitol Hill. I was not much impressed with his *Life of Taney*, of which that Chief Justice wrote the best part himself, and abruptly ended it without later particulars.

After I built a summer residence near Frederick city I examined Taney's obscure house,[127] noted his grave by his mother, found no clue to his father and visited his wife's brother's place toward Pennsylvania —the lawyer bard, Francis Scott Key.[128]

In the meantime I had composed a Maryland novel[129] on Colonel George Talbot,[130] the border trooper of Maryland, who committed a

---

[126] Possibly Sir William Hamilton of Preston (1788-1856), the most erudite and famous philosopher of the Scottish School. Although Tyler's compendium was published after Hamilton died, the Scotsman could have been familiar with parts of it before then. But several other scholars bearing the title and name Sir William Hamilton are also known of.

[127] Roger Brooke Taney, after coming to Frederick, Maryland in 1801 and starting a law practice with Francis Scott Key, married Key's sister Anne in 1806. Prospering, he built a two-story brick house in Frederick during 1815 and was elected to the state senate the following year. His defense of the abolitionist German Methodist preacher Gruber occurred in 1819. Taney was appointed Attorney General of Maryland in 1827, and in 1831 President Andrew Jackson named him Attorney General of the United States. When Supreme Court Chief Justice John Marshall died in 1835, Jackson appointed Taney to fill the vacancy.

[128] Francis Scott Key (1779-1843), born in Frederick, Maryland, began practicing law there in 1801 with friend and future brother-in-law Roger Brooke Taney. In 1805 he moved to Georgetown in the District of Columbia to enter a partnership with his uncle Philip Barton Key (see Note 138 below). Nine years later, near the end of the War of 1812, Key penned the "Star-Spangled Banner" while aboard a British warship trying to negotiate the release of a friend. Taney later wrote a detailed account of this episode.

[129] *Talbot's Hawks* was written, by Gath's own account, in 1898, but never published or typed because he felt there was no market for it. The location of the manuscript, if it still survives, is not known.

[130] Colonel George Talbot of Castle Rooney, County of Rosscommon, Ireland, was a cousin of Cecil Calvert, second Lord Baltimore. To gain colonists, Calvert in 1680 granted his cousin a 32,000-acre tract on the upper Chesapeake and lower Susquehanna if Talbot would bring and settle at his own cost "580 persons of British or Irish descent here to inhabit." Talbot built a fortified dwelling on Susquehanna Manor, as he called his estate, using a company of mounted rangers to protect his lands from Indian attacks.

murder[131] on [here the name "Chris" has been written, then scratched through] the popular leader of the colony in the time of Charles II.[132] Talbot was an Irishman, cousin of the Lords Baltimore & his important crime only came fully out in the Maryland Archives. He lived above the mouth of the Susquehanna, where my father was a pastor in my sixth year. I examined his "castle," the cliff where John P. Kennedy[133]

---

[131] In 1684, Lord Baltimore, found himself out of favor with Charles II. The 1680 Restoration having put the Stuart monarchy back on the English throne, court favorites were again jockeying for wealth and power. The Calverts, who owed their proprietary rights in Maryland to an earlier grant from Charles I, were now seeing their province threatened both by William Penn and the Virginia colony. While Calvert was in England fighting for his rights at Court, a warship commanded by Captain Thomas Allen of His Majesty's Royal Navy sailed into the Patuxent and anchored. Allen made a point of consorting with the King's Collectors of taxes and duties in Maryland, including one Christopher Rousby. Col. Talbot, left in charge during Calvert's absence, went aboard the warship to protest insults made by Allen and Rousby to the Proprietor's authority. When he tried to return to shore, he was prevented, and, losing his temper, drew a knife and stabbed Rousby to death. He was immediately placed under arrest, carried to Virginia and locked up in Gloucester Prison. When requests from Maryland for his release were ignored, his wife and a band of supporters went to Virginia, freed Talbot from jail and returned him to Susquehanna Manor. But, being a fugitive from justice, he could not remain in his manor house, so he hid out in the surrounding countryside, moving often. At times he stayed in the homes of friends, but his main refuge was a cave hollowed out of a granite cliff fronting the Susquehanna about four miles up from the river's mouth. There, legend has it, he was sustained by two falcons which brought back game to feed him. In 1685, at Calvert's request, he surrendered and was returned to Virginia to be tried for the murder of Rousby, but while the trial was in progress, a ship arrived from England bearing a royal pardon for him. Talbot returned to Ireland in 1687 to live out the rest of his life.

[132] Gath's memory appears to have failed him here. He writes that Talbot "committed a murder on Chris," but crosses through "Chris," not recalling, it seems, the slain man's full name. Then he writes "the popular leader of the colony." It is questionable whether the King's Collector of taxes in the area would also be "the popular leader of the colony." In any case, the evidence indicates that Talbot was protecting what he felt were Calvert's rights against the King's officers, and that Calvert was instrumental in getting a royal pardon for Talbot. Paul Tillich, in *Tidewater Maryland* says Talbot "was in fact a warm-hearted, courageous and impetuous Irishman, although full of bluster and devil-may-care courage which gave much romance to his life" (p. 182).

[133] Antebellum Maryland writer/statesman John Pendleton Kennedy (1795-1870) wrote into his 1838 novel *Rob of the Bowl* the old legend that Talbot, an expert

wrote that his hawks fed him, and explored old St. Mary's[134] and Mattapany[135] and the colonial relics.

I was in the habit of buying all the books printed in the early country printing offices and among these was the trial of Rev. Jacob Gruber,[136] a German Methodist, for denouncing slavery at a Maryland camp meeting, about the year 1819. Taney as one of his lawyers assailed slavery and was at the time as radical a federalist as Josiah Quincy [137] or Philip Barton Key,[138] uncle of his brother in law and a British Tory officer.

---

falconer, had used two trained hawks to supply him with meat while hiding out on the Susquehanna.

[134] St. Mary's City, the earliest capital of Maryland, was founded following the landing of the first Europeans in that colony in 1634. It is on the St. Mary's River, which empties into the Potomac just before that river flows into Chesapeake Bay.

[135] "Mattapany" (there are variant spellings) on the Patuxent near Millstone Landing was a thousand-acre tract originally granted to Henry Sewall, Secretary of the Province of Maryland, from 1661 to his death in 1665. His widow Jane then married Governor George Calvert, later third Lord Baltimore after Cecil Calvert died. When Maryland's Catholic deputies had to flee St. Mary's City during the Protestant Revolution , they took refuge at "Mattapany," later executing the formal articles of surrender there in 1689.

[136] Gath's poem "Jacob Gruber" is on pages 23-25 of *Poems of Men and Events*. See Note 144 below.

[137] Josiah Quincy (1772-1864), born in Boston as son of a notable orator and patriot, was elected to the Massachusetts state senate in 1804, where he vigorously urged his state to ask Congress for a Constitutional amendment striking the clause permitting slave states to count three-fifths of their slaves in determining the number of representatives they could seat in the House. Elected to Congress, Quincy stoutly opposed every measure put forth by the Jefferson and Madison administrations. He later was president of Harvard.

[138] Philip Barton Key (1757-1815), born in Cecil County, Maryland, to a family of landed aristocrats, was educated in England and entered the British army after the Declaration of Independence. In 1778 he was commissioned as an officer in the Maryland Loyalists Regiment, becoming its captain in 1782 and taking his troops to Jamaica. Serving in Florida, he was taken prisoner. Released on parole, he returned to England, but after the war he came back to Maryland in 1785 to practice law. He represented the Annapolis district in the state legislature before being elected to Congress in 1807, where, like Quincy, he was an ardent Federalist opposing Jefferson's and Madison's policies. Having been, as Gath notes, a British Tory officer, he was also an uncle of Francis Scott Key, composer of the *Star-Spangled Banner* and law partner of Roger Taney.

Chief Justice Roger Taney who handed down the Supreme Court Decision in the Dred Scott Case.

I began to explore the subterranean mole work of old Maryland politics, chiefly to be had in *Niles's Register* [139] of which I owned a full set indexed. Chief Justice Taney had been pushed at the Northern public by statues at Annapolis and in Baltimore.

One day I was talking at La Plata[140] with Judge Frederick Stone, whose father studied law with Francis Scott Key, when Stone suddenly said: "Townsend, Taney's father murdered a man and fled this region. I forget all the particulars. If Colonel Sothoron[141] were living he could tell, for it is a sore point in his family that Taney borrowed a thousand dollars to escape upon and his son, the Chief Justice, would not pay it."

This Colonel Sothoron had murdered a Union officer about a slave, been tried after escaping South, and was dead. This crime was mixed up with Booth's.[142]

I thought it strange that the Chief Justice who wrote the inexorable Dred Scott[143] decision forty years after he excoriated slavery should

---

[139] *Niles' Weekly Register,* published in Baltimore by Hezekiah Niles, was one of the best and most widely circulated American newspapers of the early 19th Century.

[140] A town in Charles County, Maryland.

[141] Colonel Marshall Sothoron is probably the individual to whom Gath refers. An ancestor, Henry Greenfield Sothoron, having through intermarriage come into possession of the Jowles family property, "The Plains," on the Patuxent River near Battle Creek, built a large brick dwelling on the site prior to the Revolution. Nearby was the home of Michael Taney, who had married into the prominent Brooke family. In this latter dwelling Roger Brooke Taney had been born in 1777.

[142] No information has been found thus far to confirm or elucidate Col. Sothoron's murder of a Union officer or tie this to Booth's conspiracy.

[143] Dred Scott and his family had been Negro slaves owned by a Dr. Emerson who had moved to Missouri. When Emerson died, Scott claimed he and his family were then free by virtue of the fact that they lived in a free territory (as established by the Missouri Compromise). The case came to the U. S. Supreme Court in 1856, where Chief Justice Roger Brooke Taney, writing for a majority of the Court, held that Scott was not entitled to bring a suit in federal court since he was not a citizen. Going further to consider the larger question of Negro citizenship, Taney wrote that, for more than a century prior to the Declaration of Independence, all Negroes, whether slave or free, had been regarded "as beings of an inferior order, and altogether unfit to associate with the white race, either in social or political relations; and so far inferior that they had no rights which the white man was bound to respect." To cap the decision, the Court, with two dissenting votes, denied that Congress had the power to exclude slavery from any territory of the U. S.,

have been unscathed at that time with a family crime in his origin. Gruber's life[144] had been published by the Methodist Church, as a holy wag.(?) I hunted out the camp meeting woods where he preached against slavery and started my novel[145] upon him. Henry Williams[146] of the Weems[147] line of steamers sent me a pass to go up the Patuxent River, so near Washington city though a century distant, and the base of the British expedition that burned Washington in 1814.[148] There I passed Michael Taney's house and the scenes of Taney's autobiography. Twice I made that excursion.

---

effectively ending Congressional efforts to find compromises between free and slave interests.

[144] Jacob Gruber (1778-1850), born in Lancaster County, Pa., to German Lutheran parents, converted to Methodism at age 15. Forced to leave home for a time, he was allowed to return briefly, but left again at age 21. Walking to Lancaster, he met a Methodist preacher who told him of a vacancy in a nearby circuit. Gruber went there and began preaching, and was later accepted into the Philadelphia Conference, becoming an itinerant in the mid-Atlantic states. Decribed as colorful, eccentric, witty and often sarcastic, he was also an ardent abolitionist, and one of his sermons at a Maryland camp meeting in 1819 led to his arrest and trial for inciting insurrection against state laws supporting slavery. Thanks to Taney's defense, Gruber was acquitted, but he was warned by Methodist authorities to tone down his rhetoric in future sermons.

[145] Gath probably refers here to *The Taneys*, not to a separate novel about Gruber.

[146] Henry Williams (1840-1916), born in Calvert County, Maryland, educated in Baltimore, was admitted to the Maryland bar in 1861. In 1868 he married Georgeanna Weems, daughter of Mason Locke Weems the younger, President of the Weems Steamboat Company, and granddaughter of Mason Locke Weems the elder —"Parson" Weems—most noted for his *Life of Washington* (1800), a didactic, somewhat fictionalized biography for juveniles which, as it grew in revised reprintings, added in the "cherry tree" story and other anecdotes which never happened during Washington's lifetime. In 1874, when his father-in-law died, Henry Williams took over management of the Weems line, also serving several terms in the Maryland legislature. He and Gath were apparently good friends and fellow book collectors. Williams's collection was bequeathed to Johns Hopkins University.

[147] The Weems line operated vessels from Baltimore upon the Chesapeake and up the Potomac, Rappahannock and Patuxent Rivers. Gath used these ships for many of his excursions to historical places in tidewater Maryland.

[148] When the British sent the expedition which burned Washington during the War of 1812, it traveled up the Patuxent, not the better-guarded Potomac.

My attention was called to a book called *The Old Plantation* (of Maryland).[149] The which, on a second reading, I found contained [,] with names disguised, the murder of John Magruder by Michael Taney.[150] It turned out to have been in 1819, the same year Roger Taney defended Gruber.

Here were great materials for a story but how to draw out the long forgotten and unrecorded facts was a problem. *Niles's Register* was dumb; Niles and Taney were fellow Federalists and townsmen.[151]

I concluded to challenge that tragedy in the New York *Sun*,[152] Dan[a]'s paper. As I expected, it exasperated the *Baltimore Sun* to stamp it as a lie. They sent to Henry Williams: "Yes," said he[,] "Taney's father killed a man about a woman and fled. When his body

---

[149] The book referred to is *The Old Plantation, and What I Gathered There in an Autumn Month* by James Hungerford (N.Y.: Harper & Bros.,1859).

[150] In Chapter XLIII of *The Old Plantation*, on pages 300-303, the murder of young Magruder by Michael Taney is related in a narrative which thinly disguises details and names. Michael Taney, for example, is called "Aylmer Tiernay" while Magruder is named "Bruce Macgregor." In this version the older man, a widower, having lost out to his younger rival for a neighboring lady's affections, picks a quarrel, then stabs his bachelor neighbor through the heart and flees on a fast horse. The murdered man's brothers ride in pursuit, but cannot catch or find the felon, who "had hidden himself in a retired part of Virginia, and had died there with no one to attend his hours of sickness but an old negro man, his body-servant, who had learned the way to his master's retreat, it is said, through communication from the latter to one of his sons." One son (obviously Roger Taney) is described as "now a very aged man [who] occupies one of the highest judicial positions in the country...." Gath's poem on Magruder (see pages 25-28 of *Poems of Men and Events*) is placed and dated "Frederick, Md., August 30, 1898."

[151] Hezekiah Niles (1777-1839), raised in Wilmington, Delaware, and in the printing business there from 1795-1805, moved to Baltimore in the latter year and in 1811 started his *Weekly Register,* which soon became one of the leading periodicals of the period. Taney moved to Baltimore in 1822. Townsend surmises that Niles' failure to run news of Magruder's murder by the elder Taney in 1819 was to spare the younger Taney, Niles' political ally and fellow Baltimorean, great embarrassment.

[152] Townsend's article in The New York *Sun* revealed to most of the nation for the first time that Chief Justice Taney's father was a murderer who had escaped justice.

was brought back it was identified by the teeth, which the brothers of the man he killed kicked in."[153]

In the further effort to disprove the crime, the Baltimore paper extracted witnesses of Judge Taney's wilful temper and finally an old woman of the Taney blood told the tale and another person produced a copy of the county paper revealing the inquest. Some eighty years had ensued. I had drawn the materials to my hand.

I sat down in my mountain retreat and wrote *The Taneys*. The old Revolutionary soldier culprit had escaped to that region of Virginia accessible to his son at Frederick,[154] a mountain-enfolded hamlet.

The two novels on the western lobe of Maryland I have never submitted to a publisher. They required to be type written, a matter of expense, and I had found Maryland a nearly dead field for remuneration. I put them by till a quicker generation should come out of hibernation.

While examining colonial Maryland I saw the fallacy of "imported bricks"[155] attributed to every old smoke house and shamble, though the clay pits could be found close by. There was a shriek of despair among some old gossips when I read my paper before the District of Columbia Historical Society,[156] but after that the brick myth disappeared. People who could not remember a great family crime

---

[153] The Maryland WPA Guide to the history of Maryland states that the Magruders crushed the skull of Michael Taney with a stone in its casket. In *The Old Plantation* version, the brothers merely opened the casket to see if the body was Taney's.

[154] In 1819 Roger Brooke Taney was living and practicing law in Frederick, Maryland. The nearest point of Virginia was only about ten miles south across the Potomac.

[155] Gath himself had previously been misled into accepting uncritically the lore that many of the earliest American houses had been made of bricks imported from England. In his article "The Chesapeake Peninsula" (*Scribner's Monthly*, Vol. III, No. 5 [March 1872], p. 514) he had written: "The landholders, whose roomy residences, built of English brick—the ballast of their returning produce vessels—still beautify the banks of the Wye and the Choptank ...." But having discovered, while researching around Old St. Mary's City, that he (along with many other people) had been fooled by this mistaken information, he decided to set the record straight.

[156] See "Houses of Bricks Imported from England," *Records of the Columbia Historical Society*, Vol. 7. (Washington: Published by the Society, 1904), pp. 195-210.

Charles Anderson Dana, one of America's most prominent newspapermen, and publisher of *The New York Sun*.

knew all the imported brick houses. Among the deluders of his parishioners was Bishop Meade, in his *Old Churches and Families of Virginia*.[157]

A certain hardihood is important for a literary restorer in those colonies where slavery encouraged family bragging, especially among the run-down members.

Drawing my history from the soil, fertilized by books, I began to see the general nothingness of our colonial story before the Era of Cromwell.[158] He was seventeen years old when Shakspere died and lived himself to 1658, thirty years before the English Revolution.[159] His restoration from his letters and speeches by Carlyle[160] aroused me to make him the inquest of one of my summer trips to England.

Perhaps I was partly led by my study of the English Revolution in New York and Maryland,[161] under [word illegible] kin of mine, Jacob Milbourne,[162] my mother's name.

---

[157] William Meade, D. D., served as bishop of the Protestant Episcopal Church of Virginia during the mid-19th Century. His *Old Churches, Ministers and Families of Virginia*, first appearing in 1857, went through several printings.

[158] While Oliver Cromwell lived from 1599 to 1658, Townsend apparently means by "the Era of Cromwell" that period between 1653 and 1658 when Cromwell was in power as Lord Protector in England.

[159] The so-called "Glorious Revolution" of 1688 occurred when English Protestants forced Catholic monarch James II to abdicate the throne and replaced him with William of Orange and his wife Mary.

[160] In 1845 Thomas Carlyle published his *Cromwell's Life and Letters*, which "completely revolutionized the public estimate of its subject," states *Chambers's Encyclopaedia*. Until then, Cromwell had gotten the historic reputation of being a trickster and tyrant. Using original letters and documents to prove the contrary, Carlyle showed the Protector in a far more favorable light.

[161] The English Revolution of 1688 also had profound effects in the American colonies, particularly New York and Maryland. Gath, believing some of his own ancestors had been involved in these events, studied this period of colonial history with keen interest.

[162] Gath's genealogical research led him to conclude that his mother Mary Milbourne Townsend was a direct descendant of Jacob Milborne, one of the "Protestant martyrs" of New York, who, with his father-in-law Jacob Leisler, led a popular rebellion in 1688 and seized the fort protecting Albany, New York, "for the protection of the Protestant religion." Leisler and Milborne felt they would have the backing of the new monarchs, William and Mary, but their political enemies in the colony had them arrested, tried for treason, convicted and executed. Soon after, Jacob Milborne's surviving family migrated to Eastern Shore Maryland. One

I did discover in Valentine[163] that Milbourne's wife's uncle, Loockermans,[164] had large land tracts in St. Mary's County, Md. and I found Milburn[165] graves at old St. Mary's.[166] "We came from the banks of the Potomac," said an old aunt. Genealogies soon die out where there's no record. So do books where there are no booksellers. At Leonardtown[167] they complained to me at the small library they vaunted that they did not know where to get Kennedy's novel, *Rob of the Bowl*,[168] the scenes located in that county, though it was still in print.

Maryland, in fact, was a composite state, raked up from the adjacent Dutch, Swede and Virginia colonies.[169] The Stones were from

descendant, according to Gath, was the maternal ancestor who in 1800 willed his best hat and nothing else to one of his sons. Learning of this legacy had led Townsend to begin writing *The Entailed Hat*.

[163] Probably a reference to *Valentine's Manuals, City of New York* (circa 1821) a copy of which Townsend had bought for his library. Both David Thomas Valentine (1801-1869) and Ferdinand Charles Valentine (dates unknown) wrote about the early history of New York.

[164] Probably Jacob Loockermans (1650-1730), second son of Govert Loockermans (died 1670), said to have been the wealthiest man in North America and leader of an opposition party to Peter Stuyvesant, governor of New Amsterdam, during the height of Dutch rule in America. Jacob Loockermans moved to Eastern Shore Maryland around 1681 and established a large plantation near Easton. His son Nicholas early in the 18th Century moved to Kent County, Delaware, where a descendant would give the Loockerman name [the 's' being dropped] to the main street of the state capital, Dover.

[165] A chief reason for Gath's visits to the Delmarva Peninsula in the 1870s and '80s was to trace his own ancestry. Ruthanna Hindes feels he never did entirely succeed in establishing his lineage on either his paternal or maternal side back to early colonial times, but he often gave the impression that he had.

[166] Maryland's first capital, originally settled by the Calverts in 1634. The fact that Milburns—presumably ancestors of his mother—were buried there gave Gath a claim to descent from one of the early English families in America.

[167] This present-day seat of St. Mary's County is situated a few miles northwest of Old St. Mary's City.

[168] Largely set in St. Mary's City during the Protestant uprising of 1681, *Rob of the Bowl* (1838) is considered by some to be Kennedy's best work of fiction.

[169] While Maryland is often considered the "Catholic colony" founded under the proprietorship of the Calverts, its assembly in 1649 passed the first act of religious toleration in the New World to attract non-Catholic settlers. Gath correctly points out that many Protestants came to Maryland from Virginia and from Dutch and Swedish settlements in New York, New Jersey, Pennsylvania and the Three Lower Counties on Delaware. William Penn's long-standing feud with Col. Talbot sprang

Northampton Co.[,] Virginia, who had undertaken to subdue the Puritans on Severn[170] and lost their capital. A material element of all that tidewater country was redemptioners or runaways.[171] When General Washington was pedigreed by British heralds he replied that he had no knowledge and small curiosity on that subject. He was too honest to assume beyond his daily necessity.

Grigston[172] says the parent Randolph was a barn builder.[173] I charged the Masons and Tilers to those trades,[174] as they named their Virginia county Staffordshire where are the British potteries. John

---

from the latter's "raiding" New Castle County by luring inhabitants to Bohemia Manor with inducements.

[170] One Richard Bennett, encouraged by William Claiborne (the Virginian who had established a colony at Kent Island and was challenging Lord Baltimore for primacy in the region), led a Puritan revolt from the Severn River area (near the future site of Annapolis) and took over the government at St. Mary's City, forcing Gov. William Stone (earliest American ancestor of Judge Frederick Stone) and others to flee to Virginia. Agreements between Lord Baltimore and Cromwell's emissaries later restored Stone as governor.

[171] In colonial times, redemptioners were immigrants from Europe who paid for their passage to America by serving as bondsmen for a specified period. Runaways were those who fled such obligations.

[172] Possibly Francis Grigson, compiler of *Genealogical Memoranda Relating to the Family of Bisse* (London: Mitchell & Hughes, 1886). To date no writer about the Randolph family named Grigston as been found.

[173] Evidently William Randolph of Warwickshire, described in Henry Randall's *The Life of Thomas Jefferson* as "the son of a cavalier whose fortunes had been broken in the civil wars." According to Randall, William Randolph came to America around 1660 as the first of his line here, arriving with "some small remains of a former family fortune." Settling on Turkey Island in the James River below Richmond, he became wealthy and well-respected before his death in 1711. He apparently took a "hands-on approach" to running his estate, for Randall notes, "He saw several of his sons established on their estates before his death, and, with the paternal solicitude and determined energy which marked his character, went in person with his slaves to make the commencement of their improvements, and even to aid them in the erection of their buildings." This may be how Grigston had gotten the impression that "the parent Randolph was a barn-builder."

[174] In mentioning these surnames of "First Families of Virginia," Gath is implying that their ancestors in England were probably common tradesmen to have been so named, and likely came from Staffordshire in the Midlands where many English potteries are located.

Rolfe[175] married Pocahontas before there was a prejudice against color. The Weems steamers which took me up the Patuxent were in the family of the [word illegible] colporteur[176] who wrote the Washington [words illegible].

I went to England for the express purpose (on my fourth or fifth voyage) of realizing Cromwell.[177] Francis Bannock,[178] the English companion of Hawthorne, got me a two weeks ticket to the British Museum where Robert Chambers[179] had bestowed me a whole winter twenty years before. Chambers called on me in 1862 at my humble lodgings in Islington. In that country literature is as it is called an Estate; in America they want to see the Estate alone and beshrew the Literature.

After I examined the Cromwell literature I went to Holland House,[180] and the city resorts of Cromwell, thence to Arundel Castle in Sussex,[181] next to Cambridge,[182] where I inspected the cast of

---

[175] John Rolfe (1585-1622), who came to America in 1610, is said to have been the first colonist to cultivate tobacco. He married Pocahontas, rescuer of Captain John Smith, in 1613, and took her to England in 1616, where she soon died. Rolfe returned to Virginia in 1617 and was a member of the ruling council and a wealthy planter before dying at age 37.

[176] A colporteur is a peddler of devotional literature. While some manuscript words are not legible here, Gath is apparently saying that the Weems steamers were owned by a family one of whose members was Mason Locke Weems. See Note 146.

[177] Oliver Cromwell (1599-1658), leader of the Puritan army which overthrew the British monarchy and deposed Charles I in 1645, became Lord Protector of England and Great Britain until his death, at which time the Protectorate he had established began to fall apart, leading to the restoration of Charles II to the throne in 1660. Gath had become convinced that in Cromwell's Protectorate lay the foundations of the U. S. Presidency, leading him to research and "realize" the Protector in order to write *President Cromwell*.

[178] No information has been found to date about Francis Bannock.

[179] Robert Chambers was one of two publishing brothers in Edinburgh and London who produced encyclopaedias, popular cultural journals, local histories, etc.

[180] A historic mansion at Kensington, west of London. Built by Sir Walter Cope, a Stuart courtier, in 1607, it became the seat of Henry Rich, Baron Kensington and Earl of Holland, when he married Cope's daughter. A royalist, he was beheaded by the Puritans in 1649 and the Parliamentary generals Fairfax and Lambert occupied the dwelling.

[181] Arundel Castle on the Arun River is in Sussex some 50 miles south of London.

Cromwell[183] and Cooper's portrait of him at Sydney Sussex college,[184] thence to St. Ives,[185] where he was king of the Fens,[186] and to Huntingdon,[187] his birthplace and the seat of the Cromwells at Sandwich Manse[188] close by. Finally I went to Berwick on Tweed[189] and Dunbar.[190] Nottingham[191] and Warwick Castle[192] I had already visited. Later I went to Drogheda.[193]

---

[182] Cromwell had attended Cambridge University's Sidney Sussex College as a youth, but left without receiving a degree. In Gath's time a museum containing Cromwellian relics and likenesses was evidently there.

[183] A Cromwell museum at Cambridge included the cast of a statue which had been made of him.

[184] In 1766, Sidney Sussex College received from an anonymous donor (later identified as Thomas Holles) an impressive portrait of Cromwell painted by artist Samuel Cooper.

[185] A town near Huntingdon in Cambridgeshire through which the Ouse River runs.

[186] The Fens of that area had largely been made habitable and arable by draining the marshes of the Ouse. When Charles I tried to gain revenue for the Treasury by laying claim to some 95,000 acres of the Fens, Cromwell, representing the district in Parliament, led the opposition to this move, which earned him the appellation, "Lord of the Fens."

[187] Huntingdon, northwest of Cambridge was, as Gath notes, the Cromwell family homestead where the Protector was born and raised. His paternal grandfather was Sir Henry Cromwell, while another ancestor had been Earl of Essex.

[188] The name of the ancestral Cromwell family seat.

[189] Berwick-upon-Tweed is a seacoast town at the northmost part of Northumberland near the Scottish border.

[190] Situated on the southeast coast of Scotland above Berwick-upon-Tweed, this site is where Cromwell and his army defeated the Scots in 1650.

[191] Where Charles I in 1642 rallied the Cavalier army for the first battle of the Civil War, which the Royalists won. Subsequently Oliver Cromwell, realizing the need for a more effective Parliamentary army, assembled and trained the troopers who became known as "Cromwell's Ironsides." It was this band and others modeled upon it which enabled the Parliamentary forces to win battles consistently against the Royalist armies.

[192] During the Rebellion, Roundheads at Warwick Castle, on the Avon River in the Midlands, successfully withstood a royalist siege. The castle contains Cromwell relics.

[193] Drogheda, on Ireland's Boyne River above Dublin, was a town where Cromwell's forces, during the invasion and conquest of that country in 1649, stormed the fortified garrison of that port and put its conquered defenders to the sword.

After I came home I extra illustrated two sets of Cromwelliana so that I had all the people of the Protector's time in rehearsal.

As often happens with too much material, this had been silted on the mill dam which penned it up. My true treatment should have been a poetical drama for reading, not for playing. But I fell in with a rugged, Cromwell-like actor, named Sheridan,[194] who desired to play the Protector as he would suit Americans. We draw our Inauguration form of Presidents from the Protector's swearing in, on the Scriptures. That installation I made the climax of my play and introduced Charles II[195] in disguise as a suitor of Cromwell's daughter, Frances,[196] and also Sindercome, the Leveller,[197] who would blow Cromwell up. I printed the play,[198] but Sheridan was lost at sea soon after and beyond dedicating the piece to President Cleveland I let it rest among my archives.

One of my stories[,] *Crutch the Page*,[199] upon the subject of Beau Hickman, a high vagrant about old Washington, was long in request. It is included in Collyer's library of short stories. In sequel I wrote seven novelletes for *Tales of Washington,* and the Supreme Court[,] some of

---

[194] Probably William Edward Sheridan (born 1840, birthplace unknown).

[195] Prince Charles, son of the beheaded Charles I, was then still in exile after royalist elements in Scotland unsuccessfully tried to overthrow Cromwell's forces and install "Bonnie Prince Charlie" on the throne of England. He would remain so until 1660, when Cromwell's son's inability to fill his father's shoes and maintain a stable government led to a restoration of the monarchy. But Gath fancifully decided to bring him into this play as a disguised character wooing Cromwell's daughter, evidently to give a foretaste of the young man as Britain's next king. Townsend sometimes took liberties with historical fact in order to create works of fiction based on historical figures and events.

[196] Cromwell had four children, including one daughter named Elizabeth, (not Frances).

[197] Various groups opposed the rule of Cromwell and plotted to assassinate him. The Levelers, a faction in the army, felt he had attained too much power and encouraged mutinies. A few leaders were tried, convicted and executed, ending the threat.

[198] A 200-copy edition of Gath's four-act play *President Cromwell* was published in 1884 by his son-in-law E. F. Bonaventure, presumably at Townsend's expense. It has never been performed.

[199] "Crutch the Page" is found on pp. 87-109 of Gath's *Tales of the Chesapeake*. This story drew praise from E. C. and Dr. Oliver Wendell Holmes among others.

which appeared as Christmas annuals.[200] I also wrote *Tales of Gapland, or Mountain Maryland*,[201] most of which were published as a serial issued by Mr. Pangborn at Baltimore.[202] Short stories seldom get a connected preservation. Besides, the jigglery of hunting a publisher was disagreeable to me. I discovered that with all the ado of American book publishers none of them had any authoritative eclat. Washington Irving published *The Sketch Book* himself and Sir Walter Scott had to intercede with his publisher to promote it.

The newspaper occupation, also, was sporadic. For a period of years I was worked to death, then, machinery, special telegraph wires, newspaper exchanges, suddenly put a clamp on special correspondence and one had to be a demi-machine and syndicate his writings, which took the focus and acid[?] out of them.

Yet I found the non-reliability of newspapers a better literary opportunity.

After I completed the Army Correspondents Memorial by subscription, in 1896, I used the same support to publish *Poems of Men and Events*. In this handsome book I wrote numerous poems for the first time on themes reposing in my mind and made its illustrations a souvenir of my quarter century at Gapland.

CHAPTER IV. HELPFUL SPRITES

Cultivating Literature for its own reward is right well rewarded: seldom was I congratulated on news feats but all my fancies found friends. Among these a helpful one was General, afterward President, Garfield,[203] whom I had heard of in his district while lecturing there in

---

[200] Christmas annuals, as the name suggests, were anthologies done up into gift books, often with handsome bindings, meant to be given as presents. No copies of these novelletes by Townsend have yet been found.
[201] Thus far, no serial copies of these *Tales of Gapland* have been located.
[202] J. G. Pangborn and C. K. Lord were the chief officers of the Lorborn Publishing Company of Baltimore. In the Townsend Collection at the Maryland Archives is a letter to Gath from one H. J. Lord, dated November 9, 1887, on this firm's letterhead.
[203] James Abram Garfield (1831-1881) was, after the early death of his father, a self-made man who became president of Hiram College in Ohio in 1857, being also admitted to the bar. In 1861 he entered the service and, after distinguishing himself

1865-66.[204] His subject thus early was upon our currency, or paper money.[205]

I found Garfield in Congress shy and disappointing for some time. He did not bristle to my newspaper letters, but when he called at my house (within the present Capitol grounds)[206] he asked me to repeat a poem called *Paul on the Hellespont*.[207] This, I think, is included in an article on me called "A Neglected Poet" by Montgomery Schuyler in the *North American Review*.[208]

Slowly Garfield became tractable, even confidential. I was familiar without his telling me, of his hard grapple with renowning life. The constituent expects his representative to be opulent and Garfield's constituents thought his salary was opulence, so plain do many of our people live. His most awful offence in their eyes was voting to raise his own salary to $5000 a year, nearly doubling it. He was less reprehensible for being on Oakes Ames's Credit Mobilier memoranda[209]

---

in battle, became the youngest brigadier general in the Union army in 1862. Promoted to major general after gallantry at Chickamauga, he resigned his commission and was elected a member of Congress in 1863, and, after being reelected eight times, was elevated to the Senate in January, 1880. He was elected President the same year as the Republican candidate.

[204] Townsend's postwar lecture tour had taken him to Ohio in the winter of 1865-66.

[205] Garfield, who had experienced a hardscrabble youth due to the early death of his father, made finances one of his areas of expertise. In Congress he would chair the House Appropriations Committee, also serving on the House Banking and Currency Committee.

[206] In Washington City, Gath is known to have resided at 319 North B Street and at 229 First Street, N.E. at different times. He was living at the latter address around 1899.

[207] Found on pages 97-98 of Townsend's *Poems* (1870).

[208] This article, by a respected writer and critic of the period, appeared on pages 694-710 of the *North American Review*'s May, 1900 issue. In it Schuyler wrote that "Mr. Townsend seems to me a genuine poet, who comes as near to being spokesman in verse for his own generation as anyone our country has produced...."

[209] The Credit Mobilier affair became a major scandal in the election year of 1872, when Grant was running for a second term as President. Congressman Oakes Ames (1804-1873) of Massachusetts, who was also an entrepreneur, had helped gain control of an inactive Pennsylvania corporation, change its name to Credit Mobilier of America, and take over the building of the Union Pacific Railroad across the United States. Ames and his partners were said to have overbilled and gotten rich at the expense of Union Pacific common shareholders and, indirectly, the U. S.

and for taking a fee to recommend a patent pavement for Washington City, through the Appropriations Committeeman.[210] The last he was inducted to by Parsons,[211] Marshal of the Supreme Court, a hypocrite and lobbyist, and it was the usual lawyers' solace, that the service is worth the fee. He had hardly any understanding of Credit Mobilier, and when he ran for President Sylvester Everett[212] told me he did not comprehend a pass book and check book for the bank, where they deposited for him a postage fund. Garfield had been a preacher, a vocation which praises God for benevolences and does not look a gift mare in the mouth. He was guilty of the monstrous crime in America, poverty with opportunities.

Government as well, since public lands had been given to the railroad builders as incentives. Dana's New York *Sun* led a campaign to expose the matter as an example of shady politics. Garfield, named by Ames as one of the committee chairs who had received stock, denied it, and Ames, at first confirming Garfield's version, then changed his story and said Garfield had taken the stock on credit. Garfield claimed he did not know of the stock's railroad connection and considered the stock a loan, which he later paid back. Charges of bribery were nonetheless leveled against Garfield and others, and a number of prominent officials were embarassed, including Garfield and Vice President Schuyler Colfax, who was knocked off the ticket for the 1872 election. Garfield, however, was able to convince a majority of his constituents that, since he had acted mainly from ignorance and had repaid the "loan," he was not guilty of wrongdoing. The episode did not hurt him enough politically to prevent his being elected President in 1880.

[210] An issue brought up in the 1874 campaign was that of the DeGolyer Pavement scandal. In the early 1870s, midway through Grant's first term, Washington City government had been reorganized and granted home rule. One of the first tasks undertaken was the paving of the city's dirt roads. The DeGolyer McClelland Company of Chicago wanted to pave with wood, and, in competing for the contract, hired Congressman Richard Patterson of Ohio, also an attorney, to present its case before the Board of Public Works. On having to leave town for a while, Parsons asked Garfield to stand in for him, and subsequently Garfield received a $5,000 share of Parsons' total bill of $16,000. Garfield's defense was that he was only receiving a legal fee for work done, and there was no conflict, since he was not voting in the matter, which was a city expense not funded by Congress. While the issue was clouded by the revelation that DeGolyer had also been spreading other money around to buy influence, Garfield's explanation of his own role again satisfied most of his constituents that he had done no wrong personally, and he was again re-elected to Congress.

[211] Possibly Theophilus Parsons the younger, who served as a Supreme Court Justice.

[212] Evidently a family friend of Townsend since boyhood days in Chestertown.

I beheld in the President of Hiram country college[213] a man greater than he seemed or perhaps believed himself, and wished to save him for better things. He was the best supporting legislator, a large man with large endowments physically heroic, mentally enthusiastic, morally a slump when brutal things were thrown in his face, such as Ben Butler's "Say nothing but good of the dead."[214] A large country boy grown into a musketeer legislator, probably sapped by the demi-priest's profession, he seemed to me to need public championing. When at his lowest, I published in the *Washington Star* [215] as a defiance to his pullers down:[216]

---

[213] Garfield was president of Hiram College, which he had attended as a student, from 1857 to 1861 when he entered the Union army.

[214] Benjamin Franklin Butler (1818-1893), New England lawyer and politician, Civil War general, Radical Republican Congressman who was a leader in impeachment proceedings against President Andrew Johnson. Throughout his career, Butler seemed to make more enemies than friends. While serving briefly as governor of Massachusetts, he was not infrequently called "oily," "a charlatan," and other unflattering terms. Gath's characterization of his insult to Garfield as "brutal" is consistent with the impression many of Butler's contemporaries had of him.

[215] A prominent afternoon daily in the nation's capital, the Washington *Evening Star* commenced publication as a daily in 1852 and continued operating until recent times.

[216] This poem was reprinted six years later at the end of an 1880 campaign pamphlet titled *A Talk With Business Men* published by the Republican National Committee. Besides the title essay by E. V. Smalley, it also contained some of Garfield's own views, as given previously in speeches, on business and financial questions.

TO JAMES A. GARFIELD

Thou who did'st ride on Chickamauga's day,

All solitary down the fiery line,

And saw the ranks of battle rusty shine,

Where grand old Thomas held them from dismay,

Regret not now, while meaner pageants play

Their brief campaigns against the best of men!

For those spent balls of scandal pass their way,

And thou shalt see the victory again.

Modest and faithful, though these broken lines

Of party reel and thine own honor bleeds,

That mole is blind which Garfield undermines,

That dart falls short which hired malice speeds,

That man will stay whose place the State assigns,

And whose high mind a mighty people needs.

1874

President James Abram Garfield in 1862 who had been
the youngest Brigadier General in the Union Army.
Courtesy of General Collection: Portraits, Delaware State Archives.

This was six years before he beat Grant's third term. I did not expect him to be President, only to survive clamor.[217] In fact, David Dudley Field[218] had told me that Charles A. Dana[219] related to Field how, after General Rosecrans was defeated at Chicamauga, Garfield rode alone to General Thomas's wing of the same army[220] and helped recover the lost day.

Rosecrans came to my house at Gapland and was severe on Garfield, his staff officer, for advising Washington powers that Rosecrans was infirm of purpose, but I believed that he saw the fatal imperfections of that commander in zeal for his government.

Garfield appeared to have read my books and wrote me a very long letter on the romaunt *Lost Abroad*, much like a professor revising a lad's composition. One day as we were walking to his house he said, "George, there is a deliberate attempt to [word illegible] me: little Mac(Cullough)[221] is insinuating in the *Cincinnati Commercial* [222] that I

---

[217] In 1874, when Townsend wrote the poem defending Garfield, its subject was still a committee chairman in the House under fire for his role in the Credit Mobilier affair.

[218] David Dudley Field (1805-1894), American jurist and legal reformer, was born in Connecticut but settled in New York, where he was appointed in 1857 to prepare revised versions of that state's political, civil and penal codes. His reforms being adopted in many other states as well, he then turned to international law, helped form a world committee to offer revisions, but did much of the work himself, presenting a 700-page report in 1873 which laid the groundwork for revising the laws of nations. Among other proposals, Field's method substituted arbitration for war as the legal way to settle disputes between countries. In 1890, at age 85, he presided over the London Peace Conference.

[219] Charles Anderson Dana (1819-1897) was one of 19th-Century America's most prominent newspapermen. As a youthful idealist, Dana took part in the famed Brook Farm experiment, later became managing editor of Horace Greeley's New York *Tribune* from 1848 to 1862, helping make it the strongest of major abolitionist journals. After a falling-out with Greeley, Dana worked in the War Department and was soon Assistant Secretary under Stanton, from which position his strong support of Grant made Lincoln a believer as well. After the war, he raised enough capital to buy the New York *Sun* and made it the leading newspaper of the period while waging vigorous editorial battles with Lawrence Godkin's New York *Post*. Abandoning much of his early idealism, Dana became an advocate of *laissez-faire* capitalism, but deplored the corruption of the Grant Era.

[220] See Note 204.

[221] Hugh McCullough (1808-1895) of Indiana, Secretary of the Treasury under Lincoln and Johnson, and later under Chester A. Arthur. McCullough's main

have mysterious wealth, own a Washington house, etc. Now, I had a fee in a law case and Swayne,[223] my business appointee, bought a lot with it which he mortgaged to erect the house." I forthwith attacked the imputator. When Garfield died in agony, his last words were "O Swayne, Swayne!"[224] And President Arthur[225] dismissed Swayne on

contribution in the postwar years was to return the country to specie payment (gold and silver in lieu of paper money) to restore credit. John Sherman was committed to the same policy.

[222] An important Ohio newspaper of the period, the daily Cincinnati *Commercial*, founded in 1843, was later (1896) the Cincinnati *Commercial Gazette,* then (1898) the Cincinnati *Commercial Tribune* before being merged into the Cincinnati *Enquirer*.

[223] Gath has here confused the names Swayne and Swaim. Noah Swayne was a U.S. Supreme Court Justice of the period, but the individual he refers to was David Swaim. Biographer John M. Taylor, in *Garfield of Ohio: The Available Man*, writes that Swaim, having served in the Union volunteer army under Garfield in Tennessee and assisted him in setting up a military intelligence system to curb smuggling and illegal trade, also helped him and his family get settled in Washington. Earlier, Garfield had left his family in Ohio and lived a bachelor existence in a Washington boarding house. But, Taylor writes, "in 1869, Garfield determined to build a home of his own. Aided by a loan from his Army of the Cumberland comrade, David Swaim, he purchased a lot on the corner of Thirteenth and I Streets and was able to build a comfortable brick house on it for a total of about $10,000." Gath gives a slightly different version, but in neither case are the circumstances suspicious enough to indicate that Garfield, as his accusers were charging, was getting rich at the public's expense. Therefore Gath felt no compunction about coming to the Ohio Congressman's defense, though he was evidently the only newsman to do so.

[224] Gath's memoir misleads readers somewhat here by implying that Garfield died with Swaim's ("Swayne's") name on his lips as a sign of regret for the business about Garfield's house. The individual in question, a close and trusted friend, was in fact at Garfield's bedside for much of the time after the shooting, and with him when he died. Taylor gives this account of the President's last moments: "[Dr. D. W.] Bliss [the attending physician] left the room and moments later Garfield awakened. The [P]resident recognized his old friend Swaim, and stirred slightly. 'How it hurts here!' he whispered, pressing his hand to his heart. At Garfield's request Swaim procured a glass of water, and raised the patient's head while he drank. Again he complained of severe pain in his chest, and Swaim applied a cool cloth to his forehead. Then Garfield, with a main artery collapsed and hemorrhaging, raised both arms crying, 'Swaim, can't you stop this? Oh, Swaim!' and lost consciousness. Swaim, unable to rouse the patient, called the household. At 10:35 the feeble heartbeat stopped."

complaint of a Washington City stock broker. The Conkling set[226] determined to terrorize and destroy Garfield, for supplementing Grant's well-laid scheme of the Senators.[227] John Russell Young[228] told me that Grant recoiled from the third term plot, and that Robert Lincoln was most persistent in it.[229]

---

[225] Vice President Chester Alan Arthur (1830-1886) of New York became the nation's 16th President on the death of James A. Garfield in 1881.

[226] Conkling's "set" of conservative Republicans was collectively known as the "Stalwarts." They were opposed by the "Half-Breeds," a liberal, reformist group of Republicans who opposed patronage and worked for civil service reform, return to specie payment, etc. Rutherford B. Hayes defeated Conkling at the Republican convention in 1876, and was named President by the House of Representatives after a close and hotly- disputed election contest against Samuel Tilden was not resolved by the electoral vote. In 1880, the Half-Breeds, lining up behind Blaine and Sherman, could not get their candidates the nomination, but prevented Grant from being nominated for a third term, allowing Garfield to win.

[227] Conkling and some fellow Stalwarts, when Garfield refused to cave into their demand to withdraw his appointment of a New York convention delegate who had broken ranks and voted for Garfield instead of Grant, insisted they had the right to dictate patronage jobs in their state. To push the power struggle to a crisis, Conkling and his ally Platt resigned from the Senate, counting on New York voters to re-elect them to the offices they had vacated and strengthen their hand against the incoming President. This was a serious miscalculation. They were not re-elected, and after the Republican convention they sulked for much of the campaign. Only at the eleventh hour did Conkling and Grant agree to support and work for the Republican ticket in the 1880 election.

[228] John Russell Young (1840-1899), born in Ireland to Scottish parents, came to America in his youth and, in 1857, started as a copy boy on the new Philadelphia *Press,* soon working his way up to editorial writer and reporter. He and Townsend may have become friends in 1861 when they were almost the same age and working for the same newspaper. Young became the *Press*'s chief war correspondent and covered the first Battle of Bull Run with such skill that publisher Forney promoted him to be managing editor of both the *Press* and the Washington *Morning Chronicle.* In 1870, Young moved north to edit the New York *Tribune,* having won the admiration of Horace Greeley. He later went to the New York *Herald* and spent some years in London and Paris while authoring a number of books, including *Around the World with General Grant* (1879). As an intimate of Grant (Gath once referred to him as "Grant's Boswell"), he was well-placed to know the former President's personal opinions about the third-term attempt. He was appointed Librarian of Congress in 1897 by President McKinley.

[229] Robert Todd Lincoln (1843-1926), eldest son of Abraham Lincoln, served as captain on Grant's staff during the Civil War and was at the Ford Theater when his father was assassinated. (Curiously, he was also with Garfield, as his Secretary of

After Garfield became President he yielded again to his timid spirit. He had left out the worldly side of his public life and felt the great constraint of a most worldly office, unsustained by any physical events. I met him at Elberon,[230] when his wife was brought there. He could scarcely "say that his soul was his own." And yet he had been a burly, athletic soldier. His wife, his most spunky part, I saw at Allerton with his mother after his eventful nomination. I sometimes think his passiveness had him shot. Mrs. Garfield[231] was privately known to me as her husband's mainstay. I therefore was astonished when Roosevelt[232] said to me in the White House, about her Cabinet son[233] "he is his mother's boy." I recollect no other President with such prescience.

Garfield wanted me to write his life but I was missing. So did Hancock's publisher.[234] I wrote the biography of Vice President Morton to accompany Lew Wallace's Benjamin Harrison.[235]

Numerous invitations generally from my poetical work came to me to give addresses. I wrote *Lincoln*[236] as its Captain for the Army of the

---

War, when that President was shot by Guiteau in 1881, and arrived in 1901 at a scheduled meeting with President McKinley in Buffalo just moments after Leon Czolgosz had mortally wounded that chief executive. He was at hand, therefore, for the shooting of three U. S. Presidents.)

[230] Elberon, a seaside town in New Jersey, was the place Garfield was taken to recuperate after being shot, and where he died. As his condition from the gunshot wound worsened in the summer of 1881, Garfield was taken to Elberon on September 6 and died there September 19.

[231] Lucretia "Crete" Rudolph married Garfield November 11, 1858, in Hiram, Ohio, and bore him seven children, five of whom lived past infancy.

[232] President Theodore Roosevelt (1858-1919).

[233] President Garfield's second son, James Rudolph Garfield (1865-1950), was appointed by TR as Secretary of the Interior in 1907.

[234] Former Gen. Winfield Scott Hancock was Garfield's Democratic opponent in the 1880 election. His campaign biography was written by John Russell Young (See Note 228).

[235] Levi Parsons Morton (1824-1920) of New York was the Republican nominee for Vice President in the 1888 election, while Benjamin Harrison of Indiana headed the ticket. Former Union General Lew Wallace, famous as the author of *Ben Hur*, was chosen to write the campaign biography, *Life of Gen. Benjamin Harrison* (Philadelphia: Hubbard Brothers, 1888), which also contained Townsend's "Life of the Hon. Levi P. Morton."

Potomac anniversary in Washington,[237] addressed the New York state press association in a long poem at Rochester,[238] poetized Delaware State[239] and Dickinson[240] colleges, spoke a poem on Caesar Rodney's Ride in my native town,[241] spoke before the Marquette Club at Chicago at the same time with Theodore Roosevelt long before he became President, on the subject of "Father Marquette,"[242] opened a theatre in St. Louis with a poem,[243] and addressed a poem on Washington's Mother at her monument-making at Fredericksburg,[244] spoke poems to Henry M. Stanley[245] and Bartholdi the sculptor [246] at the Lotos Club,[247]

---

[236] This poem, *Commander Lincoln*, appears on pp. 99-104 of Gath's *Poems of Men and Events*.

[237] Gath wrote and delivered his Lincoln poem as an address for the 20th Anniversary celebration of the Army of the Potomac Society at Washington in 1883.

[238] *Poem Read Before the New York State Press Association, at Rochester, June 17, 1879*, appears on pp. 14-23 of Townsend's *Poetical Addresses* published in 1881.

[239] *Poem Read Before Delaware College, Newark, Delaware, Commencement, 1868* is found on pp. 27-33 of *Poetical Addresses*, and on pp. 66-72 of Gath's *Poems of the Delaware Peninsula*. The address was actually given in 1871, not 1868.

[240] *Poem Read Before the Literary Societies of Dickinson College, Carlisle, Pennsylvania, June 28, 1881*, is on pp. 5-13 of *Poetical Addresses*.

[241] *Caesar Rodney's Fourth of July, 1776, Read by Mr. Townsend at his Birth-Place, Georgetown, Sussex County, Delaware, July 4, 1880* appears on pp. 34-42 of *Poetical Addresses*. Correspondence between Gath and Samuel Bancroft, Jr., prior to publication of *Poems of the Delaware Peninsula*, shows that Bancroft wanted to include this poem in the book as well, but Gath could not provide a copy of it at the time.

[242] Gath's verses on *Father Marquette* are on pp. 18-20 of his 1870 book *Poems*. His appearance on the same podium with Theodore Roosevelt in Chicago was probably at least one or two decades after this, and he may have given a speech on Marquette instead of, or in addition to, reading this poem.

[243] The poem *Prologue Delivered at the Opening of Pope's New Theatre, St. Louis, Mo.*, was read by Gath on September 22, 1879, at the dedication of this playhouse which had previously been a Unitarian church. It is printed on pp. 24-26 of his *Selected Poetry*.

[244] Gath read his *Mary Washington* poem to dedicate her monument at Fredericksburg, Maryland, on May 10, 1894. It is on pp. 209-213 of *Poems of Men and Events*.

[245] Townsend read his poem *Henry M. Stanley* to a gathering of the Lotos Club on November 22, 1886. Born John Rowlands in Wales, Stanley (1841-1904) took the

and for the State authorities of Delaware wrote a poem they delivered at the 300th Anniversary of Cape Henlopen.[248]

President Hayes was foully slandered after the Electoral Commission awarded him the Presidency, and on his visit to New York City Dana published his head with "Fraud" upon it.[249] As Dana had

name he was to make famous from a New Orleans merchant who employed him after he had worked his way across the Atlantic as a cabin boy. Later he served first in the United States Navy, then the Confederate Army, at length becoming a war correspondent and winning a reputation for his stories. The New York *Herald* continued to employ him after the war, first sending him to Ethiopia, then returning him to Africa to search for the Scottish missionary/explorer David Livingston, who had been reported lost somewhere in the heartland of that continent. Starting inland from Zanzibar in 1871, Stanley tracked down the missing explorer several months later, and his greeting—"Dr. Livingstone, I presume?"—soon became one of the most repeated sayings in the language. Stanley's written accounts of his exploits not only made himself and Livingstone famous to the point of being legends, they also elevated the status of the "special correspondent," a fact Townsend acknowledged in his poem to his friend and fellow war correspondent.

[246] Frederic Auguste Bartholdi (1834-1904) was the French sculptor responsible for conceiving and creating the Statue of Liberty guarding the New York City harbor. Gath delivered his poem *Bartholdi's Pharos* at a Lotos Club dinner honoring the sculptor on November 14, 1884. While the female figure has since become known as "Miss Liberty," Townsend's name for it—Pharos—recalls an island lighthouse off the coast of ancient Greece. The printed poem is found on pp. 255-57 of his *Poems of Men and Events*.

[247] The Lotos Club, founded in New York City around 1870, included as members some of the age's most illustrious men, who gathered regularly to enjoy fellowship, eat and drink, and deliver or listen to speeches on literature and the arts, exploration, politics and other topics of intellectual interest. Mark Twain was a member and frequent speaker, as were Theodore Roosevelt and Woodrow Wilson. Gath's membership is a measure of the esteem he was held in by leaders of his time.

[248] Townsend was asked to compose a poem to be read at a celebration of the 300th aniversary of Cape Henlopen held on September 22, 1909. The event memorialized was the entrance of Henry Hudson, English-born but sailing for the Dutch, into Delaware Bay in September of 1609. Gath's poem for the 1909 celebration—read by someone else since he was too ill to attend—is on pp. 161-62 of his *Poems of the Delaware Peninsula*.

[249] Charles A. Dana, whose *Sun* had backed New York attorney Tilden, was known to be zealously partisan on some occasions. This was apparently one of them.

called me The Hired Poet of the Ring,[250] I let fly a poem to molest him when Hayes died:[251]

R. B. HAYES

The silent taker of abuse

Not friendless proves when death, as still,

Takes him into the camp of truce

And beats the taps on good and ill:

Soldier, who did life's work fulfil,

However compromised by fame!

The sunny world respects thy end,

The states united speak thy name,

The soldiery thy grave attend,

And wives of gentles do the same,

To join thee to the beauteous mold

Who waits her bridegroom in that wood,

Where but the good denotes the bold.

And all of beauty is the good.

ExPresident Cleveland also went to Hayes's funeral. Vice President Hendricks[252] said to me, "I do not think we ought to abuse Hayes for

---

[250] The time and circumstances of Dana's charging Gath with being a ""hired poet" are not presently known, but it is evident that Townsend did view many powerful Republicans in a favorable light and translate his opinions into newspaper verses. It is also true that Townsend's writings gained him friends and influence in the Republican party hierarchy. So Dana's calling Gath the "Hired Poet of the Ring" might have contained a germ of truth.

[251] Hayes died on January 17, 1893.

winning the award."[253] I printed this and Hayes went to Hendricks's funeral. Amenities buried newspapers in civilities.

When Washington City was renovated by its local promoter, Alexander H. Shepherd,[254] I took my stand upon the sentiment that three of my children were born there and the city should arise nobly. Nearly alone I stood the nearly united traduction of the entire American press. It was a severe trial, but after that I was formidable enough to

---

[252] Thomas A. Hendricks (1819-1885) of Indiana had run with Tilden and lost as the Democratic Vice Presidential candidate in the contested 1876 election. In 1884, running with Cleveland, he won but served less than a year, dying in office on Nov. 25, 1885.

[253] "The award," as used here, means the Presidency. While serving as Vice President in 1885, Hendricks had evidently told Townsend0 that he felt the Democrats should stop abusing Hayes, who had declined to run for a second term in 1880.

[254] James G. Blaine, on pages 547-49 of his memoir *Twenty Years of Congress* (1886) notes that, in 1871, toward the end of Grant's first term, Congress granted the District of Columbia home rule. One power given under this act was the right to borrow money up to five per cent of assessed property value in the District. "It was a radical change," says Blaine, who then goes on to defend it. Alexander R. Shepherd, he tells, a resident of the District and a personal friend of the President, was appointed by Grant as Governor and encouraged to initiate progressive programs. "In the course of a little more than three years," writes Blaine, "an astonishing change was effected in the character and appearance of the city of Washington. From an ill-paved, ill-lighted, unattractive city, it became a model of regularity, cleanliness, and beauty. No similar transformation has ever been so speedily realized in an American city, the model being found only in certain European capitals where public money has been lavishly expended for adornment."
"Of course," Blaine continues, "so great an improvement involved the expenditure of large sums, and the District of Columbia found itself in debt to the amount of several millions. An agitation was aroused against what was alleged to be the corrupt extravagance of the government; the law authorizing it was repealed and the District placed under the direction of three Commissioners, who have since administered its affairs. Whatever fault may be found, whatever charges may be made, the fact remains that Governor Shepherd wrought a complete revolution in the appearance of the Capital. Perhaps a prudent and cautious man would not have ventured to go as fast and as far as he went, but there was no proof that selfish motives had inspired his action. He had not enriched himself, and when the government ended he was compelled to seek a new field of enterprise .... The prejudice evoked towards Governor Shepherd has in large part died away, and he is justly entitled to be regarded as one who conferred inestimable benefits upon the city of Washington."

be killed by silence.[255] The attacks were made against General Grant.[256] Colonel Roosevelt[257] asked me in the White House about 1905 what Grant had done that was good.[258] I replied: "changed the political into a war galaxy and recreated Washington."[259]

Mr. Dana was the worst victim of his personal feelings but a literary minded editor, and in the intervals of our feuds he published much matter for me, as my visits to the statesmen's homes of New York, Seward, [260] Jay, [261] the Clintons, [262] Rufus King,[263] etc. I know of no mental pleasure like realizing ancient men where they inhabited. I tried

---

[255] Not backing away from the war in the newspapers, Gath stood his ground until his critics stopped replying to his arguments.

[256] Having destroyed the District's self-rule and chased Shepherd out of the city and the country, the critics turned their guns on the President who had made the appointment.

[257] Theodore Roosevelt was President at the time, but Gath here uses his military rank, as he did with President Grant in the previous sentence of the memoir.

[258] By this time Grant had come to be considered as one of the worst of America's Presidents and as having done little to stop the corruption taking place during his administration. Gath, while not exonerating him entirely, does partly defend him.

[259] "Chang[ing] the political into a war galaxy" means that Grant had appointed many Union officers to high positions in government, displacing politicians and their cronies. "Recreat[ing] Washington" pertains to the improvements made under Grant's appointee Governor Shepherd (see Note 254).

[260] William Henry Seward (1801-1872), who, as Lincoln's and Johnson's Secretary of State, was responsible for the U. S. purchase of Alaska, long called "Seward's Folly."

[261] John Jay (1745-1829), Revolutionary War statesman, was first Chief Justice of the U. S. Supreme Court and co-author, with James Madison and Alexander Hamilton, of the *Federalist Papers*.

[262] Notable New York Clintons included James (1736-1812) who served in the French and Indian War, then was a brigadier general during the Revolution; his brother George (1739-1812), New York's first governor and U. S. Vice President during Jefferson's second term, replacing Aaron Burr; and De Witt (1769-1828), son of James and nephew of George, who served as mayor of New York City, U. S. Senator, and Governor of New York. The Erie Canal was built due to Clinton's influence as governor.

[263] Rufus King (1755-1827), long-time U. S. Senator from New York known for his sound judgment, oratorical skills, knowledge of finance, and firm opposition to slavery. He was a candidate for Vice President in 1804, running with Charles Cotesworth Pinckney, but the slate was defeated by Thomas Jefferson and George Clinton. Near the end of his life, King served as U. S. ambassador to Britain.

the same thing in Pennsylvania, going to the homes of Ingham, [264] Wilmot,[265] etc. but the Philadelphia ken was not locally reverent. After reading John Quincy Adams's twelve volumes of Diary[266] through I felt uneasy till I had seen Calhoun's[267] seat of Fort Hill, where I wrote a poem on the Cotton Mill camped on his lawn. The study of nature in these towns is equally interesting. Perished communities once athletic have a fascination like Holy Land.

I went to the funerals of President Buchanan and Thaddeus Stevens at Lancaster, saw the meeting at Cozzens' near West Point of Generals Grant and Scott,[268] visited Athens, Georgia, to get the college flavor,[269]

---

[264] Samuel Delucenna Ingham (1779-1860), born in Great Springs, Pa., was, after several terms in the U. S. House of Representatives, appointed Secretary of the Treasury by President Andrew Jackson, serving from 1829-1831 and helping develop an inland canal system, railroad transportation and anthracite coal mining.

[265] David Wilmot (1814-1868), born in Bethany, Pa., was a Democratic member of the U. S. House of Representatives during 1845-1851. During the Mexican War era he introduced into Congress an amendment to a Polk administration funding bill with the intent of prohibiting slavery in any territory acquired from Mexico as a result of the settlement of that war. This amendment, the "Wilmot Proviso," passed the House but not the Senate, where South Carolina's John C. Calhoun had enough allies to stop it. Wilmot's Proviso helped intensify the debate between pro-slavery and anti-slavery forces and states. He later bolted the Democratic Party and helped found the Free Soil Party, forerunner of the Republican Party, which he also helped found. In 1857, Wilmot was picked to serve in the U. S. Senate, filling the seat of Simon Cameron, whom Lincoln had appointed as his first Secretary of War.

[266] The *Memoirs* of John Quincy Adams (1767-1848), edited by his son Charles Francis Adams, were published in twelve volumes during 1874-1877. They constitute one of the fullest and most accurate personal accounts of U. S. governmental history during the first part of the 19th Century.

[267] John C. Calhoun (1782-1850) of South Carolina served variously as Congressman, Senator, cabinet official and Vice President of the United States. He was not born into aristocratic wealth, but, through inheritance, marriage and thrift, Calhoun acquired a large plantation homestead near Pickens, S.C., in the northwest part of the state.

[268] In June of 1865, the victorious General U. S. Grant, being given a hero's welcome throughout the North, stopped at West Point, where he had not been since his cadet days of the early 1840s. There he visited retired General Winfield Scott, a legendary figure who had served his country both as a soldier (from the War of 1812 through the Civil War) and as a peacemaker possessed of excellent diplomatic skills. Grant had long admired Scott to the point of adulation, having served under him during the Mexican War. He was also aware that only three men in American history had ever been promoted to the rank of lieutenant general: George

stood by old Jackson's garden grove at the Hermitage,[270] followed Van Buren[271] to Kinderhook, Lindenwald[272] and Hudson City, saw General Harrison's "palace" at old Vincennes,[273] dined at Monroe's Oak Hill,[274] went to Monticello[275] with Mr. Levy its owner, and explored the naked halls of Madison's Montpelier.[276]

Washington, Winfield Scott, and himself. It was surely a proud moment for Grant when Scott, at the meeting Gath mentions, presented him a gift carrying the inscription: "From the oldest general to the greatest." The Cozzens referred to may be Frederick Swarthout Cozzens (1818-1869), a noted New York writer, winegrower, merchant and connoisseur.

[269] Founded in 1785, the University of Georgia at Athens is the oldest chartered state college in the nation.

[270] Andrew Jackson (1767-1845), the nation's seventh President, had acquired in 1795, as a young attorney in Tennessee, a large tract of land near Nashville which he named "The Hermitage" and made into a cotton plantation. He would reside there the remainder of his life between forays into the military and political arenas.

[271] Martin Van Buren (1782-1862), of Dutch descent, was born in Kinderhook, New York, where his family had long been settled. A farmer's son, he became interested in law and politics as a young man, later practiced law in nearby Hudson City and was elected to Congress as a Democrat, where he became a strong supporter of President Andrew Jackson. During early 1832, Jackson's quarrel with then-Vice President John C. Calhoun of South Carolina led to Calhoun's resigning and taking his old seat in the Senate. At the Democratic convention that year, Jackson, after being unanimously renominated, hand-picked Van Buren as his Vice Presidential running mate and likely successor as President.

[272] "Lindenwald," the country estate where Van Buren would spend his last years, had once belonged to his great-great-grandfather. The land had been sold in 1780 to Judge Peter Van Ness, who in 1797 built a Palladian mansion upon it. In 1839, the Van Buren family bought it back, and Martin retired there after leaving the White House in 1841.

[273] General William Henry Harrison (1773-1841), the nation's ninth President, defeated Van Buren in the election of 1840 after losing to him in the election of 1836. Becoming ill soon after his inauguration, he died after serving only 32 days in office. Gath's reference to his "palace" in old Vincennes is tongue-in-cheek. It was said of Harrison by supporters of Van Buren during the 1840 election campaign that, being on the frontier in Indiana, he had "nothing but a log cabin to live in, and only hard cider to drink."

[274] James Monroe (1758-1831), America's fifth President, had to sell his Oak Hill plantation near Leesburg, Virginia, late in his life because of debts accumulated during his many years of public service.

[275] Naval Lieutenant Uriah Phillips Levy, according to Townsend, was a "bachelor of means" and a career Navy officer who, upon hearing in 1835 that Jefferson's home (which he had spent much of his life and fortune building) had passed into

At Orange Court House[277] I interviewed at home his nephew secretary, Mr. Willis.[278] Sam Houston's[279] and Albert Sydney Johnson's[280] dusts I contemplated, looked on Clay's relics,[281] and took in alone the stately basilica of Garfield.[282]

Of the living Presidents I knew Hayes, Harrison, Arthur and McKinley well.

---

the hands of a political enemy who vowed "not to leave one brick of the house upon another," went to then-President Andrew Jackson and said, "I have been thinking about buying Monticello in honor of Mr. Jefferson, whom I love." Jackson is said to have responded with fervor, "I order you, sir, to buy it," to which Levy responded, "I always obey the orders, Mr. President, of my superior." Levy's quick action, says Gath, enabled Monticello to be saved for posterity.

[276] Montpelier, in Orange County, Virginia, was the family seat of President James Madison, who died there in 1836.

[277] Orange Court House, in Orange County, Virginia, is near Montpelier.

[278] Actually his nephew-in-law, married to Madison's niece, who was at the former President's bedside when he died.

[279] Sam Houston (1793-1863), Virginia-born civil and military leader who was elected to Congress from Tennessee, then served as governor of that state before resigning, renouncing civilized society, and going off to live with the Cherokees. In 1832 he moved to Texas, became involved in the fight for independence from Mexico and, as commander-in-chief of the Texan army, defeated and captured Santa Anna. Twice elected President of Texas, he represented the new state in the U. S. Senate once it was annexed in 1845. In 1859 he was elected Governor of Texas, and tried hard but unsuccessfully to keep it in the Union when other Southern states seceded.

[280] Albert Sydney Johnson (1803-1862), Kentucky-born, graduated from West Point, served in the Black Hawk and Mexican Wars, then led U. S. Forces in putting down the Mormon Uprising in 1857. During the Civil War, as a Confederate general, he was put in charge of the Department of the West, defending Kentucky and Tennessee from Union army and naval forces. He was leading a successful charge near Pittsburgh Landing, Tennessee, in 1862 against Sherman when he was shot and killed. Subsequently his second-in-command, General Beauregard, ordered the Confederate troops under Bragg to pull back, halting what many students of the war have since felt would have been a Confederate victory had Johnson's plan been carried through.

[281] Henry Clay (1777-1852), a Virginian by birth, came to Congress from his adopted state of Kentucky, becoming known as one of the most powerful and eloquent legislators of the pre-Civil War period. Several times a Whig candidate for the Presidency, he was never able to achieve the nation's highest office, but his reputation endures.

[282] Garfield's tomb in Lakeview Cemetery, Cleveland, Ohio.

OTHER SELECTED WRITINGS

OF

GEORGE ALFRED TOWNSEND

TWO DAYS OF BATTLE.

PUBLISHED IN

THE CALIFORNIAN.

c. 1865

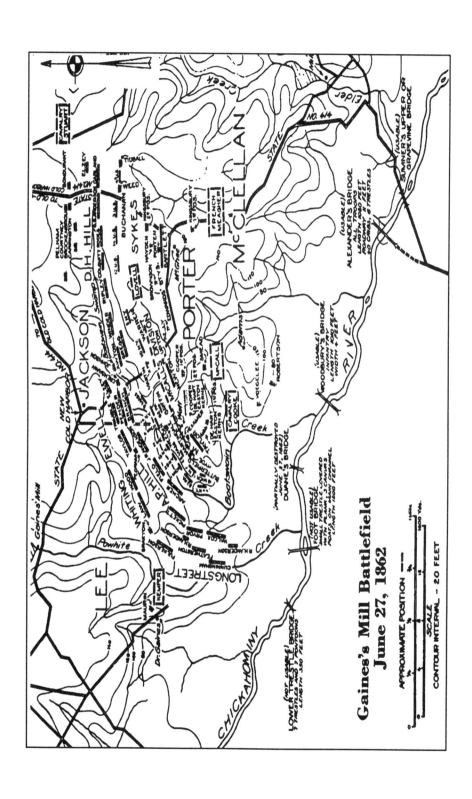

TWO DAYS OF BATTLE.

The Confederates had been waiting two months for McClellan's advance. Emboldened by his delay they had gathered the whole of their available strength from remote Tennessee, from the Mississippi, and from the coast, until, confident and powerful they crossed Meadow Bridge on the 26th of June, 1862, and drove in our right wing at Mechanicsville. The Reserves of Gen. McCall were stationed here; they made a wavering resistance—wherein four companies of Bucktails were captured bodily—and fell back at nightfall upon Porter's Corps, at Gaines' Mill. Fitz John Porter commanded the brigades of Gens. Sykes and Morrell—the former made up solely of regulars. He appeared to have been ignorant of the strength of the attacking party, and he telegraphed to McClellan early on Thursday evening that he required no reinforcements, and that he could hold his ground. The next morning he was attacked in front and back: Stewart's cavalry fell on his right and turned it at Old Church. He formed at noon in new line of battle, from Gaines' House, along the mill road to New Coal Harbor; but stubbornly persisted in the belief that he could not be beaten. By three o'clock he had been driven back two miles, and all his energies were unavailing to recover a foot of ground. He hurled lancers and cavalry upon the masses of Jackson and the Hills, but the brilliant infantry formed impenetrable squares, hemmed in with rods of steel, and as the horsemen galloped around them, searching for pervious points, they were swept from their saddles with volleys of musketry. He directed the terrible fire of his artillery upon them, but though the grey footmen fell in heaps, they steadily advanced, closing up the gaps, and their lines were like big stretches of blaze and ball. Their fire never slackened nor abated. They loaded and moved forward, column on column like so many immortals that could not be vanquished. The scene from the battle, as Lowe informed, was awful beyond all comprehension—of puffing shells and shrieking shrapnel, with volleys that shattered the hills and filled the air with deathly whispers. Infantry, artillery, and horse turned the Federal right from time to time, and to preserve their order of battle the whole line fell back toward Grape Vine Bridge. At five o'clock Sherman's Division of volunteers crossed the creek from the south side, and made a desperate dash upon the solid columns of the Confederates. At the same time Toombs' Georgia Brigade charged Smith's redoubt from the south side, and there was a probability of the whole of both armies engaging before dark.

My fever of body had so much relinquished to my fever of mind that at three o'clock I called for my horse and determined to cross the bridge, that I might witness the battle.

It was with difficulty that I could make my way along the narrow corduroy, for hundreds of wounded were limping from the field to the safe side and ammunition wagons were passing the other way, driven by reckless drivers who should have been blown up momentarily. Before I had reached the north side of the creek, an immense throng of panic-stricken people came surging down the slippery bridge. A few carried muskets, but I saw several wantonly throw their pieces into the flood and, as the mass were unarmed, I inferred that they had made similar dispositions. Fear, anguish, cowardice, despair, disgust, were the predominant expressions on their upturned faces. The giant trees, towering from the current, cast a solemn shadow upon the bustling throng and as the evening dimness was falling around them, it almost seemed that they were engulfed in some cataract. I reined my horse close to the side of a team, that I might not be borne backward by the crowd; but some of the lawless fugitives seized him by the bridle, and others attempted to pull me from the saddle.

"Gi up that hoss." said one, "what business you got wi a hoss?"

"That's my critter, and I am in for a ride; so you get off," said another.

I spurred my pony vigorously with the left foot, and with the right struck the man at the bridle under the chin. The thick column parted left and right, and though a howl of hate pursued me, I kept straight to the bank, cleared the swamp and took the military route parallel with the creek toward the nearest entrance. At every step of the way, I met wounded persons. A horseman rode past me bending over his pommel, with blood streaming from his mouth and hanging in bouts from his saturated beard. The day had been relentlessly hot, and black boys were besetting the wounded with buckets of cool lemonade. It was a common occurrence for the couples that carried the wounded on stretchers to stop on the way, purchase a glass of the beverage, and drink it. Sometimes the blankets on the stretchers were closely folded, and then I knew that the man within was dead. A little fellow, who used his sword for a cane, stopped me on the road and said:

"See yer! This is the ball that just fell out o'my boot."

He handed me a lump of lead as big as my thumb, and pointed to a rent in his pantaloons, whence the drops rolled down his boots."

"I wouldn't part with that for suthin' handsome," he said, "it'll be nice to hev to home."

As I cantered away he shouted after me:

"Be sure you spell my name right: It's Smith, with an "E"—Smithe."

In one place I met five drunken men escorting a wounded Sergeant. He had been wounded in the jaw and when he attempted to speak the blood choked his articulation.

Battle of the Chickahominy, June 27, 1862.

"You le' go him, pardner," said one of the staggering brutes, "he's not your Sergeant. Go 'way."

"Now, Sergeant," said the other idiotically, "Ill see you all right, Sergeant. Com, Bill, Fetch him over to the corncrib and we'll give him a drink."

Here the first speaker struck the second, and the sergeant in wrath knuckled them both down. All this time the enemy's cannon were booming close at hand.

I came to an officer of rank, whose shoulder emblem I could not distinguish riding upon a limping field horse. Four men held him to his seat, and a fifth led the animal. The officer was evidently wounded, though he did not seem to be bleeding, and the dust of battle had settled upon his blanched stiffening face, like grave mould upon a corpse. He was swaying in the saddle, and his hair—for he was bare-headed—shook across his white eyeballs. He reminded me of the famous Old whose body was sent forth to scare the Saracens.

A mile, or more, from Grape Vine Bridge, on a hill top, lay a frame farm-house, with cherry trees encircling it, and along the declivity of the hill were some cabins, corn-sheds and corn-bins. The house was now a surgeon's headquarters and the wounded lay in the yard and lane, under the shade, waiting their turns to be hacked and maimed. I caught a glimpse through the door of the butchers and their victims, some curious people were peeping through the window at the operation. As the procession of freshly wounded went by the poor fellows, lying on the backs, looked mutely at me, and their great eyes smote my heart.

Something has been written in the course of the war upon straggling from the ranks, during battle. But I have seen nothing that conveys an adequate idea of the number of cowards and idiots that so stroll off. In this instance, I met squads, companies, almost regiments of them. Some came boldly along the road; others skulked in woods, and made long detours to escape detection; a few were composedly playing cards or heating their coffee, or discussing the order and consequence of the fight. The rolling drums, the constant clatter of file and volley-fire—nothing could remind them of the requirements of the time or their own infamy. Their appreciation of duty and honor seemed to be forgotten; neither hate, ambition, nor patriotism could force them back; but when the columns of mounted provosts charged upon them, they sullenly resumed their muskets and returned to the field. At the foot of the hill to which I have referred the ammunition wagons lay in long lines, with the horses' heads turned from the fight. A little beyond stood the ambulances; and between both sets of vehicles, fatigue parties were going and returning to and from the field. At the top of the next hill sat many of the Federal batteries, and I was admonished by the shriek of shells that passed over my head and burst far behind me, that I was again to look upon carnage and share the perils of the soldier.

The question at once occurred to me: Can I stand fire? Having for some months penned daily paragraphs relative to death, courage and victory, I was surprised to find that those words were unusually significant. "Death" was a syllable to me before; it was a whole dictionary now. "Courage" was natural to every man a week ago; it was rarer than genius to-day. "Victory" was the first word in the lexicon of youth yesterday noon: "discretion" and safety" were at present of infinitely more consequence. I resolved, notwithstanding these qualms, to venture to the hill-top; but at every step flitting projectiles took my breath. The music of the battle-field, I have often thought, should be introduced in opera. Not the drum, the bugle, or the fife, though these are thrilling after their fashion; but the music of modern ordnance and projectile, the beautiful whistle of the minie ball, the howl of shell that it makes unearthly havoc with the air, the whiz-z-z of solid shot, the chirp of bullets, the scream of grape and canister, the yell of immense conical cylinders that fall like red hot stoves and spout burning coals.

All these passed over, beside, beneath, before, behind me. I seemed to be an invulnerable something at whom some cunning juggler was tossing steel, with an intent to impinge upon, not to strike him. I rode like one with his life in his hand, and, so far as I remember, seemed to think of nothing. No fear, *per se*; no regret; no adventure; only expectancy. It was the expectancy of a shot, a choking, a loud cry, a stiffening, a dead, dull, tumble, a quiver, and—blind-ness. But with this was mingled a sort of enjoyment, like that of the daring gamester who has played his soul and is waiting for the decision of the cards. I felt all his suspense, more than his hope; and with all, there was excitement in the play. Now a whistling ball seemed to pass just under my ear, and before I commenced to congratulate myself upon the escape, a shell, with a showery and revolving fuse, appeared to take the top off my head. Then my heart expanded and contracted, and somehow I found myself coining rhymes. At each clipping ball—for I could hear them coming—a sort of coldness and paleness rose to the very roots of my hair, and was then replaced by a hot flush. I caught myself laughing, hysterically, and shrugging my shoulders, fitfully. Once the rhyme that came to my lips—for I'm sure there was no mind in the initiation—was the simple nursery prayer:

"Now I lay me down to sleep." and I continued to say "down to sleep," "down to sleep," "down to sleep," till I discovered myself, when I ceased. Then a shell, apparently just in range, dashed toward me and the words spasmodically leaped up: "Now's your time. This is your billet." With the same insane pertinacity I continued to repeat, "Now's your time, now's your time," and "billet, billet, billet," till at last I came up to the nearest battery, where I could look over the crest of the hill; and, as if I had looked into the crater of a volcano, or down the fabled abyss into hell, the whole grand horror of a battle burst upon my sight. For a moment I could neither feel nor think. I scarcely beheld, or beholding did not understand or perceive. Only the roar of guns, the blaze that flashed along a zig-zag line and was straightway smothered with smoke, the creek lying glassily beneath me, the gathering twilight and the brownish blue of woods! I only knew that some thousands of fiends were playing with fire and tossing brands at heaven—that some pleasant slopes, dells and highlands were lit as if the conflagration of universes had commenced. There is a passage of Holy Writ that come to my mind as I write, which explains the sensation of the time better than I can do:

"He opened the bottomless pit; and there arose a smoke out of the pit, as the smoke of a great furnace; and the sun and the air were darkened by reason of the smoke of the pit."

"And there came out of the smoke locusts upon the earth."

—Revelations, ix. 2, 3.

In a few moments, when I was able to compose myself, the veil of cloud blew away or dissolved, and I could see fragments of the long columns of infantry. Then from the far end of the lines puffed smoke, and from man to man the puff ran down each line, enveloping the columns again, and that they were alternately visible and invisible. At points between the masses of infantry lay field pieces, throbbing with rapid deliveries, and emitting volumes of white steam. Now and then the firing slackened for a short time, when I could remark the Federal line, fringed with bayonets, stretching from the low meadow on the left up the slope, over the ridge and up and down the crest, until its right disappeared in the gloaming of wood and distance. Standards flapped here and there above the column, and I knew from the fact that the line became momentarily more distinct, that the Federal were falling stubbornly back. At times a battery would dash a hundred yards forward, unlimber, and fire a score ofttimes, and directly would return two hundred yards and blaze again. I saw a regiment of lancers gather at the foot of a protecting swell of field; the bugle rang thrice, the red pennons went upward like so many song birds, the mass turned the crest and disappeared, then the whole artillery belched and bellowed. In twenty minutes a broken, straggling, feeble group of horsemen returned: the red pennons still fluttered, but I knew that they were redder for the blood that dyed them. Finally, the Federal infantry fell back to the foot of the hill on which I stood; all the batteries were clustering around me, and suddenly a column of men shot up from the long sweep of the abandoned hill, with batteries on the left and right. Their muskets were turned toward us—a crash and a whiff of smoke swept from flank to flank, and the air around me rained buck, slug, bullet and ball!

The incidents that now occurred in rapid succession were so thrilling and absorbing that my solicitude was lost in their grandeur. I sat like one dumb, with my soul in my eyes and my ears, stunned, watching the terrible column of Confederates. Each party was now straining every energy—the one for victory, the other against annihilation. The darkness was closing in, and neither cared to prolong the contest after night. The Confederates, therefore, aimed to finish their success with the rout or capture of the Federals, and the Federals aimed to maintain their ground till nightfall. The musketry was close, accurate and uninterrupted. Every second marked by a discharge—the one firing, the other replying promptly. No attempt was now made to remove the wounded; the coolness of the fight had gone by, and we witnessed only its fury. The stragglers seemed to appreciate the desperate emergency and came voluntarily back to relieve their comrades; the musketry ceased for the time, and shrieks, steel-strokes, the crack of carbines and revolvers succeeded. Shattered, humiliated, sullen, the horse wheeled and returned. The guns thundered again, and by the blaze of the pieces, the clods and turf were revealed, fitfully strewn with men and horses.

The vicinity of my position now exhibited traces of the battle. A caisson burst close by and I heard the howl of dying wretches, as the fires flashed like meteors. A solid shot struck a field carriage not thirty yards from my feet and one of the flying splinters spitted a gunner as if he had been pierced by an arrow. An artilleryman was standing with folded arms so near that I could have reached to touch him: a whistle and a thumping shock, and he fell beneath my horse's head. I wonder, as I calmly recall these episodes now, how I escaped the death that played about me, chilled me, thrilled me—but spared me!

"They are fixing bayonets for a charge. My God! See them come down the hill!"

In the gathering darkness, through the thick smoke, I saw or seemed to see the interminable column roll steadily downward. I fancy that I beheld great gaps cut in their ranks but closing solidly up, like the imperishable Gorgon. I may have heard some of this next day, and so confounded the testimonies of eye and ear. But I know that there was a charge, and that the drivers were ordered to stand by their saddles, to run off the guns at any moment. The descent and bottom below me, were now all ablaze, and directly, above the din of cannon, rifle, and pistol, I heard a great cheer, as of some situation achieved.

"The rebels are repulsed! We have saved the guns!"

A cheer greeted this announcement from the battery-men around me. They reloaded, rammed, swabbed and fired, with naked arms, and drops of sweat furrowed the powder stains upon their faces. The horses stood motionless, quivering not half so much as the pieces. The gristly officers held to their match strings, smothering the excitement of the time. All at once there was a running hither and thither, a pause in the thunder, a quick consultation:

"S'death! They have flanked us again." In an instant I seemed overwhelmed with men. For a moment I thought the enemy had surrounded us.

"It's all up." said one. "I shall cross the river."

I wheeled my horse, fell in with the stream of fugitives, and was borne swiftly through field and lane, and trampled fence to the swampy margin of the Chickahominy. At every step the shell fell in and among the fugitives adding to their panic. I saw officers who had forgotten their regiments or had been deserted by them, wending with the mass. The wounded fell and were trodden upon. Personal exhibition of valor and determination there were; but the main body had lost heart; and were weary and hungry.

As we approached the bridge there was confusion and altercation ahead. The people were borne back up on me. Curses and threats ensued.

"It is the Provost-guard," said a fugitive, "driving back the boys."

"Go back" called a voice ahead. "Ill blow you to h—l if you don't go back! Not a man shall cross the bridge without orders."

The stragglers were variously affected by this intelligence. Some cursed and threatened: some of the wounded blubbered as they leaned languidly upon the shoulders of their comrades. Others stoically threw themselves on the ground and tried to sleep. One man called aloud that the "boys" were stronger than the Provosts and that therefore the "boys" ought to "go in and win."

"Where's the man that wants to mutiny?" said the voice ahead; "let me see him."

The man slipped away, for the Provost officer spoke as though he meant all he said.

"Nobody wants to mutiny!" cried others.

"Three cheers for the Union."

The wounded and well threw up their hats together, and made a sickly hurrah. The grim officer relented, and he shouted stentoriously that he would take the responsibility of passing the wounded. These gathered themselves up and pushed through the throng; but many skulkers pled injuries and so escaped. When I attempted to follow, on horseback, hands were laid upon me, and I was refused exit. In that hour of terror and sadness, there were yet jests and loud laughter. However keenly I felt these things, I had learned that modesty amounted to little in the army; so I pushed my nag steadily forward and scattered the camp vernacular, in the shape of imprecations, left and right.

"Colonel," I called to the officer in command—the line of bayonets edged me in. "May I pass out? I am civilian.."

"No." said the Colonel, wrathfully. "This is no place for a civilian."

"That is why I want to get away."

"Pass out!"

I followed the winding of the woods to Woodbury's Bridge—the next above Grapevine Bridge. The approaches were clogged with wagons and field pieces, and I understood that some panic-stricken people had pulled up some of the timbers to prevent a fancied pursuit. Along the sides of the bridge many of the wounded were washing their wounds in the water, and the cries of the teamsters echoed weirdly through the trees that grew in the river. At nine o'clock we got under way—horsemen, batteries, ambulances, ammunition teams, infantry, and finally some great siege 32's that had been hauled from Gaines' House. One of those pieces broke down the timbers again, and my impression is that it was cast into the current. When we emerged from the swamp timber, the hills before us were found brilliantly illuminated with burning camps. I made toward headquarters, in one of Trent's fields; but all the tents save one had been taken down, and lines of white covered wagons streamed southward until they were lost in the shadows. The tent of Gen. McClellan alone remained and beneath an arbor of pine boughs, close at hand, he sat, with his Corps Commanders and Aides, holding a council of war. A ruddy fire lit up the historical group and I thought at the time, as I have said a hundred times since, that the consultation might be selected for a grand national painting. The crisis, the hope, the subjects, the removed participants, peculiarly fit in for pictorial commemoration.

The young commander sat in a chair, in full uniform uncovered. Hentzelman was kneeling upon a fagot, earnestly speaking. DeJoinville sat apart, by the fire, studying a map. Fitz John Porter was standing back of McClellan, leaning upon his chair. Keyes, Franklin, and Summer were listening attentively. Some soldiers paced to and fro, to keep out vulgar curiosity. Suddenly, there was a nodding of heads, as of some policy decided: they threw themselves upon their steeds, and galloped off toward Michie's.

As I reined at Michie's porch, at ten o'clock, the bridges behind me were blown up, with a flare that seemed a blazing of the Northern lights. The family were sitting upon the porch, and Mrs. Michie was greatly alarmed with the idea that a battle would be fought around her house next day.

O'Hanlon, of Meagher's staff, had taken the fever and sent anxiously for me, to compare our symptoms.

I bade the good people adieu before I went to bed, and gave the man "Pat" a dollar to stand by my horse while I slept, and to awake me at any disturbance, that I might be ready to scamper. The man "Pat," I am bound to say, woke me up thrice by the exclamation of:

"Sure, your honor, there's —well—to pay in the yard! I think ye and the Doctor had better ride off."

On each of those occasions, I found that the man "Pat" had been lonesome, and wanted somebody to speak to.

What a sleep was mine that night! I forgot my fever. But another and a hotter fever burned my temples—the fearful excitement of the time! Whither were we to go, cut off from the York, beaten beside Richmond—perhaps even now surrounded—and to be butchered tomorrow, till the clouds should rain blood? We were to retreat one hundred miles down the hostile Peninsula—a battle at every rod, a grave at every footstep? Then I remembered the wounded heaped at Gaines's Mill, and how they were groaning without remedy, ebbing at every pulse, counting the flushing drops, calling for water, for mercy, for death. So I found heart: for I was not buried yet. And somehow I felt that fate was to take me, as the great poet took Dante, through other and greater horrors. *N.Y. Citizen.*

An American War Correspondent in England.

A Union soldier from Delaware's Pierce family.

AN AMERICAN WAR CORRESPONDENT IN ENGLAND.

The boy's vague dream of foreign adventure had passed away; my purpose was of a tamer and more practical cast; it was resolved to this problem: "How could I travel abroad and pay my expenses?"

Evidently no money could be made by home correspondence. The new order of journals had no charity for fine moral descriptions of church steeples, ruined castles, and picture galleries; I knew too little of foreign politics to give the republic its semi-weekly "sensation;" and exchange was too high at the depreciated value of currency to yield me even a tolerable reward. But might I not reverse the policy of the peripatetics, and instead of turning my European experiences into American gold, make my knowledge of America a bill of credit for England?

What capital had I for this essay? I was twenty-one years of age; the last three years of my minority had been passed among the newspapers; I knew indifferently well the distribution of parties, the theory of the government, the personalities of public men, the causes of the great civil strife. And I had mounted to my saddle in the beginning of the war, and followed the armies of McClellan and Pope over their sanguinary battle-fields. The possibility thrilled me, like a novel discovery, that the old world might be willing to hear of the new as I could depict it, fresh from the theatre of action. At great expense foreign correspondents had been sent to our shores whose ignorance and confidence had led them into egregious blunders; for their traveling outlay merely, I would have guaranteed thrice the information, and my sanguine conceit half persuaded me that I could present it as acceptably. I did not wait to ponder upon this suggestion. The guns of the second action of Bull Run growled a farewell to me as I resigned my horse and equipments to a successor. With a trifle more money than that with which Bayard Taylor set out, I took passage on a steamer, and landed at Liverpool on the 1st of October, 1862.

Among my acquaintances upon the ship had been a semi-literary adventurer from New England. I surmised that his funds were not more considerable than my own; and indeed, when he comprehended my plans, he confessed as much, and proposed to join enterprises with me.

"Did you ever make a public lecture?" he asked.

Now I had certain blushing recollections of having entertained a suburban congregation, long before, with didactic critiques upon Byron, Keats, and the popular poets. I replied, therefore, misgivingly, in the affirmative, and Hipp, the interrogator, exclaimed at once:

"Let us make a lecturing tour in England, and divide the expenses and the work; you will describe the war, and I will act as your agent."

With true Yankee persistence Hipp developed his idea, and I consented to try the experiment, though with grave scruples. It would require much nerve to talk to strange people upon an excitable topic; and a camp fever, which among other things I had gained on the Chickahominy, had enfeebled me to the last degree.

However, I went to work at once, inditing the pages in a snug parlor of a modest Liverpool inn, while Hipp sounded the patrons and landlord as to the probable success of our adventure. Opinions differed; public lectures in the old world had been generally gratuitous, except in rare cases, but the genial Irish proprietor of the *Post* advised me to go on without hesitation.

We selected for the initial night a Lancashire sea-side town, a summer resort for the people of Liverpool, and filled at that time with invalids and pleasure-seekers. Hipp, who was a sort of American Crichton, managed the business details with consummate tact. I was announced as the eye-witness and participator of a hundred actions, fresh from the bloodiest fields and still smelling of saltpetre. My horse had been shot as I carried a General's orders under fire of a score of batteries, and I was connected with journals whose reputations were world-wide. Disease had compelled me to forsake the scenes of my heroism, and I had consented to enlighten the Lancashire public, through the solicitation of the nobility and the gentry. Some of the latter had indeed honored the affair with their patronage.

We secured the three village newspapers by writing them descriptive letters. The parish rector and the dissenting preachers were waited upon and presented with family tickets; while we placarded the town till it was scarcely recognizable to the oldest inhabitant.

On the morning of the eventful day I arrived in the place. The best room of the best inn had been engaged for me, and waiters in white aprons, standing in rows, bowed me over the portal. The servant girls and gossips had fugitive peeps at me through the cracks of my door, and I felt for the first time all the oppressiveness of greatness. As I walked on the quay where the crowds were strolling, looking out upon the misty sea, at the donkeys on the beach, and at the fishing smacks huddled under the far-reaching pier, I saw my name in huge letters borne on the banner of a bill-poster, and all the people stopping to read as he wound in and out among them.

How few thought the thin, sallow young man, in wide breeches and square-toed boots, who shambled by them so shamefacedly, to be the veritable Mentor who had crossed the ocean for their benefit. Indeed the embarrassing responsibility I had assumed now appeared to me in all its vividness.

My confidence sensibly declined; my sensitiveness amounted to nervousness; I had half a mind to run away and leave the show entirely to Hipp. But when I saw that child of the Mayflower stolidly, shrewdly going about his business working the wires like an old operator, making the largest amount of thunder from so small a cloud, I was rebuked of my faintheartedness. In truth, not the least of my misgivings was Hipp's extraordinary zeal. He gave the townsmen to understand that I was prodigy of oratory, whose battle-sketches would harrow up their souls and thrill them like a martial summons. It brought the blush to my face to see him talking to knots of old men after the fashion of a town-crier at a puppet-booth, and I wondered whether I occupied a more reputable rank, after all, than a strolling gymnast, giant, or dwarf.

As the twilight came on my position became ludicrously unenviable. The lights in the townhall were lit. I passed pallidly twice or thrice, and would have given half my fortune if the whole thing had been over. But the minutes went on; the interval diminished: I faced the crisis at last and entered the arena.

There sat Hipp, taking money at the head of the stairs, with piles of tickets before him; and as he rose, gravely respectful, the janitor and some loiterers took off their hats while I passed. I entered the little bare dressing-room; my throat was parched as fever, my hands were hot and tremulous; I felt my heart sag. How the rumble of expectant feet in the audience-room shook me! I called myself a poltroon, and fingered my neck-tie, and smoothed my hair before the mirror. Another burst of impatient expectation made me start: I opened the door, and stood before my destiny.

The place was about one-third filled with a representative English audience, the males preponderating in number. They watched me intently as I mounted the steps of the rostrum and arranged my port-folio upon a musical tripod; then I seated myself for a moment, and tried to still the beating of my foolish heart.

How strangely acute were my perceptions of every thing before me! I looked from face to face and analyzed the expressions, counted the lines down the corduroy pantaloons, measured the heavily-shod English feet, numbered the rows of benches and the tubes of the chandeliers, and figured up the losing receipts from this unremunerative audience.

Then I rose, coughed, held the house for the last time in severe review, and repeated:

"Ladies And Gentlemen,—A grand contest agitates America and the world. The people of the two sections of the great North American Republic having progressed in harmony for almost a century, and become a formidable power among the nations, are now divided and at enmity; they have consecrated with blood their fairest fields, and built monuments of bones in their most beautiful valleys," etc.

For perhaps five minutes every thing went on smoothly. I was pleased with the clearness of my voice; then, as I referred to the origin of the war, and denounced the traitorous conspiracy to disrupt the republic, faint mutterings arouse, amounting to interruptions at last. The sympathies of my audience were in the main with the secession. There were cheers and counter cheers; storms of "Hear, hear," and "No, no," until a certain youth, in a sort of legal monkey-jacket and with ponderously professional gold seals, so distinguished himself by exclamations that I singled him out as a mark for my bitterest periods.

But while I was thus the main actor in this curious scene, a strange, startling consciousness grew apace upon me; the room was growing dark, my voice replied to me like a far, hollow echo: I knew-I knew that I was losing my consciousness—that I was about to faint! Words can not describe my humiliation at this discovery. I set my lips hard and straightened my limbs; raised my voice to a shrill, defiant pitch, and struggled in the dimming horror to select my adversary in the monkey-jacket and overwhelm him with bitter apostrophes. In vain! The novelty, the excitement, the enervation of that long, consuming fever mastered my overtaxed physique. I knew that if I did not cease I should fall senseless to the floor. Only in the last bitter instant did I confess my disability with the best grace I could assume.

"My friends," I said, gaspingly, " this is my first appearance in your country, and I am but just convalescent; my head is a little weak. Will you kindly bear with me a moment while the janitor gets me a glass of water?"

A hearty burst of applause took the sting from my mortification. A bald old gentleman in the front row gravely rose and said, "Let me send for a drop of brandy for our young guest." They waited patiently and kindly till my faintness passed away, and when I rose a genuine English cheer shook the place.

I often hear it again when, here in my own country, I would speak bitterly of Englishmen, and it softens the harshness of my condemnation.

But now I addressed myself feverishly to my task, and my disgrace made me vehement and combative. I glared upon the individual in the monkey-jacket as if he had been Mr. Jefferson Davis himself, and read him a scathing indictment. The man in the monkey-jacket was not to be scathed. He retorted more frequently than before; he was guilty of the most hardy contempt of court. He was determined not to agree with me, and said so.

"Sir," I exclaimed at last, "pray reserve your remarks till the end of the lecture, and you shall have the platform."

"I shall be quite willing, I am sure," said the man in the monkey-jacket with imperturbable effrontery.

Then, as I continued, the contest grew interesting; explosions of "no, no" were interrupted with volleys of "Ay, ay" from my adherents. Hipp, who had squared accounts, made all the applause in his power, standing in the main threshold, and the little auditory became a ringing arena, where we fought without flinching, standing foot to foot and drawing fire for fire. The man in the monkey-jacket broke his word: silence was not his forte; he hurled denials and counter-charges vociferously; he was full of gall and bitterness, and when I closed the last page and resumed my chair he sprang from his place to claim the platform.

"Stop," cried Hipp, in his hard nasal tone, striding forward; "you have interrupted the lecturer after giving your parole; we recall our promise, as you have not stood by yours. Janitor, put out the lights!"

The bald old gentleman quietly rose. "In England," he said, "we give everybody fair play; tokens of assent and dissent are commonly made in all our public meetings; let us have a hearing for our townsman."

"Certainly," I replied, giving him my hand at the top of the stairs; "nothing would afford me more pleasure."

The man in the monkey-jacket then made a sweeping speech, full of loose charges against the Americans, and expressive of sympathy with the rebellion; but, at the finishing, he proposed, as the sentiment of the meeting, a vote of thanks to me, which was amended by another to include himself. Many of the people shook hands with me at the door, and the bald old gentleman led me to his wife and daughter, whose benignities were almost parental.

"Poor young man!" said the old lady; "a must take care of 'is 'elth' will a come hoom wi' Tummas and me and drink a bit o' tea?"

I strolled about the place for twenty-four hours on good terms with many townsmen, while Hipp, full of pluck and business, was posting me against all the dead walls of a farther village. Again and again I sketched the war-episodes I had followed, gaining fluency and confidence as by degrees my itinerant profession lost its novelty, but we as steadily lost money. The houses were invariably bad; we had the same fiery discussions every evening, but the same meagre receipts, and in every market town of northwestern Lancashire we buried a portion of our little capital, till once, after talking myself hoarse to a respectable audience of empty benches, Hipp and I looked blankly into each other's faces and silently put our last gold pieces upon the table. We were three thousand miles from home, and the possessors of ten sovereigns apiece. I reached out my hand with a pale smile:

"Old fellow," I said, "let us comfort ourselves by the assurance that we have deserved success. The time has come to say good-by."

"As you will," said Hipp; "it is all the fault of this pig-headed nation. Now I dare say if we had brought a panorama of the war along it would have been a stunning success; but standing upon the high literary and forensic ground, of course they can't appreciate us. Confound 'em!"

I think that Hipp has since had but two notions—the exhibition of that panorama, or, in the event of its failure, a declaration of war against the British people. He followed me to Liverpool, and bade me adieu at Birkenhead, I going Londonward with scarcely enough money to pay my passage, and he to start next day for Belfast, to lecture upon his own hook, or failing (as he afterward did), to recross the Atlantic in the steerage of a ship.

My feelings, as the train bore me steadily through the Welsh border, by the clustering smoke-stacks of Birmingham, by the castled tower of Warwick, and along the head waters of the Thames and Avon, were not of the most enthusiastic description. I had no money and no friends; I had sent to America for a remittance, but in the interval of six weeks required for a reply, must eat and drink and lodge, and London was wide and pitiless, even if I dared stoop to beg assistance.

Let no young man be tempted to put the sea between his home and himself, how seductive soever be the experiences of book-makers and poetic pedestrians. One hour's contemplation of poverty in foreign lands will line the boy's face with the wrinkles of years, and burn into his soul that withering dependency which will rankle long after his privations are forgotten.

In truth my circumstances were so awkward that my very desperation kept me calm. I had a formal letter to one English publisher, but not any friendly line whatever to any body; and as the possibilities of sickness, debt, enemies, came to mind, I felt that I was no longer the hero of a romance, but face to face with a hard, practical terrible reality. It was night when I landed at the Paddington Station, and taking an omnibus for Charing Cross, watched the long lines of lamps on Oxford Street, and the glitter of the Haymarket theatres, and at last the hard splash of the fountains in Trafalgar Square, with the stony statues grouped so rigidly about the column to Nelson.

I walked down Strand with my carpet-bags in my hands, through Fleet Street and under Temple Bar, till, weary at last from sheer exercise, I dropped into a little ale-house under a great, grinning lantern which said, the crisp tone of patronage, the one word, "beds." They put me under the tiles, with the chimney-stacks for my neighbors, and I lay awake all night meditating expedients for the morrow; so far from regret or foreboding, I longed for the daylight to come that I might commence my task, confident that I could not fail where so many had succeeded. They were, indeed, inspirations which looked in upon me at the dawn. The dome of St. Paul's guarding Paternoster Row, with Milton's school in the back-ground, and hard by the Player's Court, where, in lieu of Shakespeare's company, the American presses of the *Times* shook the kingdom and the continent. I thought of Johnson as I passed Bolt Alley, of Chatterton at Shoe Lane, of Goldsmith as I put my foot upon his grave under the caves of the Temple.

The public has nothing to do with the sacrifice by which my private embarrassment received temporary relief. Though half the race of authors had been in similar straits, I would not, for all their success, undergo again such self-humiliation. It is enough to say that I obtained lodgings in Islington, close to the home of Charles Lamb, and near Irving's Canterbury tower; and that between writing articles on the American war, and strategic efforts to pay my board, two weeks of feverish loneliness drifted away.

I made but one friend: a young Englishman of radical proclivities, who had passed some years in America among books and newspapers, and was now editing the foreign column of the *Illustrated London News*. He was a brave, needy fellow, full of heart, but burdened with a wife and children, and too honestly impolitic to gain money with his fine abilities by writing down his own unpopular sentiments. He helped me with advice and otherwise.

"If you mean to work for the journals," he said, "I fear you will be disappointed. I have tried six years to get upon some daily London paper. The editorial positions are always filled; you know too little of geography and society of the town to be a reporter, and such miscellaneous recollections of the war as you possess will not be available for a mere newspaper. But the magazines are always ready to purchase if you can get access to them. In that quarter you might do well."

I found that the serials to which my friend recommended me shared his own advanced sentiments, but were unfortunately without money. So I made my way to the counter of the Messrs. Chambers, and left for its junior partner an introductory note. The reply was to this effect. I violate no confidence, I think, in reproducing it:

"Sir,—I shall be glad to see any friend of ____ ____, and may be found," etc., etc. "I fear that articles upon the American war, written by an American, will not however, be acceptable in this journal as the public here take a widely different view of the contest from that entertained in your own country, and the feeling of horror is deepening fast."

Undeterred by this frank avowal I waited upon the publisher at the appointed time—a fine, athletic, white-haired Scotchman, whose name is known where that of greater authors can not reach, and who has written with his own hand as much as Dumas *père*. He met me with warm cordiality, rare to Englishmen, and when I said,

"Sir, I do not wish the use of your paper to circulate my opinions—only my experiences," he took me at once to his editor, and gave me a personal introduction. Fortunately I had brought with me a paper which I submitted on the spot; it was entitled, "Literature of the American War," collated from such campaign ballads as I could remember, eked out with my own, and strung together with explanatory and critical paragraphs. The third day following I received this announcement in shockingly bad handwriting:

"D'r S'r,

"Y'r article will suit us.

"The ed. C. J."

For every word in this communication I afterward obtained a guinea. The money not being due till after the appearance of the article, I anticipated it with various sketches, stories, etc., all of which were largely fanciful or descriptive, and contained no paragraph which I wish to recall. In other directions I was less successful. Of two daily journals to which I offered my services, one declined to answer my letter and the other demanded a quarto of credentials.

So I lived a fugitive existence, a practical illustration of Irving's "Poor Devil Author," looking as often into pastry-shop windows, testing all manner of cheap Pickwickian veal-pies, breakfasting upon a chop, and supping upon a herring in my suburban residence, but keeping up pluck and *chique* so deceptively that nobody in the place suspected me of poverty.

I went for some American inventors to a rifle ground, and explained to the Lords of the Admiralty the merits of a new projectile; wrote letters to all the Continental sovereigns for an itinerant and independent ambassador, and was at last so poor that my only writing papers were a druggist's waste bill-heads. An article with no other "backing" than this was fortunate enough to stray into the *Cornhill Magazine*. I found that its proprietor kept a banking-house in Pall Mall, and doubtful of my welcome on Cornhill, ventured one day in my unique American costume—slouched hat, wide garments, and square-toed boots—to send to him directly my card. He probably thought from its face that a relative of Mr. Mason's was about to open an extensive account with him. As it was, once admitted to his presence, he could not escape me. The manuscript lay in his hands before he fully comprehended my purpose. He was a fine specimen of the English publisher—robust, ruddy, good-naturedly acute—and as he said with a smile that he would waive routine and take charge of my copy, I knew that the same hands that had fastened upon the crude pages of Jane Eyre, and the best labors of Hazlitt, Ruskin, Leigh Hunt, and Thackeray.

Two more weary weeks elapsed; I found it pleasant to work, but very trying to wait. At the end my courage very nearly failed. I reached the era of self-accusation; to make myself forget myself I took long, ardent marches into the open country; followed the authors I had worshiped through the localities they had made reverend; lost myself in dreaminesses—those precursors of death in the snow—and wished myself back in the ranks of the North, to go down in the frenzy, rather than thus drag out a life of civil indigence, robbing at once my brains and my stomach.

One morning as I sat in my little Islington parlor, wishing that the chop I had just eaten had gone farther, and taking a melancholy inventory of the threadbare carpet and rheumatic chairs, the door-knocker fell; there were steps in the hall; my name was mentioned.

A tall young gentleman approached me with a letter: I received him with a strange nervousness; was there any crime in my record, I asked fitfully, for which I had been traced to this obscure suburb for condign arrest and decapitation? Ha! ha! it was my heart, not my lips, that laughed. I could have cried out like Enoch Arden in his dying apostrophe:

"A sail! a sail!
I am saved!"

for the note in the publisher's own handwriting said this, and more:

"Dear sir,—I shall be glad to send you fifteen guineas immediately in return for your article on General Pope's Campaign, if the price will suit you."

But I suppressed my enthusiasm. I spoke patronizingly to the young gentleman. Dr. Johnson at the brewer's vendue could not have been more learnedly sonorous.

"You may say in return, Sir, that the sum named will remunerate me."

At the same time the instinct was intense to seize the youth by the throat and tell him that if remittance was delayed beyond the morning I would have his heart's-blood! I should have liked to thrust him into the coal-hole as a hostage for its prompt arrival, or send one of his ears to the publishing house with a warning, after the manner of the Neapolitan brigands.

That afternoon I walked all the way to Edmonton, over John Gilpin's route, and boldly invested two-pence in beer at the time-honored Bell Inn. I disdained to ride back upon the omnibus for the sum of three-pence, but returned on foot the entire eight miles, and thought it only a league. Next day my check came duly to hand—a very formidable check, with two pen-marks drawn across its face. I carried it to Threadneedle Street by the unfrequented routes, to avoid having my pockets picked, and presented it to the cashier, wondering if he knew me to be a foreign gentleman who had written for the *Cornhill Magazine*. The cashier looked rather contemptuous I thought, being evidently a soulless character with no literary affinities.

"Sir," he said curtly, "this check is crossed."

"Sir!"

"We can't cash the check; it is crossed."

"What do you mean by crossed?"

"Just present it where you got it, and you will find out."

The cashier regarded me as if I had offered a ticket of leave rather than an order for the considerable amount of seventy-five dollars. I left that banking house a broken man, and stopped with a long, long face at a broker's to ask for an explanation.

"Yeah, yeah," said the little man, whose German silver spectacles sat upon a bulbously Oriental nose; "ze monish ish never paid on a croshed shequc. If one hash a bank-account, you know, zat ish different. Ze gentleman who gif you dis shequc had no bishness to crosh it if you have no banker."

I was too vain to go back to Cornhill and confess that I had neither purse nor purser; so I satisfied the broker that the affair was correct, and he cashed the bill for five shillings.

That was the end of my necessities; money came from home, from this and that serial; my published articles were favorably noticed, and opened the market to me. Whatever I penned found sale; and some correspondence that I had leisure to fulfill for America brought me steady receipts.

Had I been prudent with my means, and prompt to advantage myself of opportunities, I might have obtained access to the best literary society, and sold my compositions for correspondingly higher prices. Social standing in English literature is of equal consequence with genius. The poor Irish governess can not find a publisher, but Lady Morgan takes both critics and readers by a storm. A duchess's name on the title-page protects the fool in the letter-press; irreverent republicanism is not yet so great a respecter of persons. I was often invited out to dinner, and went to the expense of a dress-coat with kids, without which one passes the genteel British portal at his peril; but found that both the expense and the stateliness of "society were onerous." In this department I had no perseverance; but when one evening I sat with the author of "Vanity Fair" in the concert rooms at Covent Garden, as Colonel Newcome and Clive had done before me, and took my beer and mutton with those kindly eyes measuring me through their spectacles, I felt that such grand companionship lifted me from the errantry of my career into the dignity of a renowned art.

I moved my lodgings after three months to a pleasant square of the West End, where I had for associates, among others, several American artists. Strange men were they to be so far from home; but I have since found that the poorer one is the farther he travels, and the majority of these were quite destitute. Two of them only had permanent employment; a few, now and then sold a design to a magazine; the mass went out sketching to kill time, and trusted Providence for dinner. But they were good fellows for the most part, kindly to one another, and meeting in their lodgings, where their tenure was uncertain, to score Millais, or praise Rosetti, or overwhelm Frith.

My own life meantime passed smoothly. I had no rivals of my own nationality; though one expatriated person, whose name I have not heard, was writing a series of prejudiced articles for *Fraser,* which he signed "A White Republican." I thought him a very dirty white. One or two English travelers at the same time were making amusingly stupid notices of America in some of the second-rate monthlies; and Maxwell, a bustling Irishman, who owns *Temple Bar,* the *Saint James,* and *Sixpenny Magazine,* and some half dozen other serials, was employing a man to invent all varieties of rubbish upon a country which he had never beheld nor comprehended.

After a few months the passages of the war with which I was cognizant lost their interest by reason of later occurrences. I found myself, so to speak, wedged out of the market by new literary importations. The enforcement of the draft brought to Europe many naturalized countrymen of mine, whose dislike of America was not lessened by their unceremonious mode of departure from it; and it is to these, the mass of whom are familiarly known in the journals of this country, that we owe the most insidious, because the best informed, detraction of us. *Macmillian's Magazine* did us sterling service through the papers of Edward Dicey, the best literary *feuilletonist* in England; and Professor Newman, J. Stuart Mill, and others, gave us the limited influence of the *Westminster Review.* The *Cornhill* was neutral; *Chambers's* respectfully inimical; *Bentley* and *Colburn* antagonistically flat; Maxwell's tri-visaged publications grinningly abusive; *Good Words* had neither good nor bad words for us; *Once a Week* and *All the Year Round* gave us a shot now and then. *Blackwood* and *Fraser* disliked our form of government and all its manifestations. The rest of the Reviews, as far as I could see, pitied and berated us pompously. It was more than once suggested to me to write an experimental paper upon the failure of republicanism; but I knew only one American—a New York correspondent—who lent himself to a systematic abuse of the Government which permitted him to reside in it. He obtained a newsboy's fame, and, I suspect, earned considerable. He is dead: let any who love him shorten his biography by three years.

However, I at last concluded a book—if I may so call what never resulted in a volume—at which, from the first, I had been pegging away. I called it "The War Correspondent," and made it the literal record of my adventures in the saddle. When some six hundred M.S. pages were done I sent it to the publisher; he politely sent it back. I forwarded it to a rival house; in this respect only both houses were agreed. Having some dim recollection of the early trials of authors I perseveringly gave that copy the freedom of the city; the verdict upon it was marvelously identical, but the manner of declension was always soothing. They separately advised me not to be content with one refusal, but to try some other house, though I came at last to think, by the regularity of its transit to and fro, that one house only had been its recipient from the first.

At last, assured of its positive failure, I took what seemed to be the most philosophic course—neither tossing it into the Thames, after the fashion of a famous novelist, nor littering my floor with its fragments, and dying amidst them like a *chiffonnier* in his den: I cut the best paragraphs out of it, strung them together, and published it by separate articles in the serials. My name failed to be added to the British Museum Catalogue; but that circumstance is, at the present time, a matter of no regret whatever.

When done with the war I took to story-writing, using many half-forgotten incidents of American police-reporting, of border warfare, of the development of civilization among the pioneers, of thralldom in the South, and the gold search on the Pacific. The majority of these traveled across the water, and were republished. And when America, in the garb of either fact or fiction, lost novelty, I entered the wide field of miscellaneous literature among a thousand competitors.

An author's ticket to the British Museum Reading-room put the whole world so close around me that I could touch it every where. I never entered the noble rotunda of that vast collection without an emotion of littleness and awe. Lit only from the roof, it reminded me of the Roman Pantheon; and truly all the gods whom I had worshiped sat, not in statue, but in substance, along its radiating tables, or trod its noiseless floors. Half the literature of our language flows from thence. One may see at a glance grave naturalists keep-deep in ichthyological tomes, or buzzing over entomology; pale zealots copying Arabic characters, with the end to rebuild Bethlehem or the ruins of Mecca; biographers gloating over some rare original letter; periodical writers filching from two centuries ago for their next "new " article. The Marquis of Lansdown is dead: you may see the *Times* reporter yonder running down the events of his career. Poland is in arms again, and the clever compiler farther on means to make twenty pounds out of it by summing up her past risings and ruins. The bruisers King and Mace fought yesterday, and the plodding person close by from *Bell's Life* is gleaning their antecedents. Half the *literati* of our age do but like these bind the present to the past. A great library diminishes the number of thinkers; the grand fountains of philosophy and science ran before types were so facile or letters became a trade.

The novelty of this life soon wore away, and I found myself the creature of no romance, but plodding along a prosy road with very practical people.

I carried my MSS. into Paternoster Row like any body's book-keeper, and accused the world of no particular ingratitude that it could not read my name with my articles, and that it gave itself no concern to discover me. Yet there was a private pleasure in the congeniality of my labor, and in the consciousness that I could float upon my quill even in this vast London sea. Once or twice my articles went across the Channel and returned in foreign dress. I wonder if I shall ever again feel the thrill of that first recognition of my offspring coming to my knee with their strange French prattle.

I was not uniformly successful, but, if rejected, my MSS. were courteously returned, with a note from the editor. As a sample I give the following. The original is a lithographed facsimile of the handwriting of Mr. Dickens, printed in blue ink, the date and the title of the manuscript being in another handwriting:

OFFICE OF "ALL THE YEAR ROUND."
A WEEKLY JOURNAL CONDUCTED BY CHARLES DICKENS.
No. 26 WELLINGTON STREET, STRAND, LONDON, W.C.
January 27, 1863.

Mr. Charles Dickens begs to thank the writer of the paper entitled "A Battle Sunday" for having done him the favor to offer it as a contribution to these pages. He much regrets, however, that it is not suited to the requirements of the "All the Year Round."

The manuscript will be returned, under cover, if applied for as above.

The prices of miscellaneous articles in London are remunerative. Twenty-four shillings a magazine page is the common valuation; but specially interesting papers rate higher. Literature as a profession, in England, is more certain and more progressive than with us. It is not debased with the heavy leaven of journalism. Among the many serial publications of London, ability, tact, and industry should always find a liberal market. There is less of the vagrancy of letters—Bohemianism, Mohicanism, or what not—in London than in either New York or Paris.

I think we have the cleverer fugitive writers in America, but those of England seemed to me to have more self-respect and conscientiousness. The soul of the scribe need never be in pledge if there are many masters.

While a good writer in any department can find work across the water, I would advise no one to go abroad with this assurance solely. My success—if so that can be called which yielded me life, not profit—was circumstantial, and can not be repeated. I should be loath to try it again upon purely literary merits.

After nine months of experiment I bade the insular metropolis adieu, and returned no more. The Continent was close and beckoning; I heard the confusion of her tongues, and saw the shafts of her Gothic Babels probing the clouds, and for another year I roamed among her cities, as ardent and errant as when I went afield on my pony to win the spurs of a War Correspondent.

THE LIFE, CRIME, AND CAPTURE

OF

JOHN WILKES BOOTH

WITH A FULL SKETCH OF THE

Conspiracy of which he was the Leader,

AND THE

PURSUIT, TRIAL AND EXECUTION OF HIS ACCOMPLICES

BY GEORGE ALFRED TOWNSEND,

A SPECIAL CORRESPONDENT.

Dick & Fitzgerald, Publishers: New York, 1865

John Wilkes Booth.
From the cover of *The Life, Crime and Capture of J. Wilkes Booth.*

Editor's note: The original investigation included nine sections called "Letters." They totalled 85 pages and were presumably addressed to the public. Their focus was John Wilkes Booth, and they include "The Murder," describing the actual event in Ford's Theater, "The Murderer," describing the Booth family and his motivation. A third letter, "The Assassin's Death," covers Booth's capture and the ninth letter vividly delineates the execution of Booth's compatriots. Lincoln's funeral, the conspiracy plan, the detectives involved in exposing it and a special reminiscence of Lincoln by the author were not included here but are available in the complete works of "Life, Crime, and Capture."

THE LIFE, CRIME, AND CAPTURE
OF JOHN WILKES BOOTH

EXPLANATORY.

One year ago the writer of the letters which follow, visited the Battle Field of Waterloo. In looking over many relics of the combat preserved in the Museum there, he was particularly interested in the files of journals contemporary with the action. These contained the Duke of Wellington's first despatch announcing the victory, the reports of the subordinate commanders, and the current gossip as to the episodes and hazards of the day.

The time will come when remarkable incidents of these our times will be a staple of as great curiosity as the issue of Waterloo. It is an incident without a precedent on this side of the globe, and never to be repeated.

Assassination has made its last effort to become indigenous here. The public sentiment of Loyalist and Rebel has denounced it: the world has remarked it with uplifted hands and words of execration. Therefore, as long as history shall hold good, the murder of the President will be a theme for poesy, romance and tragedy. We who live in this consecrated time keep the sacred souvenirs of Mr. Lincoln's death in our possession; and the best of these are the news letters descriptive of his apotheosis, and the fate of the conspirators who slew him.

I represented the *World* newspapers at Washington during the whole of those exciting weeks, and wrote their occurrences fresh from the mouths of the actors.

PREFATORY.

It has seemed fitting to Messrs. Dick & Fitzgerald to reproduce the *World* letters, as a keepsake for the many who received them kindly. The Sketches appended were conscientiously written, and whatever embellishments they may seem to have grew out of the stirring events,—not out of my fancy.

Subsequent investigation has confirmed the veracity even of their speculations. I have arranged them, but have not altered them; if they represent nothing else, they do carry with them the fever and spirit of the time. But they do not assume to be literal history; We live too close to the events related to decide positively upon them. As a brochure of the day,—nothing more,—I give these Sketches of a Correspondent to the public. *G.A.T.*

FORD'S THEATER

LETTER I.
THE MURDER.

Washington, April 17.

Some very deliberate and extraordinary movements were made by a handsome and extremely well-dressed young man in the city of Washington last Friday. At about half-past eleven o'clock A.M., this person, whose name is J. Wilkes Booth, by profession an actor, and recently engaged in oil speculations, sauntered into Ford's Theater, on Tenth, between E and F streets, and exchanged greetings with the man at the box-office. In the conversation which ensued, the ticket agent informed Booth that a box was taken for Mr. Lincoln and General Grant, who were expected to visit the theater, and contribute to the benefit of Miss Laura Keene, and satisfy the curiosity of a large audience. Mr. Booth went away with a jest, and a lightly-spoken "Good-afternoon." Strolling down to Pumphreys' stable, on C street, in the rear of the National Hotel, he engaged a saddle horse, a high-strung, fast, beautiful bay mare, telling Mr. Pumphreys that he should call for her in the middle of the afternoon.

From here he went to the Kirkwood Hotel, on the corner of Pennsylvania avenue and Twelfth street, where, calling for a card and a sheet of note-paper, he sat down and wrote upon the first as follows:

For Mr. Andrew Johnson:—
I don't wish to disturb you; are you at home?
J. W. Booth

To this message, which was sent up by the obliging clerk, Mr. Johnson responded that he was very busily engaged. Mr. Booth smiled, and turning to his sheet of note-paper, wrote on it. The fact, if fact it is, that he had been disappointed in not obtaining an examination of the Vice-President's apartment and a knowledge of the Vice-President's probable whereabouts the ensuing evening, in no way affected his composure. The note, the contents of which are unknown, was signed and sealed within a few moments. Booth arose, bowed to an acquaintance, and passed into the street. His elegant person was seen on the avenue a few minutes, and was withdrawn into the Metropolitan Hotel.

At 4 P.M., he again appeared at Pumphreys' livery stable, mounted the mare he had engaged, rode leisurely up F street, turned into an alley between Ninth and Tenth streets, and thence into an alley leading to the rear of Ford's Theater, which fronts on Tenth street, between E and F streets. Here he alighted and deposited the mare in a small stable off the alley, which he had hired some time before for the accommodation of a saddle-horse which he had recently sold. Mr. Booth soon afterward retired from the stable, and is supposed to have refreshed himself at a neighboring bar-room.

At 8 o'clock the same evening, President Lincoln and Speaker Colfax sat together in a private room at the White House, pleasantly conversing. General Grant, with whom the President had engaged to attend Ford's Theater that evening, had left with his wife for Burlington, New-Jersey, in the 6 o'clock train. After this departure Mr. Lincoln rather reluctantly determined to keep his part of the engagement, rather than to disappoint his friends and the audience. Mrs. Lincoln, entering the room and turning to Mr. Colfax, said, in a half laughing, half serious way, "Well, Mr. Lincoln, are you going to the theater with me or not?" "I suppose I shall have to go, Colfax," said the President, and the Speaker took his leave in company with Major Rathbone, of the Provost-Marshal General's office, who escorted Miss Harris, daughter of Senator Harris, of New-York. Mr. and Mrs. Lincoln reached Ford's Theater at twenty minutes before 9 o'clock.

The house was filled in every part with a large and brilliantly attired audience. As the presidential party ascended the stairs, and passed behind the dress circle to the entrance of the private box reserved for them, the whole assemblage, having in mind the recent Union victories, arose, cheered, waving hats and handkerchiefs, and manifesting every other accustomed sign of enthusiasm. The President, last to enter the box, turned before doing so, and bowed a courteous acknowledgment of his reception. At the moment of the President's arrival, Mr. Hawks, one of the actors, performing the well-known part of *Dundreary*, had exclaimed: "This reminds me of a story, as Mr. Lincoln says." The audience forced him, after the interruption, to tell the story over again. It evidently pleased Mr. Lincoln, who turned laughingly to his wife and made a remark which was not overheard.

The box in which the President sat consisted of two boxes turned into one, the middle partition being removed, as on all occasions when a state party visited the theater. The box was on a level with the dress circle; about twelve feet above the stage. There were two entrances—the door nearest to the wall having been closed and locked; the door nearest the balustrades of the dress circle, and at right angles with it, being open and left open after the visitors had entered. The interior was carpeted, lined with crimson paper, and furnished with a sofa covered with crimson velvet, three arm chairs similarly covered, and six cane-bottomed chairs. Festoons of flags hung before the front of the box against a background of lace.

President Lincoln took one of the arm-chairs and seated himself in the front of the box, in the angle nearest the audience, where, partially screened from observation, he had the best view of what was transpiring on the stage.

Mrs. Lincoln sat next to him, and Miss Harris in the opposite angle nearest the stage. Major Rathbone sat just behind Mrs. Lincoln and Miss Harris. These four were the only persons in the box.

The play proceeded, although "Our American Cousin," without Mr. Sothern, has, since that gentleman's departure from this country, been justly esteemed a very dull affair. The audience at Ford's, including Mrs. Lincoln, seemed to enjoy it very much. The worthy wife of the President leaned forward, her hand upon her husband's knee, watching every scene in the drama with amused attention. Even across the president's face at intervals swept a smile, robbing it of its habitual sadness.

About the beginning of the second act, the mare, standing in the stable in the rear of the theater, was disturbed in the midst of her meal by the entrance of the young man who had quitted her in the afternoon. It is presumed that she was saddled and bridled with exquisite care.

Having completed these preparations, Mr. Booth entered the theater by the stage door; summoned one of the scene shifters, Mr. John Spangler, emerged through the same door with that individual, leaving the door open, and left the mare in his hands to be held until he (Booth) should return. Booth, who was even more fashionably and richly dressed than usual, walked thence around to the front of the theater, and went in. Ascending to the dress circle, he stood for a little time gazing around upon the audience and occasionally upon the stage in his usual graceful manner. He was subsequently observed by Mr. Ford, the proprietor of the theater, to be slowly elbowing his way through the crowd that packed the rear of the dress circle toward the right side, at the extremity of which was the box where Mr. and Mrs. Lincoln and their companions were seated. Mr. Ford casually noticed this as a slightly extraordinary symptom of interest on the part of an actor so familiar with the routine of the theater and the play.

The curtain has arisen on the third act, *Mrs. Mountchessington* and *Asa Trenchard* were exchanging vivacious stupidities, when a young man, so precisely resembling the one described as J. Wilkes Booth that he is asserted to be the same, appeared before the open door of the President's box, and prepared to enter.

The servant who attended Mr. Lincoln said politely, "this is the President's box, sir, no one is permitted to enter." "I am a senator," responded the person, "Mr. Lincoln has sent for me." The attendant gave way, and the young man passed into the box.

As he appeared at the door, taking a quick, comprehensive glance at the interior, Major Rathbone arose. "Are you aware, sir," he said, courteously, "upon whom you are intruding? This is the President's box, and no one is admitted." The intruder answered not a word. Fastening his eyes upon Mr. Lincoln, who had half turned his head to ascertain what caused the disturbance, he stepped quickly back without the door.

Without this door there was an eyehole, bored it is presumed on the afternoon of the crime, while the theater was deserted by all save a few mechanics. Glancing through this orifice, John Wilkes Booth espied in a moment the precise position of the President; he wore upon his wrinkling face the pleasant embryo of an honest smile, forgetting in the mimic scene the splendid successes of our arms for which he was responsible, and the history he had filled so well.

The cheerful interior was lost to J. Wilkes Booth. He did not catch the spirit of the delighted audience, of the flaming lamps flinging illumination upon the domestic foreground and the gaily set stage. He only cast one furtive glance upon the man he was to slay, and thrusting one hand in his bosom, another in his shirt pocket, drew forth simultaneously his deadly weapons. His right palm grasped a Derringer pistol, his left a dirk.

Then, at a stride, he passed the threshold again, levelled his arm at the President and bent the trigger.

A keen quick report and a puff of white smoke,—a close smell of powder and the rush of a dark, imperfectly outlined figure,—and the President's head dropped upon his shoulders: the ball was in his brain.

The movements of the assassin were from henceforth quick as the lightning, he dropped his pistol on the floor, and drawing a bowie-knife, struck Major Rathbone, who opposed him, ripping through his coat from the shoulder down, and inflicting a severe flesh wound in his arm. He leaped then upon the velvet covered balustrade at the front of the box, between Mrs. Lincoln and Miss Harris, and, parting with both hands the flags that drooped on either side, dropped to the stage beneath. Arising and turning full upon the audience, with the knife lifted in his right hand above his head, he shouted, "*sic temper tyrannis*—Virginia is avenged!" Another instant he had fled across the stage and behind the scenes. Colonel J. B. Stewart, the only person in the audience who seemed to comprehend the deed he had committed, climbed from his seat near the orchestra to the stage, and followed close behind. The assassin was too fleet and too desperate, that fury incarnate, meeting Mr. Withers, the leader of the orchestra, just behind the scenes, had stricken him aside with a blow that fortunately was not a wound; overturning Miss Jenny Gourlay, an actress, who came next in his path, he gained, without further hindrance, the back door previously left open at the rear of the theater; rushed through it; leaped upon the horse held by Mr. Spangler, and without vouchsafing that person a word of information, rode out through the alley leading into F street, and thence rapidly away. His horse's hoofs might almost have been heard amid the silence that for a few seconds dwelt in the interior of the theater.

Then Mrs. Lincoln screamed, Miss Harris cried for water, and the full ghastly truth broke upon all—"The President is murdered!" The scene that ensued was as tumultuous and terrible as one of Dante's pictures of hell. Some women fainted, others uttered piercing shrieks, and cries for vengeance and unmeaning shouts for help burst from the mouths of men. Miss Laura Keene, the actress, proved herself in this awful time as equal to sustain a part in real tragedy as to interpret that of the stage. Pausing one moment before the footlights to entreat the audience to be calm, she ascended the stairs to the rear of Mr. Lincoln's box, entered it, took the dying President's head in her lap, bathed it with the water she had brought, and endeavoured to force some of the liquid through the insensible lips. The locality of the wound was at first supposed to be in the breast. It was not until after the neck and shoulders had been bared and no mark discovered, that the dress of Miss Keene, stained with blood, revealed where the ball had penetrated.

This moment gave the most impressive episode in the history of the Continent.

The Chief Magistrate of thirty millions of people—beloved, honored, revered,—lay in the pent up closet of a play-house, dabbling with his sacred blood the robes of an actress.

As soon as the confusion and crowd was partially overcome, the form of the President was conveyed from the theater to the residence of Mr. Peterson, on the opposite side of Tenth street. Here upon a bed, in a little hastily prepared chamber, it was laid and attended by Surgeon-General Barnes and other physicians, speedily summoned.

In the meanwhile the news spread through the capital, as if borne on tongues of flame. Senator Sumner, hearing at his residence, of the affair took a carriage and drove at a gallop to the White House, when he heard where it had taken place, to find Robert Lincoln and other members of the household still unaware of it. Both drove to Ford's Theater, and were soon at the President's bedside. Secretary Stanton and the other members of the cabinet were at hand almost as soon. A vast crowd, surging up Pennsylvania avenue toward Willard's Hotel, cried, "The President is shot!" "President Lincoln is murdered." Another crowd sweeping down the avenue met the first with the tidings, "Secretary Seward has been assassinated in bed." Instantly a wild apprehension of an organized conspiracy and of other murders took possession of the people. The shout "to arms!" was mingled with the expressions of sorrow and rage that everywhere filled the air. "Where is General Grant?" or "where is Secretary Stanton!" "Where are the rest of the cabinet?" broke from thousands of lips. A conflagration of fire is not half so terrible as was the conflagration of passion that rolled through the streets and houses of Washington on that awful night.

The attempt on the life of Secretary Seward was perhaps as daring, if not so dramatic, as the assassination of the President. At 9:20 o'clock a man, tall, athletic, and dressed in light coloured clothes, alighted from a horse in front of Mr. Seward's residence in Madison place, where the secretary was lying, very feeble from his recent injuries. The house, a solid three-story brick building, was formerly the old Washington Club-house. Leaving his horse standing, the stranger rang at the door, and informed the servant who admitted him that he desired to see Mr. Seward. The servant responded that Mr. Seward was very ill, and that no visitors were admitted. "But I am a messenger from Dr. Verdi, Mr. Seward's physician; I have a prescription which I must deliver to him myself." The servant still demurring, the stranger, without further parley, pushed him aside and ascended the stairs. Moving to the right, he proceeded towards Mr. Seward's room, and was about to enter it, when Mr. Frederick Seward appeared from an opposite doorway and demanded his business. He responded in the same manner as to the servant below, but being met with a refusal, suddenly closed the controversy by striking Mr. Seward a severe and perhaps mortal blow across the forehead with the butt of a pistol. As the first victim fell, Major Seward, another and younger son of the secretary, emerged from his father's room. Without a word the man drew a knife and struck the major several blows with it, rushing into the chamber as he did so; then, after dealing the nurse a horrible wound across the bowels, he sprang to the bed upon which the secretary lay, stabbing him once in the face and neck. Mr. Seward arose convulsively and fell from the bed to the floor. Turning and brandishing his knife anew, the assassin fled from the room, cleared the prostrate form of Frederick Seward in the hall, descended the stairs in three leaps, and was out of the door and upon his horse in an instant. It is stated by a person who saw him mount that, although he leaped upon his horse with most unseemly haste, he trotted away around the corner of the block with circumspect deliberation.

Around both the house on Tenth street and the residence of Secretary Seward, as the fact of both tragedies became generally known, crowds soon gathered so vast and tumultuous that military guards scarcely sufficed to keep them from the doors.

The room to which the President had been conveyed is on the first floor, at the end of the hall. It is only fifteen feet square, with a Brussels carpet, papered with brown, and hung with a lithograph of Rosa Bonheur's "Horse

Fair," and engraved copy of Herring's "Village Blacksmith," and two smaller ones of "The Stable" and "The Barn Yard," from the same artist. A table and bureau, spread with crotchet work, eight chairs and the bed, were all the furniture. Upon this bed, a low walnut four-poster, lay the dying President; the blood oozing from the frightful wound in his head and staining the pillow. All that the medical skill of half a dozen accomplished surgeons could do had been done to prolong a life evidently ebbing from a mortal hurt.

Secretary Stanton, just arrived from the bedside of Mr. Seward, asked Surgeon-General Barnes what was Mr. Lincoln's condition. "I fear, Mr. Stanton, that there is no hope." "Oh, no, general; no, no," and the man, of all others, apparently strange to tears, sank down beside the bed, the hot, bitter evidences of an awful sorrow trickling through his fingers to the floor. Senator Sumner sat on the opposite side of the bed, holding one of the President's hands in his own, and sobbing with kindred grief. Secretary Welles stood at the foot of the bed, his face hidden, his frame shaken with emotion. General Halleck, Attorney-General Speed, Postmaster General Dennison, M.B. Field, Assistant Secretary of the Treasury, Judge Otto, General Meigs, and others, visited the chamber at times, and then retired. Mrs. Lincoln—but there is no need to speak of her. Mrs. Senator Dixon soon arrived, and remained with her through the night. All through the night, while the horror-stricken crowds outside wept and gathered along the streets, while the military and police were patrolling and weaving a cordon around the city; while men were arming and asking each other, "What victim next?" while the telegraph was sending the news from city to city over the continent, and while the two assassins were speeding unharmed upon fleet horses far away—his chosen friends watched about the death-bed of the highest of the nation. Occasionally Dr. Gurley, pastor of the church where Mr. Lincoln habitually attended, knelt down in prayer. Occasionally Mrs. Lincoln and her sons, entered, to find no hope and to go back to ceaseless weeping. Members of the cabinet, senators, representatives, generals, and others, took turns at the bedside. Chief-Justice Chase remained until a late hour, and returned in the morning. Secretary McCulloch remained a constant watcher until 5 a.m. Not a gleam of consciousness shone across the visage of the President up to his death—a quiet, peaceful death at last—which came at twenty-two minutes past seven a.m. Around the bedside at this time were Secretaries Stanton, Welles, Usher, Attorney-General Speed, Postmaster-General Dennison, M.B. Field, Assistant Secretary of the Treasury, Judge Otto, Assistant Secretary of the Interior, General Halleck, General Meigs, Senator Sumner, F.R. Andrews, of New-York, General Todd, of Dacotah, John Hay, private secretary, Governor Oglesby, of Illinois, General Farnsworth, Mrs. and Miss Kenny,

Miss Harris, Captain Robert Lincoln, son of the President and Drs. E.W. Abbott, R.K. Stone, C.D. Gatch, Neal Hall and Leiberman. Rev. Dr. Gurley, after the event, knelt with all around in prayer, and then, entering the adjoining room where were gathered Mrs. Lincoln, Captain Robert Lincoln, Mr. John Hay, and others, prayed again. Soon after 9 o'clock the remains were placed in a temporary coffin and conveyed to the White House under a small escort.

In Secretary Seward's chamber, a similar although not so solemn a scene prevailed; between that chamber and the one occupied by President Lincoln, visitors alternated to and fro through the night. It had been early ascertained that the wounds of the secretary were not likely to prove mortal. A wire instrument, to relieve the pain which he suffered from previous injuries, prevented the knife of the assassin from striking too deep. Mr. Frederick Seward's injuries were more serious. His forehead was broken in by the blow from the pistol, and up to this hour he has remained perfectly unconscious. The operation of trepanning the skull has been performed, but little hope is had of his recovery. Major Seward will get well. Mr. Hansell's condition is somewhat doubtful.

Secretary Seward, who cannot speak, was not informed of the assassination of the President, and the injury of his son, until yesterday. He had been worrying as to why Mr. Lincoln did not visit him. "Why doesn't the President come to see me?" he asked with his pencil. "Where is Frederick—what is the matter with him?" Perceiving the nervous excitement which these doubts occasioned, a consultation was had, at which it was finally determined that it would be best to let the secretary know the worst. Secretary Stanton was chosen to tell him. Sitting down beside Mr. Seward's bed, yesterday afternoon, he therefore related to him a full account of the whole affair. Mr. Seward was so surprised and shocked that he raised one hand involuntarily, and groaned. Such is the condition of affairs at this stage of the terror. The pursuit of the assassins has commenced; the town is full of wild and baseless rumors; much that is said is stirring, little is reliable. I tell it to you as I get it, but fancy is more prolific than truth: be patient!

[The facts above had been collected by Mr. Jerome B. Stillson, before my arrival in Washington: the arrangement of them is my own.]

LETTER III.
THE MURDERER.

Washington, April 27th

Justice is satisfied, though blinder vengeance may not be. While the illustrious murdered is on the way to the shrine, the stark corpse of his murderer lies in the shambles. The one died quietly, like his life; the other died fighting, like his crime. And now that over all of them the darkness and the dew have descended, the populace, which may not be all satisfied, may perhaps be calmed. No triumphal mourning can add to the President's glory; no further execration can disturb the assassin's slumbers. They have gone for what they were into history, into tradition, into the hereafter both of men and spirits; and what they were may be in part concluded. Mr. Lincoln's career passes, in extent, gravity, and eventful association, the province of newspaper biography; but Booth is the hero of a single deed, and the delineation of him may begin and be exhausted in a single article. I have been at pains, since the day of the President's obsequies, to collect all valid information on the subject of his assassin, in anticipation of the latter's capture and death. Now that these have been consummated, I shall print this biography.

The elder Booth in every land was a sojourner, as all his fathers were. Of Hebrew descent, and by a line of actors, he united in himself that strong Jewish physiognomy which, in its nobler phases, makes all that is dark and beautiful, and the combined vagrancy of all men of genius and all men of the stage. Fitful, powerful, passionate, his life was a succession of vices and triumphs. He mastered the intricate characters of dramatic literature by intuition, rather than by study, and produced them with a vigor and vividness which almost passed the depicting of real life. The stage on which he raved and fought became as historic as the actual decks of battle ships, and his small and brawny figure comes down to us in those paroxysms of delirious art, like that of *Harold*, or *Richard*, or *Prince Rupert*. He drank to excess, was profligate but not generous, required but not reliable, and licentious to the bounds of cruelty. He threw off the wife of his bosom to fly from England with a flower-girl, and, settling in Baltimore, dwelt with his younger companion, and brought up many children, while his first-possessed went down to a drunken and broken-hearted death. He himself, wandering westward, died on the way, errant and feverish, even in the closing moments. His widow, too conscious of her predecessor's wrong, and often taunted with them, lived apart, frugal and discreet, and brought her six children up to honorable maturity. These were Junius Brutus, Edwin Forrest (though he drops the Forrest for professional considerations), John Wilkes, Joseph, and the girls. All of the boys are known to more or less of fame; none of them in his art has reached the renown of the father; but one has sent his name as far as that of the great playwright to whom they were pupils; wherever Shakespeare is quoted, John Wilkes Booth will be named, and infamously, like that Hubert in "King John," who would have murdered the gentle Prince Arthur.

It may not be a digression here to ask what has become of the children of the weird genius I have sketched above. Mrs. Booth, against whom calumny has had no word to say, now resides with her daughters in Nineteenth street, New-York. John S. Clarke dwells in princely style in Philadelphia, with the daughter whom he married; he is the business partner of Edwin Booth, and they are likely to become as powerful managers as they have been successful "stars." Edwin Booth, who is said to have the most perfect physical head in America, and whom the ladies call the beau ideal of the melancholy Dane, dwells also on Nineteenth street. He has acquired a fortune, and is, without doubt, a frankly loyal gentleman. He could not well be otherwise from his membership in the Century Club where literature and loyalty, are never dissolved. Correct and pleasing without being powerful or brilliant, he has led a plain and appreciated career, and latterly, to his honor, has been awakening among dramatic authors some emulation by offering handsome compensations for original plays. Junius Brutus Booth, the oldest of them all, most resembles in feature his wild and wayward father; he is not as good an actor as was Wilkes, and kept in the West, that border civilization of the drama; he now lies, on a serious charge of complicity, in Capitol Hill jail. Joseph Booth tried the state as an utility actor and promptly failed. The best part he ever had to play was *Orson* in the "Iron Chest," and his discomfiture was signal; then he studied medicine but grew discouraged, and is now in California in an office of some sort. A son of Booth by his first wife became a first-class lawyer in Boston. He never recognized the rest of the family. Wilkes Booth, the third son, was shot dead on Wednesday for attempting to escape from the consequences of murder. Such are the people to whom one of the greatest actors of our time gave his name and lineaments. But I have anticipated the story:

Although her family was large, it was not so hard sailing with Mrs. Rosalie Booth as may be inferred. Her husband's gains had been variably great, and they owned a farm of some value near Baltimore. The boys had plain but not sufficient schooling, though by the time John Wilkes grew up Edwin and Junius were making some little money and helping the family. So Wilkes was sent to a better school than they, where he made some eventful acquaintances. One of these won his admiration as much in the playground as in subsequent life upon the field of battle; this was Fitzhugh Lee, son of the great rebel chieftain. I have not heard that Lee ever had any friendship for young Wilkes, but his port and name were enough to excite a less ardent imagination—the son of a soldier already great, and a descendant of Washington. Wilkes Booth has often spoken of the memory of the young man, envied his success, and, perhaps, boasted of more intimacy than he ever had. The exemplars of young Wilkes, it was soon seen, were anything but literary. He hated school and pent-up life, and loved the open air. He used to stroll off to fish, though that sort of amusement was too sedentary for his nature, but went on fowling jaunts with enthusiasm. In these latter he manifested that fine nerve, and certain eye, which was the talk of all his associates; but his greatest love was the stable. He learned to ride with his first pair of boots, and hung around the grooms to beg permission to take the nags to water. He grew in later life to be both an indurated and a graceful horseman. Toward his mother and sisters he was affectionate without being obedient. Of all the sons, Wilkes was the most headstrong in-doors, and the most contented away from home. He had a fitful gentleness which won him forgiveness, and of one of his sisters he was particularly fond, but none had influence over him. He was seldom contentious, but obstinately bent, and what he willed, he did in silence, seeming to discard sympathy or confidence. As a boy he was never bright, except in a boy's sense; that is, he could run and leap well, fight when challenged, and generally fell in with the sentiment of the crowd. He therefore made many companions, and his early days all passed between Baltimore city and the adjacent farm.

I have heard it said as the only evidence of Booth's ferocity in those early times that he was always shooting cats, and killed off almost the entire breed in his neighborhood. But on more than one occasion he ran away from both school and home, and once made the trip of the Chesapeake to the oyster fisheries without advising anybody of his family.

While yet very young, Wilkes Booth became an habitue at the theater. His traditions and tastes were all in that direction. His blood was of the stage, like that of the Keans, the Kembles, and the Wallacks. He would not commence at the bottom of the ladder and climb from round to round, nor take part in more than a few Thespian efforts. One night, however, a young actor, who was to have a benefit and wished to fill the house, resolved for the better purpose to give Wilkes a chance. He announced that a son of the great Booth of tradition, would enact the part of *Richmond*, and the announcement was enough. Before a crowded place, Booth played so badly that he was hissed. Still holding to his gossamer hopes and high conceit, Wilkes induced John S. Clarke, who was then addressing his sister, to obtain him a position in the company of the Arch Street Theater at Philadelphia.

For eight dollars a week, Wilkes Booth, at the age of twenty-two, contracted with William Wheatley to play in any piece or part for which he might be cast, and to appear every day at rehearsal. He had to play the *Courier* in Sheridan Knowles's "Wife" on his first night, with five or ten little speeches to make; but such was his nervousness that he blundered continually, and quite balked the piece. Soon afterward he undertook the part of one of the Venetian comrades in Hugo's "Lucretia Borgia," and was to have said in his turn—"Madame, I am Petruchio Pandolfo;" instead of which he exclaimed: "Madame, I am Pondolfio Pet—, Pedolfio Pat—, Pantuchio Ped—; damn it? what am I?"

The audience roared, and Booth, though full of chagrin, was compelled to laugh with them.

The very next night he was to play *Dawson*, an important part in Moore's tragedy of "The Gamester." He had bought a new dress to wear on this night, and made abundant preparation to do himself honor. He therefore invited a lady whom he knew to visit the theater, and witness his triumph. But at the instant of his appearance on the stage, the audience, remembering the Petruchio Pandolfo of the previous night, burst into laughter, hisses, and mock applause, so that he was struck dumb, and stood rigid, with nothing whatever to say. Mr. John Dolman, to whose *Stukely* he played, was compelled, therefore, to strike *Dawson* entirely out of the piece.

These occurrences nettled Booth who, protested that he studied faithfully but that his want of confidence ruined him. Mr. Fredericks the stage manager made constant complaints of Booth, who by the way, did not play under his full name, but as Mr. J. Wilkes—and he bore the general reputation of having no promise, and being a careless fellow. He associated freely with such of the subordinate actors as he liked; but being, through Clarke, then a rising favourite, of better connections, might, had he chosen, advanced himself socially, if not artistically. Clarke was to have a benefit one evening, and to enact, among other things, a mock *Richard III.*, to which he allowed Wilkes Booth to play a real *Richmond*. On this occasion for the first time, Booth showed some energy, and obtained some applause. But, in general, he was stumbling and worthless. I myself remember, on three consecutive nights, hearing him trip up and receive suppressed hisses. He lacked enterprise; other young actors, instead of waiting to be given better parts, committed them to memory, in the hope that their real interpreter might not come to hand. Among these I recall John McCullough, who afterwards became quite a celebrated actor. He was getting, if I correctly remember, only six dollars a week, while Booth obtained eight. Yet Wilkes Booth seemed too slow or indifferent to get on the weather side of such chances. He still held the part of third walking gentleman, and the third is always the first to be walked off in case of strait, as was Wilkes Booth. He did not survive forty weeks engagement, nor make above three hundred dollars in all that time. The Kellers arrived; they cut down the company, and they dispensed with Wilkes

Booth. He is remembered in Philadelphia by his failure as in the world by his crime.

About this time a manager named Kunkle gave Booth a salary of twenty dollars a week to go to the Richmond Theater. There he played a higher order of parts, and played them better, winning applauses from the easy provincial cities, and taking, as everywhere the ladies by storm. I have never wondered why many actors were strongly predisposed toward the South. There, their social status is nine times as big as with us. The hospitable, lounging, buzzing character of the southerner is entirely consonant with the cosmopolitanism of the stage, and that easy "hang-up-your-hat-ativeness," which is the rule and the demand in Thespianship. We place actors outside of society, and execrate them because they are there. The South took them into affable fellowship, and was not ruined by it, but beloved by the fraternity. Booth played two seasons in Richmond, and left in some esteem.

When the John Brown raid occurred, Booth left the Richmond Theater for the scene of strike in a picked company with which he had affiliated for some time. From his connection with the militia on this occasion he was wont to trace his fealty to Virginia. He was a non-commissioned officer, and remained at Charleston till after the execution, visiting the old pike man in jail, and his company was selected to form guard around the scaffold when John Brown went, white-haired, to his account. There may be in this a consolation for the canonizers of the first arm-bearer between the sections, that one whose unit swelled the host to crush out that brave old life, took from the scene inspiration enough to slay a merciful President in his unsuspecting leisure. Booth never referred to John Brown's death in bravado; possibly at that gallows began some such terrible purpose as he afterward consummated.

It was close upon the beginning of the war when Booth resolved to transform himself from a stock actor to a "star." As many will read this who do not understand such distinctions, let me preface it by explaining that a "star" is an actor who belongs to no one theater, but travels from each to all, playing a few weeks at a time, and sustained in his chief character by the regular or stock actors. A stock actor is a good actor, and a poor fool. A star is an advertisement in tights, who grows rich and corrupts the public taste. Booth was a star, and being so, had an agent. The agent is a trumpeter who goes on before, writing the impartial notices which you see in the editorial columns of country papers and counting noses at the theater doors. Booth's agent was one Matthew Canning, an exploded Philadelphia lawyer, who took to managing by passing the bar, and J. Wilkes no longer, but our country's rising tragedian. J. Wilkes Booth opened in Montgomery, Alabama, in his father's consecrated part of *Richard III*. It was very different work between receiving eight dollars a week and getting half the gross proceeds of every performance. Booth kept northward when his engagement was done, playing in many cities such parts as *Romeo*, the *Corsican Brothers*, and *Raphael* in the *"Marble Heart;"* in all of these he gained applause, and his journey eastward, ending in eastern cities like Providence, Portland, and Boston was a long success, in part deserved. In Boston he received especial commendation for his enactment of *Richard*.

I have looked over this play, his best and favorite one, to see how closely the career of the crookback he so often delineated resembled his own. How like that fearful night of Richard on Bosworth field must have been Booth's sleep in the barn at Port Royal, tortured by ghosts of victims all repeating.

"When I was mortal my anointed body
By thee was punched full of deadly holes:
Think on the Tower and me! Despair and die!"

Or this, from some of Booth's female victims:

"Let me sit heavy on thy soul to-morrow!
I that was washed to death with fulsome wine;
Poor Clarence, by thy guile betrayed to death:
To-morrow in the battle think on me; despair and die!"

These terrible conjurations must have recalled how aptly the scene so often rehearsed by Booth, sword in hand, where, leaping from his bed, he cried in horror:

"Give me another horse! bind up my wounds!
Have mercy, Jesu! Soft! I did but dream.
Oh! coward conscience how thou dost afflict me!
The lights burn blue. It is now dead midnight!
Cold, flareful drops stand on my trembling flesh.
What do I fear? Myself? there is none else by:
Is there a murderer here? No!—Yes!—I am!
Then fly,—what from myself?

* * * * * * *

My conscience hath a thousand several tongues,
And every tongue brings in a several tale,
And every tale condemns me for a villain!
Perjury, perjury in the highest degree:
Murder, stern murder in the direst degree:
All several sins, all used in each degree,
Throng to the bar, crying all, *Guilty! Guilty!*"

By these starring engagements, Booth made incredible sums. His cashbook, for one single season, showed earnings deposited in banks of twenty two odd thousand dollars. In New York he did not get a hearing, except at a benefit or two: where he played parts not of his selection. In Philadelphia his earlier failure predisposed the people to discard him, and they did. But he had made enough, and resolved to invest his winnings, The oil fever had just begun; he hired an agent, sent him to the western districts and gave him discretionary power; his investments all turned out profitable.

Booth died, as far as understood without debts. The day before the murder he paid an old friend a hundred dollars which he had borrowed two days previously. He banked at Jay Cook's in Washington, generally; but turned most of his funds into stock and other matters. He gave eighty dollars eight month's ago for a part investing with others in a piece of western oil land. The certificate for this land he gave to his sister. Just before he died his agent informed him that the share was worth fifteen thousand dollars. Booth kept his accounts latterly with great regularity, and was lavish as ever, but took note of all expenditures, however irregular. He was one of those men whom the possession of money seems to have energized; his life, so purposeless long before, grew by good fortune to a strict computation, and of what use was the gaining of wealth, to throw one's life so soon away, and leap from competence to hunted infamy.

The beauty of this man and his easy confidentiality, not familiar, but marked by a mild even dignity, made many women impassioned of him. He was licentious as men, and particularly as actors go, but not a seducer, so as far as I can learn. I have traced one case in Philadelphia where a young girl who had seen him on the stage became enamored of him.

She sent him bouquets, notes, photographs and all the accessories of an intrigue. Booth, to whom such things were common, yielded to the girl's importunities at last and gave her an interview. He was surprised to find that so bold a correspondent was so young, so fresh, and so beautiful. He told therefore, in pity, the consequences of pursuing him; that he entertained no affection for her, though a sufficient desire, and that he was a man of the world to whom all women grew fulsome in their turn.

"Go home," he said, "and beware of actors. They are to be seen, not to be known."

The girl, yet more infatuated, persisted. Booth, who had no real virtue except by scintillations, became what he had promised, and one more soul went to the isles of Cyprus.

In Montgomery, if I do not mistake, Booth met the woman from whom he received a stab which he carried all the rest of his life. She was an actress, and he visited her. They assumed a relation creditable only in La Boheme, and were as tender as love without esteem can ever be. But, after a time, Booth wearied of her and offered to say "good bye." She refused—he treated her coldly; she pleaded—he passed her by.

Then, with a jealous woman's frenzy, she drew a knife upon him and stabbed him in the neck, with the intent to kill him. Being muscular, he quickly disarmed her, though he afterward suffered from the wound poignantly.

Does it not bring a blush to our faces that a good, great man, like he who has died—our President—should have met his fate from one so inured to a life of ribaldry? Yet, only such an one could have been found to murder Abraham Lincoln.

The women persecuted Booth more than he followed them. He was waylaid by married women in every provincial town or city where he played. His face was so youthful, yet so manly, and his movements so graceful and excellent, that other than the coarse and errant placed themselves in his way. After his celebrated Boston engagement, women of all ages and degrees pressed in crowds before the Tremont House to see him depart. Their motives were various, but whether curiosity or worse, exhibited plainly the deep influence which Booth had upon the sex. He could be anywhere easy and gentlemanly, and it is a matter of wonder that with the entry which he had to many well-stocked homes, he did not make hospitality mourn and friendship find in his visit shame and ruin. I have not space to go into the millionth catalogue of Booth's intrigues, even if this journal permitted further elucidation of so banned a subject. Most of his adherents of this class were, like Heine's Polish virgins, and he was very popular with those dramatic ladies—few, I hope and know, in their profession—to whom divorce courts are superfluous. His last permanent acquaintance was one Ella Turner, of Richmond, who loved him with all the impetuosity of that love which does not think, and strove to die at the tidings of his crime and flight. Happy that even such a woman did not die associated with John Wilkes Booth. Such devotion to any other murderer would have earned some poet's tear. But the daisies will not grow a whole rod from his grave.

Of what avail, may we ask, on the impossible supposition that Booth's crime could have been considered heroic, was it that such a record should have dared to die for fame? Victory would have been ashamed of its champion, as England of Nelson, and France of Mirabeau.

I may add to this record that he had not been in Philadelphia a year, on first setting out in life, before getting into a transaction of the kind specified. For an affair at his boarding-house he was compelled to pay a considerable sum of money, and it happily occurred just as he was to quit the city. He had many quarrels and narrow escapes through his license, a husband in Syracuse, N. Y., once followed him all the way to Cleveland to avenge a domestic insult.

Booth's paper "To Whom I May Concern" was not his only attempt at influential composition. He sometimes persuaded himself that he had literary ability; but his orthography and pronunciation were worse than his syntax. The paper deposited with J. S. Clarke was useful as showing his power to entertain a deliberate purpose. It has one or two smart passages in it—as this:

"Our once bright red stripes look like bloody gashes on the face of heaven."

In the passages following there is common sense and lunacy:

"I know how foolish I shall be deemed for undertaking such a step as this, where, on the one side, I have many friends and everything to make me happy, where my profession alone has gained me an income of more than twenty thousand dollars a year, and where my great personal ambition in my profession has such a great field for labor. On the other hand, the South have never bestowed upon me one kind word; a place now where I have no friends, except beneath the sod; a place where I must either become a private soldier or a beggar. To give up all of the former for the latter, besides my mother and sisters, whom I love so dearly (although they so widely differ with me in opinion) seems insane; but God is my judge."

Now, read the beginning of the manifesto, and see how prophetic were his words of his coming infamy. If he expected so much for capturing the President merely, what of our execration at slaying him?

"Right or wrong, God judge me, not man. For be my motive good or bad, of one thing I am sure, the lasting condemnation of the North.

"I love peace more than life. Have loved the Union beyond expression. For four years have I waited, hoped and prayed for the dark clouds to break, and for a restoration of our former sunshine. To wait longer would be a crime. All hope for peace is dead. My prayers have proved as idle as my hopes. God's will be done. I go to see and share the bitter end."

To wait longer would be a crime. Oh! what was the crime not to wait! Had he only shared the bitter end, then, in the common trench, his memory might have been hidden. The end had come when he appeared to make of benignant victory a quenchless revenge. One more selection from his apostrophe will do. It suggests the manner of his death:

"They say that the South has found that 'last ditch' which the North have so long derided. Should I reach her in safety, and find it true, I will proudly beg permission to triumph or die in that same 'ditch' by her side." The swamp near which he died may be called, without unseemly pun—a truth, not a *bon mot*—the last ditch of the rebellion.

None of the printed pictures that I have seen do justice to Booth. Some of the *cartes de visite* get him very nearly. He had one of the finest vital heads I have ever seen. In fact, he was one of the best exponents of vital beauty I have ever met. By this I refer to physical beauty in the Medician sense—health, shapeliness, power in beautiful poise, and seemingly more powerful in repose than in energy. His hands and feet were sizable, not small, and his legs were stout and muscular, but inclined to bow like his father's. From the waist up he was a perfect man; his chest being full and broad, his shoulders gently sloping, and his arms as white as alabaster, but hard as marble. Over these, upon a neck which was its proper column, rose the cornice of a fine Doric face, spare at the jaws and not anywhere over-ripe, but seamed with a nose of Roman model, the only relic of his half-Jewish parentage, which gave decision to the thoughtfully stern sweep of two direct, dark eyes, meaning to woman snare, and to man a search warrant, while the lofty square forehead and square brows were crowned with a weight of curling jetty hair, like a rich Corinthian capital. His profile was eagleish, and afar his countenance was haughty. He seemed throat full of introspections, ambitious self-examinings, eye-strides into the future, as if it withheld him something to which he had a right. I have since wondered whether this moody demeanor did not come of a guilty spirit, but all the Booths look so.

Wilkes spoke to me in Washington for the first time three weeks before the murder. His address was winning as a girl's, rising in effect not from what he said, but from how he said it. It was magnetic, and I can describe it therefore by its effects alone. I seemed, when he had spoken, to lean toward the man. His attitude spoke to me; with as easy familiarity as I ever observed he drew near and conversed. The talk was on so trite things that it did not lie a second in the head, but when I left him it was with the feeling that a most agreeable fellow had passed by.

The next time the name of Wilkes Booth recurred to me was like the pistol shot he had fired. The right hand I had shaken murdered the father of the country.

Booth was not graceful with his feet, although his ordinary walk was pleasant enough. But his arms were put to artistic uses; not the baser ones like boxing, but all sorts of fencing, manual practice, and the handling of weapons.

In his dress, he was neat without being particular. Almost any clothes could fit him; but he had nothing of the exquisite about him; his neckties and all such matters were good without being gaudy. Nature had done much for him. In this beautiful palace an outlaw had builded his fire, and slept, and plotted, and dreamed.

I have heard it said that Booth frequently cut his adversaries upon the stage in sheer wantonness or bloodthirstiness. This is a mistake, and is attributable to his father, the elder Booth, who had the madness of confounding himself with the character. Wilkes was too good a fencer to make ugly gashes; his pride was his skill, not his awkwardness. Once he was playing with John McCullough in the last act of "Richard." They were fighting desperately. Suddenly the cross-piece on the hilt of McCullough's sword flew off and cut the owner deeply in the forehead. Blood ran down McCullough's face, though they continued to struggle, and while, ostensibly, Booth was imitating a demon, he said in a half whisper:

"Good God, John, did I hurt you?"

And when they went off the stage, Booth was white with fear that he had gashed his friend.

As an actor, Booth was too energetic to be correct; his conception of Richard was vivid and original, one of the best that we have had, and he came nearer his father's rendering of the last act than any body we have had. His combat scene was terrific. The statement that his voice had failed had no valid foundation; it was as good when he challenged the cavalry-men to combat as in the best of his Thespian successes. In all acting that required delicate characterization, refined conception or carefulness, Booth was at sea.

But in strong physical parts, requiring fair reading and an abundance of spring and tension, he was much finer than hearsay would have us believe.

His Romeo was described a short time ago by the Washington Intelligencer as the most satisfactory of all renderings of that fine character. He played the Corsican Brothers three weeks on a run in Boston. He played Pescara at Ford's Theater—his last mock part in this world—on to-morrow (Saturday) night, six weeks ago.

He was fond of learning and reciting fugitive poems. His favorite piece was "The Beautiful Snow," comparing it to a lost purity. He has been known by gentlemen in this city to recite this poem with fine effect, and cry all the while. This was on the principle of "guilty people sitting at a play." His pocket-book was generally full of little selections picked up at random, and he had considerable delicacy of appreciation.

On the morning of the murder, Booth breakfasted with Miss Carrie Bean, the daughter of a merchant, and a very respectable young lady, at the National Hall. He arose from the table at, say eleven o'clock. During the breakfast, those who watched him say that he was lively, piquant and self-possessed as ever in his life.

That night the horrible crime thrilled the land. A period of crippled flight succeeded. Living in swamps, upon trembling hospitality, upon hopes which sank as he leaned upon them. Booth passed the nights in perilous route or broken sleep, and in the end went down like a bravo, but in the eyes of all who read his history, commanding no respect for his valor, charity for his motive, or sympathy for his sin.

The closing scenes of these terrible days are reserved for a second paper. Much matter that should have gone into this is retained for the present.

LETTER IV.
THE ASSASSIN'S DEATH.

Washington, April 28—8 p.m.

A hard and grizzly face overlooks me as I write. Its inconsiderable forehead is crowned with turning sandy hair, and the deep concave of its long insatiate jaws is almost hidden by a dense red beard, which can not still abate the terrible decision of the large mouth, so well sustained by searching eyes of spotted gray, which roll and rivet one. This is the face of Lafayette Baker colonel and chief of the secret service. He has played the most perilous parts of the war, and is the capturer of the late President's murderer. The story that I am to tell you, as he and his trusty dependents told it to me, will be aptly commenced here, where the net was woven which took the dying life of Wilkes Booth.

When the murder occurred, Colonel Baker was absent from Washington. He returned on the third morning, and was at once besought by Secretary Stanton to join the hue and cry against the escaped Booth. The sagacious detective found that nearly ten thousand cavalry, and one-fourth as many policemen, had been meantime scouring, without plan or compass, the whole territory of Southern Maryland. They were treading on each other's heels, and mixing up the thing so confoundedly, that the best place for the culprits to have gone would have been in the very midst of their pursuers. Baker at once possessed himself of the little the War Department had learned, and started immediately to take the usual detective measures, till then neglected, of offering a reward and getting out photographs of the suspected ones. He then dispatched a few chosen detectives to certain vital points, and awaited results.

The first of these was the capture of Atzeroth. Others, like the taking of Dr. Mudd, simultaneously occurred. But the district supected being remote from the railway routes, and broken by no telegraph station, the colonel, to place himself nearer the theater of events, ordered an operator, with the necessary instrument, to tap the wire running to Point Lookout, near Chappells Point, and send him prompt messages.

The same steamer which took down the operator and two detectives brought back one of the same detectives and a negro. This negro, taken to Colonel Baker's office, stated so positively that he had seen Booth and another man cross the Potomac in a fishing boat, while he was looking down upon them from a bank, that the colonel was at first skeptical; but when examined the negro answered so readily and intelligently, recognizing the men from the photographs, that Baker knew at last that he had the true scent.

Straightway he sent to General Hancock for twenty-five men, and while the order was going, drew down his coast survey-maps. With that quick detective intuition amounting almost to inspiration, he cast upon the probable route and destination of the refugees, as well as the point where he would soonest strike them. Booth, he knew, would not keep along the coast, with frequent deep rivers to cross, nor, indeed, in any direction east of Richmond, where he was liable at any time to cross our lines of occupation; nor, being lame, could he ride on horseback, so as to place himself very far westward of his point of debarkation in Virginia. But he would travel in a direct course from Bluff point, where he crossed to Eastern Tennessee, and this would take him through Port Royal on the Rappahannock river, in time to be intercepted there by the outgoing cavalrymen.

When, therefore, twenty-five men, under one Lieutenant Dougherty, arrived at his office door, Baker placed the whole under control of his former lieutenant-colonel, E. J. Conger, and of his cousin, Lieutenant L. B. Baker—the first of Ohio, the last of New York—and bade them go with all dispatch to Belle Plain on the Lower Potomac, there to disembark, and scour the country faithfully around Port Royal, but not to return unless they captured their men.

Conger is a short, decided, indomitable, courageous fellow, provincial in his manners, but fully understanding his business, and collected as a housewife on Sunday.

Young Baker is large and fine-looking—a soldier, but no policeman—and he deferred to Conger, very properly, during most of the events succeeding.

Quitting Washington at 2 o'clock p.m. on Monday, the detectives and cavalrymen disembarked at Belle Plain, on the border of Stafford county, at 10 o'clock, in the darkness. Belle Plain is simply the nearest landing to Fredericksburg, seventy miles from Washington city, and located upon Potomac creek. It is a wharf and warehouse merely, and here the steamer John S. Ide stopped and made fast, while the party galloped off in the darkness. Conger and Baker kept ahead, riding up to farm-houses and questioning the inmates, pretending to be in search of the Maryland gentlemen belonging to the party. But nobody had seen the parties described, and, after a futile ride on the Fredericksburg road, they turned shortly to the east, and kept up their baffled inquiries all the way to Port Conway, on the Rappahannock.

On Tuesday morning they presented themselves at the Port Royal ferry, and inquired of the ferry-man, while he was taking them over in squads of seven at a time, if he had seen any two such men. Continuing their inquiries at Port Royal, they found one Rollins a fisherman, who referred them to a negro named Lucas, as having driven two men a short distance toward Bowling Green in a wagon. It was found that these men answered to the description, Booth having a crutch as previously ascertained.

The day before Booth and Harold had applied at Port Conway for the general ferry-boat, but the ferryman was then fishing and would not desist for the inconsiderable fare of only two persons, but to their supposed good fortune a lot of confederate cavalrymen just then came along, who threatened the ferryman with a shot in the head if he did not instantly bring across his craft and transport the entire party. These cavalrymen were of Moseby's disbanded command, returning from Fairfax Court House to their homes in Caroline county. Their captain was on his way to visit a sweetheart at Bowling Green, and he had so far taken Booth under his patronage, that when the latter was haggling with Lucas for a team, he offered both Booth and Harold the use of his horse, to ride and walk alternately.

In this way Lucas was providentially done out of the job, and Booth rode off toward Bowling Green behind the confederate captain on one and the same horse.

So much learned, the detectives, with Rollins for a guide, dashed off in the bright daylight of Tuesday, moving southwestward through the level plains of Caroline, seldom stopping to ask questions, save at a certain halfway house, where a woman told them that the cavalry party of yesterday had returned minus one man. As this was far from circumstantial, the party rode along in the twilight, and reached Bowling Green at eleven o'clock in the night.

This is the court-house town of Caroline county—a small and scattered place, having within it an ancient tavern, no longer used for other than lodging purposes; but here they hauled from his bed the captain aforesaid, and bade him dress himself. As soon as he comprehended the matter he became pallid and eagerly narrated all the facts in his possession. Booth, to his knowledge, was then lying at the house of one Garrett, which they had passed, and Harold had departed the existing day with the intention of rejoining him.

Taking this captain along for a guide, the worn out horsemen retraced, though some of the men were so haggard and wasted with travel that they had to be kicked into intelligence before they could climb to their saddles. The objects of the chase thus at hand, the detectives, full of sanguine purpose, hurried the cortege so well along that by 2 o'clock early morning, all halted at Garrett's gate. In the pale moonlight three hundred yards from the main road, to the left, a plain old farmhouse looked grayly through its environing locusts. It was worn and whitewashed, and two-storied, and its half-human windows glowered down upon the silent cavalrymen like watching owls which stood as sentries over some horrible secret asleep within. The front of this house looked up the road toward the Rappahannock, but did not face it, and on that side a long Virginia porch protruded, where, in the summer, among the honeysuckles, the humming bird flew like a visible odor. Nearest the main road, against the pallid gable, a single-storied kitchen stood, and there were three other doors, one opening upon the porch, one in the kitchen gable, and one in the rear of the farmhouse.

Dimly seen behind, an old barn, high and weather-beaten, faced the roadside gate, for the house itself lay to the left of its own lane; and nestling beneath the barn, a few long corn-cribs lay with a cattle shed at hand. There was not a swell of the landscape anywhere in sight. A plain dead level contained all the tenements and structures. A worm fence stretched along the road broken by two battered gate posts, and between the road and the house, the lane was crossed by a second fence and gate. The farm-house lane, passing the house front, kept straight on to the barn, though a second carriage track ran up to the porch.

It was a homely and primitive scene enough, pastoral as any farm boy's birth-place, and had been the seat of many toils and endearments. Young wives had been brought to it, and around its hearth the earliest cries of infants, gladdening mothers' hearts, had made the household jubilant till the stars came out, and were its only sentries, save the bright lights at its window-panes as of a camp-fire, and the suppressed chorusses of the domestic bivouac within, where apple toasting and nut cracking and country games shortened the winter shadows. Yet in this house, so peaceful by moonlight, murder had washed its spotted hands, and ministered to its satiated appetite. History—present in every nook in the broad young world—had stopped to make a landmark of Garrett's farm.

In the dead stillness, Baker dismounted and forced the outer gate; Conger kept close behind him, and the horsemen followed cautiously. They made no noise in the soft clay, nor broke the all-foreboding silence anywhere, till the second gate swung open gratingly, yet even then nor hoarse nor shrill response came back, save distant croaking, as of frogs or owls, or the whizz of some passing night-hawk. So they surrounded the pleasant old homestead, each-horseman, carbine in poise, adjusted under the grove of locusts, so as to inclose the dwelling with a circle of fire. After a pause, Baker rode to the kitchen door on the side, and dismounting, rapped and halloed lustily. An old man, in drawers and night-shirt, hastily undrew the bolts, and stood on the threshold, peering shiveringly into the darkness.

Baker seized him by the throat at once, and held a pistol to his ear. "Who—who is it that calls me?" cried the old man. "Where are the men who stay with you?" challenged Baker. "If you prevaricate you are a dead man!" The old fellow, who proved to be the head of the family, was so overawed and paralysed that he stammered, and shook, and said not a word. "Go light a candle," cried Baker, sternly, "and be quick about it." The trembling old man obeyed, and in a moment the imperfect rays flared upon his whitening hairs and bluishly pallid face. Then the question was repeated, backed up by the glimmering pistol, "where are those men?" The old man held to the wall, and his knees smote each other. "They are gone," he said. "We haven't got them in the house. I assure you that they are gone." Here there were sounds and whisperings in the main building adjoining, and the lieutenant strode to the door. A ludicrous instant intervened, the old man's modesty outran his terror. "Don't go in there," he said, feebly; "there are women undressed in there." "Damn the women," cried Baker; "what if they are undressed? We shall go in if they haven't a rag." Leaving the old man in mute astonishment, Baker bolted through the door, and stood in an assemblage of bare arms and night robes. His loaded pistol disarmed modesty of its delicacy and substituted therefore a seasonable terror. Here he repeated his summons, and the half light of the candle gave to his face a more than bandit ferocity. They all denied knowledge of the strangers' whereabouts.

In the interim Conger had also entered, and while the household and its invaders were thus in weird tableaux, a young man appeared, as if he had risen from the ground. The muzzles of everybody turned upon him in a second; but, while he blanched, he did not lose loquacity. "Father," he said, "we had better tell the truth about the matter. Those men whom you seek, gentlemen, are in the barn, I know. They went there to sleep." Leaving one soldier to guard the old man—and the soldier was very glad of the job, as it relieved him of personal hazard in the approaching combat—all the rest, with cocked pistols at the young man's head, followed on to the barn. It lay a hundred yards from the house, the front barn door facing the west gable, and was an old and spacious structure, with floors only a trifle above the ground level.

The troops dismounted, were stationed at regular intervals around it, and ten yards distant at every point, four special guards placed to command the door and all with weapons in supple preparation, while Baker and Conger went direct to the portal. It had a padlock upon it, and the key of this Baker secured at once. In the interval of silence that ensued, the rustling of planks and straw was heard inside, as of persons rising from sleep.

At the same moment Baker hailed:

"To the persons in this barn. I have a proposal to make; we are about to send in to you the son of the man in whose custody you are found. Either surrender to him your arms and then give yourselves up, or we'll set fire to the place. We mean to take you both, or to have a bonfire and a shooting match."

No answer came to this of any kind. The lad, John M. Garrett, who was in deadly fear, was here pushed through the door by a sudden opening of it, and immediately Lieutenant Baker locked the door on the outside. The boy was heard to state his appeal in under tone. Booth replied:

"Damn you. Get out of here. You have betrayed me."

At the same time he placed his hand in his pocket as for a pistol. A remonstrance followed, but the boy slipped quickly over the reopened portal, reporting that his errand had failed, and that he dared not enter again. All this time the candle brought from the house to the barn was burning close beside the two detectives, rending it easy for any one within to have shot them dead. They observed, the light was cautiously removed, and everybody took care to keep out of its reflection. By this time the crisis of the position was at hand, the cavalry exhibited very variable inclinations, some to run away, others to shoot Booth without a summons, but all excited and fitfully silent. At the house near by the female folks were seen collected in the doorway, and the necessities of the case provoked prompt conclusions. The boy was placed at a remote point, and the summons repeated by Baker:

"You must surrender inside there. Give up your arms and appear. There is no chance for escape. We give you five minutes to make up your mind."

A bold, clarion reply came from within, so strong as to be heard at the house door:

"Who are you, and what do you want with us?"

Baker again urged: "We want you to deliver up your arms and become our prisoners."

"But who are you?" hallooed the same strong voice.

Baker:—"That makes no difference. We know who you are, and we want you. We have here fifty men, armed with carbines and pistols. You cannot escape."

There was a long pause, and then Booth said:

"Captain, this is a hard case, I swear. Perhaps I am being taken by my own friends." No reply from the detectives.

Booth—"Well, give us a little time to consider."

Baker—"Very well. Take time."

Here ensued a long and eventful pause. What thronging memories it brought to Booth, we can only guess. In this little interval he made the resolve to die. But he was cool and steady to the end. Baker, after a lapse, hailed for the last time.

"Well, we have waited long enough; surrender your arms and come out, or we'll fire the barn."

Booth answered thus: "I am but a cripple, a one-legged man. Withdraw your forces one hundred yard from the door, and I will come. Give me a chance for my life, captain. I will never be taken alive."

Baker—"We did not come here to fight, but to capture you. I say again, appear, or the barn shall be fired."

Then with a long breath, which could be heard outside, Booth cried in sudden calmness, still invisible, as were to him his enemies:

"Well, then, my brave boys, prepare a stretcher for me."

There was a pause repeated, broken by low discussions within between Booth and his associate, the former saying, as if in answer to some remonstrance or appeal, "Get away from me. You are a damned coward, and mean to leave me in my distress; but go, go. I don't want you to stay. I won't have you stay." Then he shouted aloud:

"There's man inside who wants to surrender."

Baker—"You are the man that carried the carbine yesterday; bring it out."

Harold—"I haven't got any."

This was said in a whining tone, and with an almost visible shiver. Booth cried aloud, at this hesitation: "He hasn't got any arms; they are mine, and I have kept them."

Baker—"Well, he carried the carbine, and must bring it out."

Booth—"On the word and honor of a gentleman, he has no arms with him. They are mine, and I have got them."

At this time Harold was quite up to the door, within whispering distance of Baker. The latter told him to put out his hands to be handcuffed, at the same time drawing open the door a little distance. Harold thrust forth his hands, when Baker, seizing him, jerked him into the night, and straightway delivered him over to a deputation of cavalrymen. The fellow began to talk of his innocence and plead so nosily that Conger threatened to gag him unless he ceased. Then Booth made his last appeal, in the same clear unbroken voice:

"Captain, give me a chance. Draw off your men and I will fight them singly. I could have killed you six times to-night, but I believe you to be a brave man, and would not murder you. Give a lame man a show."

It was too late for parley. All this time Booth's voice had sounded from the middle of the barn.

Ere he ceased speaking, Colonel Conger, slipping around to the rear, drew some loose straws through a crack, and lit a match upon them. They were dry and blazed up in an instant, carrying a sheet of smoke and flame through the parted planks, and heaving in a twinkling a world of light and heat upon the magazine within. The blaze lit up the black recesses of the great barn till every wasp's nest and cobweb in the roof was luminous, flinging streaks of red and violet across the tumbled farm gear in the corner, plows, harrows, hoes, rakes, sugar mills, and making every separate grain in the high bin adjacent, gleam like a mote of precious gold. They tinged the beams, the upright columns, the barricades, where clover and timothy, piled high, held toward the hot incendiary their separate straws for the funeral pile. They bathed the murderer's retreat in beautiful illumination, and while in bold outline his figure stood revealed, they rose like an impenetrable wall to guard from sight the hated enemy who lit them. Behind the blaze, with his eye to a crack, Conger saw Wilkes Booth standing upright upon a crutch. He likens him at this instant to his brother Edwin, whom he says he so much resembled that he half believed, for the moment, the whole pursuit to have been a mistake. At the gleam of the fire Wilkes dropped his crutch, and carbine in both hands, crept up to the spot to espy the incendiary and shoot him dead. His eyes were lustrous like fever, and swelled and rolled in terrible gutteral beauty, while his teeth were fixed, and he wore the expression of one in the calmness before frenzy. In vain he peered with vengeance in his look; the blaze that made him visible concealed his enemy. A second he turned glaring at the fire as if to leap upon it and extinguish it, but it had made such headway that this was a futile impulse and he dismissed it. As calmly as upon the battle-field a veteran stands amidst the hail of ball and shell, and plunging iron, Booth turned at a man's stride, and pushed for the door, carbine in poise, and the last resolve of death, which we name despair, set on his high, bloodless forehead.

As so he dashed, intent to expire not unaccompanied, a disobedient sergeant at an eye-hole drew upon him the fatal bead. The barn was all glorious with conflagration and in the beautiful ruin this outlawed man strode like all that we know of wicked valor, stern in the face of death. A shock, a shout, a gathering up of his splendid figure as if to overtip the stature God gave him, and John Wilkes Booth fell headlong to the floor, lying there in a heap, a little life remaining.

"He has shot himself!" cried Baker, unaware of the source of the report, and rushing in, he grasped his arms to guard against any feint or strategy. A moment convinced him that further struggle with the prone flesh was useless. Booth did not move, nor breathe, nor gasp. Conger and two sergeants now entered, and taking up the body, they bore it in haste from the advancing flame, and laid it without upon the grass, all fresh with heavenly dew.

"Water," cried Conger, "bring water."

When this was dashed into his face, he revived a moment and stirred his lips. Baker put his ear close down, and heard him say:

"Tell mother—and die—for my country."

They lifted him again, the fire encroaching in hotness upon them and placed him on the porch before the dwelling.

A mattress was brought down, on which they placed him and propped his head, and gave him water and brandy. The women of the household, joined meantime by another son, who had been found in one of the corn cribs, watching as he said, to see that Booth and Harold did not steal the horses, were nervous, but prompt to do the dying man all kindnesses, although waived sternly back by the detectives. They dipped a rag in brandy and water, and this being put between Booth's teeth he sucked it greedily. When he was able to articulate again, he muttered to Mr. Baker the same words, with an addenda. "Tell mother I died for my country. I thought I did for the best." Baker repeated this, saying at the same time, "Booth, do I repeat it correctly." Booth nodded his head. By this time the grayness of dawn was approaching; moving figures inquisitively coming near were to be seen distinctly, and the cocks began to crow gutturally though the barn was a hulk of blaze and ashes, sending toward the zenith a spiral line of dense smoke. The women became importunate that the troops might be ordered to extinguish the fire, which was spreading toward their precious corn-cribs. Not even death could banish the call of interest. Soldiers were sent to put out the fire, and Booth, relieved of the bustle around him, drew near to death apace. Twice he was heard to say, "kill me, kill me." His lips often moved but could complete no appreciable sound. He made once a motion which the quick eye of Conger understood to mean that his throat pained him. Conger put his finger there, when the dying man attempted to cough, but only caused the blood at his perforated neck to flow more lively. He bled very little, although shot quite through, beneath and behind the ears, his collar being severed on both sides.

A soldier had been meanwhile despatched for a doctor, but the route and return were quite six miles, and the sinner was sinking fast. Still the women made efforts to get to see him, but were always rebuffed, and all the brandy they could find was demanded by the assassin, who motioned for a strong drink every two minutes. He made frequent desires to be turned over, not by speech, but by gesture, and was alternately placed upon his back, belly and side. His tremendous vitality evidenced itself almost miraculously. Now and then his heart would cease to throb, and his pulses would be as cold as a dead man's. Directly life would begin anew, the face would flush up effulgently, the eyes open and brighten, and soon relapsing, stillness re-asserted, would again be dispossessed by the same magnificent triumph of man over mortality. Finally the fussy little doctor arrived, in time to be useless. He probed the wound to see if the ball were not in it, and shook his head sagely and talked learnedly.

Just at his coming Booth had asked to have his hands raised and shown him. They were so paralyzed that he did not know their location. When they were displayed he muttered, with a sad lethargy, "Useless, useless." These were the last words he ever uttered. As he began to die the sun rose and threw beams into all the tree-tops. It was of a man's height when the struggle of death twitched and fingered in the fading bravo's face. His jaw drew spasmodically and obliquely downward; his eyeballs rolled toward his feet, and began to swell; lividness, like a horrible shadow, fastened upon him, and, with a sort of gurgle and sudden check, he stretched his feet and threw his head back and gave up the ghost.

They sewed him up in a saddle blanket. This was his shroud; too like a soldier's. Harold, meantime, had been tied to a tree, but was now released for the march. Colonel Conger pushed on immediately for Washington; the cortege was to follow. Booth's only arms were his carbine, knife, and two revolvers. They found about him bills of exchange, Canada money, and a diary. A venerable old negro living in the vicinity had the misfortune to possess a horse. This horse was a relic of former generations, and showed by his protruding ribs the general leanness of the land. He moved in an eccentric amble, and when put upon his speed was generally run backward. To this old negro's horse was harnessed a very shady and absurd wagon, which rattled like approaching dissolution, and each part of it ran without any connection or correspondence with any other part. It had no tail-board, and its shafts were sharp as famine; and into this mimicry of a vehicle the murderer was to be sent to the Potomac river, while the man he had murdered was moving in state across the mourning continent. The old negro geared up his wagon by means of a set of fossil harness, and when it was backed to Garrett's porch, they laid within it the discolored corpse. The corpse was tied with ropes around the legs and made fast to the wagon sides. Harold's legs were tied to stirrups, and he was placed in the centre of four murderous looking cavalrymen. The two sons of Garrett were also taken along, despite the sobs and petitions of the old folks and women, but the rebel captain who had given Booth a lift, got off amidst the night's agitations, and was not rearrested. So moved the cavalcade of retribution, with death in its midst, along the road to Port Royal. When the wagon started, Booth's wound till now scarcely dribbling, began to run anew.

It fell through the crack of the wagon, dripping upon the axle, and spotting the road with terrible wafers. It stained the planks, and soaked the blankets; and the old negro, at a stoppage, dabbled his hands in it by mistake; he drew back instantly, with a shudder and stifled expletive, "Gor-r-r, dat'll never come off in de world; it's murderer's blood." He wrung his hands, and looked imploringly at the officers, and shuddered again: "Gor-r-r, I wouldn't have dat on me fur tousand, tousand dollars." The progress of the team was slow, with frequent danger of shipwreck altogether, but toward noon the cortege filed through Port Royal, where the citizens came out to ask the matter, and why a man's body, covered with sombre blankets, was going by with so great escort. They were told that it was a wounded confederate, and so held their tongues. The little ferry, again in requisition, took them over by squads, and they pushed from Port Conway to Belle Plain, which they reached in the middle of the after noon. All the way the blood dribbled from the corpse in a slow, incessant, sanguine exudation. The old negro was niggardly dismissed with two paper dollars. The dead man untied and cast upon the vessel's deck, steam gotten up in a little while, and the broad Potomac shores saw this skeleton ship flit by, as the bloody sun threw gashes and blots of unhealthy light along the silver surface.

All the way associate with the carcass, went Harold, shuddering in so grim companionship, and in the awakened fears of his own approaching ordeal, beyond which it loomed already, the gossamer fabric of a scaffold. He tried to talk for his own exoneration, saying he had ridden, as was his wont, beyond the East Branch, and returning, found Booth wounded, who begged him to be his companion. Of his crime he knew nothing, so help him God, &c.

But nobody listened to him. All interest of crime, courage, and retribution centered in the dead flesh at his feet. At Washington, high and low turned out to look on Booth. Only a few were permitted to see his corpse for purposes of recognition. It was fairly preserved, though on one side of the face distorted, and looking blue-like death, and wildly bandit-like, as if beaten by avenging winds.

Yesterday the Secretary of War, without instructions of any kind, committed to Colonel Lafayette C. Baker, of the secret service, the stark corpse of J. Wilkes Booth. The secret service never fulfilled its volition more secretively. "What have you done with the body?" said I to Baker. "That is known" he answered, "to only one man living besides myself. It is gone. I will not tell you where. The only man who knows is sworn to silence. Never till the great trumpeter comes shall the grave of Booth be discovered." And this is true. Last night, the 27th of April, a small row boat received the carcass of the murdered; two men were in it, they carried the body off into the darkness, and out of that darkness it will never return. In the darkness, like his great crime, may it remain forever, impalpable, invisible, nondescript, condemned to that worse than damnation,—annihilation. The river-bottom may ooze about it laden with great shot and drowning manacles. The earth may have opened to give it that silence and forgiveness which man will never give its memory. The fishes may swim around it, or the daisies grow white above it; but we shall never know. Mysterious, incomprehensible, unattainable, like the dim times through which we live and think upon as if we only dreamed them in perturbed fever, the assassin of a nation's head rests somewhere in the elements, and that is all; but if the indignant seas or the profaned turf shall ever vomit his corpse from their recesses, and it receive humane or Christian burial from some who do not recognize it, let the last words those decaying lips ever uttered be carved above them with a dagger, to tell the history of a young and once promising life—useless! useless!

LETTER IX
THE EXECUTIONS.

Washington, Friday, July 7th.

The trial is over; four of the conspirators have paid with their lives to a penalty of the Great Conspiracy; the rest go to the jail, and with one exception for the remainder of their lives.

Whatever our individual theories may be, the great crime is ended, and this is the crowing scene:

It was a long and dusty avenue, along which rambled soldiers in bluishly white coats, cattle with their tongues out, straying from the herd, and a few negroes making for their cabins, which dotted the fiery and vacant lots of the suburbs. At the foot of this avenue, where a lukewarm river holds between its dividing arms a dreary edifice of brick, the way was filled with collected cabs, and elbowing people, abutting against a circle of sentinels who kept the arsenal gate. The low, flat, dust-white fields to the far left were also lined with patrols and soldiers lying on the ground in squads beside their stacked muskets. Within these a second blue and monotonous line extended. The drive from the arsenal gate to the arsenal's high and steel-spiked wall was beset by companies of exacting sabremen, and all the river bank to the right was edged with blue and bayonets. This exhibition of war was the prelude to a very ghastly but very popular episode—an execution. Three men and a woman were to be led out in shackles and hung to a beam. They had conspired to take life; they had thrilled the world with the partial consummation of their plot; they were to reach the last eminence of assassins, on this parched and oppressive noon, by swinging in pinioned arms and muffled faces in the presence of a thousand people.

The bayonets at the gate were lifted as I produced my pass. It was the last permission granted. In giving it away the General seemed relieved, for he had been sorely troubled by applications. Everybody who had visited Washington to seek for an office, sought to see this expiation also. The officer at the gate looked at my pass suspiciously. "I don't believe that all these papers have been genuine," he said. Is an execution, then, so great a warning to evil-doers, that men will commit forgery to see it?

I entered a large grassy yard, surrounded by an exceedingly high wall. On the top of this wall, soldiers with muskets in their hands, were thickly planted. The yard below was broken by irregular buildings of brick. I climbed by a flight of rickety outside stairs to the central building, where many officers were seated at the windows, and looked awhile at the strange scene on the grassy plaza. On the left, the long, barred, impregnable penitentiary rose. The shady spots beneath it were occupied by huddling spectators. Soldiers were filling their canteens at the pump. A face or two looked out from the barred jail. There were many umbrellas hoisted on the ground to shelter civilians beneath them. Squads of officers and citizens lay along the narrow shadow of the walls. The north side of the yard was enclosed on three sides by columns of soldiers drawn up in regular order, the side next to the penitentiary being short to admit of ingress to the prisoner's door; but the opposite column reached entirely up to the north wall.

Within this enclosed area a structure to be inhabited by neither the living nor the dead was fast approaching completion. It stood gaunt, lofty, long. Saws and hammers made dolorous music on it. Men, in their shirt sleeves, were measuring it and directing its construction in a business way. Now and then some one would ascend its airy stair to test its firmness; others crawled beneath to wedge its slim supports, or carry away the falling debris.

Toward this skeleton edifice all looked with a strange nervousness. It was the thought and speculation of the gravest and the gayest.

It was the gallows.

A beam reached, horizontally, in the air, twenty feet from the ground; four awkward ropes, at irregular intervals, dangled from it, each noosed at the end. It was upheld by three props, one in the center and one at each end. These props came all the way to the ground where they were morticed in heavy bars. Midway of them a floor was laid, twenty by twelve feet, held in its position on the farther side by shorter props, of which they were many, and reached by fifteen creaking steps, railed on either side. But this floor had no supports on the side nearest the eye, except two temporary rods, at the foot of which two inclined beams pointed menacingly, held in poise by ropes from the gallows floor.

And this floor was presently discovered to be a cheat, a trap, a pitfall.

Two hinges only held it to its firmer half. These were to give way at the fatal moment, and leave only the shallow and unreliable air for the bound and smothering to tread upon.

The traps were two, sustained by two different props.

The nooses were on each side of the central support.

Was this all?

Not all.

Close by the foot of the gallows four wooden boxes were piled upon each other at the edge of four newly excavated pits, the fresh earth of which was already dried and brittle in the burning noon.

Here were to be interred the broken carcasses when the gallows had let go its throttle. They were so placed as the victims should emerge from the gaol door they would be seen near the stair directly in the line of march.

And not far from these, in silence and darkness beneath the prison where they had lain so long and so forbodingly, the body of John Wilkes Booth, sealed up in the brick floor, had long been mouldering. If the dead can hear he had listened many a time to the rattle of their manacles upon the stairs, to the drowsy hum of the trial and the buzz of the garrulous spectators; to the moaning, or the gibing, or the praying in the bolted cells where those whom kindred fate had given a little lease upon life lay waiting for the terrible pronouncement.

It was a long waiting, and the roof of a high house outside the walls was seen to be densely packed with people. Others kept arriving moment by moment; soldiers were wondering when the swinging would begin and officers arguing that the four folks "deserved it, damn them!" Gentlemen of experience were telling over the number of such expiations they had witnessed. Analytic people were comparing the various modes of shooting, garroting, and guillotining. Cigars were sending up spirals of soothing smoke. There was a good deal of covert fear that a reprieve might be granted. Inquiries were many and ingenuous for whisky, and one or two were so deeply expectant that they fell asleep.

How much those four dying, hoping, cringing, dreaming felons were grudged their little gasp of life? It was to be a scene, not a postponement or a prolongation. "Who was to be the executioner?" "Why had not the renowned and artistic Isaacs been sent for from New York?" "Would they probably die game, or grow weak-kneed in the last extremity?" Ah, the gallows' workmen have completed the job! "Now then we should have it."

Still there was delay. The sun peeped into the new-made graves and made blistering hot the gallows' floor. The old pump made its familiar music to the cool plash of blessed water. The grass withered in the fervid heat. The bronzed faces of the soldiers ran lumps of sweat. The file upon the jail walls looked down into the wide yard yawningly. No wind fluttered the tow battle standards condemned to unfold their trophies upon this coming profanation. Not yet arrived. Why? The extent of grace has almost been attained. The sentence gave them only till two o'clock! Why are they so dilatory in wishing to be hanged?

Suddenly the wicket opens, the troops spring to their feet, and stand at order arms, the flags go up, the low order passes from company to company; the spectators huddle a little nearer to the scaffold; all the writers for the press produce their pencils and note-books.

First came a woman pinioned.

A middle-aged woman, dressed in black, bonnetted and veiled, walking between two bare-headed priests.

One of these held against his breast a crucifix of jet, and in the folds of his blue-fringed sash he carried an open breviary, while both of them muttered the service for the dead.

Four soldiers, with musket at shoulder, followed, and a captain led the way to the gallows.

The second party escorted a small and shambling German, whose head had a long white cap upon it, rendering more filthy his dull complexion, and upon whose feet the chains clanked as he slowly advanced, preceded by two officers, flanked by a Lutheran clergyman, and followed, as his predecessor, by an armed squad.

The third, preacher and party, clustered about a shabby boy, whose limbs tottered as he progressed.

The fourth, walked in the shadow of a straight high stature, whose tawny hair and large blue eye were suggestive rather of the barbarian striding in his conqueror's triumph, than the assassin going to the gallows.

All these, captives, priests, guards, and officers, nearly twenty in all, climbed slowly and solemnly the narrow steps; and upon four arm chairs, stretching across the stage in the rear of the traps, the condemned were seated with their spiritual attendants behind them.

The findings and warrants were immediately read to the prisoners by General Hartrauft in a quiet and respectful tone, an aid holding an umbrella over him meantime. These having been already published, and being besides very uninteresting to any body but the prisoners, were paid little heed to, all the spectators interesting themselves in the prisoners.

There was a fortuitous delicacy in this distribution, the woman being placed farthest from the social and physical dirtiness of Atzerott, and nearest the unblanched and manly physiognomy of Payne.

She was not so pale that the clearness of her complexion could not be seen, and the brightness of the sun made her vail quite transparent. Her eyes were seen to be of a soft gray; her brown hair lay smoothly upon a full, square forehead; the contour of her face was comely, but her teeth had the imperfectness of those of most southern women, being few and irregular. Until the lips were opened she did not reveal them. Her figure was not quite full enough to be denominated buxom, yet had all the promise of venerable old age, had nature been permitted its due course. She was of medium height, and modest—as what woman would not be under such searching survey? At first she was very feeble, and leaned her head upon alternate sides of her armchair in nervous spasms; but now and then, when a sort of wail just issued from her lips, the priest placed before her the crucifix to lull her fearful spirit. All the while the good fathers Wigett and Walter murmured their low, tender cadences, and now and then the woman's face lost its deadly fear, and took a bold, cognizable survey of the spectators. She wore a robe of dark woolen, no collar, and common shoes of black listing. Her general expression was that of acute suffering, vanishing at times as if by the conjuration of her pride, and again returning in a paroxysm as she looked at the dreadful rope dangling before her. This woman, to whom the priests have made their industrious moan, holding up the effigy of Christ when their own appeals became of no avail, perched there in the lofty air, counting her breaths, counting the winkfuls of light, counting the final wrestles of her breaking heart, had been the belle of her section, and many good men had courted her hand. She had led a pleasant life, and children had been born to her—who shared her mediocre ambition and the invincibility of her will. If the charge of her guilt were proven, she was the Lady Macbeth of the west.

But women know nothing of consequences. She alone of all her sex stands now in this thrilled and ghastly perspective, and in immediate association with three creatures in whose company it is no fame to die: a little crying boy, a greasy unkempt sniveller, and a confessed desperado. Her base and fugitive son, to know the infamy of his cowardice and die of his shame, should have seen his mother writhing in her seat upon the throne his wickedness established for her.

Payne, the strangest criminal in our history, was alone dignified and self-possessed. He wore a closely-fitting knit shirt, a sailor's straw hat tied with a ribbon, and dark pantaloons, but no shoes. His collar, cut very low, showed the tremendous muscularity of his neck, and the breadth of his breast was more conspicuous by the manner in which the pinioned arms thrust it forward. His height, his vigor, his glare made him the strong central figure of this interelementary tableaux. He said no word; his eyes were red as with the penitential weeping of a courageous man, and the smooth hardness of his skin seemed like a polished muscle. He did not look abroad inquisitively, nor within intuitively. He had no accusation, no despair, no dreaminess. He was only looking at death as for one long expected, and not a tremor nor a shock stirred his long stately limbs; withal, his blue eye was milder than when I saw him last, as if some bitterness, or stolidness, or obstinate pride had been exorcised, perhaps by the candor of confession. Now and then he looked half-pityingly at the woman, and only once moved his lips, as if in supplication. Few who looked at him, forgetful of his crime, did not respect him. He seemed to feel that no man was more than his peer, and one of his last commands was a word of regret to Mr. Seward.

I have a doubt that this man is entirely a member of our nervous race. I believe that a fiber of the aboriginal runs through his tough sinews. At times he looked entirely an Indian. His hair is tufted, and will not lie smoothly. His cheek-bones are large and high set. There is a tint in his complexion. Perhaps the Seminole blood of his swampy state left a trace of its combative nature there.

Payne was a preacher's son, and not the worst graduate of his class. He real name is Lewis Thornton Powell.

He died without taking the hand of any living friend.

Even the squalid Atzerott was not so poor. I felt a pity for his physical rather than his vital or spiritual peril. It seemed a profanation to break the iron column of his neck, and give to the worm his belted chest.

But I remember that he would have slain a sick old man.

The third condemned, although whimpering, had far more grit than I anticipated; he was inquisitive and flippant-faced, and looked at the noose flaunting before him, and the people gathered below, and the haggard face of Atzerott, as if entirely conscious and incapable of abstraction.

Harold would have enjoyed this execution vastly as a spectator. He was, I think, capable of a greater degree of depravity than any of his accomplices. Atzerott might have made a sneak thief, Booth a forger, but Harold was not far from a professional pickpocket. He was keen-eyed, insolent, idle, and, by a small experience in Houston street, would have been qualified for a first-class "knuck." He had not, like the rest, any political suggestion for the murder of the heads of the nation; and upon the gallows, in his dirty felt hat, soiled cloth coat, light pantaloons and stockings, he seemed unworthy of his manacles.

A very fussy Dutchman tied him up and fanned him, and he wept forgetfully, but did not make a halt or absurd spectacle. Atzerott was my ideal of a man to be hung—a dilution of Wallack's rendering of the last hours of Fagan, the Jew; a sort of sick man, quite garrulous and smitten, with his head thrown forward, muttering to the air, and a pallidness transparent through his dirt as he jabbered prayers and pleas confusedly, and looked in a complaining sort of way at the noose, as if not quite certain that it might not have designs upon him.

He wore a greyish coat, black vest, light pantaloons and slippers, and a white affair on his head, perhaps a handkerchief.

His spiritual adviser stood behind him, evidently disgusted with him.

Atzerott lost his life through too much gabbing. He could have had serious designs upon nothing greater than a chicken, but talked assassination with the silent and absolute Booth, until entrapped into conspiracy and the gallows, much against his calculation. This man was visited by his mother and a poor, ignorant woman with whom he cohabited. He was the picture of despair, and died ridiculously, whistling up his courage.

These were the dramatis personae, no more to be sketched, no more to be cross-examined, no more to be shackled, soon to be cold in their coffins.

They were, altogether, a motley and miserable set. Ravaillac might have looked well swinging in chains; Charlotte Corday is said to have died like an actress; Beale hung not without dignity, but these people, aspiring to overturn a nation, bore the appearance of a troop of ignorant folks, expiating the bloodshed of a brawl.

When General Hartrauft ceased reading there was momentary lull, broken only by the cadences of the priests.

Then the Rev. Mr. Gillette addressed the spectators in a deep impressive tone. The prisoner, Lewis Thornton Powell, otherwise Payne, requested him to thus publicly and sincerely return his thanks to General Hartrauft, the other officers, the soldiers, and all persons who had charge of him and had attended him. Not one unkind word, look, or gesture, had been given to him by any one. Dr. Gillette then followed in a fervent prayer in behalf of the prisoner, during which Payne's eyes momentarily filled with tears, and he followed in the prayer with visible feeling.

Rev. Dr. Olds followed, saying in behalf of the prisoner, David E. Harold, that he tendered his forgiveness to all who had wronged him, and asked the forgiveness of all whom he had wronged. He gave his thanks to the officers and guards for kindnesses rendered him. He hoped that he had died in charity with all men and at peace with God. Dr. Olds concluded with a feeling prayer for the prisoner.

Rev. Dr. Butler then made a similar return of thanks on behalf of George A. Atzerott for kindness received from his guards and attendants, and concluded with an earnest invocation in behalf of the criminal, saying that the blood of Jesus cleanses from all sin, and asking that God Almighty might have mercy upon this man.

The solemnity of this portion of the scene may be imagined, the several clergyman speaking in order the dying testament of their clients, and making the hot hours fresh with the soft harmonies of their benedictions.

The two holy fathers having received Mrs. Surratt's confession, after the custom of their creed observed silence. In this, as in other respects, Mrs. Surratt's last hours were entirely modest and womanly.

The stage was filled with people; the crisis of the occasion had come; the chairs were all withdrawn, and the condemned stood upon their feet.

The process of tying the limbs began.

It was with a shudder, almost a blush, that I saw an officer gather the ropes tightly three times about the robes of Mrs. Surratt, and bind her ankles with cords. She half fainted, and sank backward upon the attendants, her limbs yielding to the extremity of her terror, but uttering no cry, only a kind of sick groaning, like one in the weakness of fever, when a wry medicine must be taken.

Payne, with his feet firmly laced together, stood straight as one of the scaffold beams, and braced himself up so stoutly that this in part prevented the breaking of his neck.

Harold stood well beneath the drop, still whimpering at the lips, but taut, and short, and boyish.

Atzerott, in his grovelling attitude, while they tied him began to indulge in his old vice of gabbing. He evidently wished to make his finale more effective than his previous cowardly role, and perhaps was strengthening his fortitude with a speech, as we sometimes do of dark nights with a whistle.

"Gentlemen," he said, with a sort of choke and gasp, "take ware," He evidently meant "beware," or "take care," and confounded them.

Again, when the white death-cap was drawn over his face, he continued to cry out under it, once saying, "Good bye, shentlemens, who is before me now;" and again, "May we meet in the other world." Finally he drifted away with low, half-intelligible ebullitions, as "God help me," "oh! oh!" and the like.

The rest said nothing, except Mrs. Surratt, who asked to be supported, that she might not fall, but Harold protested against the knot with which he was to be dislocated, it being as huge as one's double fist.

In fact all the mechanical preparations were clumsy and inartistic, and the final scenes of the execution, therefore, revolting in the extreme. When the death-caps were all drawn over the faces of the prisoners, and they stood in line in the awful suspense between absolute life and immediate death, a man at the neck of each adjusting the cord, the knot beneath the ears of each protruded five or six inches, and the cord was so thick that it could not be made to press tightly against the flesh.

So they stood, while nearly a thousand faces from the window, roof, wall, yard and housetop, gazed, the scaffold behind them still densely packed with the assistants, and the four executioners beneath, standing at their swinging beams. The priests continued to murmur prayers. The people were dumb, as if each witness stood alone with none near by to talk to him.

An instant this continued, while an officer on the plot before, motioned back the assistants, and then with a forward thrust of his hand, signaled the executioners.

The great beams were darted against the props simultaneously. The two traps fell with a slam. The four bodies dropped like a single thing, outside the yet crowded remnant of the gallows floor, and swayed and turned, to and fro, here and there, forward and backward, and with many a helpless spasm, while the spectators took a little rush forward, and the ropes were taut as the struggling pulses of the dying.

Mrs. Surratt's neck was broken immediately; she scarcely drew one breath. Her short woman's figure, with the skirts looped closely about it, merely dangled by the vibration of her swift descent, and with the knot holding true under the ear, her head leaned sideways, and her pinioned arms seemed content with their confinement.

Payne died a horrible death; the knot slipped to the back of his neck, and bent his head forward on his breast, so that he strangled as he drew his deep chest almost to his chin, and the knees contracted till they almost seemed to touch his abdomen. The veins in his great wrists were like whip-cords, expanded to twice their natural dimensions, and the huge neck grew almost black with the dark blood that rushed in a flood to the circling rope. A long while he swayed and twisted and struggled, till at last nature ceased her rebellion and life went out unwillingly.

Harold also passed through some struggles. It is doubtful that his neck was broken. The perspiration dripped from his feet, and he swung in the hot noon just living enough to make death irritable.

Atzerott died easily. Life did not care to fight for his possession.

The two central figures lived long after the two upon the flanks.

There they hung, bundles of carcass and old clothes, four in a row, and past all conspiracy or ambition, the river rolling by without a sound, and men watching them with a shiver, while the heat of the day seemed suddenly abated, as if by the sudden opening of a tomb.

The officers conversed in a half-audible tone; the reporters put up their books; the assistants descended from the gallows; and the medical men drew near. No wind stirred the unbreathing bodies, they were stone dead.

The bodies were allowed to hang about twenty minutes, when surgeon Otis, U.S.V., and Assistant Surgeons Woodward and Porter, U.S.A., examined them and pronounced all dead. In about ten minutes more a ladder was placed against the scaffold preparatory to cutting the bodies down. An over-zealous soldier on the platform reached over and severed the cord, letting one body fall with a thump, when he was immediately ordered down and reprimanded. The body of Atzerott was placed in a strong white pine box, and the other bodies cut down in the following order, Harold, Powell, and Mrs. Surratt.

The carcasses thus recovered were given over to a squad of soldiers and each placed in the pits prepared for them, and directly all but the memory of their offense passed from the recording daylight.

In the gloomy shadow of that arsenal lies all the motive, and essay of a crime which might have changed the destinies of our race. It will be forever a place of suspicion and marvel, the haunted spot of the Capitol, and the terror of all who to end a fancied evil, cut their way to right with a dagger.

THE LIFE AND BATTLES

OF

GARIBALDI,

AND

HIS MARCH ON ROME IN 1867.

BY

GEORGE ALFRED TOWNSEND

LATE SPECIAL CORRESPONDENT OF THE NEW YORK "TRIBUNE,"
AND THE NEW YORK "WORLD"
WITH THE ARMIES OF ITALY AND PRUSSIA.

———oo)o(oo———

AMERICAN NEWS COMPANY,
NEW YORK
(1867)

Giuseppe Garibaldi, "Liberty does not fail those who are determined to have it." Photograph taken in Naples, November 1860.

PREFACE.

For seven years I have been a special newspaper correspondent from many lands to many journals. Earnest to qualify myself by versatile experiences, both at home and abroad, for an influential and useful position among my countrymen, I have been careless in all things but adventure and observation. My letters have insensibly given me recognition. I wish more independence of thought and expression than is permitted upon the staff of a newspaper. Therefore I have projected an irregular succession of Special Letters upon all-absorbing occurrences, to be as simplifying and vivid as I can write them, fresh from their fields, and to be published in the form of pamphlet bulletins, resembling the present issue. If I am encouraged, I shall spare no distance nor expense to go in person to all scenes of interest and reproduce them in a dignified popular literature. My theory of descriptive journalism has always been to convey not only incidents but their impressions, as strongly as a cheerful, open-air American mind can seize them. I believe that I have the impulsions and sympathies of the masses of the American people, and there is no more noble object to which they are now directed than the representative soldier of Italian and human liberty, whom I have selected for this first *Brochure*. Young men, come round me! I open to you a recruiting office for Giuseppe Garibaldi!

GEORGE ALFRED TOWNSEND.

Garibaldi's American home, Clifton, Staten Island. Century, May, 1907.

LIFE OF GARIBALDI.

Garibaldi Cottage, Staten Island, October, 1867.

Last summer I lived a little while beside the Narrows on this most beautiful island. For neighbors, I had a colony of Italians, chatty, cheerful, hopeful, people, who spoke scarcely intelligible English, and these inhabited small cottages a quarter of a mile back from the Bay, where they made a self-amusing, anomalous community, so merry and innocent that I often wished I could be their countryman to be admitted into their circle. They drank wines imported by themselves from Italy,—good Capri Sec, Marsala and Montepulciano,—lived upon bare floors as they had done at home, and were surrounded by parrots, dogs, and chickens.

I sometimes went over to see them, and felt keenly the contrast of their light-heartedness with the anxious, money-getting, money-talking nature of our Americans. They were all Republicans, and patriots to both their native and adopted lands, and it was amongst them that Garibaldi lived parts of the years 1850, 51-52.

He was then a banished man, freshly smarting with wounds of body and heart, his wife buried in a mountain grave, his children orphans across the ocean, and his own sixteen years of hard battle for freedom in both worlds hardly accounted his honor. But he never mourned nor despaired, and all his record on Staten Island was of truthfulness, pleasantness, and toil. Few knew him, but his face was remembered still for its most benevolent eloquence and beauty, and the love that I had learned to bear him from some knowledge of his life, made my daily evening walk a visit to the Italian colony.

At the head of this colony was Signor Meucci, an elderly man of dignity and genius. He was an inventor and manufacturer, and his house was the home of the Exile, to whom his factory gave employment. The house was a low frame dwelling in a green yard, with wooded hills reaching up behind it. On the porch, of twilights, when the Italians sat smoking, I used to steal past, humoring the conceit that I heard the soft voice of the great soldier of freedom. They had letters from him often, and some of his earlier portraits, and he always wrote to M. Meucci as "My dear old Boss."

Next door to the house, across a fence, was Meyer's Brewery, called now, by everybody, "The Garibaldi Brewery," and in it the guest worked even with the long hospitality of his friend, moulding candles and drawing wicks, but he was never regarded as less than an honored companion, and at noon he knocked off work and took to reading. The history and poetry of his ancient land were his relief, for he was a man of large, bold, intelligences, and when the old love of the sea came back to him, now and then, he shipped upon a voyage, and lived close to the face of Nature as next beloved to Freedom's.

I seemed to be gladder and better that this great man had once lived near my cottage. It is a disheartening neighborhood that has never been entered by great good presence. He made a feature of all the woods and lanes. The ferry boats to town were haunted by him. I wondered if I should not some time shake his hand.

At last this good time came. It came at Brescia, when I saw him in his camp,—happy, child-like veteran, whose broad shoulder had tumbled thrones,—and I walked into the magnetism of his eye with the bold word on my tongue of "neighbor!" but the love and dignity he looked made me quite silent. I only shook his hand and felt that I had passed the great moment of my life.

Here let me sit upon Herr Meyer's stool, with a foamy mug of lager before me, and run down the thread of this career of sacrifice. It is a study to stir and soften mankind!

On the 4th of July, sixty-one years ago, a day memorable to freedom, the wife of a sailor-before-the-mast brought forth in the city of Nice a boy whom she named Giuseppe or Joseph. He was one of several boys, and his father helped to sail his grandfather's vessel. They were all poor and affectionate together. Giuseppe was of a gentle sympathizing nature, but stout and strong; a swimmer and a rover, and while at school he saved the lives of three persons from drowning. There was no braver son to any mother. "One of the sorrows of my life," he wrote on Staten Island, "is that I am not able to brighten the last days of my good parents, whose path I have strewn with many griefs by my adventurous career." He had simple religious feelings, and believed always in the power of his mother's prayers. Loving the open air more than school, they sent him to sea, for he had already tried twice to make a runaway voyage. His second harbor was the port of Rome, and he soon had visited all places on the Mediterranean from Constantinople to Gibraltar.

The Italians of the coasts near to Nice have always been redoubtable sailors. Columbus was born upon the same beach with Garibaldi, and both of them were of that hardy Ligurian race that lived under the shadows of the Alps at the brink of the Sea,—grand nature at their back, grand history before.

Young Garibaldi had a little schooling, and he read all the story of his native coasts, the glory of his race, and the griefs it had inherited; the heroisms of its towns, the everlasting hopefulness of his land, and how its beauty made it the spoil of strong conquerors. One time he sailed up the Black Sea and met among the crew a member of a secret patriotic Society, who broke to him a republican dream of unity and freedom for Italy. "Columbus," he says, "did not enjoy so much satisfaction on the discovery of America as I experienced hearing that the redemption of our country was meditated."

Straightway he joined the *Carbonari*, or "Charcoal Burners," so named from their wild spots of rendezvous, by the smouldering light of charcoal fires. "Quitting one of these outlawed meetings," he says, "on the fifth of February, 1834, I passed out of a gate of Genoa in the disguise of a peasant, 'a proscript.' At that time my public life commenced, and a few days afterward I saw my name for the first time in a newspaper: but it was in a sentence of death."

Let me make plain the condition of a land that compelled so desperate conspiracy, and punished it with so cruel a sentence. Before the birth of Christ Rome was the metropolis of the earth. Glutted with glory and riches, her climate attracted all the barbarians of the world. They overran the Alps, and first devastating Italy, settled upon it. The Christian Church made Rome its capital, converted the conquered and the conqueror, and arose to a power scarcely less than that of ancient Rome. Italy was a land of genius still, and by her discoveries and learning at once sent Christianity into all lands, and made a ferment in the human mind for a freer, fuller destiny than even religion gave. So, powerful cities arose and became republics, and the Church which had crushed the spirits of Kings found them too stubborn for her. She invited foreign monarchs to support her claims, encouraged municipal intrigues and usurpations, till Italy became a geographical term rather than the name of a nation, and divided into a horde of petty despotisms. All the great kingdoms made her their battle-field. Everything was ruined but the Church, which played tyrant against tyrant, and all against the people. The wail of the beautiful land pierced the hearts of mankind. But out of this grief arose thoughtful literature. Poets dimly ventured to hint of a great nation to be born out of this chaos. At last the rise of the American republic stimulated the great rebellion against tyranny known as the French revolution, and one after another the indignant people overthrew their tyrants, Italians among the first. While freedom was not quite won, the successful soldier of the people, Napoleon Bonaparte, by his tremendous military genius, mastered republicanism and changed it from an emancipation into a conquest. The hate he aroused among all nations but his own, gave the ruined Kings control again. The "reaction," or return tide of monarchy, put Europe once more in chains, and Italy was still a piecemeal misery. But the instrumentalities to nationality were all prepared. A common language was spoken from the Alps to Sicily; in the revolutionary wars the people of different cities had mingled; local prejudices had nigh disappeared; a few magnetic men developed, who formed the patriotic youths of all the lands into secret societies, and the greatest of these was Joseph Mazzini. He was a man of genius and indomitable purpose, working forever and by stealth. He gave a grand unrest to all the generation of which Garibaldi was a member. Frugal, unrelenting, uncompromising, his dark eyes, grand thoughtful forehead, and fervid eloquence, made him the inspirer of young Garibaldi, whose aid, being a sailor, Mazzini wished, to circulate his appeals in various ports. Seeing a mysterious influence at work among their subjects, the Italian despots adopted all cruel tortures to suppress revolt, but in vain. Mutinies sprang up in every city; at last all the monarchs combined against the people, and Garibaldi, proscribed, hunted down, sailed for South America.

Still, he knew no despair. "In cases of difficulty or danger," he says, "I have never in all my life been disheartened." His simpler, fresher spirit, unable to adopt the dark, moody plans of Mazzini, resolved by franker means to work for the same great end: the liberty and union of Italy! His voyage to South America was not a flight but a design. Mazzini had taught him that the only hope for freedom in one's own land was to labor for it in all. There were many Italians in South America. These he resolved to organize, and by the hard school of war in strange republics, make them fit to do battle at home. He launched a fishing boat immediately on his arrival at Rio Janeiro, and calling it "The Mazzini," sailed to do battle for the infant republic of Uruguay.

His career here extended over fourteen years, and he has himself written a full history of it, in a style of child-like modesty. He was the most electrical energy of all the South American wars, equally daring and successful on foot, on deck, or on horseback; now shot down at the head of his boarders; now nigh drowning; now galloped over by cavalry; insane with fever; naked and hungry; but all the while, with an eye single to freedom, and he never drew his sword for a doubtful or a personal cause. He was tortured, put in a dungeon, banished, but not a revengeful period, nor a private enmity, appears in his life. Indeed, except upon public grounds, Garibaldi never quarreled with any person. While he thus gave the romance of his young manhood to the South Temperate zones, the broad and breezy nature over which he fought inspired him with feelings beyond the powers of cities to give. "I caught sight of the Pampas," he says, in one place; "for the first time in my life I saw those vast plains, and was thrilled with admiration; wild-horses and cattle were running free and unrestrained, feeding, resting, and racing, at will. My mind was filled with new, sublime, and delightful emotions."

At length Garibaldi found himself the last remaining member of the little band of Italians with whom he had first taken the field. He was lonely, but not weary; and says plaintively of his parents: "I felt the love of them warm in my heart. At last I knew that I must go to Montevideo to see an Italian ship, something that had been within sight of my home." He had no money, and the republic gave him a drove of cattle, numbering nine hundred, to pay his way to Montevideo. He drove them himself two hundred miles, and on the way they nearly all died of hunger and fatigue. He reached the city with a few hides merely. There was no pleasant news from his country, petty despotism being absolute and high-handed everywhere; and with a trustful sadness he turned his face to the forest again. Upon his banished life a new and gentle feeling came at last. He saw a face, and loved it. In the city of Laguna he looked up at a window one day by chance, and met the gaze of a young girl. It made him alter the rule of his life, which was to know no wife but Italy and no children but her sons. He was already beloved by this brave girl; and when he told her that his mission would not permit the quietness of a fireside life, she answered that she could ride and fight at his side. Therefore they were married, and woman won in Anita a place in the fame of Garibaldi. He speaks thus beautifully of their first campaign:

"Among the many sufferings of my stormy life I have not been without happy moments, and among them I count that in which, at the head of a few men remaining to me, I first mounted and commenced my march with my wife at my side, in a career which had always attractions for me, even greater than the Sea's. It seemed to me of little importance that my entire property was that which I carried, and that I was in the service of a poor Republic unable to pay anybody. I had a sabre and a carbine, which I carried on the front of my saddle. My wife was my treasure, and no less fervent in the cause of the people than myself. Whatever might happen, she gave me smiles; and the more wild the extensive and desert American plains appeared, the more beautiful and delightful they seemed to our eyes. I was in a dutiful cause, the good of my fellow-men, and love and freedom made me happy!"

It is sad to follow the brave devotion of this lion-hearted wife. She aimed the guns of his vessel, stood cutlass in hand to repel boarders, charged with the cavalry, deployed with skirmishers, rode down the enemy with lance and lasso, and after the combat, cooked and comforted, leading so a two-fold life. Menotti Garibaldi, her first son, was born at San Simon, Uruguay, on the 10th of September, 1840. His mother fought in an action four days before his birth; and twelve days afterward the party of soldiers with whom she quartered were surprised and nearly all slain, so that she climbed upon a horse with her baby, and galloped into the forest. At this time Garibaldi had gone twenty miles to find food and clothing for the mother and child, swimming two rivers on the way. For three months this future young invader of the Roman territory was carried on horseback by his father, suspended in a handkerchief from Garibaldi's neck, and kept warm with his breath. Wild as this career may have been for a woman, it was like that of the Maids of Orleans and Saragossa. Freedom's necessities and Love's nerved without unsexing her. All her life long she was held in almost superstitious regard; and the boy, whose cradle was on horseback, and whole lullabies were the peals of the cannon, drawing breath from two continents, is, while I write, bearing down upon the last stronghold of Italian tyranny with his father's watchword of "Rome or death!"

Our age is practical and close to define the sphere of woman. Let us who live in this cool northern zone, little advised of the desperate straits of freedom in the south, remember Anna Garibaldi as her countrymen revere her, a chaste and consecrated life to the high devotion of her husband. They have made the broad pampas wonderful with their recollection—the married apostles of freedom, giving a kiss on the brink of battle, then riding down upon the foe. When the victory was won they searched among the fallen for each other. Their bivouacs were full of tender fears; an agony fell into the first flush of every triumph till both were found unharmed. Banished existences, their lonely shadows blended in the blowing grasses that bound the horizons, and in the perfect freedom of the prairies they felt that breadth of distance akin to their destiny, whose motto was: "Where freedom is not there is my country!"
I do not find in all history an episode like theirs: so simple, yet so dramatic; so linked to the world's heart by aims, so far from it by space. They won little reputation, since the great aggregation of men were ignorant of their valor, fighting in the wilderness. The late stormy revolution of Europe absorbed men's minds; and no one saw the common sailor moving with his brood among the long grasses of the new world, almost as savage to the eye as the plunging bulls he startled. But in the vast solitude, troubled only by tyrants, this common man learned all the lessons of primitive democracy: to despise rank and birth, the value of strength and strategy, self-reliance and independence. He stood like some eagle upon a bold mountain beyond the clamor of Europe, gazing into it. His looks developed all the past of Italy: the milestone men to freedom—the Gracchi, Rienzi, Masaniello, Francesco Ferruci.

With his Italian troops he talked, calm and resolute, of all the points of strategy upon the peninsula, and they conquered that azure land for freedom, in all knowledge and in spirit, ten years before a red-cap passed the walls of Rome. Let no tyranny feel ever secure. There are eyes over the oceans. There are swords on the other side of the Earth. Subdue all space ere you have subdued all freedom!

At last Garibaldi resolved to quit America. His practical work had been to make Uruguay a republic and afterward to defend her against ambitious

Buenos Ayres. His prospective work had been to discipline a thousand Italian patriots and imbue them with the love of Italy and freedom. In the spring of 1848 he set sail for Italy with his wife and a part of the Italian legion. Arriving in sight of Nice, his birthplace, the soldier comrade of Garibaldi, Colonel Anzani, worn down with wounds and consumption, asked to be brought on deck to look at the bright land. They set his face toward shore, all purple with mountains. He caught the scent of the groves of fruit, and sighed for joy, and died.

The soldier of South American freedom, after a dozen years of exile, poor as when he departed, was now to plunge from prairie warfare into the political struggle of a dense and elderly civilization. Scarcely known, he made his way to the field of battle in Piedmont and offered his sword to the King of Sardinia. His wife remained with his old mother in Nice.

I must make you see the condition of Italy at this time, or I shall have written in vain.

Italy is a nation of people numbering twenty-four millions, and its territory is just about three times as large as Pennsylvania. You will observe, therefore, that two-thirds of the whole strength of United States is condensed in Italy into a territory no bigger than the State of California.

To make this still plainer, imagine Italy a long Flemish boot, with the top of the leg folded over, such as actors wear sometimes. The fold is Piedmont, Lombardy, and Venice; the leg is mainly Tuscany and Naples; the instep, heel and tie is Naples. This boot is kicking a rock out of the water: the rock is Sicily. All this is but true; for Italy is shaped almost precisely like a boot, and Sicily is an island at the boot-toe.

In this year of 1848 a terrible mutiny raged throughout Europe. France had expelled from her throne that compromising King, Louis Philippe, who sought to consolidate the realm into a family property, and following the successful example of the French, the Italians rose against their thirty tyrants. The great boot pulsed as if Ætna and Vesuvius were belching in it. With servile fear the despots were proposing compromise. All tyranny cried out for order, all freedom said, "Advance!" Mazzini and his fifty thousand carbonari were ubiquitously active. The strong monarchs to the north of the Alps, themselves paralyzed, were unable to march, as they had been wont, down upon the beautiful peninsula and strangle it.

Over this sea-bound country there were three tyrants: in Lombardy, Venice and Tuscany, the Austrian; in Sicily and Naples the Bourbons, a bloody-minded house; in Rome a weak Pope, whose vanity sought to postpone the full development of his tyranny till he might first get some show of popular applause. In the smaller States the spawn of the great royal families ruled.

The spy was unevadible, the dungeon dumb; tortures were practised upon all patriots, speaking or suspected; it was the glut of a reactionary tyranny, full of ingenuities to crush the last hope of mankind. The Christian churchmen, lazily luxurious in their vast untaxed properties, used the holy confessional as a detective police office. Garrisons of mercenaries,—dull, savage Germans, heartless Swiss, the refuse peasants of churchmen and satraps, in uniform, these, to the number of six hundred thousand, were fettered upon Italy. Around the coasts the fleets of all the monarchies of Europe cruised; the sea was prostituted to drown liberty. One monarch only showed a little leaning toward human kindness, Charles Albert, the King of Sardinia. He had been a repelled relative of the grim feudal house of Savoy, and suddenly raised to the throne, exhibited, by turns, a love of the people and a terror of them. Mazzini called him aptly the "Hamlet of Monarchs,"—sad, philosophical, irresolute, honorable. But his subjects were implacable democrats, men of Turin, of Genoa, of Nice, mountaineers and hardy sailors, descendants of the stern and simple Vaudoise, the Swiss of Italy! They rose to arms at the first rumor of the expulsion of Louis Philippe of France; for France and Austria were the two hereditary interveners in the concerns of Italy. Charles Albert driven to his palace, his Ministers menaced, Europe in confusion,—came out to the leaders of the people in person and asked them the price of order.

"You shall have a liberal constitution," he said.

"No!" was the reply, "we demand more: war with Austria and the word *Italy* on our flag instead of Sardinia."

A generous impulse came to the King, strengthened by an Austrian threat: he answered, "I will sacrifice my crown for the independence of Italy. Raise me an army!"

This was the origin of the connection of the House of Savoy with the popular movement in the peninsula. An army sprang up at once; the King put himself at its head, and they crossed the boundary of Lombardy, the whole able-bodied population of the kingdom.

When Garibaldi set sail for Italy he was accompanied by fifty-six of the Italian legion, and a few Orientals, among them a coal black negro, named Aguyar. They had unitedly hardly enough money to buy a ferry ticket, having declined all offers of land in recompense for their services, but the Republic they had established gave them two cannon and eight hundred muskets, and a brig was chartered by contribution to convey them. Some of these itinerants of liberty even sold their shirts before starting, and had to lie naked in bed for the whole passage.

Clad in a worn red blouse with green and white facings, Garibaldi waited upon King Carlo Alberto at Genoa and asked a command. The King, only half-earnest in the cause, and distrustful of the people, looked ruefully upon this sunburnt and unshorn republican:

"Go to Turin!" he said, haughtily. "See the Minister of War."

The Minister of War said: "You might be useful to us as a *corsair*. Go to Venice and try your luck with a fishing vessel or two. That is all I can do for you."

He disdained to reply to either King or Minister, but hastened to the city of Milan, which had, after a desperate contest with the Austrian garrison, just gained its independence. The Provisional government of Lombardy gave him the title of General, and his prowess in South America being known over all Italy, five thousand young men joined his legion at once. He named it after Anzani, his dead comrade, and a common soldier of it was Joseph Mazzini. It was hard for Garibaldi to get ammunition, rations, or clothes, all the officers being prejudiced against him. They called him a brigand, *sabreur,* a penniless fellow. At last he marched to Bergamo, but the city of Milan capitulated behind him; the King made peace with Austria, and excepted the legion of Garibaldi from the list of his army. That chieftain, hemmed round with Austrians, fell back on Como, proclaimed his King a traitor to Italy, and prepared to continue independent warfare with the invaders. The land was all in despair. Out of the vast plain of Lombardy a wail like its vapors climbed up the Alps. Milan that had so nobly manned her barricades, fighting from house to house, her women and her girls in arms beside their children and sweethearts, awoke to find the army of the King outflanked, and the Austrian eagle soaring over the magnificent cathedral. In all the North of Italy but two men stood in arms, Daniel Manin in Venice and Joseph Garibaldi in Lombardy. Against them, beleaguered, Haynau and Radetzky proclaimed no quarter. Garibaldi used all burning eloquence to inspire his men, but they fell away in despair, and at last he was left with but four hundred. While the whole army of Piedmont was retreating back to Turin, this little band marched against the Austrians. All the world looked at them as at madmen or martyrs. Their General formed them across the bold country of blue lakes and Alpine spurs that divides Italy from Switzerland. A quick military eye directed every movement. If beaten, he could retire to a neutral country, and so flanked by the lakes Como, Varese, and Maggiore, he advanced and struck sharp, bloody blows at Lerino, Varese, Ligumo, and Merazzene, his little expatriated band in every case outnumbered five to one. He himself had a burning fever, but on his horse, a central figure in every combat, he fought seven days from dawn to night, till at last twenty thousand Austrians in three columns marched upon him. They hoped to cut him off from Switzerland and Piedmont, and drive him into the deep lake of Lugano. All the Swiss mountains were full of spectators to see this strange being at war with the empire of Austria. Through the gloom of Lombardy nothing flashed but his individual sword. Twenty-five millions of weeping men looked through their tears and saw no Italy left but Garibaldi. He hoped by his example to call all these to arms. It was in vain. Bruised, bullet-rent, a wild-eyed starveling, he did not give up the field till quite deserted; then, alone, by a rugged path, he walked by night into Switzerland, where the government refused to demand his sword. In three months he had won a name wide as Europe, and given the only lustre to the last despair of the war.

The object of Garibaldi, in encouraging the people to rise, had been in vain. Tuscany was a republic; Sicily did not expire without another struggle. The Roman state was altogether free, and for the first time since Rienzi the terms of liberty, toleration, open justice, and frank speech were patent in the Eternal city. The States of the Roman Church, accumulated out of the dying piety of tyrants, or the generous treaties of confederate monarchs, had been for two years under the sway of Pope Pius the Ninth, a weak prelate, with some love of applause, and when the ferment among the people began in 1848, this Pope alternately banned and blessed his countrymen, granted a few reforms, and then discovered that the love of freedom is an eternal hunger. The Roman people swept over the Pope like a cage of lions, loosened, past a boy who would feed them with crumbs! He fled to Gaeta and in the solemn capital of the republic which had lived before the birth of Christ, new Rome assembled her elected delegates, made three triumvirs, of whom was Mazzini, and while the causes of the people were falling all round them, the National Assembly sat solemnly in the hearing of cannons and excommunications to draft a constitution. "Romans," they said, "for many years the Pope has lost the power to love and bless. Excited for a moment by the immense spectacle of the resurrection of a people, Pius IX, two years ago, murmured a benediction to Italy, and that accent of love sounded so new and unusual on the lips of a Pope that all Europe imagined a second era for the papacy, and became intoxicated with enthusiasm, ignorant of the history of past ages respecting him who had pronounced it. Italians! you are not a race born to be slaves of the Pope or of the Austrian whip; you are twenty-six millions of people, created free, equal, brethren; all children of God and servants of nothing but his law."

These were the words of neither atheists nor protestants, for it is convenient to stigmatize our enemies by these names. Through what wrongs had the superstition of a Roman people graduated to utter them? The Catholic Church arose against the Catholic churchmen, and the head of these, himself an Italian, was cheering the French, Swiss, Austrian, and Neapolitan mercenaries, who marched down upon his countrymen. Mankind had found that love of country and the claims of Pontiffs were irreconcilable. To all who prayed that Italy might be happy and man free, the Pope had shut the ear of God. It is remarkable that at this impious spectacle the nation of Italy did not plunge into excesses of unbelief. On the contrary, every mother made her prayer as before; no church was spoiled in any village; the worshipers only arose and set aside a clerical traitor, and like men about to die, asked absolution of God in the name of freedom.

The reaction had come over the face of the world. France had fallen into the hands of Louis Napoleon, a perjured adventurer, and he was stifling, banishing, and speciously lying as he has continued to do ever since. While Austria bombarded Venice, it was meet that he should throttle Rome; for those two cities were reminders of two glorious episodes, ancient republicanism and feudal republicanism. Rome drove her Tarquins out while Europe was yet a baby; Venice, saved out of the sack of Rome, lay nursing freedom in her blue lagoon, till Garibaldi should be born to restore freedom to Rome again.

Garibaldi rode out of Ravenna, from the tomb of Dante, in the cold month of January, and crossed the Rubicon as Cæsar had done two thousand years before. His companions were Colonel Medici, Nino Bexio, his ordnance officer, Captain Sacchi, and Aguyar his negro, with a little lame dog, wounded in an American battle. He had been elected a delegate to the Roman Assembly. A strange procession it was, bound on an eventful errand. America marching on Rome with less than John Brown's pikemen that marched on slavery. A tamer of wild horses, his herdmen, and a coal black African! The Goths and Vandals showed no such picture, nor Hannibal floating down from the clouds on the back of his elephant. Their lassoes were tied to their Buenos Ayres saddles; they wore the red blouse faced with white and green, and under their broad *sombreros* floated their sunburnt beards. Garibaldi was swollen with rheumatism and could not get on his boot. They climbed into the Appenines by a bridle path, dogged all the way by Bourbon spies and the retainers of fat convents. Wild winter roses grew in the sight of snow; the lemon trees, as all year round, hung full of golden fruit on the slopes of villa-gardens. The sunsets looked wonderingly at them, going down in a softer west than they had ever known, and on the promontories reeled to decay, with a grinning defiance, the castles of feudal slavery, dark as their bloody age, in which all hereditary rank is lost. In the ruins of Etruscan walls they cooked the sheep they had purchased, and early in the saddle threaded gorges where Titanic nature had made the mid-day terrible as night. The flag they carried was the tri-color; its bright dyes stained the crystal pools of mountain torrents, and flashed along the margins of lakes where ignorance only had traced its stolid shadow. At last they burst from a peak-top upon the valley of the Tiber where the dense populace lay in the early breaths of freedom, laughing like their vineyards. Far off the purple mountains curtained Rome. They looked almost in tears to feel the glory and the shame that had been crowned there. Winding down into the broad campagna they seemed to feel that nature had already prepared them in a similar land to figure on these historic pampas. For, soft as the Sabine mountains the Andes had looked down on them, and like the buffaloes of the Parana roamed the Roman bulls. They felt their pulses leap to believe that perhaps they were the consecrated pioneers of democracy, moving on Rome with the banner of our century. No thoughts or conquest fell in those simple hearts, great to refuse as to conquer a crown. Crusaders from the land of Columbus they saw the historic Jerusalem basking on her hills with the crown of St. Peter on his dome. Perhaps in that glimpse the vision of the Apocalypse received its translation:

"And the nations of them which are saved shall walk in the light of it.

"And the gates of it shall not be shut at all by day: for there shall be no night there.

"And they shall bring the glory and honor of the nations into it.

"And there shall in no wise enter into it any thing that defileth, neither whatsoever worketh abomination, or maketh a lie."

It was on the 28th of April that they passed the city gates, where the commander of the French, General Oudinot, had already demanded admission and been refused. The people were in the first doubt of resistance; the Triumvirate had been ordered by the Assembly to meet force with force; they had mounted the walls with cannon and armed boys and greybeards; suddenly Garibaldi appeared at the head of his troops, and he rode down the *Corso* to the capital with flowers strewn in his way, and the Eternal city ringing with *vivas*: "Hail! Garibaldi! soldier of the people! God's man to men! Welcome to Rome!" All jealousy, all bigotry, all conservatism had in vain decried him as an Adventurer, a Brigand, a mere Cavalryman, a Corsair, a *sabreur,* Anti-Christ; these creatures of conventionality did not know the schooling one gets on the broad prairies of nature, nor what virtue there is in her winds. A diligent scholar of books and men, he was really the only soldier of the age who could fight a fleet, and handle cavalry, artillery and infantry equally well. Avezzana, the Minister of War, made him actual commander but gave another the nominal title. He reviewed his troops in the broad Piazza of the People, all Rome standing round.

And this is a picture of Garibaldi in Rome, written by Gustave de Hoffstiller:

"A man of the middle height, his countenance scorched by the sun, but marked by lines of antique purity. He sat his horse calmly and firmly as if he had been born there; beneath his hat, broad-brimmed, with a narrow loop, and ornamented with a black ostrich feather, was spread a forest of hair. A red beard covered the whole of the lower part of his face. Over his red-shirt was thrown an American *poncho*, white, lined with red like his shirt. His staff wore red blouses. Behind him galloped his groom, a vigorous negro who had followed him from America; he was dressed in a black cloak, and bore a lance, with a red *banderolle*. All who came with him from America wore pistols and poniards of a fine workmanship in their belts, and carried whips of buffalo skin in their hands."

The army of defence of Rome consisted of 1,650 regular troops, including the South Americans, and the militia of the city was fourteen thousand strong. The population within the walls, all told, was one hundred and fifty thousand. To these thirty thousand Frenchmen were opposed; from the South twenty thousand Neapolitans were advancing; from the North thirty thousand Austrians were coming down. The claims of these three monarchies were different, their designs were the same: to shackle Italy again and plunder it, and to silence Liberty. Not France, but Louis Napoleon, was the real invader. Rome had not been attacked by a foreign army since the days of the Reformation, under Charles V., and but once since the time of the Barbarians. Against the Pope Louis Napoleon had first made battle, a private soldier, before his days of destiny had come, and now he was President of France, the real ally of Rome, using Republican troops to subdue a republic. By what right France assumed to forbid Italians from assisting an Italian city when her own whole history down to to-day is a constant interference in the politics of Italy is plain only to that astute Emperor, who can prove by his spies that France is free, and show by a row of new houses that his usurpation is just. Well did he write the life of Caesar, who also crossed the Rubicon to expel the Roman Senate. His inglorious bombardment of Rome will rank with the sack of many a city by many a bandit forgotten but for his lusts.

The city of Rome on the 30th day of April, 1849, was a wonderful instance of the revolutionary soul beating beneath feudal armor. The turbid Tiber, with frequent grimy bridges dividing the city unequally, leaves upon the north the Vatican and Saint Peter's, on the South the capital. The settled city lies all in a dense huddle, with towers, and battlements, and monuments overhanging it, not much beyond a mile square; and without this is a rolling plain spotted with mighty ancient ruins and beautiful modern villas, the whole enclosed by a Roman wall, crowned with towers and pierced with gates. At the north of the city this wall comes boldly up to the town, almost to the shadow of the Pope's palace and Saint Peter's; in the centre of the city, hanging, on its memorable hill, the Capitol lifts up its one square tower, and in and around the city are other hills, up whose slopes the houses undulate. More than three hundred churches lie in these dense blocks of palaces and dwellings; heathen and Christian architecture lie neighbors; beyond the walls the hard Roman roads go off to the blue and purple mountains, and so do the stately aqueducts stalk on their strong arches to the mountain springs. Outside the walls it is a broad plain, bare or grassy, where a group of houses stands here and there, or a walled-villa lies in its orange groves. But on this day the streets of Rome are spiky and beetling with barricades. The lava pavements lie in heaps; old Roman stones close up the walks; the loop-holed houses are defended by dark-haired women, and on the housetops walk girls and grandmothers ready to unfix the tiles and hurl them down. The tri-color flag waves upon the Capitol. In the open square the citizens stand under arms. The gardens of the Vatican, where the Aurelian wall comes closest, are filled with grim citizen reserves. Upon the dome of Saint Peter's a signal flag is waving; steady in the midst of the resolved town, like the conscript fathers of old, the republican Assembly calmly debates the Constitution. All the republican intelligence of Italy is there, save that which holds Venice against the Austrians, and of this Congress fully one-half the members were born Gentlemen and Noblemen in the conservative sense. Yonder the triumvirs sit: Armelini, Mazzini, Saffi. Receiving his instructions, Avezzana, the Minister of War, leans upon his scabbard. Beside him are Carnesuchi, Cattabeni, and Caldesi, the Committee on barricades, warm with grave toil. In the midst, presiding, is the face of Allocaletti, his grey hairs like the ashes upon a burning coal.

Without, standing among the people infrequently, are a few valorous priests, musket in hand, fighting for the Republic. The girls of the Campagna carry water to the men, clad in their rich head-dresses; and gigantic Roman peasants, with untanned sheep skins wrapped about them, heightened by their peaked hats, man the defiling batteries. A winkful of this scene is worth more to freedom than all the processions of the Church. At early day the roll of drums hastens the muster of men. All the boys from the schools are under arms. The French are seen defiling across the plain, coming from Civita Vecchia, the port of Rome. Now batteries upon the walls and in towers play upon them. They deploy across the plain, eight thousand strong, a full *corps d'armee*—twelve pieces of cannon divided between their wings—the divine and the evil principles are at war beneath the Aurelian walls! Garibaldi commanded on the Italian left, the Colonel Masi on the right, the reserves were in the public squares under Savini, Manara, Galletti. Garibaldi began the battle, issuing orders from a tower, attacking the French in flank and doubling them up like a cramp masqued in a whirlwind. They had been divided into two columns, one marching upon the Vatican, the other upon the Gate San Pancrazio; it was the latter that Garibaldi demoralized, as it deployed, by sending shells into it rapidly. The reformed French line of battle was beautiful, and it advanced with a shout, the greyish-blue uniforms of the Chasseurs and the red breeches of the line mingled. The Roman music played the *Marsellaise*, more worthy of that song than the countrymen of its author, and over their infantry the French artillery, excellently served, dismounting some guns upon the bastions, enabled the foot to creep into the protection of the high walls. Then Garibaldi mounted his horse and with the tigers of Montevideo, darting out of the gate, charged bayonets upon the lions of Algiers. It was the first time that an American column had ever fought upon the soil of Europe, and they engaged picked regiments of France. The people peeping from the walls ceased to fire, and Rome looked down upon the soldiers of the pampas parrying cold steel. Such Italians the French had never found. In individual combat, thrusting and wrestling, the short rolling oaths of the French and the cries of the graver Latins mingled as they measured strength and suppleness. Their feet were on the Christian catacombs. Five centuries of Gallic arrogance gave the invaders confidence, the Italians hate. Above them all, likened by Dumas to a statue of brass, the streaming hairs of Garibaldi, sabre in hand, rode the field, like old Marcus Aurelius galloped down from his pedestal on the Capitoline Hill. At sight of him old Roman men recalled the exploits of their immortal ancestors. No Napoleon calmly following his ten thousands with the field-glass, but personally in the front, like the young general of Lodi, dealing bronze-armed blows that killed when they touched! The light French infantry saw the Southern Bayard, and a fear fell into their hearts. For four hours the swaying combatants interlapped, the artillery meanwhile dumbly poised and almost sentient, staring blackly down; they cut the French column in two, flung back its left in panic into the open country and penned the right into a house and garden where they laid down their arms with their Lieutenant-Colonel at their head, three hundred prisoners of war. Meanwhile, behind the Vatican, where they had crept through vineyards and behind walls, the other French column debouched into the sunlight, and at the first flash of their bayonets the old Vatican roared down a palpable thunder. The artillery of the Castle of Saint Angelo raked them down by dozens. In their rear, from the fortified hill of Monte Mario, riflemen picked them off. They ran into the summer houses, among the olive trees, and surrendered separately. All this the General Oudinot beheld, far off, and his hope of an easy victory expired when the fugitive Chasseurs fled to his feet.

He had no cavalry. His troops had pushed so far that it was doubtful they could return to Civita Vecchia.

Garibaldi sent a courier to Avezzana: "Send me one regiment and the French shall never regain their vessels!"

But Mazzini advised to the contrary. "France," he said, "opposes this expedition of Napoleon. Let us not excite the national pride by a complete defeat."

The battle had lasted ten hours. At its close the French were in full retreat. One prisoner only they carried off with them. Fifteen hundred of his men prisoners and dead, made Oudinot wonder if the ghost of Camillus had not repulsed the Gauls again from the walls of Rome.

"People!" proclaimed the government, "yesterday commenced the entrance of the French into Rome. They entered by the Porta San Pancrazio to the number of five hundred—as prisoners!"

That night the ancient city was illuminated. Bands of music played in every square. Garibaldi was alert all night, preparing to pass the walls at dawn and attack the enemy on the open plains. At four o'clock he was under way with twelve hundred infantry and a hundred dragoons. He attacked fiercely five miles from Rome. In the first glow of the battle the French general sent a flag of truce for an armistice. The Triumvirs accepted it, and they granted a cessation of hostilities for forty days.

The news of this event thrilled Italy and astonished Europe. Legitimacy looked aghast. The Pope in Gaeta upbraided Antonelli, his Jesuit Minister, and refused to be comforted. Venice heard the story, and the eyes of her people, stricken of the plague, brightened as they expired.

Debarred from attacking the French, Garibaldi resolved to sally from Rome and engage the twenty thousand Neapolitans who were advancing through the southern mountains. He took with him four thousand men. As he emerged from the city the whole population were assembled. Every habit and incident of his life were now subjects of interest. Not in vain had he learned the art of war in a far wild land; for every energetic probation is eventual success. But this man had more than "parts:" he had honesty, sincerity, and devotion. A great unconscious actor, he had no dramatic intents. A man, loving the open air and despising war as a profession, he saw that the history of mankind's progress was written with the inevitable sword. They looked upon him as a human St. Michael, long lost among the free savages of the West, and seeing how his men lassoed their nags, slaughtered their steers by the ruined fountains of the Roman emperors, rode bareback, went on far fearless scouts, reckoned death an incident and not a climax, a superstition arose in their souls: the church believed in its saints; why not the republic?

The surprise column, marching in the fresh, brilliant night encamped the second evening beyond the mountain of Tivoli, where Zenobia had dwelt, in the solemn ruins of the villa of Adrian.

It was a fortress, and in its subterranean chambers they laid down to sleep to the sentry-cry of the owls, droning a long "all's well!" The fourth day they entered the city of Palestrina, and the sixth day, at noon, espied the Neapolitan army advancing in line of battle. To the notes of the trumpet the little army of Rome deployed. A volley on either flank; a general advance along the whole front with the bayonet, and the troops of Bomba wheeled and fled, leaving a hundred dead on the field. Their trembling prisoners were laden down with images, relics, and amulets. Garibaldi smiled upon them sadly. Next day he pushed ten miles further south. Without cavalry to pursue, it was impossible to overtake the pale-hearted tyrant of Naples. Two nights they quartered in an Augustin convent, where a ludicrous scene ensued, of soldiers robed in Dominican hats and long white robes, patroling with long wax candles, and reading aloud the private correspondence of the monks, much of which made even these *sabreurs* blush.

A second expedition, fifty miles from Rome, engaged the bulk of the army of Naples at Velletri, with nineteen hundred soldiers of Italy. The only doubtful part of the battle was a charge of five hundred royalists. Garibaldi, with sixty horse, dashed down upon them midway. The concussion unhorsed the General and flung him headlong ten paces; he arose and cleared a space around him with his sabre, while his trained stallion walked to his side. His troops thought him dead, till he waved his hat upon his sword, and then their acclamations were full of joy. The gallant Bersaglieri of Lombardy, their black feathers floating in the wind, every man a nobleman's son, arrived in the pitch of peril. The rear guard opened to let them pass; they defiled by the sound of the trumpet.

"*Vivent les Bersaglieri!*" burst from every mouth.

"*Vive Garibaldi!*" was the answer of Lombardy.

In a moment the enemy, driven from position to position, fled within the walls of Velletri, and next day were flying to Naples. Garibaldi entered Rome in a triumph like the old conquerors. The army of Naples never reappeared, and that of Spain, five thousand strong, hearing of this prowess, never dared come to battle.

The President of France at last compelled the friends of Rome in the National legislature to fly to England. Then his General, the Duke Oudinot, gave notice that the French armistice would conclude on the 4th of June. Under this agreement Oudinot dishonorably surprised the Roman out-works the night of June 2nd, poniarded the sentries and occupied a strong mansion called the Villa Corsini, close to the city walls, and set upon a commanding hill. Twenty thousand men made this surprise; Garibaldi had four thousand.

The battle for the recovery of this place was more desperate than we had ever fought before Petersburg or Fredericksburg. The villa stood upon terraces; the lawn before it, full of busts, statues, summer-houses, hedges and clumps of trees, was enclosed by strong walls that converged to one massive gate, on which cannon and muskets concentrated a murderous and incessant fire. With his white poncho and plumed hat rendering him a target, Garibaldi led the Italian legion and the Bersaglieri at a charge through the gateway and up the broad walk. From every marble effigy a death's head aimed; the orange trees dropped shells; every belvedere was full of French tirailleurs; the great villa seemed a volcano, belching fire. His cloak and hat riddled with balls, he leaped the terraces, waving his sword, and cried, "Surrender!" From the great stairways, and the luxurious saloons the reply came like an earthquake. He was alone with a handful, and the flower of Italy lay dead in the garden walks. Beaten back to the gate the trumpet sounded again; again the lawn and terraces were filled with dead. The third charge saw him on the stairs, immortal but alone. Now the Lombard legion advanced, with Henry Dandalo at its head, to give one hour of that blind old Doge, his ancestor. To the sound of eight trumpets these two divisions climbed the stairs; every officer was slain at the cannon's mouth. Thrice again the assault was made, against fresh French reserves, each time a march into a vault. Now Garibaldi mounted at the head of his lancers, infantry behind him; the dying in the gardens saw in the broad daylight his waving plume darken up the path, and cheered him as he galloped. He spurred to the marble stairs and ascending them, wheeled on the landing place, like an equestrian statue in apotheosis, and flourished his sabre. A fusillade rang out, and horse and rider reeled and disappeared. He was up again, and on foot, in time to lead the infantry, bayonet in hand; they cleared the long saloons, swept the halls, drove the French over the balustrades and out of the windows; all bloody and gasping while they stopped for breath, a French reserve flowed in like a deluge; there were no men left to continue the assault. A thousand men had been slain outright, one hundred of them officers, and of these were the noble names of Masina, Dandolo, Daverio, and Scoriani.

The failure to retake the Villa Corsini sealed the fate of Rome. "From the moment an army of forty thousand men, having thirty-six pieces of seige cannon, can perform their works of approach," said Garibaldi, "the taking of a city is nothing but a question of time. It must fall one day or other; the only hope it has left is to fall gloriously."

He established his quarters within half carbine shot of the French tirailleurs, in an ancient casino. The walls were strengthened with inner works; Gavazzi and Bixio, the two eloquent priests of freedom, went through the city and the provinces preaching a stern resistance; the ladies gave their ear-rings to buy arms. The grand old city, standing alone against two-thirds of Europe, contained within it as much genius as Florence when under Ferruci, and the great engineer, Michael Angelo, she made a defense that was the climax of her glories. On the night of the 4th of June the trenches were opened three hundred yards from the walls, and two siege batteries began to batter the city. Shells and shot rained into the precious galleries; nothing was respected of the past nor the future. On the 10th of June, Garibaldi made a sally with half his command. An accident discharged some of the muskets of his own men, and in the panic of the darkness that ensued, Garibaldi, with his gaucho whip struck left and right to stem the tide of retreat. It was too late; the French were already under arms. Time after time the Romans sprang counter-approaches against the French parallels and engaged in bloody combats on the enemy's parapets. The fire of the invaders made havoc in the city. In the midst of the unceasing hurricane, Anita, the wife of Garibaldi, slipped through the French lines and joined her husband in the city. At the moment he was condemning to death a Neapolitan spy. As he pressed her to his heart she asked that the man's life be spared. The example was needful for the good of Rome; her request was in vain; the man was shot. By the thirteenth of June, seven batteries made breaches in the walls; the French dared not assault. On the twenty-first they had cleared a space with cannon into which an army might be marched. Through this Garibaldi resolved to make the last desperate assault. At dawn next day the tocsin sounded. Boys, students, monks, veterans, peasants were under arms and impatient to be led. The French beheld them grimly embattled, and refusing to repel their forlorn charge, withdrew to their flanking batteries. For three days more bombs poured into every quarter of Rome, striking the Capitol, the Pantheon, the Colosseum. Mothers fled from their falling houses clasping their babes, but not a voice in the Eternal city cried "surrender." As every shell burst in the streets, the people cried jeeringly: "A benediction from the Pope." Till the 28th the Italian cannons conducted a marvellous defence. For two days the troops of the line worked the guns, not an artillerist being left alive. The town was choked with mutilated men. On the evening of the 29th the last gun was dismounted. It was the festival of Saint Peter. Rome was all illuminated. The cupola of the Vatican was hung with colored lanterns; the Corso was an aisle of fire; up the slopes of the Capitol flambeaux flashed; the winding Tiber was lurid with the glow of Christian rejoicing, while all the while from the hills without the walls, where the flags of France and the Pope floated together, iron rockets trailed against the sky, and by their explosion the banner of the republic was seen spread upon the tower of the Capitol, within which sat the grave of death. At midnight, from three quarters of the city, three cannons gave the signal for the last struggle. The breaches were full of French. Garibaldi, resolving to be killed, led the remnant of the army of Rome. Singing the national song, the devoted Republicans, debouching through all the narrow streets, marched by the light of the enemy's bursting bombs upon the mouths of the cannon. The Jews in the Ghetto looked out on them and trembled; the nuns from convent windows peeped and grew pallid, half praying in their hearts that Italy might live for such devotion; the wounded heard their singing, and wished to die twice in such companionship. Like the fall of armor, like the toppling down of St. Peter's, like the mountains tumbling, the defenders of Rome threw themselves into the breaches, and by the flash of pistols, magnified upon the crossing bayonets, you could almost see the Angel and Apollyon contending over head. Two soft languages blended in the word "murder;" two brave kindred races immolated that a Pope might have a throne; two principles wrestling with death for arbiter, and Rome, the mother of nations, standing darkly back, looking through the wrinkles of centuries upon the valor she inspired: This was the battle!

Everywhere, anywhere, so that he might die, Garibaldi sought an enemy.

Says Vecchi, the historian, himself present: "Garibaldi that night was greater than I had ever seen, greater than any body had ever seen him. His sword was like lightning: every man he struck fell dead. The blood of a new adversary washed off the blood of him who had just fallen. I trembled in expectation of seeing him fall, from one instant to another; but no! he remained as erect as destiny."

Here, almost at his side, the negro Agayar, holding his horse, was struck by a ball and fell dead. "I lost much more than a servant," said Garibaldi, "I lost a friend!"

In this wild rage of interlocked despair, their feet amongst the corpses, their souls only conscious, Lombard and Sicilian, Savoyard and Venitian, Tuscan and Roman, hacked and parried, with bleeding faces and garments rent, crying, as they separately perished: "Life to Italy!" "Garibaldi! *Morituri te Salutant!*" You could hear the yell of the French *chasseurs*, like the wild beasts of the arena, munching Christian bones. You could hear the huzzas around the crosses of the martyrs. At dawn the awful combat slackened. Mazzini, standing up in the assembly, related the story of the night. They sent for Garibaldi.

When he appeared at the door of the chamber all the deputies arose and applauded. He was covered with blood. His clothes were pierced with balls and bayonet thrusts; his sabre was so bent that it would not enter its sheath halfway.

"To the Tribune! to the Tribune!" they cried.

He mounted it, mild and beautiful as a saint condemned.

"Defence is henceforth a waste of Italian life," he said, "unless we are resolved to make Rome another Saragossa. I will withdraw with my brave men to the mountains that Rome may not be sacked, leaving the glories and monuments of art intact till a better day shall come."

In tears they proclaimed their decree:

The Roman Republic: In the name of God and the people! The Roman Constituent Assembly discontinues a defence which has become impossible. It has its post.

On the 2nd of July, after sixty-five days of heroic defence, Garibaldi assembled his troops in the square before Saint Peter's. He advanced into the centre of them and announced his plan of warfare in the Marshes and Provinces.

"In recompense for the love you may show your country," he said, "I offer you hunger, thirst, cold, war and death; who accepts these terms let him follow me!"

Amidst weeping and wailing the little army defiled through the Tivoli gate. It was their hope to cross Italy, embark upon the Adriatic, and go the relief of Venice. Sherman's march to the sea was not more skilful. French were in their rear, Austrians before. Eighty thousand men hemmed them round. Fighting at St. Angelo, at Orvieto, at San Marino, they evaded every ambush; at last their gallantry provoked from the Austrian offers of amnesty. Garibaldi and two hundred and ninety of his men, among them the renowned republic priest Nino Bixio, refused it, and pushed from San Marino to the Adriatic.

It was at the little seaport of Cesenantico that the troops found boats to sail for Venice. All night they toiled on the beach, getting the barges afloat, filling and provisioning them, while poor sick Anita, whose life had been a man's toil, and a woman's many childbirths, sat upon a rock wearily waiting, with death in her eyes. At dawn they all got afloat, and turned their bows for Venice. Still holding bravely out against siege, pestilence and famine, she had survived the fall of Rome, it seemed meet that she should, in the future day, anticipate that capital's deliverance, so that Rome might lie in the mire till the last, trailed over by serpents, when in the sight of mankind this stalwart architect shall lift her on his sword to be the Keystone of Italy.

Very soon a storm arose and scattered the flotilla, wrecking some of the boats. Three cruisers appeared bearing the Austrian flag, and they sank many barges with grapeshot, driving others ashore to the foot of the mountains, and worrying them with shells. In the boat with Garibaldi were Hugo Bassi, once a priest, and always a comrade of the chieftain, Ciceronacchio, and his two sons, and the dying wife of the hunted soldier. She was quite cold and lost in mind, murmuring now of battle, and now of her children, while Garibaldi holding her on his lap, pulled with a breaking heart for the shore, shot playing about his head, water from the enemy's shell bathing the brow of his wife. With all steam up the Austrian bore down upon the dying minutes of this poor loving woman, the flag of "our dear son in Jesus Christ, Francis Joseph," flying at the maintop and marksmen in the shrouds and rigging drawing sight upon the red breeches of Bassi. The artillery of an absolute monarch, never so fitly employed, was concentrated upon these five refugees. Agony covered the face of the great soldier. His bruises and wounds were all forgotten; for he saw the grey hand of death laid on the temples he had kissed, and laying down the paddle at last, he took the chilled head into his arms and called it every name of endearment. They glided into the shore, still howled at from behind by the ashamed iron, and then Garibaldi with the helpless form across his shoulders, plunged up the bed of a torrent and faced for the mountain. Few of his party even reached Venice ere she fell. I spoke to one of them the day she yielded her huzzaing gates to the King of Italy, and he said: "I do not see anything beautiful; Garibaldi has not come!" After a whole day of wretchedness, without any thing to eat, with Anita delirious, uttering sighs that stabbed him, Garibaldi laid her down to die at dusk, Hugo and the rest gathering around full of misery and sympathy. The stricken soldier knelt beside her and made a prayer to the one God who orders all things well. Tears fell upon his beard; they groaned to see him in this agony. Suddenly a farm house was seen by them, as if mercy had answered Garibaldi's cry. He tottered towards it with the body, while, meantime, prowling figures were seen in ambush, waiting to bind and sell them. A Bolognese farmer came out from the old house, and his sons pleaded with him to receive the dying Amazon. While they deliberated, cries and rifle shots were heard approaching. Anita opened her eyes and said:

"Giuseppe, fly!"

"Never!" he answered hoarsely.

"I am dying," she murmured, "but you must live for our children."

"I must die with my love," he sobbed.

Once more she spoke with difficulty, her face hardening into the lines that never melt but to the worm, and her wish had therefore all the power of a dying adjuration:

"Live for Italy!"

He burst into tears. His friend Hugo carried her into the house. "Countrymen," he said, "keep this wife of General Garibaldi, if you ever loved your own!"

They all turned pale. There was a price on the head of Garibaldi, his wife, and his friends.

"I will guard this woman's body with mine!" said the Bolognese. Basso looked again into Anita's face: "Here is one who will spare you the trouble, farmer!" he said; "it is death!"

They called Garibaldi. He lifted the poor brave soul into his arms, and drank her last breath into a kiss.

They buried her in a field, all swearing to keep her rest a sacred secret, and in the night they hurried away, the country lusting for the price of their blood.

The last good-by of Basso to Garibaldi was to say: "General! my red breeches will make you discovered. Save your life for Italy."

Within twelve hours Basso was hunted down and dragged to Bologna. The Pope's friend, and afterwards Legate to the United States, the infamous Bedini, ordered him to be "desecrated" before execution because he had once been a priest, and he was flayed in the head and hands. All bleeding with these wounds, the soldier of two worlds was marched to execution. Ciceronacchio and his boys were chased into a swamp and murdered. A priest discovering where Anita had died, informed upon the farmer, and all his family barely escaped being fusiladed. A lonely man, the country up against him, Garibaldi walked on foot by night a hundred miles across the peninsula of Italy, barefooted at last, and almost naked, cursed of the church, his motives and the purity of his life libelled, his name an unholy one, the soul of his wife excommunicated as her love had been slandered.

> "I tell thee churlish priest,
> A ministering angel shall my sister be,
> When thou liest howling!"

The death of Anita will be in that coming age of freedom, when we shall not look for heroines at the feet of thrones, the beloved episode of womankind. Perhaps the church will think its hatred over, and canonize her as it has hated most of the saints we know best. But Garibaldi has canonized Anita already. He has written her life in his simple, truthful periods, saying of her death scene.

"Soil of generous men! press lightly on the grave of the brave daughter of America. God, protector of the innocent, preserve the children of the Martyr and the Proscript! And my sons, when you are asked where are your parents? say: We are orphans for Italy."

How paltry to this lost month of the Mountain hunter, are the incidents of savage Marius hiding at Carthage, or Napoleon raging on his rock in the ocean. Some weep with Marie Antoinette climbing the scaffold stairs; her life in all its acts had not the devotion of one pulse of Anita, and her husband, though made a saint, was not fit to walk in Garibaldi's shadow. He lived literally with beasts, and the wild brigands in their caves gave him meat and drink. Emerging upon the coast of Piedmont, he found that the King, Carlo Alberto, had abdicated on the field of battle to save some shadow of a crown for his son, and his son, King Victor Emmanuel, banished Garibaldi from his realm. He sailed to Algiers, then to New York, cheerfully waiting for Freedom's good time.

In New York he was treated with distinction, but the Press, timid of giving offence to the catholic clergy—a class of men that to my experience, read the newspapers less, and influence them more than any other in America,—gave him little encomium. Boarding awhile with Signor Pastacaldi in Irving place, he moved to his friend Meucci's, on Staten Island. Meucci was clever and poor. Garibaldi, the successor Rienzi, moulded candles three years for his bread, setting democracy its cardinal examples. Meucci had a hard struggle to get along, and Garibaldi sailed as captain of a ship at last to San Francisco. Some years he kept at sea, nourishing his dreams of freedom yet, and hearing that amnesty had been proclaimed in Sardinia, he departed for Nice in time to see his mother die, and for her virtues and his valor all the city followed her body by torchlight to the grave. She had given birth to him in the same house and the same chamber where Marshal Massena was born. Italy has named this sailor's wife its Mary Washington.

Dwelling with his three children in beloved retirement at Nice, Garibaldi appeared no more till 1859. Meantime Louis Napoleon had overthrown the republic of France, and pursuing a crooked policy with Italy, seemed to reserve that unhappy land for a theatre on which to play his melodramas. Having married his cousin to King Victor Emmanuel's daughter, and an uneasy lull having occurred in his own dominions, he suddenly resolved to make some martial show against the Austrians that he might conciliate the republic sentiment of Europe and redeem some of his promise that he was only an elective monarch, ruling in behalf of progress and the people. The Austrians, in 1859, ordered Victor Emmanuel tersely to disarm. Cavour, his Prime Minister, had long been seeking an alliance between Italy and France; at the moment of the Austrian menace this was accomplished. When the Austrians moved toward Turin they found themselves opposed not only to Sardinia, but to France. Then they called upon the same Garibaldi they had rejected eleven years before. The people everywhere compelled the King to give him a command. He led the left wing of the grand allied army, his soldiers being named "the Hunters of the Alps." Napoleon was the General-in-Chief. He promised never to relinquish the cause of Italy till she were made free from the Alps to the Adriatic. At this oath the glorious peninsula felt a glow of gratitude, forgiveness, and valor. The broad army of Italian unity extended across the country, a hundred and fifty thousand strong; they were met by as many Austrians commanded by the Count Giulay. In quick succession occurred the great battles of Magenta and Solferino.

What was Magenta? An all-day battle fought by the Austrian Giulay, with 150,000 men to save the city of Milan by defending the passage of the Tessino River. Twelve thousand men were killed or wounded in it. Next day Milan was evacuated.

What was Solferino? A line of battle fifteen miles long, foolishly delivered by the Emperor of Austria and Benedek, his General, in front of the river Mincio, outside of the "Quadrilateral." Four hundred thousand men were engaged. Thirty thousand were killed and wounded. The Austrians retired to their fortresses in the angle of the Quadrilateral. At these victories Italy felt a thrill of joy such as Europe had not known since the French revolution. Venice extended her arms. Rome was in revolt. Praises and prayers for Napoleon ascended from twenty-six millions of people.

In both these battles Garibaldi fought like a lion. He swept the mountain slopes like a uniform avalanche along all the Alps. His personal stature arose above that of either King. At Varese, Lugano, Bergamo, Como, and Brescia he gained swift victories, his flank of the army always in advance, and the young men flocked to his standard till the Alps were full of red-shirts resistlessly advancing.

In the midst of the joy, like a sentence of death, came word that Napoleon had made peace on the battle-field of Solferino, and on such terms that freedom was dishonored and Italy surrendered. He had broken his oath; satisfied with a laurel and animated by no single principle of sacrifice, he withdrew to Paris to enjoy a little triumph, and curses followed him from every Italian home and tent. To add to his treason, he afterward wrenched from the weak King, in payment for his paltry services, the province of Savoy and the city of Nice, the one the birth-place of the King, the other of Garibaldi. So while Italy—increased by but one city—the kingdom of Sardinia and Lombardy merely, felt all the grief of blasted patriotism, and Lombardy was disconsolate to find herself liberated and not her sisters, a silence of shame fell over the land, succeeded by a fierce cry of "We are betrayed, Oh! King! *Itala fara de se!*"

The oppressed provinces, that had so manfully risen, holding out their hands to Piedmont, saying "King Victor, we entreat thee to receive us for sweet union's sake!" fell to weeping, and shouted with Mazzini, "the league of Kings has failed; now let the league of the peoples begin!"

But one man had no tears. With his young son at his side, a cheerful, hopeful, placid presence, Giuseppe Garibaldi drew his free spirits around him, and silently prepared to declare war in the name of humanity and the people. On the island of Caprera he met, at his simple residence, set upon a rocky hill, in sight of the soft volcanic archipelago, all those fervid youths and grave old men whose hearts were full of yearnings for liberty everywhere. There was Kossuth, the Hungarian, his eloquent voice that went round the world in indignant periods, stilled to calm advice, and he listened to Garibaldi as to a saint of freedom come down from Heaven. Mazzini looked into the beautiful eyes of his disciples, and said; "At best I am John Baptist. Your mind is healthier than mine. In your acts only I am speaking best. Go on!" Absent in the body, the words of Victor Hugo came over the Mediterranean; "Garibaldi, we are growing old and bookish; you have drunk of the waters of perpetual youth. Subject of poesy yet unsung! advance!"

On the 6th of May, 1860, Garibaldi descended from the Villa Spinola, in Genoa, the mansion of one of his intimate literary friends, to the beach within the crescent of the harbor. A thousand and seven men were drawn up in silence; two green lamps, without the lights of the mole, showed where two steamers darkly lay to carry these liberators to Sicily. One after another the boats departed, to muffled oars; the General quitted the shore last, and his few friends, forbidden to cheer, came up and wept and kissed him. With twenty thousand dollars for a military chest, four field pieces, and five thousand muskets, this individual man sailed upon two old steamers, the *Lombardo* and the *Piemonte*, to conquer the kingdom of Naples and Sicily, defended by sixty thousand troops, and numbering six millions of people.

The tyrant of the two Sicilies was Francis II., called "Bomba," because he shelled the cities of his own people—a man whose ingenuities of cruelty almost passed belief. He was a goodly ally of the Church, a personal craven, and the thumb-screw was his Prime Minister. The terror and stench of his acts smote all Europe.

On the night of the 11th of May, while before the low rocky promontory of Marsala, the extreme city of Sicily, a royal fifty-gun frigate and two steam-sloops were cruising, two steamboats flying the flags of Italy and the United States, coming up slowly and gravely, pushed between the hulls of their enemies, and while one got aground, the other landed at the mole. Quietly disembarking, every man went to his place, a mounted figure in a red shirt giving the orders.

And while the people, with trembling joy, saw these dark bodies fall in solid order, and go up at dusk toward the walls of the town, there seemed to stand to some old men too frail for battle, other spectators in the soft Sicilian sunset,—the galaxy of Italy's loving genius, spectrally defined against the sky, smiling through eyes of eternal sadness; the frail stature of Rienzi; Dante's gaunt, grand face; Savonarola, full of burning speech; the gnarled countenance of Michael Angelo, like his rough marble speaking, the toughest republican of them all; Galileo, with the pinch of the rack upon his soul, saying; "it moves at last." These the old men heard with vesper-voices, reaching out their laurels, say: "Brother and Master! march on to victory!" Up the shore, into the town of Marsala, the mild-eyed soldier passed, where Cicero had ruled and Scipio given battle, and where, in the old Cathedral, the battle-flag of Lepanto hung, which gave the ocean to the Christian faith. In solid body, stepping fast and strong, the deliverers passed the city portal; a few shots rang down the narrow winding streets; the populace timidly huzzaing when they saw how few these bold adventurers were, still looked no good to the troops of Bomba, and in the space of a calm thought's birth, the red-shirted skirmish line had flanked the town, shot off the sentries, picketed all the landside, while the main body, at a swinging gait, pressed up the middle of the city, and dropped post-guards at every grim old open piazza. A volley or two completed the surprise. Timid Marsalians stole forth at last, and their *vivas* thrilled the evening. They opened recruiting places at once. To the sound of the Neapolitan men-of-war shelling their empty steamers, the young men of Sicily enrolled their names in the Peoples' Army of Italy, and Garibaldi, quietly issuing orders from an armchair, was told directly that the *Lombardo* and the *Piemonte* had sunk. Like Cortes only in this, that his ships were burnt behind him, Garibaldi, with scarcely that conqueror's army, broke bivouac at midnight and marched to Palermo!

With his "Hunters of the Alps" Garibaldi came up to the troops of the tyrant, commanded by the General Landi, on the fifteenth of May. He was posted along the highest mountainous ridge of that part of Sicily, overlooking the town of Calatafimi, and near the venerable Greek ruin of Segeste. Green mountain downs extended below them, far and bare, wild peaks obtruding on the horizon, and the blue coast, in jagged outlines, looked as if the sea had lifted up to look at what a thousand men could do against a kingdom. Animated by witnesses like theirs, defeat would be a miracle, for round about them the monuments and graves of Saracen, Carthagenian, Roman, Catalonian, Greek and Phoenician lay.

Garibaldi disposed his men with all his calmness, then lit them with all his fire. In an hour he had lost two hundred of his soldiers, but won the victory. Fleeing before him, daggered by their consciences, the mercenary men of Francis hid in the city of Palermo. Curses were their milestones; to Garibaldi every blade of grass arose and freshened.

The olive trees wore a brighter gray to freedom's people; the dry beds of the torrent seemed to fill and overflow with joy when they appeared; the hedges of figs sprang into blossoms; the locust trees wore a glossier foliage. The huzzaing Contadini came out to swell his ranks, wearing sometimes their strange Albanian costumes; and he turned aside the day after the battle and made a flank march over the wild mountains till he appeared at Misilmeri near Palermo on the twenty-sixth of May, only seven miles from the capital of Sicily. At daylight on the twenty-seventh of May, he looked down from the sides of his amphitheatre upon Palermo, lying in its ancient plain, the city of the "Golden Shell," overhung by all beautiful fruits, the grape, the orange, the peach, the olive, the dangling lemon groves. Two hundred thousand of his fellow men lay gasping for freedom within those grimy walls, beneath the perpetual menace of two frowning castles, within whose dungeons the rack was the answer to prayer. Within its mole the royal ships lay with shotted guns; twenty-five thousand soldiers lined the walls; Garibaldi looked and descended. He placed his troops in line of battle before a venerable gate, and led them on himself through a terrible cross-fire; they scaled the walls, picked the sharpshooters out of the towers, dragged down the warm cannons, and charged into the city. From the sea the ships threw shells into Palermo; the people did not heed them, fighting themselves the retreating troops from cellars and housetops, women and girls hurling tiles and stones. At every cool fountain there was a struggle for the barricades; out of every griffin-dominated gate some revengeful citizen took aim; before the noble cathedral there was a tussle of despair with despotism. The red-shirt of the grant liberator was seen in every quarter, at every scene of death. He had lived beyond the knowledge of pain. Before night the ships of war were gone; the people, hoarse with their huzzas of delivery, had demolished the jails and the castles, and hanged upon their wrecks the menials of the despot in sight of the very wretches who but yesterday writhed in the chair of torture.

Now a new ally came upon the scene; to replace his sunken steamers, the *Oregon* and the *Washington*, American vessels, flying the stars and stripes, bore up to Sicily, filled with arms and volunteers from every country. Here were Poles, Hungarians, Americans, Englishmen, French, Swiss, Belgians, anxious to add their lives to the great cause of Italy. These swept on to Milazzo, where there was a seige and assault in which representatives of the whole brotherhood of man engaged. Garibaldi was ridden over by Neapolitan cavalry, but rising with his drawn sword he cut down three men at the head of his skirmishers; over him, contending, his main body charged; they made the gray old town ring with their cries of "Union and Freedom!"

He was soon in Messina, with Sicily behind him emancipated in every part. Here his proclamation spoke to the world:

"Diplomacy has not been able to check me and I positively refuse to compromise with it."

In the ship *Franklin*,—strange name to be on this adventure,—he crossed the straits of Messina and landed on the mainland of Naples. The whole world was ringing with his name. Noblemen and princes sent him gratulations. Authors were in his train, anxious to make fresh records of his triumphs. The people sprang to arms, blessing his face wherever he appeared. The priest Gavazzi carried a bowie-knife, riding in his staff. Dumas, the author, was there, writing as fast as Garibaldi could fight. At Reggio, Cajazzo and Volturno he fought two great actions, making panic in Bomba's capitol, and with all the six millions of this monarch's subjects delivered from the presence of bondage, he rode into the city of Naples on the 7th of September, in advance of his army, preceded by the battle bulletin of "Victory along the whole line." That beautiful city could find no words to thank him. They made him "dictator" almost in worship. The servile pens and rostrums of Europe that had named him an adventurer, hastened to call him the Great General of the age. He was the same man still, a common soldier of freedom, wearing his red shirt. No aspirations of a throne arose in his heart. He gave to Victor Emmanuel all his conquests, saying: "King of Italy, *Re Galantuomo*! rule for the people and by the people!"

Seated beside the king he soon made that formal entry into Naples which was the great pageant of our time, and then retired to the wild island of Caprera, the same simple man that had sailed before the mast, declining riches, rank and title.

The success of this conquest of Southern Italy stimulated the rising of all the populations. At the end of the year 1860, Italy was a united nation in every part, except Venice and Rome. In 1862, Garibaldi resolved that Rome should be delivered, and he marched upon her again. Fettered by cowardly treaties, too selfish or too irresolute to pluck his own while there was chance, Victor Emmanuel resolved to crush Garibaldi, jealous, perhaps, of his fame, and not great enough in mind to appreciate the heroic self-abnegation of that incomparable General. At Aspromonte the troops of the very king he had aggrandized shot Garibaldi in the foot. Rome's destiny was only postponed. The hero lived to serve in the army of the same king in the war of 1866, fighting valiantly as ever in the mountains, till Venice was delivered.

With the delivery of Venice, five millions more were added to free Italy. I was present in that City in October, 1866, when, at the Cathedral of St. Mark, King Victor Emmanuel returned thanks to God.

St. Mark, as the world knows, was the elected patron of the Venitians; they brought his relics home with great pomp from the East, and built for him, upon the model of the Church of St. Sophia at Constantinople, a cathedral in the most elaborate Byzantine architecture. Five cupolas domineer above it; within and without it is covered with huge and beautiful mosaics, many of them nine centuries old, but as fresh in color and as durable as ever, and they cover, unitedly, 40,000 square feet of surface. Five hundred columns of rare serpentine, porphyry, and verd antiques support or ornament this structure; the floors, arches and walls are plentiful with these precious materials; the cupolas and front are faced with pure gold. The exterior, towards which the King advanced with the ecclesiastic, showed one broad, gilded screen pierced with mighty arches, and over the central of these the four bronze horses of St. Mark looked down through the tarnish of 2,000 years. Behind them a second screen arose, labyrinthine with niches, pinnacles, pediments and statues, and over this again, the domes went afar, capped with bulbous Eastern cupolas. No earnestness of description can make visible to you this extraordinary *basilica*, so overloaded with ornament, come down from an architectural age when we searched for builders close to the grave of Christ, and they hurled upon their structures all the gorgeous imagery and materials of the East. It is so grotesque, that its grandeur is not at first apparent; over its splendid adornments the grayness of age has somewhat fallen; but, on this day, young with tri-color robes flung from every pinnacle and angle, crowded above the screen with women's faces and drapery, every perch in its architecture a human statue, glinted with an Autumnal southern sun, and crossed with shadows of green and crimson, the aspect of it, as the procession entered, was reconcilable in no respect with the century in which we live. Pageant and architecture were of remotest feudality. It seemed that some great Crusader was coming back from war, carried along on the thunder of cannon, and bells, and voices, and repairing straightway to the altar in thankfulness for victory. As he disappeared under the deep portal, a silence almost devout fell upon the thousands of faces, and directly they heard the *Te Deum* bursting the doors and trembling up the great square like the escape of birds. In an instant the people in the open air took up the measure, music being intuitive here, and half of Venice followed the great organ and the bands of brass, making such praise that I doubt it has been excelled since the Army of the Cross entered Jerusalem. Up the narrow canals, from house-tops, from shipping in the harbor, the cadences arose, and the daylight was a solemn serenade, where thankfulness and happiness seemed to have improvised the same glorious song out of the perfect accord of half a million. Christ come again could scarce have such a welcome.

Within St. Mark's the scene was softer, darker, stranger. Out of the great nave reached golden-groined arches; the mosaics were rich in the ceilings, touched with concentrated light; venerably delicate baptismal fonts and urns of holy water stood against the rich pillars of black and white porphyry; the floor was one great surface of mosaics, so that you walked with self-upbraiding to crush such sensitive dyes; across the choir, dividing it from nave and transepts, a screen of marble, with fourteen statues in its architrave, lifted the crucifix, where Christ dies forever amid his gorgeous antiquites. Seen through the fissures of the screen beyond the carved chairs of the choir, set amid prized bas-reliefs and elderly bronzes the high altar of Greek marble, rose into a canopy of verd-antique, furnished to-day with the most brilliant jewels in the treasury, and covering with its base the body of St. Mark, the Evangelist. The body of the church, where the spectators stood, was very dim, the light lying warmest around the ceilings, yet one could see the flash of sword-hilts and epaulettes and the shining decorations on the breasts of the rewarded, even the features and eyes of those around the King, as they stood, bending, before the altar, all uncovered and still. You could hear the pace of the soft-footed priests, the echoes to whispers of prayer that fell abrupt, like kisses, against the domes; the murmur, as of surprise, for a moment, at the weirdness of the building, into which, most probably, the majority of the King's party had never before entered; and then—so universal, with such space to resound in, with such sweet energy and inspiration pronounced, that it seemed to have neither choristers nor abode—the *Te Deum* pealed along the aisles and arches, like tuneful thunder loosened.

One's memories of grand emotions are apt to err in favor of the latest. If I should say that this *Te Deum* was the most wondrous music I ever heard, perhaps I might be repeating what I have said of other occasions. The glorious harmony of a full military band going into action, the serenade on the waters, the camp-meetings hymns in green woods, the diapason of opera, sustained by a multitude; these recollections come back to me weaker than ever before, for the lifting up of this *Te Deum* was like the flight of men's souls, burst out of them with song. They stood so listlessly below, the melody was so strong and sonorous above, that the discrepancy of cause and effect made of them, to the mind, automatons merely, like fountain-statues, motionless, that fling up mighty water-jets. Into the cornet, drum and organ the human song poured like the cheer of an army into one bugle-blast, and every glad emotion went up to Gods with the dignity of men whose faith in the end met it with no surprise. It was a song for Calvin to have heard, reconciling faith and destiny as he only believed it. It was a song to be given by the people of Moses when the last wave rolled over their enemies. Calm thankfulness, so calm that out of its good consciousness and self satisfaction it drew power, swelled at last into one mighty climax of praise, tenaciously prolonged, the last comprehensiveness of gratitude; and then fell absolute quiet upon king, priest and soldier.

While Venice is thus a fire at sea, a city of light-houses, a great beacon burning down the Mediterranean, a new Stromboli, with souls for coals in its working crater, every sister city in Italy has leaped into flames to honor her. There are burning torches at Palermo; Massena is belting her famed Strait with fire; the Bay of Naples is a beach of blaze; Florence hoists the tricolor lamp to all her towers and campiniles; Ravenna, in her remote and venerable repose, cries *vivas* for Venice at Dante's tomb; in Pisa, the leaning tower swings to the reverberating cheers; Sienna's checkered Cathedral flares in the illumination; every glorious pinnacle at Milan is white in the flash of happy windows; Genoa, the crescent of the sea, no longer threatens to bridle the horses of Saint Mark, but wreathes their counterfeits in laurel; and every city under the Alps becomes a bonfire, to make this liberation an equal outburst of humanity and love wherever the language of the South is a household utterance. One of the galaxy of great municipalities alone stands dark and sullen among her mountains. There is no streak of light upon her hills. Around her forum there are those who keep watch to murder him who cheers for Venice. Her churches are dumb to the choral song of a waiting people redeemed and made glad by freedom. Crumbling sternly and unbendingly to ruin like her barbaric Coliseum, Rome, that cannot be Mistress of the World, can at least rail upon it. From under the great dome of St. Peter's, flung over it by the Republican arm of Michael Angelo, a strange, discordant reproof fell upon Venice the day that her people crowded to the polls. Not a word of all hail for the fulfilment of suffering years. No earnest of "Be happy, Italy, our native land!" But a mad wail and rail, and termagant shout against the deliverers and delivered of "our dear son in Jesus Christ, Francis Joseph of Austria!"

The home of the great chief had been established some time on the island of Caprera. The furniture of Garibaldi, down to 1861, consisted of one chair without a back. The officers of the steamer *Washington* gave him a couple of dozen maple chairs after his victory at Naples. He sleeps on an iron bedstead; a line across his bedroom holds his clothes; there is no carpet on the floor;

papers and books lie around in confused heaps; on the wall, in a frame, is a lock of his brave wife's hair, some portraits of his slain comrades, and the memorable sword of Tour D'Auvergne, the first grenadier of France. His meals are commonly made upon maccaroni, fresh fish, and wild boar; he has common Capri wine on the table, but drinks cold water only himself. He goes to bed at ten o'clock, after reading the newspapers, and rises at three in the morning and reads again. At four he takes coffee, and then gardens till breakfast. His daughter sings the Marsellaise beautifully. His horses are, "Marsala," given to him on arriving in Sicily, "Said," the gift of the Pacha of Egypt, and "Borboni," from whom Menotti, at Reggio, pulled off a man by main force. Garibaldi's house is white and small, set on a level spot among stone walls, and backed by tumbled rocks. The gate to it is a pole turning on a pivot; it has one story and an attic merely, and vines grow round it, climbing upon poles. The island is fifteen miles in circumference, unapproachable from the sea at many places by its rugged vertical rocks, and wild goats and eagles dwell upon it, in sight of the minute islets that cluster around it. The nearest neighbor of Garibaldi was, until of late, Collins, an eccentric Englishman, who used to pen up the Chief's donkeys and chargers when they trespassed; in return Menotti Garibaldi killed a couple of his pigs, and then Collins sued the whole family.

The advance of Garibaldi on Rome in this year of 1867 is animated by the intensest of all the feelings of his life. He is an old man; looking from his rocky island he sees all his race made prosperous and united by his individual devotion, except the Romans. So long as Rome is constrained Italy is incomplete, and working from that excepted spot, ambitious churchmen, as in the past will foment intestine discord in Italy, or allure the rapacious stranger. It is not sought to banish the Christian church, but to dethrone a political churchman, who does not love Italy, intelligence, nor freedom; whose personal will is despotism; and who, entrenched upon the national soil, excommunicates the King and the patriot together. If the Papacy is founded in the needs of any vast body of mankind, its own usefulness will preserve it; but it has no right to forbid competition and slander civilization,—a military fortress where Christ is dishonored to be the chief of a detective police. It claims the right to hold free of taxation vast ecclesiastical establishments over all Italy, which are but strongholds of mutiny, and no nation dare respect itself that admits its monstrous pretensions. I have found, as an American journalist, that sympathy with Italy is made a political offence in America. When I have sometimes said a cheerful word for the greatest man of my generation, the subject of this sketch, I have been advised that it displeases some mysterious interest which I refuse to acknowledge. Any ecclesiastic, in the Pope's position, would be an enemy to freedom, Methodist, Baptist, Quaker, or Catholic. Let this man, Pius, enter the lists with other faiths; all men want the best faith, whatever it be, and all men will have freedom. I am persuaded that American Catholics value their cheerfully accorded toleration in a land of liberty too well to believe their faith endangered anywhere by the triumph of patriotism and freedom. Grand and manly is it to see this republican soldier, making all titles mean by his quiet refusal of them, dwelling at Caprera in the free air of seas, under the tinted mountains, asking no higher fame than to die under the walls of Rome.

THE REAL LIFE

OF

ABRAHAM LINCOLN.

A TALK WITH MR. HERNDON,
HIS LATE LAW PARTNER

BY

GEORGE ALFRED TOWNSEND

WITH CABINET PORTRAIT, AND MR. LINCOLN'S FAVORITE POEM.

———•✦•———

NEW YORK:
PUBLICATION OFFICE, BIBLE HOUSE,

1867

Abraham Lincoln.
Courtesy of General Collection: Portraits, Delaware State Archives.

ABRAHAM LINCOLN.

A TALK WITH THE LATE PRESIDENT'S LAW PARTNER.

The following charming description of the real life of the late President was written by the accomplished poet, lecturer, and correspondent, Mr.George Alfred Townsend, and published in the *New York Tribune*. It is dated—

SPRINGFIELD, ILL., Jan. 25, 1867.

When history makes up its mind to commemorate a place, no special correspondence can keep pace with it. After Mr. Lincoln's nomination to the Presidency—the most Republican of all *coups d'etat*—the little city of Springfield ascended at a bound from the commonplace to the memorable. Caravans of patriots from all the other States wended across the prairies to visit it. From a market town, where eggs were duly exchanged for calico, and the father of the family reported himself twice a year to get stone-drunk, it rose to be the home of a President, and sent him across the continent to usefulness and martyrdom. His body lies near by it—shrine which any city might covet—and his prim frame residence, practical and mud-colored, I have walked around these two nights, to find my curiosity shared by a half-dozen couples, looking upon it as if the tall ghost of its former owner might possibly appear.

I came here to lecture; of two days leisure spared me I have passed one-half of each in conversation with a man who knew the great citizen of Springfield for twenty years anterior to his Chief Magistracy better and closer than any human being. Until very lately you might have read upon a bare stairway, opposite the State House Square, the sign of LINCOLN & HERNDON. A year ago it gave place to the name of HERNDON & ZANE. Ascending the stairs one flight, you see two doors opening to your right hand. That in the rear leads to what was for one generation the law office of the President. Within, it is a dismantled room, strewn with faded briefs and leaves of law books; no desks nor chairs remaining; its single bracket of gas darkened in the center, by whose flame he whom our children's children shall reverently name, prepared, perhaps, his gentle, sturdy utterances; and out of its window you get a sweep of stable-roofs and dingy back yards, where he must have looked a thousand times, pondering Freedom and Empire, with his eye upon ash-heaps and crowing cocks and young Americans sledging or ball-playing. As simple an office, even for a country lawyer, as ever I saw in my life, it is now in the transition condition of being prepared for another tenant. In the middle of the room the future President sat at a table side, and in the adjoining front room this table and all the furniture of the place is still retained, while in its back corner, looking meditatively at the cylinder stove, you see Mr. Herndon, the partner and authority I have referred to.

He has given me permission to write what I choose of himself and his dead friend, and among all the men I have ever met he is the readiest to understand a question and to give even and direct answers. He resembles Mr. Lincoln so much, and in his present quarters, garb, and worldly condition, is so nearly a reproduction of A. Lincoln, lawyer, as he lived before Fame drove a chariot through this second story, that we may as well take a turn around the surviving man and the room.

Lincoln was the taller and older, and the senior partner; he had been in two or three associations with lawyers; one of his early partners, by fraud or mismanagement, got him into debt, and he carried the burden of it about ten years; his latest partner, excepting Herndon, was anxious to be a candidate for the Legislature, and as Mr. Lincoln desired the same honor at the same time, a dissolution was inevitable, and then to Herndon's great surprise, for he was very young and obscure, Lincoln said: "Billy, let us go into business together." Herndon accepted the proposition thankfully. Mr. Lincoln arranged the terms of partnership, and the new "shingle" went up directly, never to be removed till the bullet of Booth had done its errand.

How young Herndon might have looked twenty-five years ago we can scarcely infer from the saffron-faced, blue-black haired man before us, bearded bushily at the throat, disposed to shut one eye for accuracy in conversation, his teeth discolored by tobacco, and over his angular features, which suggest Mr. Lincoln's in ampleness and shape, the same half-tender melancholy, the result in both cases, perhaps, of hard frontier work, poor pay, thoughtful abstraction, and a disposition to share the sorrows of mankind.

Oh! why should the spirit of mortal be proud—is the sentiment of Herndon's face, as it was of Mr. Lincoln's—a gravity that befits greatness well, when it comes, and in the dress of the firm of Lincoln & Herndon you see this sentiment practicalized. "Mr. Lincoln," said Mr. Herndon, "cared so little about clothes that sometimes he did not put all of them on. He was brought up barefoot." Mr. Herndon, by parallel, wears to-day a bright yellow pair of breeches, turned up twice at the bottoms, and looks to be a wind-hardened farmer, rather than one of the best lawyers in the State, and, as a public man, is charged with delivering the best stump speeches in Illinois, on the Republican side, during the last election. His address is homely in form, commencing with, "Friend, I'll answer you;" and this he does without equivocation, with his long fore-finger extended, and with such fund of new information upon the revered member in question that although the Lincoln biographers, from Holland up, have talked with him, he seems to be brimful of new reminiscences. With an extraordinary memory, great facility of inference, and a sturdy originality of opinion, he had the effect upon me to stagger all my notions of the dead President's character. He has been a wonderful desultory reader, and in his law library you may see the anomalous companions for a prairie attorney of Bailey's *Festus*, Schlegel's Critique, Comte's Philosophy, Louis Blanc, and many of the disobedient essayists. He has one of the best private libraries in the West, and in this respect is unlike Mr. Lincoln, who seldom bought a new book, and seldom read one. Mr. Lincoln's education was almost entirely a newspaper one. He was one of the most thorough newspaper readers in America, and for fifteen years before his election to the Presidency subscribed regularly to *The Richmond Enquirer* and *The Charleston Mercury*. He grew slowly, therefore, as public opinion grew, and as an Anti-Slavery man was a gradual convert; whereas Herndon, years before, embraced at a leap all the social reforms, read all the agitators, and talked human liberty to Mr. Lincoln, gravely listening, till a fraternity of sentiment developed and about the year 1844 the coming emancipator declared himself an enemy of slaveholding.

It is worth while to stop and ponder that while Rhett and Wise, with Slavery in full feather, wrote every day of the inviolateness of Secession and the divinity of bondage, these two Illinois lawyers, in their little square office, read every vaunting, cruel word, paid to read it, and educated themselves out of their mutual indignations—the one to a grand agency, the other to as grand an abhorrence.

Mr. Lincoln had some six or seven places of residence during his life; he was of full age before he left his family never to return, the pleasantest of his reminiscences were of his mother, to whom he imputed the best and the brightest qualities he had inherited. He broke out once to Mr. Herndon, as they were returning from Court in another county: "Billy, all I am or can be I owe to my angel-mother."

As a boy Lincoln made a frontierman's living by hard work, poling a flatboat, getting out cedar and chestnut rails, even sawing wood. The scene of his early struggles was Indiana, and there he developed into a sort of amateur public clerk, writing letters for folks to whom a steel pen was a mystery, giving miscellaneous advice on law and business, and excelling particularly in the ingenuities of anecdote and illustrations. The story-telling reputation he retains was no fabulous qualification, nor was it an idle and gossipy recreation, but a means of making intelligence plain to rude minds. At this stage of his life he wore moccasins and a hunting-shirt, and was in great request by thick-headed people, because of his skill and clearness in narration. The jury always got from him a fair statement of any case in hand, and years later it was remarked by the Chief Justice of Illinois that when Lincoln spoke he argued both sides of the case so well that a speech in response was always superfluous. The habit he had of enforcing a fact with an anecdote so far survived his moccasin days that he seems to have been constitutional in a sense. No man ever told so many stories, and he was seldom known either to repeat one twice or to tell one that was hackneyed. His long, variable and extensive experience with common, native people made him acquainted with a thousand oddities, and he had a familiar way of relating them that was as piquant as his application of them. It is also true that some of these stories were more cogent than delicate, yet in no single case was he ever remembered to have told an exceptional anecdote for the sake of that in which it was exceptional. Mr. Herndon remembers a person who so far mistook Mr. Lincoln once as to tell a coarse story without a purpose. During the recital Mr. Lincoln's face worked impatiently. When the man had gone he said: "I had nearly put that fellow out of the office. He disgusts me."

Finally settled at Springfield, Mr. Lincoln found the law jealous and niggard. He was always able to keep a horse, and was very fond of riding; but he made a poor income, though one not incommensurate with the general smallness of his colleagues at the Illinois bar. Now and then he was pinched to distress, and went to bed with no notion of how he should meet the morrow's claims. For nearly a fifth part of his whole life he owed money that he could not pay, and although of easy disposition, the debt galled him and hastened his wrinkles. He cleared himself finally on his return from Washington City, where he sat as a Representative in Congress. When he quitted Springfield for the White House he was worth just $30,000. Never moody nor petulant, he yet loved solitude and self-communion, and has been known to sit six hours in one place, to lie on his back for example, on the floor of his house, looking absently at the ceiling, or to sun himself, sitting upon a fence, or in a hay-mow all the day, passing the processes of a plea through his mind, or forming some political judgment.

The tenderness of his nature was not always manifest, yet he had his romance in early manhood, and as of this Mr. Herndon had spoken in public, I asked particularly about it.

At Sangamon, Illinois, a pretty and high-spirited girl, without fortune, made havoc in many hearts, and Mr. Lincoln constituted one of three earnest suitors who wanted her in marriage. She preferred the addresses of a young merchant of the town, and gave the other tow their *congè*. Her affianced soon afterwards went East to buy goods, but as he returned was taken with brain fever in some wayside town, and lay raving for three months, unknown by name or resident to his entertainers. A rumor started that he had run away to avoid marrying his lady, and, waiting some time in vain to hear from him, she received anew the attentions of Mr. Lincoln. About the time when they passed from courtesy to tenderness, and marriage between them was more than hinted at, the sick man returned like a ghost, gauged the condition of affairs, and upbraided the lady with fickleness. She had a delicate sense of honor, and felt keenly the shame of having seemed to trifle with two gentlemen at once; this preyed upon her mind till her body, not very strong, suffered by sympathy, and Mr. Herndon has oral and written testimony that the girl died out of regret at the equivocal position she had unwittingly assumed. The names of all the parties he has given me, but I do not care to print them.

On the dead woman's grave Mr. Lincoln promised himself never to marry. This vow he kept very long. His marriage was in every respect advantageous to him. It whetted his ambition, did not nurse too much a penchant for home indolence that he had, and taught him particularly that there was something called society, which observed one's boots as well as his principles. He was always a loyal and reverent husband, a gentle but not positive father, and his wife saw the Presidency for him before the thought of it troubled him.

He built the frame house in Springfield, which is now so celebrated, at a comparatively recent period. I went over it yesterday with amusement at its utter practicality. It stands upon a prosaic corner, in an inferior quarter of the town, and was the design of a carpenter, not an architect. A narrow yard and palings shut it from the street; the door is in the middle, and is approached by four or five wooden steps; on the abutment beside these he stood after his nomination, in the blaze of pine torches, the thunder of huzzas breaking around his head, the only solemn man in Springfield. He might have felt that all these gratulations were such as the Aztecs spent upon the beautiful captive who was to be sacrificed in the *teocallis*.

As a lawyer, he was a close student of those cases that interested him. Slow to take them into his mind, passing in their consideration from stage to stage, and if he found beneath an embodied principle, his heart grew into the work of developing it. He frequently sat up all night, preparing some favorite argument, and never failed to present it so perspicuously that dull intellects grew appreciative and shrewd ones absorbed. Some of his legal arguments are described as having been classical. Yet, beneath all the drudgery of his craft, he was at soul a politician rather than an attorney. Every legal study carried him beyond itself to the mysteries of public infirmity. "He sat," says Mr.

Herndon, "looking through a brief to the constitution of society and the moral government of God." Now and then he shut himself up all night, and lay on his office floor in his careless garments, revolving some problem set by a village client that had expanded to a great human principle. At these times he seemed to be a dreamer reasoning. Again, he drove miles over the prairies with his lips close shut, wrinkling, softly humming, and returned again at night strangely white and exhausted.

Before his great public call came he had passed the world through his silent thought, as if it had been a legal case to be stated and argued.

"Did he ever quarrel, Mr. Herndon?"

"Seldom, friend, but sometimes. Once I saw him incensed at a Judge for giving an unfair decision. It was a terrible spectacle. As he was grand in his good nature, so he was grand in his rage. At another time I saw two men come to blows in his presence; he picked them up separately and tossed them apart like a couple of kittens. He was the strongest man I ever knew, and has been known to lift a man of his own weight and throw him over a worm fence. Once, in Springfield, the Irish voters meditated taking possession of the polls. News came down the street that they would permit nobody to vote but those of their own party. Mr. Lincoln seized an ax-handle from a hardware store, and went alone to open a way to the ballot-box. His appearance intimidated them, and we had neither threats nor collisions all that day. He was never sick during the whole of our long acquaintance; being a man of slow circulation, and of most regular habits, capable of subsisting upon a morsel, he was wiry and indurated beyond the best of our Western men, and even with Booth's bullet in his brain he lived ten hours. His life in general was smooth and unruffled. He had no prejudices against any class, preferring the Germans to any of the foreign element, yet tolerating—as I (Herndon) never could—even the Irish.

"Did he ever drink?"

"Only in Indiana, when he took whisky as ague medicine. After his nomination for the Presidency it was suggested to him that the Visiting Committee would require some hospitality. 'Very well,' he said, 'any food that is proper I authorize to be purchased.'"

"'But these gentlemen will expect some liquors.'"

"'I cannot permit to strangers what I do not do myself. No liquors, Billy! there's the tavern!'"

Of miscellaneous books Mr. Lincoln's favorites were Shakespeare and Pope. He never read Byron, and of contemporary American poets preferred the patriotic selections chiefly. Milton he knew by heart, and was a good literary reader of the Bible. His friends were selected with regard to their sincerity chiefly; he loved not cliques, and those who knew him best were younger than he. He was cautious in friendships, no hero-worshiper, and for Mr. Douglas, his most prominent antagonist, had much less admiration than repulsion. Douglas was uneasily arrogant in Lincoln's presence; the latter, never sensitive nor flurried, so grew by his imperturbability that when he reached the White House, Mr. Douglas was less surprised than anybody else. The great Senatorial campaign, in which they figured together, is remembered by every Springfielder. Douglas, with his powerful voice and facile energy, went into it under full steam. Lincoln began lucidly and cautiously. When they came out of it Douglas was worn down with rage and hoarseness, and Lincoln was fresher than ever. He prepared all the speeches of this campaign by silent meditation, sitting or lying alone, studying the flies on the ceiling. The best evidence of his superiority in this debate is the fact that the Republicans circulated both sets of speeches as a campaign document in 1860, and Mr. Douglas' friends refused to do so.

The most remarkable episode of Herndon's conversation—which I am repeating by memory only—related to Mr. Lincoln's Presidential aspirations. In common with most people, I had concluded that this great honor came to Mr. Lincoln without paving, as unexpected as it was unsolicited, and to him a staggering piece of luck, like a lottery prize. This estimate is a charming one, but it is not a true one. When the Douglas and Lincoln contest was ended, the defeated man said to his partner:

"Billy, I knew I should miss the place when I competed for it. This defeat will make me President."

He refused, in the interim, any proposition looking to his acceptance of a lesser office, and this was the concurrence of his friends and family. At the same time he took no immediate means to precipitate his opportunity, rather, like a man destined, sat more closely to study and vigilance, read all the issues as they developed, and waited for his call.

It came at last, in a special invitation to visit New York and speak in the Cooper Institute. He felt intuitively that this was the Rubicon, and, with a human thrill, paused and hesitated.

It is possible that, at this moment, had any close friend whispered "stay," the Republican might be dead and Abraham Lincoln living.

"Go, Mr. Lincoln," said Herndon, "make your best effort. Speak with your usual lucidity and thoroughness."

Home said "Go" also.

He appeared in New York, as all of you remember, and his success there drew the attention of the country to his name. The West can originate men: the East must pass them; and the firm of Lincoln & Herndon died, in reality, when the Convention met at Chicago. He had by this time reached the highest usefulness in his State of which his nature was capable.

The best lawyer in it, the hero of a debate equivalent to a Senatorship, with a mind too broad and grave for a mere gubernatorial place, and already by four years' destiny and preparation President of the United States, he went up to the post with a dignity and ease that made men stare, because they had not seen the steps he took upon the road.

At last he came to his office for the last time.

"Billy," said he, "we must say good-bye."

Both of them cried, speechlessly.

"You must keep up the firm-name, Billy, if it will be of use to you."

They shook hands upon it, with tears in their eyes.

"I love the people here, Billy, and owe them all that I am. If God spares my life to the end, I shall come back among you, and spend the remnant of my days."

He never returned to Springfield till glory brought him home under her plumes, a completed life, and the prairie, like a neighbor, opened its door to take him in.

When Mr. Herndon saw him again at Washington City he was furrowed and fretted with state cares. They talked a while of the old office, the clients, and the town, and then the war rolled between them once more.

One sentence Mr. Herndon recollects of the President before his departure for Washington that is memorable as showing his purpose.

"Billy," he said, "I hope there will be no trouble; but I will make the South a grave-yard rather than see a Slavery gospel triumph, or successful secession lose this Government to the cause of the people and representative institutions."

To this Mr. Herndon added: "Mr. Lincoln was merciless in the abstract. Battles never moved him, unless he trode among their corpses. He would have carried on the war forever, or as long as the people intrusted him its management, rather than give up."

Speaking thus, among the associations of his working life, the years of Abraham Lincoln began to return in the vividness of their monotony, bleak and unremunerated, hard and practical, full of patient walk down a road without a turning, brightened by dutifulness alone, pointed but not cheered by wayside anecdote, and successful, not so much because he was sanguine of himself, as because he rated not eminence and honor too high or too difficult. When he found himself competing for the Senatorship with the quickest, the least scrupulous, and the most flattered orator in the Union, he saw nothing odd nor dramatic about it. His Presidential opportunity surprised everybody but himself—not that he had self-conceit, but that he thought the office possible. He was none of your Richelieus, meditating aside the great uses to which Providence had put him. He never made a bid for the favor or forgiveness of history, but ruled the nation as if it were practicing law, and practiced law as if it were ruling the nation. This real greatness of mind, this obliviousness of circumstances, ascending from a practice of three thousand dollars a year to twenty-five thousand, as if there was no contrast between them, giving "Billy" permission to use the firm style as before, without a conscious poetic trait, yet ever in absent moments looking very long away pondering the distance of rewards, promises, vindications, with a longing that was poetry—these compose some of the character of one whose fame differs vastly from his life, and must do so by the anomaly of the man. The strongest of his loves and faiths was The People. He had more reverence for them in bulk than for their highest public exemplars. Religiously he was a reverent man without creed, believing in a beneficent God—no more. No denomination had a special claim to him; he was not a regular church-goer; the few clergymen whom he liked recommended themselves on personal grounds; he refused to argue on religious matters, but inclined toward Congregational independence. His mother and sisters were fond of camp-meetings, and a rather humorous letter held by Mr. Herndon says that a portion of their family was regularly converted every year, and backslid in the Winter.

I know of no better illustration of the difference between the real life and the renown of Mr. Lincoln than you get by visiting his grave. A horse railroad, two miles long, leads to it, in the cemetery of Oak Ridge. Behind you is his real life, Springfield, a Western market town, set upon the monotonous prairie, half the year noisy with the chatter of politicians, plethoric with lawyers, for all of whom there is less than enough to do, and savoring much of the frost and the frontier; a pretty prairie city, but capitalized so that what the State had not done for the town, and what the people expected it to do, make an unfinished desultoriness. All at once, as you approach the Sangamon River, the scene changes. Stalwart young oaks of natural growth become plentiful. The landscape is plowed with leafy ravines. Bold knolls start up. A creek goes plashing around the abrupt hills. Shadow, murmur, and surprises succeed the level life of the city. And among all those mysteries, itself the great mystery of our age, the vault of the President caps a hill, a temporary edifice of brick, and the great drive of one of the handsomest cemeteries in the Union winds with the winding brook beneath it:

"The last,
   As 'twere the cape of a long ridge of hill,"

and all the white tombs marshal about it; buttonwood, maple and ash trees cluster at its base: here is to be his monument. About $75,000 have been collected for it up to this time, and it is supposed the State will vote enough to make $200,000 in all. There is no sweeter spot for a tired life to rest in. It would be blasphemy to mar the dead man's grave with any mere prettiness of marble or smartness of bronze. Let the fiery, untamed Western genius be of timid chisel here. "Abraham Lincoln" is a good epitaph if plainly lettered. And, after all, will any monument be like the man, for no such one was ever a sculptor's theme before. Canova could get no notion of Mr. Lincoln. An allegory would be unlike him, a shaft too formal, a statue too inexpressive. If the Pacific Railroad could be called by his name, that would be better than either; but this man will trouble any artist in that he was so unlike any model.

MR. LINCOLN'S FAVORITE POEM.

As is well known to many persons, the exquisitely beautiful poem entitled "Mortality," referred to in the preceding sketch, was an especial favorite with our late President, but it is not generally understood that the poem was written by a young Scotchman, who died at thirty-seven—that age so fatal to Burns, Byron, Motherwell, and so many other children of song. One evening in December, 1863, Mr. Lincoln repeated this poem to Col. J.G. Wilson, then in Washington, when the latter said, "Mr. President, you have omitted a portion of it." "What! is there more of it?" responded Mr. Lincoln, with as much eagerness as did the ragged backwoodsman in the story of the Arkansas Traveler. "Yes, sir, two other stanzas;" and he thereupon repeated them to the great delight of the President. "Can you tell me who wrote it?" asked Mr. Lincoln, "for I can't find out. Some of the papers attribute it to me." "It was written," replied the Colonel, "by William Knox, a Scottish poet of considerable talent, who died at Edinburgh in 1825. He published several volumes of poems, and was well known to Sir Walter Scott, 'Christopher North,' of glorious memory, and to many other of the literary magnates of that day." As the poem has already appeared incomplete in various journals, we append it in full:

MORTALITY.

Oh! why should the spirit of mortal be proud?
Like a swift, fleeting meteor, a fast-flying cloud,
A flash of the lightening, a break of the wave,
He passeth from life to his rest in the grave.

The leaves of the oak and the willow shall fade,
Be scattered around and together be laid;
And the young and the old, and the low and the high
Shall molder to dust and together shall lie.

The infant and mother attended and loved;
The mother that infant's affection who proved;
The husband that mother and infant who blessed—
Each, all, are away to their dwellings of rest.

The maid on whose cheek, on whose brow, in whose eye,
Shone beauty and pleasure—her triumphs are by;
And the memory of those that beloved her and praised,
Are alike from the minds of the living erased.

The hand of the king that the scepter hath borne;
The brow of the priest that the miter hath worn;
The eye of the sage and the heart of the brave,
Are hidden and lost in the depths of the grave.

The peasant, whose lot was to sow and to reap;
The herdsman, who climbed with his goats up the steep;
The beggar, who wandered in search of his bread,
Have faded away like the grass that we tread.

The saint that enjoyed the communion of heaven;
The sinner that dared to remain unforgiven;
The wise and the foolish, the guilty and just,
Have quietly mingled their bones in the dust.

So the multitude goes, like the flower or the weed,
That withers away to let others succeed;
So the multitude comes, even those we behold,
To repeat every tale that has often been told.

For we are the same our fathers have been;
We see the same sights our fathers have seen;
We drink the same stream and view the same sun,
And run the same course our fathers have run.

The thoughts we are thinking our fathers would think;
From the death we are shrinking our fathers would shrink;
To the life we are clinging they also would cling:
But it speeds for us all, like a bird on the wing.

They loved, but the story we cannot unfold;
They scorned, but the heart of the haughty is cold;
They grieved, but no wail from that slumber will come;
They joyed, but the tongue of their gladness is dumb.

They died, ay! they died: we things that are now,
That walk of the turf that lies over their brow,
And make in their dwellings a transient abode,
Meet the things that they met on their pilgrimage road.

Yes! hope and despondency, pleasure and pain,
We mingle together in sunshine and rain;
And the smile and the tear, the song and the dirge,
Still follow each other, like surge upon surge.

'Tis the wink of an eye, 'tis the draught of a breath,
From the blossom of health to the paleness of death,
From the gilded saloon to the bier and the shroud.
Oh! why should the spirit of mortal be proud?

THE

MORMON TRIALS

AT

SALT LAKE CITY

BY

GEO. ALFRED TOWNSEND

NEW YORK:
AMERICAN NEWS COMPANY.
1871.

Brigham Young.

LETTER FROM UTAH TO THE CINCINNATI COMMERCIAL,
OCTOBER, 1871.

HON. W. H. HOOPER,
DELEGATE IN CONGRESS FROM UTAH TERRITORY.

My dear sir,

You wished to see the letters I wrote from Salt Lake last month, collected in pamphlet. Have your wish? Your courtesy and hospitality in the Land of the Bee exercised in the two visits I have made you this year, were seconded by the best of the Mormon people. You are an Eastern Shore Marylander like myself, and I believe in your sincerity, in your faith and sympathize with your devotion to your beautiful country and the diligent hands which have made its deserts blossom. The march of the children of Israel from Egypt around the corner of the Mediterranean was a little affair compared to the Mormon migration. They were more unlettered and idolatrous than your bands, and Moses could not turn his back but they fell to worshipping calves and serpents. They conciliated nobody much on the way, and were a very unloveable, illiberal, rapacious set of people. They had awkward notions besides on the marrying point. And yet we, who are preached at from childhood out of the old books of Exodus and Deuteronomy, refuse to see any equities, wonders, or heroisms in the history and condition of a native church, whose legends are no less miraculous. I cannot confess to a deep interest in these ecclesiastical subjects, and your friends Orson Pratt and Dr. Newman appear to me equally fatiguing. But I do take pride in the material achievements of the United States, however brought about. Religious movements, however motley, have been the making of us. Amongst the names of John Robinson, Roger Williams, William Penn, George Whitefield, Count Zinzendorf, and Lord Baltimore, founders of American communities, the name of Brigham Young will unquestionably stand. He has made the boldest, most rapid, and most remarkable colonization we have had; in a political point of view it has been fortunate to us all. I admire force of character and success achieved upon no baser principles than faith and industry, and I have said so in these letters. As to the camp-meeting jurists and their camp-followers out there, I am indifferent to their abuse and proud of their disapproval.

My friend, your people must stop polygamy, or it will stop Utah. Apart from the question of faith, it is a question of the common law. Your most generous apologists are only apologists, and they diminish in number every year. Do not tempt the democratic passions of a nation whose unanimous prejudice is law and power. Be rid of polygamy; cast out by this course the Federal officials who prey upon you, and become an American State in good faith, represented amongst us, and blessed by neighborhood rule.

GEO. ALFRED TOWNSEND.

WASHINGTON, *November 25, 1871.*

THE MORMON CITY AND CHIEF.

SALT LAKE, October 20.

The train from the East has dashed down the wild, barbaric sceneries of Weber and Echo Canyons; and, although something of Asiatic inhospitality clings to the knobs and cliffs, we feel that we are approaching an oasis of grass; this grass we perceive by the quick tests of instinct, and it is confirmed by occasional kine and sheep; patches of cultivation slip into the inlets of ravines, and bluesmoke appears to agitate the wheeling fishhawks; teams show upon the old stage road, useless now, except for neighborhood intercommunication. At last, with a whoop, brakes down, and the crack of rock echoes, the mountain gate yields; snow appears on distant ranges; there is something queer and blue hung across the dry sky—it is water. The Valley of Salt Lake, covered with cattle herds, and the town of Ogden, advise us that we are half way between the Missouri and the Pacific.

There is a darting about for baggage, many moving, people and small traders, and a change of a few paces from depot to depot; in a little while we have paid our $2.50 in gold additional fare, and received in change queer, crude shin-plasters of the corporation of Salt Lake City, and are moving slowly over the Utah Central Railway, every employé of which is said be a Saint. This being the case, we feel no sense of personal responsibility, and so look out upon the green waves of the lake destitute of a sail, note the frequent Mormon hamlets, the close and snowy mountains sending down rapid torrents for irrigation, and seek to separate the sheep from the goats, the Saints from the Gentiles. In the last endeavor we unwittingly classify a methodist doctor of divinity as the possessor of four wives, and rate one of Tammany Hall's pilgrims as a Mormon bishop. Everybody looks queerly at everybody else, suspecting one another of the patriarchal virtues, and drawing many crude conceits of this or that innocent passenger sleeping all over his premises within the same small hours.

Finally, after more than two hours' ride we enter the environs of Salt Lake, among the small and bushy orchards of apple, pear, and apricot; the lean and often low, sundried houses, of a bluish-white color; and wide, straight streets, down whose lazy declivities the snow-water gurgles, passing at every other gate into the vegetable patches and the lawns of wheat and wild oats. A cleanly depot, well officered, gives us outlet to a street full of cabmen and hotel-runners. Cries of "Townsend House", "Salt Lake House," salute us, and a one-armed Mormon, possessing two wives, single-handed, cracks his whip, with the reins between his teeth, and makes the wagon fly. We see it all in a couple of minutes, the big temple, which resembles a tortoise standing on a hundred short legs, the ugly wall enclosing the palace of Brigham and the new temple, the lone theatre, the heathen-seeming city hall, the many shops, plastered in front with a monotonous signboard of "Holiness to the Lord," and one painted eye, winking at the motto as if to satirize it. Then we are set down at the "Townsend House" a long, low, sprawling hotel, with a comfortable piazza and shade trees, growing out of the wooden pavement. The only Townsend who can keep a hotel stands whittling a stick, and lazily counting the number of newly-arriven guests; it is apparent that his hostship sits heavily upon his shoulders. Townsend has three wives, originated in Maine, and is doing his best to multiply our great breed of freemen. We feed well at the Townsend House at $4 a day, and sleep in the delicious dry air of this Wahsatch Valley; and next day we take a warm sulphur plunge bath in the environs of the town, the hot water pouring from the mountain side into a pool, and a cold shower bath standing convenient, like an ice-cream at the end of a warm dinner. I observed in this bath-house and its dressing-rooms what was altogether exceptional in American out-houses—no vulgar writings on the wall, no sporadic bits of doggerel indited by cowards for women to read. The only attestations were testimonials in lead-pencil to the pleasures of the bath, and the autographs of irrepressible travelers of vanity.

The valley and city of Salt Lake are marvels of patient, unskilled labor, directed by a few powerful native minds. The spirit of John Smith and the hands of the Puritan English meet in this mid-world colony—the brawn all peasant, the pluck all Yankee. Maine, Vermont, and New York were the fathers of this frontier, and folks out of the northwestern races of Europe—people of narrow foreheads and animal religious instincts—fell into the furrows the former opened.

The morning after my arrival I found everybody going up to see Brigham Young, some accompanied by an introducer, others falling in as interlopers. My chaperon was a bright young Mormon editor, as rosy as the sun on the mountains, who conducts a live salt newspaper, possesses a singular family, in that it is limited, and has built the first house with a Mansard roof in the heart of the continent. If he should feel distressed at any of these comments upon the Saints, my ingratitude will be great, and his paper will score me.

Passing under the small shade trees, across the flowing rills, past Godbe's flaming drug store, past Hon. Thomas Fitch's new law office, where he sits arranging his books with his cultivated wife; past the market where lake trout as big as young pigs lie speckled and fresh; past Delegate Hooper's bank, whence he looks out like one of Velasquez's Spanish gentlemen; past the chain gang of worthless Gentiles making road with manacles dragging after them;

past the theatre, and up a gentle hill among the painted adobe houses—everything flattish, low-set, quaint, but not permanent-seeming, as if all the town could be blown away by a gale—we see the sun shining hotly along the long, tall wall which encloses Brigham's palace. An eagle over a sunny gateway, a plaster or wooden bee-hive, and a lion above the roof, denote the clump of dwellings and offices just behind the wall, and seen through the gateway gap in it, where "President " Young keeps state. The scene is like pictures of scenery in Tunis or Morocco, hot, yellow, sandy, half-barbaric, as if architectural models were shaping themselves in a Darwinian way from the crude slime. He who would reign must not pick his palace, his capital, or his subjects.

A long procession of Eastern sightseers is entering the gate, and amongst them are many fine young women, many wives, many young girls and children, and they pay as much respect to Brigham as to the Grand Turk. None of them appear to stand in dislike of him, because of his much marrying, and they push aside the Mormon brethren, who stand reverently off on the porch till the hand-shaking shall be done. It is truly queer to see that fine Boston belle, tall as a queen, with the rose and blush of maidenhood dignifying her for some impending husband, shake hands with the bland old Bluebeard, whose honeymoons have been more numerous than her years. Meekly as Rebecca at the well she takes his palm, and looks honored by his consideration.

Within we see a snug office, narrow and deep, and in the recesses of it some secretaries, very like other folks' secretaries, writing. Everybody about Brigham, we may remark, is of a Gentile countenance and a worldly, business look; he does not take kindly to long faces; several of his confidential clerks have been associated with the Salt Lake theatre. This office is surrounded with portraits of the Mormon dignitaries, and it contains two large oil portraits taken from life, as I was informed—of Joseph Smith and Hyrum Smith. Both wear clerical neck-ties and look like country clergymen.

How powerful is ignorance! See it tugging away at the Column Vendome, delighted with itself, noble and earnest, wiping out the monuments and vindications of our human nature, and sparing Heaven the necessity of humiliating us. Of all queer enterprises which ignorance has undertaken, Mormonism excels. It has not yet found itself out. With superb leadership, with patient delight, with prayer and praise, it goes on dignifying nonsense, and by its success almost making us infidel to our own religion and country; for what have we done in our knowledge that they have not imitated in theirs. Their humble apostles have passed the barriers of language, and the crude Danes and Swedes are pouring into Utah as well as the English-speaking nations. Compact, disciplined, devout, no cowards, at times desperate men, yet soft and diplomatic, so that they have pacified hostile Indians and checkmated the United States, they illustrate the nobility of delusion when attended with labor, fired with purpose, and properly organized. Moses, Roger Williams, John Brown, Joe Smith, very different, yet like in material results, the politician in all of them blended with the fanatic—they put in motion greater successors, and, by the two mighty inspirers of weak masses—sympathy and success—their sects grew to columns and their columns to States.

With his hair nicely oiled in ringlets and falling around his heavy neck, hair and beard luxuriant, and but a little turned in color, a pair of silver spectacles in his hand, and his manner all bland, from his half-closed eyes to the poise of his knees and feet, Brigham Young soothes mankind with seignoral hospitality. We are all introduced, except one young man, who steps forward and says:

"As there is nobody to make me acquainted, here is my card, President Young." "It is unnecessary, Sir," replies Brigham; "quite needless! Be seated."

We see he is more perfectly at home than anybody in the crowded room, and that he has a hard, peremptory voice, plausibly toned down to reception necessities. Looking not more than sixty years of age, he is past that period by half a score, and still may have twenty years to live. Of a wonderfully robust constitution, equal to all responsibilities of polygamy, of self-pride, cool self-management, and self-will, with an education chiefly religious, and an aptness and ardor for power and avarice. Young is wonderfully devised for organizing an ignorant and solemn people, and compelling them to be productive and docile.

About everybody of ecclesiastical prominence in the Church has several wives, and such bear themselves with added dignity. According to the number of the hens so grandiosely bears himself the cock, and I remarked amongst the most polygamous elders, that easy self-consciousness and grace of carriage becoming what are truly "ladies' men."

THE FIRST CONVICTION FOR POLYGAMY.

SALT LAKE, October 24, 1871.

Today Thomas Hawkins, English, from Birmingham, better known around Salt Lake as "Tummus Awkeens," is to be sentenced in the best elocution of which Judge McKean is capable, to the Territorial Penitentiary for a term of years.

The offense of Thomas was somewhat uncommon—committing adultery with his wife, Elizabeth Mears, on complaint of his wife Harriet Hawkins, better known as Arriet Awkeens. He was also arraigned in the indictment for the same offense with his third and last wife, Sarah Davis, but no witnesses were adduced as to the criminal act, owing to the fact that Sarah quartered in the upper part of the house, and there was no way to observe what happened there, except by looking down the chimney. Voices, it is true, had been heard in that quarter, as of people sitting up or otherwise, toward morning; but it was somewhat singular that, although the first wife, complainant, had lived under the polygamous roof for several years, she swore that she had never beheld the direct offense charged but once, even with Mears, and then peeked in at a window on purpose.

As you are all anxious to realize this scene, I relate it below with all its atmospheric and personal surroundings.

"Hear ye! hear ye! The United States Court for the Third Judicial District of Utah is now in session. Hats off! Spectators will get off the jury bench!"

These were the remarks of the Deputy Marshal Furnman, who is intermarried with Mormons, but a prosecutor of the Saints, and brother-in-law of Billy Appleby, United States Commissioner in Bankruptcy. The Marshal, M. T. Patrick, had gone to Southern Utah to shoot snipe, prospect a mine, and arrest a Mormon Bishop.

The Judge on the bench, J. B. McKean, at once cleared his throat and looked over the bar and the audience. The Judge wore a blue coat, and was trim as a bank president. He sat upon a wooden chair, behind a deal table, raised half a foot above the floor; the Marshal stood behind a remnant of drygoods box in one corner, and the jury sat upon two broken settees under a hot stove-pipe and behind the stove. They were intelligent, as usual with juries, and resembled a parcel of baggage smashers warming themselves in a railroad depot between trains. The bar consisted of what appeared to be a large keno party keeping tally on a long, pine table. When some law books were brought in after a while, the bar wore that unrecognizable look of religious services about to be performed before the opening of the game.

The audience sat upon six rows of damaged settees, and a standing party formed the back-ground, over whose heads was seen a great barren, barn-like area of room in the rear, filled with the debris of some former fair. One chair on the right of the Judge was deputed to witnesses. The entire furniture of the place might have cost eleven dollars at an auction where the bidding was high. The room itself was the second story of a livery stable, and a polygamous jackass and several unregenerate Lamanite mules in the stalls beneath occasionally interrupted the Judge with a bray of delight. The audience was composed entirely of men, perfectly orderly and tolerably ragged, and spitting surprisingly little tobacco juice; almost all of them Mormons, with a stray miner here and there mingled in, wearing a revolver on his hip and a paper collar under his long beard.

At the bar table, on one side sat Baskins and Maxwell, the prosecutors, the former frowsy, cool and red headed, the latter looking as if he had overslept himself for a week, and got up mad. On the opposite side sat Tom Fitch, late member of Congress from Nevada, a rotund cosmopolitan young man, with a bright, black eye, a piece of red flannel around his bad cold of a throat, and great quantities of forensic eloquence wrapped away under his mustache. Behind him was A. Miner, the leading Mormon lawyer, turned a trifle gray, and thinned down in flesh very much since Judge McKean got on the bench; for the Judge uses Miner as the scapegoat for the sins of the bar, and threatens him with Camp Douglas and a fine every time he has a toothache. Whenever Miner gets up to apologize, the Judge makes him sit down, and when he sits down the Judge looks at him with his resinous black eyes as if he had committed solely and alone the Mountain Meadow massacre. Miner is the Smallbones of the Court, and is fed on judicial herrings. The other lawyers are all Gentiles, except Hosea Stout and one Snow, of the firm of Snow & Hayne, a Vermonter. Yonder is a square-built man with cropped hair, ex-Governor Mann, Fitch's partner; they divide the leading business here, although resident only six months, with Hempstead & Kirkpatrick, the former a slow, serious military officer, and the latter a dark-eyed Kentuckian.

Kentuckian also is Marshall, the Ancient Pistol of the bar, rare and stupendous in speech, and chiefly admired by his partner Carter, from Maryland. Marshall once did a good deal of Brigham's business, but, with the impartial eye of a lawyer, he afterward sued Brigham for Godby's fee, and lost the better client. Nothing is a bereavement to Marshall, however, for, as he frequently reminds the Court, the jurisprudence of the country reaches its perihelion in the names of " Kent, Choate and Marshall, of which latter I am a part." Smith and Earl and De Wolf are about the remainder of the Utah bar— a shrewd, clever bevy of pioneer chaps, some of whom draw large contingent fees from mining suits, others encouraged to settle here by Brigham, who does not like litigious emulation amongst his own folks. He wants his good pleaders to be preachers.

As Miner is the victim of the Court, the Court in turn is the victim of Baskins, the Prosecuting Attorney *pro tem*. Baskins comes from Ohio, and gets his red hot temper from his hair. He is related to have shot somebody in Ohio, and about six months ago he scaled the ermine slopes of Judge Hawley, one of the three luminaries of this bench. The Judge, by an order, came between Baskins and a fee. Baskins threw the paper on the floor, and ground it with his boot-heel into an inoffensive tobacco quid. The Judge, who is slender, conscious, and respects himself and his rulings, told Mr. Baskins he would fine him.

"Go ahead with your fine!" said Baskins," you're of no account."

The Judge fined Baskins one hundred dollars, and sent him to Camp Douglas for ten days. Baskins twitched the order out of the Judge's hands and said that being an "old granny" the Judge should forthwith be kicked down stairs. At this Barkins threw open the door to expedite the descent of the venerable man, and rushed upon him, like Damon upon Lucullus. The Marshal interposed to save the author of so many learned and long opinions, and Baskins went to the Camp in custody. But as this notable Bench in Utah never consult together, Strickland agreeing with McKean in everything and Hawley in nothing, Judge McKean let Baskins out on *habeas corpus* in four days; and Baskins disdained to pay his fine. It is Baskins, therefore, who insists, as Prosecuting Attorney, that the laws of the United States and the Courts thereof must be respected in Utah.

As for McKean's two Associate Judges, they are off holding District Court at Provo and Beaver, Hawley harassing some rural justice of the peace with his last printed opinion, and Strickland playing billiards for drinks, between sessions, with Bill Nye. But Judge McKean himself does not use tobacco nor a billiard cue in any form; his sole recreation is to practice elocution and parlor suavity in anticipation of his appearance in the United States Senate from the State of New York. A trim, apprehensive, not unsagacious man, with a great, burning mission to exalt the horn of his favorite denomination upon the ruins of the Mormon Bishoprick, McKean is resolved in advance that everybody is guilty who can keep awake under Orson Pratt's sermons.

There stand the guilty fold, without the bar of the court—most of them look as if they wanted a new razor and a square meal—the Mormon rank and file. Grave and listening, and so respectful as to irritate the prosecuting attorneys very much (so that they would like to make premeditated good behavior a conspiracy punishable at law), these Mormons, could they speak aloud, would swell a chorus profuse and unintelligible as on the eve of the miraculous Pentecost—Dane and Welshman, Norwegian and Finn, Westphalian and Belgian, hard, nasal Yankee, and wide-mouthed Northumbrian lads from the collieries of Newcastle, the purlieus of London, and the mills of Bradford, they look upon the United States in a blue coat with a lead pencil in its hand as if it were the Man of Sin, and combined under the same baldish sconce the peculiarities of Guy Fawkes and Judge Jeffreys.

Simple people in the main, who, with all their regard to the command to increase and multiply, feared the United States census takers as partners in their persecution, and cut down, the returns of their population by sheer shyness, from 130,000 to 86,000 odd. Docile people, as well, though not without the courage of the poor, so that when on the late occasion of the great Methodist camp meeting, Brigham said to them in the Tabernacle: "I want you all to go to this camp meeting, and listen to what is said!" They filled it to over-flowing every day, but the mourners' bench remained empty as a lion's platter. And when, on one occasion only, at some harangue upon polygamy, a mutter arose over that great congregation, Brigham, himself present, stood up and waved his finger, and the complaint hushed to utter peace. People, also, who dance and waltz between religious benedictions, and yet can listen four hours in ardent delight to dry dissertations and discussions in their Tabernacle, which might make nature snore in her processes. How infinite are the possibilities of our nature when we reflect that these grave, unrebellious people, the waifs and findings of all lands, many of them dignified in apparel and culture, and steadily ascending in the scale of comfort and possessions, hold still with the tenacity of a moral purpose to the loose and spreading life of polygamy, preferring this fantastic reproduction like the Banyan's branches to the straight and peaceful unity of the European family. I saw in the court a Jew, lineal descendant of the old Patriarchs whom these Mormons delight to exemplify. His dark, shining eyes, aquiline beak, and wavy coarseness of hair made a strong contrast with those Saxon and Scandinavian races, fair-haired and highly-colored around him. He had marched down through two thousand years of wandering to accord with the century and Europe. And these Europeans had marched back six thousand years to resume the civilization the Jew had abandoned. What a feast for skepticism is this. But whoever looked closely could see the end of all this near at hand, unless fanned by irritation to fanaticism again. The weary faces, long and hollow, told of responsibilities too burdensome and of bodies overtaxed. The bright lights which shine in the face of him who submits to the life and customs proved by time and wisdom, were often darkened here. From the windows of the court, the rolling or serrated line of mountains, enfolding a valley like the lawn of Paradise, suggested far different men and women, and a life bounded by fewer necessities and wider opportunities for them all; a life consonant with the literatures of all these people, consonant with Christian art and promising a period of rest between labor and death. Who can look at this many-wedded manhood and envy it, or believe that its direction can be prolonged beyond the breaking of the darkness out of which this Mormon wife comes, like the feeble beam of the morning near at hand?

In a chair sat Mrs. Hawkins, a darkhaired, black-eyed woman from Birmingham, where she was converted to Mormonism about thirty years ago, and married to Hawkins, also a Mormon at the time, in an English parish church. Mrs. Hawkins wears a plain bonnet, a delaine dress, and drops her H's all over the floor. She refers to Hawkins as "my husband," and seems thoroughly aroused to the necessity of correcting him for the recreations of his maturer age. In short, Mrs. Hawkins has two suits against Thomas. This one is for adultery, and the next will be for divorce. Mrs. Hawkins is accompanied by her daughter, Lizzie Hawkins, a timid, embarrassed girl of about sixteen years, and while the mother is a prompt and rather bright witness, the daughter is measurably dumb. The daughter never saw anything wrong; she knew Elizabeth Mears' children were her father's, because they called him father, but she never saw anything in the Mears and Davis end of the house, because she never went there except on a visit in daytime.

Thomas Hawkins looks like one who might enjoy married life, and yet be a rather mean husband. A square English head, bulging in the big, high, dwarf's forehead, plastered straight across from ear to ear with thin, long, yellow hair, which permits half his pale head to stand naked in front, and still be no bald-head; a light-blue, animal eye, which would pick out a woman quickest in a landscape; not in athletic body, and that clad in light, worn clothes; silent, attentive, and at times uneasy, during the trial—such is the meager hero of three marriages, brought up seven years after date to answer the charge of adultery. I have understood that Hawkins stands in doubtful odor among his church people for not equalizing himself more among his families, both socially and financially. The common expression among the Mormons is—"There's wrong on both sides in that family;" but the inevitable addenda is "just as in plenty of monogamous families."

Here is Mrs. Hawkins' testimony, in part, showing that all is not tranquil in those households, and that dissolution is proceeding of itself more rapidly than interference can promote it:

Q. Did you ever have any conversation with Thomas Hawkins on the subject of his living with these women in the house?

A. Yes, sir.

Q. What did he say about it?

A. He said they were his wives.

Q. Did you ever have more than one conversation?

A. I have had many a thousand.

Q. State their substance.

A. Well, in the first place, he allowed he was doing religious duties, and he allowed that he had got to live with some one else.

Q. Did he give you any reason why he had to live with some person else?

A. Well, no reason; only he allowed that he had got to live with some one else! That I had had my day, and he had got to have some one else.

Q. Did you say you could consent to that?

A. No sir, I did not.

Q. What did you say to him?

A. I have told him that it was a damned bad trick, and that I did not believe in any such damned doctrine.

Q. Well, what did he say? What did he do?

A. Well, it didn't matter. If I didn't like it, I could do the other thing. He appeared to feel very indifferent about it, and I suppose if I had sanctioned what be wanted me to, and would have cleared out, that would have suited him, I suppose.

(Miner Smallbones), the Mormon lawyer: You need not state what you suppose. State the facts.

Witness: I am speaking the facts. I am not to be insulted by you, Mr. Miner!

At this point, when it appeared to be coming out exactly how the inside of a heavenly mansion was conducted, and how objecting damsels were chastised, the lawyers made objections, and we returned to the matter of the adultery.

One other witness was called, the brother-in-law of Hawkins, who flew off in high dudgeon at the idea that a man's wife was "anything else" but his wife. *He* couldn't see any difference in the order of wives; 'e didn't know whether Mears was the second or sixtieth wife; it was none of 'is business, &C.

The audience laughed and applauded only once when Mrs. Hawkins testified that her husband's lawyer came to her to solicit a compromise, and said that unless she settled, the lawyers would get all the property. To this she replied that the lawyers might as well have it as "'is woman."

There seemed to be no feeling in the town except regret at the wife's suit for divorce, but a notion that the prosecution for adultery was malicious, and set on by the court and its favorite lawyers.

The oratory was mixed in the case. Maxwell, who was admitted at his own solicitation to assist Baskins in the prosecution, making the point against the Mormons that in twenty-two years their Legislature had never made a statute validating polygamy even by inference. To this Muller, the Mormon lawyer, replied that marriage was not a civil, but an ecclesiastical rite in Utah, that polygamy was established prior to the formation of any American government here, and relied upon a clause of the treaty of Guadaloupe Hidalgo, whereby the newly annexed inhabitants were guaranteed against interference with their religion. The speeches of Maxwell and Baskins were bold and acrid, but the large Mormon audience listened without a murmur.

The reliance of the prisoner and his friends was upon Hon. Thomas Fitch, who came into the case late, and made an address which extorted admiration on every side, as well for its frankness as its legal incision. He is the best public orator and pleader west of the Rocky Mountains since the death of General Baker, and in the opening of his address he proclaimed himself an opponent of polygamy on every ground, and affirmed it to be a cruel and uncompensating system of barbarism, whether indorsed by former patriarchs or latter saints.

But the prisoner was on trial for adultery, and not for polygamy, and under a statute passed by a Territorial Legislature, three-fourths of whom were polygamists, and signed by Brigham Young himself, as governor, nineteen years ago. This statute fixes a penalty so severe as to show that the adultery meant was that committed outside, or in injury of the sort of marriage relation acknowledged here, prescribing from three hundred to one thousand dollars fine, and from three to twenty years imprisonment. To carry out its relentless purposes, this court—which had announced itself as a United States Court, and nothing else, and had quashed all territorial acts as to Probate Courts, selections of juries, divorces, &c. now revives this obsolete statute, resumes for this object only a territorial jurisdiction, and punishes polygamy with the penalty of adultery.

Mr. Fitch's argument was that, as the Legislature had not defined adultery, the jury had a right to interpret the meaning of this statute according to the intent of the Legislature—the intent constituting the gist of the offense. The prisoner was clearly unaware that his offense was adultery according to any law enacted in Utah. The "Thou shalt not commit adultery" was delivered to a polygamous people, and engraved upon stone by the husband of three wives. The same public opinion and religious inculcation which enacted the statute against adultery, married the prisoner to his wives, and honored the children of them equally. The rulings of the courts in Utah, both probate and district, for twenty years, had been in accordance with this theory of marriage, and now, seven years after committing the act charged with his second wife, "a rusty law is drawn from its antique sheath," and made retroactive upon this man. The polygamists on trial in the person of the prisoner had left civilized places and entered the desert, followed by the women, to attest their belief in this dispensation, and obey it out of the way of the people.

Here the eloquent advocate touched the audience to tears, and as he proceeded, an audible "boo-hoo" went over the courtroom, two jury-men joining in the chorus, to the great alarm of the judge and Baskins, who feared that, unaware, some Mormons might have been insinuated into that packing-box. When Mr. Fitch concluded, there seemed a possibility, despite the clearness of Mrs. Hawkins' evidence as to the cohabitation between Hawkins and Mrs. H. No. 2, that the jury might hang.

To make this impossible, Judge McKean delivered a harangue to the jury answering every point made by the defense. It was a speech of three quarters of an hour, and amounted to an exhortation to convict. As to the intent of the Territorial Legislature, he said, that was no more to be conjectured than that *magna charta* could be interpreted away because King John, its grantor, was a tyrant; a statute against gambling might be similarly disproved because the enactors were proven to play at chance.

The Mormon paper, the *Herald*, tendered Judge McKean's charge and conduct of the trial as follows, on the following morning:

"You have your duties, gentlemen, and I have mine. My duty is to pick you out and pack you in; to fix the trial at such a time as will be least convenient to the defendant; to exclude all evidence that may help him, and to admit all evidence that may hurt him; to rule all points of law against him; to pick out from acts of Congress and acts of the Utah Assembly those laws which, combined, may convict him; to be first a United States Justice's Court, and then a Territorial Justice's Court, and vice versa, as the exigencies of the case may demand; to dramatize the case, and elocutionize my opinions; to follow my instructions from Rev. Dr. Newman, and avenge his death at the Tabernacle; in short, gentlemen, my duty is to secure a conviction."

Directed by this peremptory charge, the jury found a verdict of guilty in one hour, and it was heard by the large audience, standing with breathless eagerness and silence. As this case came up on complaint of a wife, and the testimony as to the second cohabitation was clear, it was thought to be the easiest case to obtain a conviction, and made comparatively little excitement. The streets of Salt Lake were quiet, as usual, and no knots of people discussed the affair unless in privacy.

The cases of Brigham Young, Wells, and Cannon are accompanied by no complaint from any wife, and are regarded by the Mormons as deliberate attempts to invite resistance and inaugurate persecution.

About the close of the trial, the only disturbance occurred between the reporter for the anti-Mormon organ and a deputy marshal. It was on the supposed occasion of the administration of sentence, and, either to express sympathy with the prisoner or to find out what might be the penalty of such wedlock, the room was filled with Mormon women. Suddenly a man came up stairs from the livery stable, and said that the floor showed signs of coming down. At this, the court was profoundly exercised. The deputy marshal, under pretence of regulating admissions, got near the door, and just at this juncture, the Gentile reporter strutted in in search of items. The marshal gave him an item by tearing his coat off his back, in the unfounded supposition that the coat was not too rotten to pitch him down stairs by it. Quantities of lead pencils and free tickets to the theater strewed the courtroom in an instant. The reporter, to whom a thousand years were but as a day, struck the marshal, and they clinched and fell down stairs, the marshal on top. The reporter was handed over to the Mormon police, and discharged that afternoon by a Mormon judge, on the ground that there was no breach of the peace committed outside of the court-room. This excitement and the fact that Judge McKean had not committed the sentence to memory so as to render it effective, led to a postponement of Hawkins' sentence.

THE FEDERAL ENEMIES OF THE SAINTS.

SALT LAKE CITY, October 23.

There are now two places in Salt Lake City of more superstitious consequence even than Brigham Young's Lion House or Camp Douglas. These are the Wahsatch Club—the headquarters of the anti-Mormon "Ring" and the United States District Court room, over a livery stable.

Except for the good counsel prevailing among the Mormons, and the powerful control Brigham Young has over these people, the $70,000,000 of real and personal property here, the accumulations of twenty-two years, and the homesteads of one hundred and thirty thousand people, might today have been ashes and desert, and the suppositious mineral wealth in this territory would have lain hidden in the mountain ores for half a century. The Union Pacific Railroad, as a separate incorporation with an independent trade, would have been bankrupt or worse. Our half-way house to the Pacific, the only oasis of any capacity or longevity in the Great American Desert, would have relapsed to plains and benches of alkali. We should have lost from Utah the only type of human labor with the patience, frugality, simplicity and directed industry to keep it under development. And we should have expedited the extermination of polygamy at the cost of more than $100,000,000 principal money, by only about two or three years. The Chief Justice of this territory, a wilder fanatic than Orson Pratt or John Taylor, would have achieved a reputation upon this lamentable commercial transaction, and might have assumed to run against Roscoe Conkling for the next vacant senatorship from New York, whence he came. But sound statesmanship, the common interest which in the end surrounds and regulates morals, our pride of empire and our jealousy of law, precedent and equity, would have suffered in the catastrophe, and there would have been a reaction, political and historical, against the reckless actors in it.

For, according to the best information I have been able to obtain, the Mormons, rank and file, believing that neither law nor equity were to be observed in dealing with them for the future, had meditated a wholesale, desertion of their country and an occupation of Mexican soil, where they had frequently been invited, and where, with their arms, discipline, cattle, and fortitude, they could maintain themselves as victoriously as had Texas under Houston and Crockett.

They were saved from this act of devotion and despair by the abnegation of their leaders and thinkers, men who had proved their resources thrice before under worse conditions of exodus. Brigham Young, the theocrat of this church; Daniel H. Wells, Mayor of Salt Lake City, and George Q. Cannon, an editor of influence and a man of property and force, appeared before the Court and gave bonds to stand trial on the charge of lewd and lascivious conduct and cohabitation with divers women. At the same time, the strong instinct for peace in the Mormon counsels compelled one Thomas Hawkins, an English member of the Church to submit to indictment, trial, and, if required, punishment, on the ground of adultery with his later wives, which he has done with dignity worthy a better cause.

I have seen the whole of this trial, being present in Salt Lake City, upon commercial business, and, although on the occasion of my last visit here, four months ago, I wrote probably as severe strictures upon the essence of this civilization, as any tourist, I have found the Mormons anxious to encourage the slightest disposition to represent them to the Eastern people, and without resentment for expressions of opinion.

Near the Townsend House, the principal hotel of Salt Lake, and a Mormon's property, in a pleasant two-story adobe house of a gray color, is a lounging place and mess-room called the Wahsatch Club, denominated here by three-fourths of the Gentiles as the "Jumpers' Club," in allusion to the tendency of the judicial judges and their satellites to "jump" or possess without right and by force the neighboring valuable mining claims.

In this club meet by accident or design the members of the Federal Administration who are moving on the Mormon works, and at the same time upon the substantial interests of Utah. As they have written themselves up copiously for the Eastern press, they may not object to taking this current and third-party opinion of their qualifications. I give them in the order of brains and consequence.

1. Chief Justice of Utah, J. B. McKean, of New York State; an officer in the volunteer army during the war, and a prominent Methodist, formerly, it is

said, a preacher. McKean came here upon a crusade against polygamy, and his fair abilities and great vanity have carried him through it thus far with about equal flourish and fearlessness. He is a wiry, medium-sized man, with a tall baldish head, gray side-locks, and very black, sallow eyes, at times resinous in color, like tar-water. He looks, however, to be in the prime of strength and will; has never communicated with Brigham Young personally since he arrived, and is absorbed in the purpose of intimidating the Mormon Church or breaking it up. His behavior on the bench has been despotic and extra-judicial to the last degree, and he has also been unfortunate enough to compromise his reputation by mining speculations which have come before his court, and received influential consideration there.

2. R. N. Baskins, the author of what is called in Congress the " Cullom Bill," and at present temporary Prosecuting Attorney before McKean's Court; a lean, lank, rather dirty and frowsy, red-headed young man, but a lawyer of shrewdness and coolness, and inflamed against Mormonism. He said, in a speech before McKean last Friday, that if Joseph Smith had been a eunuch he would never have received the revelation on polygamy. To this the Mormons retort that Baskins is married to a woman for whom he procured a divorce from a former husband, &c.

3. George R. Maxwell, an ex-officer from Michigan, with a game leg, a strong, dissipated face, and Register of the Land Office here; an indomitable man, but accused of corruption, and a chronic runner for Congress against delegate W. H. Hooper; thinks Congress is a vile body, because it will not put Hooper out of Congress for his creed, as promptly as Judge McKean would put him off a jury.

4. J. H. Taggart, United States Assessor; a person who was bitten by a dog some time ago, and charged the bite to Mormon assassins. Imperfect, indeed doubtful record in the army as surgeon, and chiefly potential as a gadder and street gossip against the Saints.

5. 0. J. Hollister, United States Collector; uninteresting man, who married the half sister of the Vice-President, and, although a determined anti-Mormon, does not agree with several of the Ring; the same is the case with several others; all want to be boss. Hollister deluges the Eastern press, from Chicago to New York, with letters of locums picked up at hearsay, and hardly reliable enough for a comic paper.

6. Dennis T. Toohy, editor and late partner with Hollister in the *Corinne Reporter*; an Irishman, witty and abusive, and incapable of working in harness. The Ring tactics have generally been to combine the Godbyites and the Gentiles in a "Liberal" or anti-Brigham party; but at a meeting of the two

sets some time ago, Toohy denounced polygamy so violently that Godby and Eli B. Kelsey, apostates but polygamists, rose up and resented it.

7. Frank Kenyon, proprietor of the *Review*, a paper which has superseded the *Salt Lake Tribune* in irritating the Mormons; a Montana man, and with so little fortitude that when the indictment of Brigham was proposed, he sent his domestic treasures to San Francisco.

8. C. M. Hawley, Associate Justice with McKean, but not servile, like O. F. Strickland, the other Judge. Hawley bores people on the streets by reading his long opinions to them. He nearly made O. P. Morton a polygamist lately by reading to him opinions the other way.

8½. C. M. Hawley, jr., son of the aforesaid, a weakish, flop-whiskered, insubstantial young man, who stood challenged at the polls in Salt Lake recently, with too many horns "into" him, and was arrested by the city police and confined two hours; he now has a suit against the corporation for twenty-five thousand dollars damages, and one of the usual packed juries may award it.

9. George A. Black, Secretary of the Territory, author of the proclamation against the Fourth of July here.

10. George L. Woods, of Oregon, the Governor; a red-headed, gristly, large man, of little mental 'heft.' Woods refused to let the Mormon militia celebrate the Fourth of July last year, and ordered, through Black, General De Trobriand to turn out his regular army garrison and fire on the Nauvoo Legion if they disobeyed. De Trobriand, who has a contempt for the Gentile Ring, like all the regular army officers, answered:

"If I do this thing, there is to be no confusion nor debate about it upon the actual field. I shall parade my troops down to the Mormon line; the second order, in proper succession, will be, 'Fire!' the last order *you* must give."

Woods refused to take the responsibility, and threatened to make General Grant remove De Trobriand. The letter told Woods to go to the devil, and said it was an outrage, anyway, to forbid the Mormons to celebrate the Fourth, as they had been doing for twenty years. De Trobriand was removed as soon as Dr. Newman, the Methodist preacher, could see Grant, and General Morrow was ordered here.

This is about all the Ring, except Strickland, a Michigander on the bench; William Appleby, the Register in Bankruptcy, and R. H. Robertson, Strickland's law partner, seeking practice under the protection of the courts.

These people represent the average character of Territorial officers; political adventurers for the most part, paid the low stipends allowed in the wisdom of the Federal Government, and possessing in common only an intense feeling, begotten of conviction and interest against every feature of the

Mormon Church. Polygamy is the objective feature, but the city and Territory completely out of debt and both with plethoric treasuries, the great cooperative store paying two per cent a month and yet unincorporated, and the value, of Salt Lake City property, for which title has never yet been given, appear to offer wonderful opportunities for plunder in case an outbreak can be devised. Utah, although the richest and most populous Territory in the Union, really affords less political pap than any other. But the mining enthusiasm, the large trade of Salt Lake, the elasticity of real estate here, and the large acquisitions of Brigham Young and others in the church, give lawyers in favor with the United States Courts unusual chances to thrive, and the anti-Mormon lawyers and the Court make a close society—so close that some time ago Justice McKean in the case of the Velocipede Mine kept the whole bar of Salt Lake from appearing against his interest, and lawyers had to be sent for from Nevada.

In this Ring McKean is the organizing spirit, and Baskins, whom McKean made Prosecutor, is the executive arm. The Court has lost its superstition in the Territory, and in criminal cases affecting Mormons the Saints say that their only chance is to fee the Ring lawyers, while the public morals of Salt Lake, which, up to two years ago, barring polygamy, had extorted the admiration of travelers, are nearly as bad as elsewhere in Nevada or Idaho. The Court has given moral support to unlicensed liquor dealers, and encouraged them to resist paying the hitherto almost prohibitory rates of license. One Engelbrecht, having set the license law at defiance, recently had his stock destroyed by Mayor Wells' police, and he brought suit against the city and got sixty thousand dollars damages. W. S. Godby, leader of the Godbyites, but a liquor dealer and a polygamist, also applied to Judge McKean for an injunction to restrain the city from suing him for violating the license law. When McKean was applied to for a dissolution of the injunction, he put it in his pocket, saying he would hold it under advisement, while meantime Godby goes on selling liquor. Prostitution, taking encouragement from these cases, has quadrupled in Salt Lake, every bagnio being composed of Gentile women. A day or two ago a streetwalker was arrested for drunkenness and swearing, but some of her friends the poker players at the Wahsatch Club, prompted her to sue the city for ten thousand dollars.

In short, the Officeholders' Ring, led by the United States Court, and supported by the liquor and lewd interests, and all who want to throw off city taxation, is engaged in an unequal grapple with the municipal corporation. The East is liberally supplied with inflammatory correspondence, charging mutiny upon the Mormons, in despite of the fact that Brigham Young has submitted to arrest and appeared, unattended, in court. The garrison has been increased to about 1,200 men, unwilling allies of the Ring. A large amount of capital invested in the rich argentiferous galena mines has been diverted to Nevada, Idaho, and Montana; and other foreign capital, apprehensive of a war, has declined to come here. Brigham Young with whom the United States has dealt upon terms of encouragement in a hundred ways while as much of a polygamist as now—using him to build telegraph and railways, to furnish supplies, to repress Indians, and carry mails—and which appointed him first Governor of Utah and continued him in the place for seven years,—this old man, at seventy years of age, is suddenly admonished that he is a criminal, and put on trial for offenses committed twenty years ago.

And yet, it is capable of demonstration that polygamous marriages have declined between September 1, 1869, and September 1, 1871, in the remarkable proportion of one hundred to six. That is, the months of 1869 and the corresponding ones of 1871, prior to September, show the decrease, and this is due to public opinion, to Gentile influx, to commercial intercourse, the awakened consciousness of the women, and the cost of keeping them. The preposterousness of polygamy dooms it in the event of peaceful competition with monogamy. The Mormon Church itself is modifying its whole internal structure, and I have heard it said that whereas two years ago Brigham Young could have emigrated to Mexico with his entire membership, he could now carry with him only three-fourths, and in another year could not persuade one-fourth to go.

Nothing can rally together from their centrifugal and gainful individual pursuits these Mormon people—who cast twenty-five thousand votes, and outnumber in armsbearing men the American regular army—except the aggressive attitude of the Federal State toward them. Fifteen years ago Brigham Young integrated the church, and kept it from crumbling by feigning a persecution, and inventing the Utah war. This time the cry of persecution is not a feint. To try the representatives of twenty-two thousand votes, a jury is picked by the United States Marshal from one-fourth of two thousand Gentiles; because less than one-fourth of the Gentiles living here indorse the action of the Court. No wife, neighbor or acquaintance of Brigham Young has made any complaint against him. The Court which is to try him packs a grand jury to do the work of inquisition, a petit jury to try him, and comes down itself amongst the lawyers to prosecute him. This is persecution, because there is no law for it. The Court enacts the Cullom Bill, which never passed Congress, and prosecutes under it by the very man who wrote it.

The present movement against Brigham Young at one time comprised a large portion of the Gentile and apostate population here, but nearly all these have fallen away, and the Ring is left nearly alone, with scarcely enough citizen material to get sufficient juries from it. The mines are ransacked to find people partial or ignorant enough to find verdicts according to the charging of the Court, and now, the only reply the Ring makes to the allegation that they are without followers, is that the timid property-holders have fallen away from them. The Ring people, however, possess no property, unless "jumped" or prospective, and several of them are merely waiting for the spoils of violence.

Bishop Tuttle, the Episcopal functionary here, to whom Brigham Young gave a liberal subscription for the Episcopal Chapel, as he gave $500 to the new Catholic Church, is said to deprecate the precipitate action of the Court, as does Father Welsh, the priest. Dr. Fuller, ex-Republican acting Governor here; ex-Secretary and Governor S. A. Mann; Major Hempstead, District Attorney here for eight years, and even General Connor, an old enemy of Brigham Young, express contempt for these sensational court processes. Connor has just written a letter to Hempstead, saying, that this action was altogether unfortunate as a repressory measure. The late Chief Justice, Charles C. Wilson, is even more pronounced in his condemnation of the Court. I. C. Bateman and D. E. Buell, as well as the Walkers, the latter the leading merchants of Salt Lake apostates, and the former two great mining capitalists, are said to be of the same mind. Joseph Gordon, late Secretary to Governor Latham, calls the Court hard names. The large law firms are nearly all in like attitude. Every Representative and Senator west of the Rocky Mountains, including, Cole, Williams, Corbett, Nye, Stewart, Sargent, and other Republicans, stand opposed to any measure which shall sacrifice Utah to blind bigotry without statesmanship. Mrs. Lippincott (Grace Greenwood), who is here, agrees with me in our mutual dislike of polygamy and of these "hot gospelers" and "notoriety hunters," who will not let it die ignobly, but must irritate it to renewed existence.

The original movement against the Mormons, through which the Salt Lake Tribune was started—the first paper here to attack the Church—began for quite a different interest. The valuable Emma Mine was then in litigation, and a decision of Judge McKean confirmed the Walker Brothers and others in the occupation and use of it, as against the claim of James E. Lyon, of Colorado. The Walkers occupied the mine jointly with W. M. Hussey, President of the opposition bank of Salt Lake, the Selovers, capitalists of New York, and Tranor W. Park, of Vermont, late financial agent of the John C. Fremont ring and candidate for the United States Senate from California. None of these wished to consummate the arrest of Brigham Young, or provoke any collision or debate in Utah, but they were forced to support McKean because his decision confirmed them in the mine. Meantime, Lyon and his attorneys,

Stewart, Hempstead, Curtis J. Hillyer, and others, preferred charges against McKean, for his corrupt transaction in the Velocipede Mine, wishing to get him off the bench in the Emma Mine case. The Walkers and Hussey—to whom McKean was necessary—started the newspaper to sustain him, and McKean himself alleged that the Mormons were behind the effort to remove him. Thus the Emma Mine quarrel gave the anti-Mormon ring a temporary appearance of power which they no longer retain; for by a compromise the mine has passed out of the hands of the court, and Benjamin Curtis, of Boston, has been made arbitrator between the claimants, while the anti-Lyon interest has relapsed to conservatism. So true is this that the Salt Lake Tribune has ceased to be the prominent ring organ, and they have started the Review, to keep up the appearance of a quarrel here.

While the effort was being made to remove McKean, the Lyon interest called upon Brigham Young to give it aid through his great, but silent, influence in Eastern circles.

"No," replied Brigham; "whoever will be sent here in his place will proceed to rob and plunder us in the same way. I have no choice between thieves, and can't help you."

When the Emma Mine litigation, the unconscious entering wedge to Mormonism, was pending, Tranor W. Park, who had lived in Nevada, and knew the desperate means often resorted to there to get ante-judicial possession of a valuable mine, became apprehensive that Lyon and his lawyers would import roughs from Nevada and seize the mine by force. He cozzened Governor Woods, therefore, for the sake of the military which Woods controlled, with the gift of the presidency of a tunnel company, and thus, perhaps, it happens that the Governor is able to swear in one of his stock transactions that he is now worth fifty thousand dollars—either a large oath or a large commercial increase in a short while.

You can see from these data how much more than the Mormon question there is out here in Utah, and all the adventurers secrete themselves behind the halloo of "polygamy." No wonder the Mormons are afraid of our judicial morals more than our justice.

During the Emma Mine controversy it is alleged that Judge McKean was afraid to put Judge Hawley, his associate, upon the bench in the Velocipede case for fear Hawley would grant an injunction upon the Park interest working the Emma Mine.

The Velocipede case has been already ventilated, and Senator Stewart denounced the Court's transactions in it publicly in the streets of Salt Lake. Here is the charge:

Judge Strickland, associate and crony of McKean, "jumped" a mine in Ophir Canon. Strickland sold his interest to McKean, who organized a company called "The Silver Shield," of which he was made President. McKean retained Baskins, the Prosecutor of Brigham Young, his attorney, and by visiting all the lawyers practicing at McKean's Bar, it was extorted from them that they would not take the case against him. McKean then commenced suit, in his own court, against the original locators of the Velocipede Mine, and called Judge Strickland to sit in his place.

The defendants declined to try the case in the District Court before Strickland, on the ground that he had sold McKean his interest, and was therefore as much interested in the case as McKean himself. They appealed to McKean as Supreme Justice of the Territory, to allow Hawley, the alternate Justice and who was disinterested, to try the issue. This McKean refused to do; the one we stuck fast in the courts; and McKean's company, the " Silver Shield," continue to claw ore from the Velocipede Mine, while Theodore Tracy, of Wells, Fargo & Co., and the Velocipede people, abuse McKean and Strickland without stint, and call them names not polite enough to put in this correspondence.

If the interior of a Mormon family is as impestuous as a Gentile's out-of-doors, the life must be worse than seductive.

The three men indicted by McKean's and Baskin's grand jury (the jury picked by Marshal M. T. Patrick, who has little or no sympathy with the court he must obey), Young, Wells and Cannon, are the vitality of the Mormon Church. Young is the organizer of the industry of Utah, and the ablest executive spirit west of the Rocky Mountains. His power is in his will, his Yankee materialism, and his position, now so long maintained as to be traditional with his people. They are proud of him, of his hale old age fearlessness, sagacious enterprises, attention to their wants, and high rank amongst the great men of the time. He has brought the mass of them out of English, Danish and Swedish beggary, to a country of land, fruit, and scenery.

He can put ten thousand men to work any day on his three railways, for their daily board, paying them wages in stock, and he needs no land grant or bonded endorsement. His enterprises generally pay speedy dividends. His tithing system brings out immigrants, who in time return the passage-money to the Church, and it reappears in large systems of mechanism and traffic. He has built five hundred miles of the Deseret telegraph line, connecting all his settlements from St. George, where the Mormons cultivate cotton and mill it; past Provo, where a granite woolen mill, seven stories high, costing two hundred thousand dollars, and adapted to five hundred hands, is about to move its infinite spindles; up to Brigham city, where his narrow-gauge road is progressing toward Idaho. He has built sixty miles of cooperative railway in Utah, one hundred and fifty miles of the Union Pacific Railroad, and many hundred miles of the Western Union Telegraph. There is no ecclesiastic in the Methodist or any other American church, with a tithe of his versatile and vigorous administrative ability. Of his sixty odd children, many are married to Gentiles, and all are endowed never with money, but with occupation. Brigham Young is still a credulous, sincere convert to the Mormon Church, and he has never pretended, himself, to receive a revelation. The church has made him, as well as he has dignified it; for he was only a painter and carpenter, with a serious nature, and an inclination for the Methodist Church, when the gospel of Joseph Smith overtook him, and drew him in. The prophet himself predicted a career for Brigham, and sent him abroad on a mission. Given thus a consequence and experience which old and beaten faiths would not have proffered, Brigham Young was ten years a traveling preacher and agent, and the doctrine of polygamy was no part of his suggestion. He accepted it as he did every other declaration of Joseph Smith; and the wife of his youth was dead before he ever saw the prophet. To this day, in all matters of mental erudition, logical analysis, and capacity to discover the illiteracy and mere cunning of Smith's writings, Brigham Young is grossly ignorant. As a theologian, he is only an exhorter and moralist. His life for all great ends began, not with education, but with a full superstitious conviction and entire allegiance to the Mormon Church. The mysteries of his faith he has never ventured to question, nor has he ever, with a learned man's skepticism, reexamined his creed. Such characters are common enough in other churches why not possible with this man whose life in all but polygamy has been abstemious, ardent and powerful, and who, considering his want of education, is, perhaps, the greatest living instance of human development without advantages?

Wells, the Mayor of Salt Lake, is a man of willing administration, entirely faithful to Young, in nothing else great, and he has a disagreeable cock-eye, but he is a diligent Mayor, and Salt Lake city is in much his creation.

Geo. Q. Cannon is one of the most intelligent Mormons, an Englishman and a good writer; outside of his family he is a pure man.

These three are selected for indictment upon the complaint of nobody but a grand jury picked especially with this object.

Bearing in mind these natures, strong men but zealous of forty years' standing (for Brigham was converted in 1832), you may imagine the situation when the indictment was served upon them.

There were gathered together in the Lion House Brigham's chief counselors: old John Taylor, who stood by Joe Smith when he was shot in

Carthage jail and was himself wounded, and would rather take his chances in the open air than go to a Gentile jail again; a tall, good-looking, severe man with gray hair.

There was George A. Smith, cousin to Joseph, and, next to Young, the highest man in the church, also a witness of the sack of Nauvoo, a polygamist, but with few wives, a fat, aged, good-humored and rather weak Saint.

There was Orson Pratt, the chief theologian and expounder, whose brother, Parley Pratt, was shot dead by the Gentiles—a venerable-looking, Mosaic sort of man, with flaming beard, and large, introspective eyes, a Greek student, and a sort of Mormon Matthew Henry. The natty and flowery Dr. Newman, of Washington, who came out here with six Hebrew roots carefully committed to memory, expecting to demolish Orson with them, found the old fellow to be capable of talking Hebrew with Moses or Daniel.

There was Joseph Young, President of the Seventies, a lean face and low forehead, with a mouth like Abraham Lincoln's—elder brother of Brigham Young.

These and others, baked dry in the furnace of old Mormon dangers which they now account their glory, gave counsel to Brigham Young as to his duty. Almost unanimously they urged that he must never give himself up: the people would rise if he were to be convicted, whether he forbade them or no. Their counsel was to cut the irrigating ditches, burn every Mormon settlement in the Territory, leave the valley of Salt Lake in desolation, and march across Arizona with their herds and portables to Mexican soil; these were their own, and they had a right to annihilate the property they had created.

Brigham Young, himself in the condition of an old lion, not uncertain that his prowess was now a part of his nature and religion, urged that he was promised safe conduct and fair treatment.

To this old John Taylor retorted:

"So was Joseph! I saw the safe treatment they gave him in jail!"

There was a general exclamation of deep feeling and cry of perfidy at this,—and I am writing no fancy sketch, but the statement of two attorneys who were present. Brigham himself was deeply moved. Perhaps the recollection of his more youthful Captaincy of the Mormon exodus across the alkali plains inspired him with enthusiasm. To this urgent statement of the Gentiles that he could not hold out a week against the United States, the old man retorted with a strange, almost childish confidence, that if he were disposed to resist, the ally of Moses, of Gideon, and of David, would appear upon his side.

Then, after a minute, Brigham closed his great square mouth and jaw, and said calmly:

"God is in courts as well as in battles and marches. There will be no resistance. I shall obey the summons."

In due time he dismounted from his buggy before the little old squalid stone stable where the United States Court meets, climbed the creaky outside stairs, and at his colossal, venerable appearance, the whole court unconsciously arose, bar and audience.

He was the overshadowing presence there, and when he answered "Not guilty," Judge McKean's elocution flew out of his head and he forgot, temporarily, to be dramatic.

The editors have chosen to remove the next two sections of "The Mormon Trials" in the interest of brevity. Those sections entitled "Interview with the Mayor of Salt Lake City" and "Salt Lake and Utah Pictures" written October 25 and 27 respectively can be found in the original paper. The final section follows.

INSIDE VIEWS OF UTAH SOCIETY.

SALT LAKE, Oct. 27.

Mr. Kinzer, a Californian, who has been developing mines in Southern Utah, told me several anecdotes which illustrate Mormon dignity and sincerity. One day, as the period of the semi-annual Mormon conference approached, he met a very old woman driving a cart to which an ox was attached. The miner peeped into her cart and saw that it contained nothing to eat except a little salt meat and a bag of meal with fodder for the ox. This was somewhere in Juab County.

"Old lady," said the miner, "where are you going?"

"Up to our conference, sir. I ha'n't been there now for two year, but I want to get my soul warmed up a little. It appeared as if I could not stay away any longer. I have been in church twenty-two years, and I always go to the conference when I can, but I live 'way down here on the Santa Clara River, and it takes me three weeks to go to Salt Lake."

This poor old zealot had actually been more than two weeks on the way to her church conference; she camped out every night, and was entirely alone and unbefriended. The miners gave her some cheese and bread and sent her on her way rejoicing.

The Mormon conferences are fearfully apostolical. Twelve thousand people often attend them. A band of music plays at the Tabernacle gate as the Saints go in and as they come out, and "Shoo Fly," " Bully for You," "High Ricketty Barlow," &c., are the class of tunes selected. Go into that vast enclosure, and you will see the Mormon Church conducting its business, the hands of its officials held up by the whole broad public sentiment. W. H. Hooper told me that for nearly twenty years he had attended these conferences, and he had never heard a half dozen nays voted against any measure propounded by the High Quorum. Brigham Young reads such an announcement as this:

"Brother William Johnson is nominated for a mission to Russia of two years, at his own expense. All in favor of that nomination will say *aye*."

A roar goes up from the great conference of Saints, and Brother William Johnson, who perhaps keeps a shop in one of the streets of Salt Lake, who does not speak any language but his own, and that indifferently well, and who has never traveled away from home, ten miles in his life, has no option but to hearken to that cry as if it were as sacred as the voice in St. Paul's dream of "Come over into Macedonia and help us."

A great many people who read this will cry out, "Despotism," but I, who am a preacher's son in the Methodist Church, have seen the heart of my mother sink down when my father was ordered off, by government as absolute as Brigham Young to live two years in some swampy part of the earth for such a salary as could be picked up,—marriage fees and presents of sausage and sparerib about Christmas thrown in.

The death of Brigham Young will be as things stand, a benefit to his people. Of Brigham's devotion, credulity and constancy as a Mormon there can be no doubt. He is as sincere a man in his church as Bishop Simpson is in the Methodist Church or Judge McKean in his. But the old man has been cramped up in Utah since 1848. Absolute authority has made him vain; want of travel to distant parts has kept his charity from expanding. To him, the whole earth lies under the thatch of the Wahsatch Mountains, and he is only aware of the fearful mightiness of democratic sentiment in America from the few troops camped in his vicinity, from the miserable character of the Federal officials who go out there to blackmail him, and from the stream of respectful visitors, for whom he holds a levee every morning, and who butter him with praises, while perhaps the same people are inditing letters to the East raising a hue and cry against his Empire. He will leave behind him in that State a name never to be rivaled in the future prosperous history of Utah. This very old man, against whom the Courts are battering, and who may soon be a fugitive on the borders of Arizona to avoid the penitentiary of Salt lake, —I dare believe the fame of Brigham Young is as indissolubly bound in the literature and reverence of the Rocky Mountain people, as the names of La Salle, John Winthrop and Hernando Cortez are embedded in other parts of the country.

I was talking one day with a distinguished apostle of the Mormon Church, and he used this curious illustration:

"Suppose, Mr. Townsend," he said, that Joseph Smith had been born 3400 years ago, and Moses in the year 1800, A.D., thus reversing the order of their several revelations,—which would be the harder to believe?"

I replied: "You ask me too much. I am not familiar with the story of Moses. My notion of Moses is obtained from one of Michael Angelo's statues; he always seemed to me to be a fair man."

"Now," said this apostle, the story of Joseph Smith is, that he discovered a set of golden plates, and he was divinely endowed to translate them. You ask where are those plates? We answer that Joseph Smith gave them back to the angel, who kept them. Moses on the other hand went up into Mount Sinai, taking no witnesses with him, and is alleged to have had a familiar talk with the Lord. The Lord gave him two tablets of stone on which the commandments are engraved; but Moses never showed the people those stone tablets, any more than Joseph Smith showed the golden plates. When Moses came down from Sinai with the tablets, he found the people worshipping a golden calf, and it says in the ninth chapter of Deuteronomy, that he cast down the tablets and broke them to pieces. Then he went up into the mountain again, as the tenth chapter of Deuteronomy discloses and was permitted by the Lord, to hew himself a new set of tablets, on which the commandments were engraved, these tablets were put into the ark, and they were everlastingly concealed from the public eye. Now had Moses been named Joseph Smith, the gentile world would have scoffed at this story, and would have said that the nonappearance of the stone tablets, the breaking of the original pair, and the re-engraving of an imitation by the prophet himself, were all subterfuges such as those which accompanied the chiseling of the Cardiff giant. But you have had preached at you for eighteen hundred years, the legend of Moses, and you take it without question while you laugh at the altogether more consistent story of the translation of the golden plates. Both instances must be accepted by faith and not by reason. Our people out here believe equally in the tale of Moses, and in that of Joseph, and you who accept one-half of the gospel, want to put us in jail and break us up for believing the other half. You came in here just like the Catholic priests got into the vales of the Waldenses. Failing to convert us or, rather to unconvert us, you begin to persecute us. It is no fault of ours that we offend you; for we left civilization fifteen hundred miles behind us, in order not to irritate you. We think that our revelation treats of matters if possible more important to human nature than the Old Testament. It solves the problem of the past history of America. It has the only new gospel and indigenous prophet and seer on this hemisphere. It has grown more rapidly than the Jewish power, and if it were not for our notion on the subject of marriage, I believe we would have more converts in the United States, than any other sect.

Mormon Utah is a congregation of all the good institutions which you separately maintain. It is a house of correction, an inebriate asylum, an almshouse, a church, an intelligence office, a system of apprenticeship, a commission of emigration, loan office, a college of agriculture, a school of mines and manufactures; in short it collects from all parts of the earth, the weak, the ignorant, and those who need spiritual and social reformation, and brings them out here removed from temptation and constructs them into a useful citizenry."

This is a case arising under Judge McKean's system of ruling Mormons off a jury in civil as well as criminal trials affecting them in any way. Engelbrecht, a liquor seller, refused to take out a city license, (the licenses here being costly, $300 a month to sell spirits over a bar; $200 a month to sell liquors wholesale and retail, not to be drank on the premises; $100 a month to keep a wholesale liquor store; $50 a month to sell ale and beer), and after being notified of the consequences by the Justice of the Peace in his ward, one Clinton, the liquors of Engelbrecht were poured into the street. He sued Clinton and the officers of the corporation for malicious destruction of his stock, under a territorial statute, making malicious damage punishable three times the value of the property destroyed. McKean ruled every Mormon off the jury on the ground of bias and incapability of giving a verdict according to the evidence. The liquor seller won the case by the packed jury, and for nineteen thousand dollars worth of liquors got an award of fifty-seven thousand dollars. The case is to be carried up to the Supreme Court and pressed for a decision in advance of its order, on the ground that this wholesale and indiscriminate trial of cases affecting the great majority of the people by juries selected from an insignificant minority, is subversive of justice in Utah, and puts the liberty and property of the people at the disposal of two men—the majority of the Court. The Mormons have a superstitious faith in the honesty of the Supreme Court of Washington, but they regard the Supreme Court of Utah as a mixture of fanaticism, dullness and draw-poker. If it be decided at Washington that McKean's way of making up juries is legal, the Mormons will quietly submit, but it is not probable that the Supreme Court, even as manipulated within the past two years, will indorse this brutal manner of violating the essential spirit of trial by jury.

In Utah, as generally in the Territories, the Federal administration is loose, discordant and slip-shod. The late Prosecutor, Hempstead, was hated by McKean, for objecting to the jury-packing system, and the present Prosecutor is appointed by the court only; the post military commanders are invariably friendly with the Mormons, because they perceive nothing admirable or lovable in the Federal officials. Judge Strickland frequently smokes cigars and whittles sticks while holding court. A vague impression, started by the preacher "Doctor" Newman, that Grant wants a general movement made on polygamy, an ambrosial notoriety seeker, he devised a trip to Utah many months ago, and the Mormons, in democratic fairness, threw open their tabernacle to him to let him say the worst against their theology. Imagine a Methodist Bishop giving up his pulpit to a Mormon in like circumstances. Newman now returns the courtesy of the Mormons by setting on foot, through the President, this whole precipitate assize against polygamy. Thus are schemes of statesmanship balked by theological pretenders, and shallow preachers are given the scope and influence of Cardinals like Richelieu and Antonelli.

Bates, who has been appointed United States Attorney for Utah within the past few days, is a burnt-out Chicago lawyer, a friend of Lyman Trumbull, and a conservative man. We shall probably hear no more of Basking's ferocious billingsgate, where he called Brigham Young a thief, assassin, &c., before the smiling Judge McKean, and reduced the associations even of the livery stable where the United States Court is held.

Senator Trumbull says these prosecutions are out of all equity, and that they should be stopped, and polygamy left to its natural enemies, prosperity, Gentile influx, opinion and competition.

There is no doubt that the successor of Brigham Young is already resolved upon by that old Moses himself, and that he is advised of his nomination. It is George A. Smith, cousin to Joseph Smith, and the Historian of the Church, and also at present one of the three members of the "First Presidency."

A man more unlike Brigham Young it would be difficult to conceive. Brigham is the incarnation of will and purpose, a materialist, a Yankee Turk. George A. Smith is the spirit of reverence, gentleness and accord, and in his hands Mormonism will cease to offend its neighbors, and resolve to a quiet, docile, but still numerous and proselytizing body of worshipers. Smith is very little of a polygamist. He has none of Brigham's consideration for money and clearheadedness upon the great unit of the interest bearing dollar. Smith is one of us literary folks, a man of the stamp of Thackeray, Peter Force and Washington Irving—not equal to them in degree, perhaps, but in nature the same—a *collaborateur*, lover of traditions and family reminiscences, and a pleasing, dignified *raconteur* and politician. He has no avarice, no love of war, no vindictiveness, and he is yet a sincere, hale, immovable Mormon, believing in Joseph's revelations without question. I am told that there is no historical society in any county or State of the Union so perfectly complete in archives as that of the Mormons. The recording angel might have gone off on a holiday as far as they are concerned; for George A. Smith has kept the account for him.

And yet, this lolling, easy Bohemian has energies of his own not to be despised, and Brigham Young is more frequently in his society than with any of the Madames Young. He has a wonderful memory, power of language and stump-speaking, and adroit political management. He loves politics and is not a bigot. The Mormons have a weakness for the Smith family as the Islamites might have for the relatives of Mohammed, and there never was any Smith with more sagacity and *bonhommie* than this one. He is a very large, heavy, and self-enjoying man in appearance—resembling ex-Senator Toombs, of Georgia, but without Toombs' opinionatedness or passion. He weighs as much as Brigham Young, wears a brownish auburn wig and spectacles, walks with a cane, and has a ready smile and a big mouth to spread it upon. Although having two or three wives, I dare believe that George Smith is at heart a chaste, tender, and religious husband, father, friend and gentleman.

Here I close my letter for the present. In conclusion, it must be said, seriously, warningly, to the Mormon leaders, that they must by the force of example and edict, stop this policy of polygamy! They are to a very great extent still the "guides, philosophers and friends" of their masses. Let them put their flourishing territory in accord with the surrounding civilized populations, take domestic example from the white man's one wife, and not from the Indian's many squaws and be, like a New Testament bishop, 'the' husband of one!" Let them bring Utah into the Union as a State, rid themselves of judiciary and Governor responsible only to a distant public opinion, and share in the profits and comforts of an expanding, a developing, and a rich nation. Of what avail are industry and polygamy yoked together, the one slaving for the other to live ahungered upon its proceeds? Even President Young's millions will go thinly around among his numerous progeny. The present conflict between the United States and the polygamous leaders may be staved off, but similar troubles will arise again and again. The nation will not put up with polygamy much longer. Governments and administrations may keep hands off, but the danger to polygamy is from the power that makes administrations and governments—the Democratic populus, the public opinion. The very courts and troops now so obnoxious in Utah may one day be the refuge of the Mormon people, and that necessity for refuge will be when the public opinion catches up and overtakes the United States Government and supersedes it as it did at Nauvoo. Heaven deliver a thrifty and sincere people from that fate and let Heaven make useful for this purpose the present leaders of the Mormon Church, so that we may see Utah saved from desolation.

A way seems to arise by which—as under our free system such communications should be brought about—the Mormon Church, the Mormon people, and the true course of law, justice and tolerance, may be secured. It was proposed at Salt Lake, to several Mormons in my presence, by a distinguished member of the church.

Namely: That the Mormon chiefs should not trifle with time, nor hesitate upon the brink of danger in this age of breech-loaders and volunteer soldiering. Let them dismiss the freak of an exodus to some other Territory, where in a few years the storm against polygamy will burst forth again. A forcible resistance, in my judgment, they never contemplated. Let them believe that many thousands of Gentiles take pride and interest in their past energy and useful acquisitions, and desire to see them protected in both and in their worship. But polygamy is not only a tenet; it is a practice, and it encounters the whole force of the creed and current of the common law of civilization. Here is a way to deal with it, extinguish it, and make a wholesome and flourishing State out of an anomaly.

Let a convention be called promptly, even at once, before Congress gets well under way with next session's business. Let this convention prepare a State constitution and concede polygamy in return for the right of local government, trial by jury, and a share in the benefits of representation in the nation. If necessary to the dignity and conscience of the Mormon people, let them throw in their preamble or codicil the responsibility for abandoning polygamy in future upon the government they petition, and concede it to the cause of peace and the prejudice of the times. The country will not be unjust enough to demand them to violate the duties of paternity and wedlock in marriages already contracted where the complaint does not arise within the marriage relation. Let them staunchly, inviolably agree and bind themselves to keep the agreements of this State constitution as they make it, and to attest the same, let them make the oath to sustain monogamous marital fidelity in all future marriages, a portion of the official oath to be taken by every State officer.

This concession will be statesmanship and sacrifice together on the part of those influential apostles, counselors and quorums who will bring it about. They will approve themselves worthy to preserve the State they have erected, and remove the last cause of interference with the civil rights and freedom of worship and faith. They will share in the benefits of a State to which they are already bound by the ties of race, interest, and neighborhood, and will find compensation for the loss of polygamy in riches, respect and stability. They will save themselves, by a speedy movement of this kind, from such political neutralization, I might say annihilation, as has overtaken the South. For, if they do not heed the warning, it may be too late. One rash act, the folly of any wretch, may blot out Utah politically, materially, ecclesiastically, even as a tradition! "Now is the accepted time, and now is the day of salvation!"

THE END.

JOHN M. CLAYTON

OF

DELAWARE

CORRESPONDENCE OF THE ENQUIRER

By Geo. Alfred Townsend

This article was copied from two newspaper clippings in the Townsend Collection, Maryland State Archives.

John M. Clayton.
Courtesy of General Collection: Portraits, Delaware State Archives.

GATH.
John M. Clayton and Delaware—It Has Been Moved to Abolish the Claton-Bulwer Treaty—Who was John M. Clayton?

CORRESPONDENCE OF THE ENQUIRER.

NEW YORK, APRIL 28, 1886.

JOHN M. CLAYTON OF DELAWARE

Delaware had an illustrious conception in the brain of the great champion of the Reformed Religion, King Gustavus Adolphus of Sweden. His apostate daughter carried out the design, and though she died at the foot of the Pope, the Lutheran religion was established in New Sweden, and the site of the venerable church at Wilmington is said to be the depository of the body of Peter Minuit and Reorus Torkillus, first Governor and first clergyman of New Sweden, who settled this realm in 1638. Mr. Irving has related in his veritable history of Knickerbocker how Peter Stuyvesant made war on those Swedes and subdued them, fighting the only decisive battle ever given on the soil of Delaware, and was in turn subdued by the English fleet of the Duke of York sailing out of the port of the American Amsterdam. When Penn sailed up the river in 1682, he saw old settlements of people from the Baltic and North Sea coasts to indicate the sites of his future cities, and he landed at New Castle to receive their o'er zealous allegiance. During his lifetime, they seceded from his political Province, but continued parts of his "territory," and received immigration from his English followers, and when the Revolutionary War was mooted, the pen of John Dickinson, a Dover gentleman, was as ready as that of Samuel Adams or Benjamin Franklin, to defend the Colonial cause. Without challenge, Delaware took her place among the old chartered Colonies, and added three names to the Declaration of Independence and five to the Constitution. The little manikin reached up for the pen and indorsed the Constitution foremost of all the States and then subsided to a long and silent growth of almost alluvial deposition, like her soil, sending two Senators and two Representatives (now one) to the seat of Government to be the more lost there in the association of so obscure a Commonwealth. The highest political promotion seemed to be irrelevant to such a Principality. It published no daily newspaper until the war of the rebellion, when the manufacturers of the City of Wilmington had given it that importance to warrant a daily press. It was off the highways of both business and pleasure travel, a mere peninsula, with one shoulder barred by a canal and a ferry railroad. The shell-fish in its coves and crocks were exposed to more worldly contact than the human inhabitancy.

Yet in the Arabian story there were mighty genii imprisoned in the smallest boxes, and it was a common copper lamp which the Prince Aladdin must rub to light to the splendors of the cave. Within the confines of this little topographical coffin have been erected all the solemn ordinances of a sovereignty. Its mild climate, easy soil and surrounding waterways gave it an early peopling, and its growth is, therefore, like the ripening of one of its peaches, uniform and mellowing, instead of spasmodic and forced, as in many of the greater States.

NO REVOLUTION

Has happened in Delaware; nothing has been developed there but what is old in mines or soils; no conquests were required nor innovations invited. Its boundary was plainly run and set with enduring stones in the middle of the last century, and immigration loitered in pastorally, as the cattle seek the fields, instead of raising the dust on the old loam highways and crying "Excelsior" where there were no mountains.

The same river drifts to the sea. At the Breakwater the light is burning in the old British tower where it was trimmed by order of the King and guided Blackbeard and his pirates. At the three county towns, two of them named for the shire towns of namesake counties in England, the same punishment of the pillory and the lash is in vogue now that used to be inflicted at the corner of Broad and Wall, where the stocks stood in the High street of New Amsterdam. Delaware affords the best opportunity on the Atlantic side of North America to see men and society as they were before machinery and corporations modified them. The peasantry and the gentlemen are scarcely relatively changed, and if the peasant has become the gentleman he is the old-style gentleman, half Quaker, half Episcopalian, unattractive in exteriors but sound and conservative within, and often luminous with the lamp of long and undiverted country thought. Delaware has been leavened without yeast, and its internal conflicts have little more reference to the outer world than the music of the sea-shell, which expires when it reaches the air. Let us place the shell to our ear for a moment, to draw from its recesses an echo of a man of affairs as nearly great as one can be, born without dominion, who could not go abroad to gain a career.

BIRTH OF JOHN M. CLAYTON.

Among the companions and privy councillors of William Penn at Philadelphia was a certain William Clayton, whose name reappears so frequently as we descend the Delaware side of the Peninsula that it is apparent he was a man of ardor and great posterity. It is ninety-five miles from the top to the southern boundary of Delaware and near this habitable conclusion of the State, at a hamlet called Dagsborough, a baby christened John Middleton Clayton, descendant of a kinsman of Penn's councillor, was born July 24, 1796.

His father was a tanner, a large, commanding person, with a good deal of brawny wit, and he was said to be a first-rate Shakespearian scholar. His mother was a native of Maryland, close by, and his sister was married to a gentleman of superior extraction, Walter Douglas, the head of a Scotch Jacobite family which had settled in the Peninsula to work the beds of bog iron ore not uncommon there. The portraits of the Douglas brothers, painted in oil, probably by Stuart, are to be seen at Dover, and their style of dress and countenance betokens a rank of commercial gentry quite above what might be expected of that flat, detached territory. But in that early period the society of the region between Cape Henlopen and Cape Charles was better than on the still uncleared highlands.

It is related that early in the eighteenth century Penn's Deputy Governor, Lloyd, sent his daughters from Philadelphia to Lewes, nearly opposite Cape May, to finish their education, and the pastor of the four Episcopal Churches of Sussex County, Rev. William Beckett, related that out of 1,750 souls there in all, there were 1,075 Church of England people, 600 Presbyterians and 75 Quakers. "The Scotch-Irish had two meeting-houses and were very bigoted." The Douglases were of this Presbyterian stock, high-mettled, "little, cymblin-headed men," who chased the Churchmen Tories to the swamps, and as their brother-in-law grew up he preferred their faith. The Presbyterians were the military stock of the Revolution in the Middle States. The Methodists had just begun to make an impression, and Clayton's mother was of this persuasion. His father was busy for a part of the time in getting out beams, flooring and shingles for great houses to the northward, among them the mansion of the Read family at Newcastle, which was built in 1801, and considered the finest residence in the State, and long afterward rented by young Clayton.

PENINSULAR LIFE IN 1800.

There is a swamp just below Dagsborough of fifty thousand acres extent, one of the greatest in America—a high, level, half-inundated basin, in which are thousands of noble sunken trees that have been for a century excavated and sawed out. While Clayton's father was at this work and buying and tanning hides, his brother-in-law, residing at a place called "The Bloomery," was making pigs of iron and sending them to the Chesapeake. The boy Clayton, for his ruddy health and aptness, attracted the attention of Walter Douglas, and his father sent him to school at Berlin, in Maryland, eighteen miles below, under the custody of a negro. Years afterward this negro drove an ox-team on Clayton's birthday annually from Dagsborough to Dover—fifty miles—to receive a present from "Moss Johnny." At Berlin the mother of Stephen Decatur had given birth to that Bayard of the seas during the Revolutionary War; the region was relatively high and healthy, and as the boy went back and forth his thought and stature grew. Dagsborough had some antiquities; the battle between the Tories and Colonel Dagworthy had taken place near by, and the old Colonel slept under the chancel of the parish church, near Clayton's birthplace, where a few months ago the rebuilders of the shrine found only three teeth of so much warrior. More slaves were held in the bay coasts adjacent than in all the rest of the State.

The tanner's house is now going to decay, its four square rooms on each floor, with corner chimney-places, huge, solid chimney-boards of wood, and great end chimneys, are for litters of houseless cats and drying peaches. The old tree, in the crotch of which tradition says that Clayton made his first speech, fell down in 1876. A railroad crosses the Clayton garden and land, and the forest encroaches upon one of the earliest settlements in Delaware.

When his father removed to the more flourishing Village of Milford, twenty miles to the northward, John was sent to such school-houses as the county afforded, and for awhile to

LEWES,

The old Cape village, still in possession of some of the importance attached to the county seat. It was an old settlement of clapboarded houses, occupied by sea captains, pilots, fishermen and perhaps a few lawyers and land-owners. The Court was removed inland to Georgetown about this time, and the old Court house, celebrated in the local annals of the Province, was falling to the utility of a meeting-house, and stable alternately. From the sand-hills, among which the hamlet was pitched, could be seen the yellow beaches of Cape May, nine miles distant, and the broad Atlantic Ocean, which had broken over the low Delaware Bar at two or three shallow inlets, and created wide salt estuaries inland, some of which had twenty-five miles of surface; and grain-boats were kedged over the bar, exposed to the furious surf, but sailing within over unruffled water to ascend the creeks to Millsborough and other hamlets. Except the exposed roadstead at Lewes, there was not a safe harbor between New York and Hampton Roads, and, as the Delaware was still the great river of commerce, the Government at this early period was planning a breakwater to shelter its navy and merchant marine. Young Clayton wandered with his gun over this region of marsh, high beach and inlet, whose scenery became the components of his imagination, and until in middle life, when his flesh grew too great and his office habits restrained him, he was an ardent lover of duck and partridge-shooting. His family surroundings were better than his fortune. Joshua Clayton had been Governor of Delaware the year John was born, and while he was still a boy his father's cousin, Thomas Clayton, entered upon a public career which did not stop short of the Senate at Washington and the Chief-Justiceship of the State. Another kinsman had been Sheriff of Kent in the Revolution and Judge of the Common Pleas. The young man's father was a politician also, though a tanner, and he kept his son at work a part of the time in the tan-yard, where he acquired the art among his father's negroes of playing the violin.

This acquirement was of the dearest solace to him through life, and an important auxiliary in politics. He never laid down the fiddle until he reached the Cabinet of General Taylor, and even there, at infrequent times, awoke the strains which summoned back the friends and recollections of boyhood, and brought to his eyes the ready tears of genial sympathy. Popular almost from the cradle, and handsome and impressive, his father was persuaded by Walter Douglas to send him to

YALE COLLEGE,

With a pledge of assistance if his own circumstances should become straitened. John entered that institution in 1811 at the age of fifteen, and passed his holidays at Milford and at Dover. A strong, inherent ambition to acquire learning and study law was intensified by a desire to relieve his father and provide for his sisters, as the family was drifting along toward that insolvency which finally overtook them. The sacrifice of this hard-working parent was repaid in a son whose filial affection never ceased while he could labor for his mother and her brood, and the wisdom of that sacrifice gave to the State of Delaware its most illustrious citizen and counselor.

At Yale College his classmate was the poet Percival. Senator James A. Bayard described the College life of Clayton in the Senate as assiduous and laborious, attended with the confidence of his instructors, and graduating with the highest honors.

It might be well to peep into the College cloister and describe the offspring of the Cypress Swamp as he leaned upon his strong physique and gave the night as well as the day to storing his head with knowledge, but that would be to lead the picture out of the frame of his native State. Calhoun, who was to be his colleague for many years in the Senate, had graduated at Yale seven years before Mr. Clayton entered there. The tanner, Clayton, had a large establishment at Milford, where the boy spent his holidays, and inhabited a painted brick mansion on the heights overlooking the Mispillon ponds and creek, old mills and shipping.

Milford is about twenty miles south-east of Dover, and has generally been regarded as the second settlement in the State, not only in population, but in the refinement and industry of its citizens. It produced in the rebellion the most distinguished miliary officer of Delaware, Major-General Alfred T. Torbert. Vessels ascend to the town by one of the navigable creeks in which the tides of the Delaware wash, and in the history of Methodism the region is celebrated as the site of Barrett's chapel, founded in 1780, where, while it was yet a new edifice—roomy for its period, but cramped and quaint in ours—Francis Asbury entered the church-door, and, seeing before him in the pulpit a small, long-haired and bright-eyed young man addressing the congregation, recognized Bishop Coke, and rushed forward and kissed him on the pulpit stairs. Coke was the first American Bishop, and was ordained by Wesley. Asbury was compelled to make his haunt during the Revolutionary War in the hidden parts of this peninsula, for he suffered elsewhere under the imputation of being one of Wesley's Englishmen, at a time when Mr. Wesley, more loyal than prudent, had pronounced against the American cause to the great prejudice of his anxious missionaries in the Western World. Asbury's resort during this period was in the forest country near the Maryland line, twenty miles south-west of Dover, at the house of Judge Thomas White. He wrote, October 6, 1782: "I preached in White's new chapel for the first time. It is one of the neatest country chapels the Methodists have on the whole Continent." Out of the flock connected by the pioneer at this place came the Methodist family of Saulsbury, who have played such an important part in the State Government in our period. The father of the Saulsburys was the Sheriff of Kent County about 1821, and he sent his sons to Dickinson College. One of them, Willard, was twice elected Senator of the United States, and is now Chancellor of Delaware, his brother, Eli Saulsbury, having been elected to his seat in the Senate. At the same time the older brother, Gove Saulsbury, was Governor of the State. Such political success in one family has seldom been equaled. Two of the brothers remain strict Methodists, and the third holds that Church in nearly equal respect. When Mr. Asbury found Dr. Coke at Barrett's Chapel, he also saw in the pulpit Bishop Whitecoat, who is buried in Dover on the site of the old Wesley Church erected in 1780, in the midst of the Revolution. The inscription over Whitecoat says that he was ordained an Elder by John Wesley in person in 1769, and sent to America with Dr. Coke to assist in organizing the Methodist Episcopal Church, and was constituted a Bishop by the General Conference in 1800, and died in great peace in Dover, 1806.

Parson Thorne Mansion in Milford, rented by the Clayton family.
Courtesy of Purnell Collection, Delaware State Archives.

AT LAW SCHOOL.

When John M. Clayton returned to Delaware, in 1815, Bachelor of Arts, he began to study law immediately in the office of his sturdy cousin, Thomas Clayton, then in Congress and a Federalist.

Thomas Clayton was a short, squarish, wedge-shaped man, with slight extremities and broad shoulders, about five feet eight inches high. He is referred to by Nathan Sergeant in his memoirs as a man of exceptionally strong mind, but he was a jurist, not an orator, and, therefore, shows in the counsels of the Senate, but not in the debates. In fact, he seldom spoke at all. He had that stability of conviction which gave even his provincial prejudices firmness and currency. "The oxen of Kent County," he used to say, "can trot faster than the horses any-where else." He said to a drover man once at Newcastle: "They do have better shad up there than we have, but I'll be plagued if I'll own it."

His students' mingled docility and force engaged and startled this able lawyer, of whom Pierce Butler, of South Carolina, said that, "after thirty years' experience, he pronounced Thomas Clayton to have the best judicial mind he had ever met in the Senate." W. W. Seaton also wrote that Thomas Clayton was "a man of few words, but of excellent powers," and that his correct habits and inflexible justice might designate him as the Aristides of the Senate. The kinsmen observed John's equal anxiety to get work and thoroughness, and seconded his desire to attend the lectures at the celebrated Law School of Tapping Reeve and James Gould, at Litchfield, Conn.

Reeve, the founder of this school, was as much a Federalist as Thomas Clayton, though the brother-in-law of Aaron Burr. Yale and Princeton education met in the founders of Litchfield. The village was the home of the Wolcotts, those furious Hamiltonians, and there, while John M. Clayton pursued his studies, Lyman Beecher was the village pastor, and his children, Henry Ward and Harriet, were "toddling" around the shady streets. Thirty-five years were to elapse, and under Secretary of State Clayton's windows at Washington the newsboys hawked the National Era with the serial chapters of "Uncle Tom's Cabin" in its columns.

Clayton's studies of Litchfield were overshadowed by family vicissitudes; his father's luck had run out, and his brother-in-law, Douglas, had become insolent. Several sisters, a brother and parents were struggling along, and he felt that he must quit his books precipitately to repay their kindness and help their necessity. In the year 1818, in the Court-house at Georgetown, in the county of his birth, he was admitted to practice in the Superior Court. No affianced lover ever sprang to the arms of his bride, after absence and delay, with more ardor than Clayton to the bar.

IN PRACTICE,

He settled immediately at the State Capital, Dover, a little village of about five hundred inhabitants at the time, but containing much of the talent of the State. Established for the purpose of a county seat in 1694, a large, open square had been left in the center of the place, kept green and planted with trees, and here was established in one edifice the Courts of the county and the chambers of Government years before Clayton had been born. There is a bill in the State House bearing the molder's date, 1765, which did service for the Commonwealth in a building yet more antique, and prior to the time when (September 20, 1776), Thomas McKean gave name to the State in these words: "The government of the Counties of Kent, Sussex and Newcastle, upon Delaware, shall hereafter, in all public and other writings, be called the Delaware State."

The hotel in which it is apocryphally said that McKean wrote the first Constitution of Delaware, "sitting up all night to compose it after having ridden in one day from Philadelphia," is still in use for its original purpose at the corner of the green. The State-house of 1785, enlarged and modernized and finally in one day relieved of its county uses, raises the same walls in the prospect. In this square, while volunteers were being enrolled for Haslett's regiment, the Declaration of Independence, transmitted by post from Caesar Rodney at Philadelphia, was read to the command, and a picture of King George was committed to the flames. At the present day there are perhaps twenty edifices around this square; at that time there were not so many, and they were plainer, but the public life of John M. Clayton, was to make milestones of many of those old walls. To the low-roofed, aged Ridgely mansion he took his wife and his books; in another corner he lived his widower life and received his earliest honors; near by he hired his first quarters and studied law. And at last he died in a third corner, close to the monument where his body lies. His life began with the decay of the Revolutionary statesmen, and reached over to the organization of the Northern Republican party. He was born in Washington's Presidency, came to the bar in Monroe's went to the United States Senate in the Adams', Jackson's, Tyler's and Pierce's, was the head of Taylor's Cabinet, and died about the time Buchanan had carried Delaware and the Presidency. His home and office were on this little green for a quarter of a century. For more than half that time he lived on his farm near Newcastle and in the latter village. Except to Saratoga and to Washington he seldom passed beyond the boundary of the State, of which

View of Walnut Street, Milford, C. 1880. *Courtesy Purnell Collection, Delaware State Archives.*

when he was in it he was nearly absolute. If he had taken his motto at the outset from the Earl of Strafford, "Thorough." he could not have fulfilled it better. As an advocate, politician, Senator, Chief Justice and statesman, he was one of the most correct and thorough men of the country. His nature was sluggish and his ambition easily satisfied, but his sense of acquitting himself well overruled both, and he could be equally patient and powerful. Such minute perceptions have not been seen in this country united with such weight, and behind the bars of that little constituency he paced like a lion in an impecunious show, all his majesty made comic by the disproportionate surroundings.

HIS FIRST FEE.

Soon after he entered the bar, a Philadelphian gave him a civil case, which he won with a display of his compact yet diverting argument, and at sunset, retiring to his little bare office, the client counted out five hundred dollars in gold. The young lawyer's immediate thought was his mother, then a widow at Milford. It was twenty miles away, but he was buoyant of body and spirits, and he set out at once to walk that distance alone.

The nights over that country have the clearness of starlight and the beauty of sunset, which seems to be peculiar to regions of sandy coast and shore. Cedars line the road with woodlands of locust and walnut, and in the rolling fields the great Spanish oak, bare of leaves held on its blasted branch the fish-hawk's bulky nest. The persimmons stiffly bear up their abundant tomato-like fruit. It was October, and the bay of hounds hunting, the raccoon by night for unwearied negroes arose in the distance, and the muskrat and the mink slipped in the ditches as he approached them. His head was full of happiness and lore. As good a Horatian scholar as any body in his walk, he had texts of Tacitus and bars of Juvenal to remember. Old chapels behind grave-yard walls blinked at him through their windows. He reached Milford at eleven o'clock, and stole to his mother's door, scarcely locked by night to this day in that country, to surprise her. The poor old lady was sitting before the chimney logs alone and bereaved. The hard times had overtaken all her family. Clayton poured the gold over her shoulder into her lap. She looked up and saw her son. "Johnny," she cried, "did you come by it honest?"

"Yes, mother; I earned it for a fee to-day, and I walked down to bring it to you and gladden your dear old heart."

The parents of Clayton are buried behind the old mansion at Milford. It was a celebrated house one hundred years ago, and the two distinct family burying-grounds are near the garden, which is laid out with rows of boxbush. The body of Colonel Benjamin Potter, who died in 1845, "aged about seventy-four," dies in one inclosure, among his family; in the other lies Rev. Sydenham Thorne, who died in 1790, aged forty-five.

The shaft to Clayton's ancestors is narrow and of above a man's height, copiously inscribed:

"This monument is erected by John M. Clayton to the memory of his father, James Clayton, and the members of his family whose mortal remains are buried within the (stone) walls which surround it.

"James Clayton was born in Kent County, Delaware, March 24, 1761, and died in his mansion house on this farm, November 24, 1820, aged fifty-nine years and eight months."

"He was the son of James, who was the son of John, who was the son of Joshua Clayton, one of the first settlers of this country, to which he emigrated with William Penn at the time of his first visit to America."

The statesman's sister, Elizabeth Clayton, his junior by five years, who died in early womanhood, 1822, is buried near by, and also his mother's mother, Elizabeth Middleton, who died at the age of sixty-six, in 1811. "She was a most affectionate parent and a woman of exemplary piety and virtue." The account of the Senator's mother is as follows:

"Sarah, the wife of James Clayton, born March 8, 1774, near Annapolis, Maryland, died at the house of her son, John M. Clayton, at Dover, Delaware, June 28, 1820, aged fifty-five. As a wife, mother and sincere Christian, she was without reproach. While dying she selected the text from which her funeral sermon was preached: Psalms cxvi, verse 7: 'Return unto thy rest, oh! my soul; for the Lord hath dealt kindly with thee.'"

Clayton also describes his father's character on the same monument: "He was a man of warm, sincere and affectionate disposition, remarkable for the strength and originality of his mind and for his activity and enterprise as a man of business. He had the rare good fortune to bear with him from his cradle to the grave the unquestionable character of an honest man." GATH

Reminiscences of the Author of the Clayton-Bulwer Treaty—A study from Old Neighbors.
CORRESPONDENCE OF THE ENQUIRER.
WASHINGTON, D. C., APRIL 12, 1882.

HIS APPEARANCE
at the Bar of Delaware was the greatest event in the civil history of the State, and unexpected as it was startling, except to those who had conducted his examination.

He had all the great motives in his nature to second his electrical temperament and robust powers. He loved to know, to tell, to work, to win. His curiosity was that of a first-class reporter. His reading was like Napoleon's—every thing offered to him—and he absorbed it like some chemical whale, which might fill its maw with a ton of animalculae, and then blow them separately, by choice, through its spiracle. He never refused to buy a book, but his standard reading was the law, the classics and history. With a prodigious memory he had a most orthodox mind, and errors made no impression upon it but to amuse. He loved affairs, and his intuitions on men were as keen as on law; but he was never suspicious. He loved society, yet of women he knew almost nothing. Bashful in their company from boyhood, he married one and led a life of such rare and brief happiness that he never disturbed its memory with another courtship, and blushed before ladies when he was a Senator.

There is still living a very old man who relates that he was the means of making Clayton acquainted with his wife.

CLAYTON'S COURTSHIP.

John Loudon had been an apprentice of Clayton's father, a tanner, at Milford, Del., and was lodging at the old Quaker settlement of Camden, four miles from Dover, when the young man's fame began to sound at the bar. In Camden was a beautiful young lady, Sally Fisher, the daughter of Dr. James Fisher, who had attracted Loudon's attention, and the old apprentice, mindful of Clayton's poverty, considered, perhaps, that she was not only lovely and amiable, but of good advantages and prospects. He insisted that John should go and see her and judge for himself.

Clayton loitered around Camden diffidently, awaiting for a pretext, and hearing that a copy of Cooper's Spy, which had just been published, was in the lady's possession, he thought he would take the Delaware privilege of borrowing it. Like the Spy he sought he entered the dwelling, and his diffidence vanished in the charms he found there.

He was six feet and an inch high, brown-haired, with a forehead of medium height, but very perfect and expressive features, clear, grayish-blue eyes, and an almost transparent skin. His frame was large to hold the great flesh he was to acquire. He had much sensibility and affection, and his suit was as successful in love as in the profession. At marriage he gave his wife a richly-bound copy of "The Spy" as a souvenir of their introduction.

Married, he was the happiest man in the State, uxorious and popular, and for a while he lived at Camden, walking to Dover and back, eight miles every day. A son was born the year following his marriage, and Clayton took the venerable Ridgely mansion on Dover Green for his home and office. A second son was born two years after his marriage, and then, at the age of twenty-five, the young bride died, leaving a woman in place of the strong man Clayton had been. He never ceased to feel her absence and her presence. "He achieved fame," said Senator James Bayard, "and acquired fortune, and his checks in pursuit of either were few and transient. This is the bright side of the picture. The reverse presents the afflictions to which he was subjected in his domestic relations. He married an accomplished lady and the object of his first affections. He cherished her memory with an almost romantic devotion, and though unusually demonstrative as to his ordinary emotions and feelings, with his deeper affections it was otherwise. The observant eye of friendship could only see from momentary glimpses how immedicable was the wound inflicted."

COMING INTO POLITICS.

He had not entered upon politics or public life when his wife died, except to be elected to the State Legislature, which sat across the Green, and he was at her decease Secretary of State for Delaware at the age of twenty-eight, appointed by Governor Polk. A scion of this house, Tursten Polk, was born in Clayton's native county, 1811, and became Governor of Missouri, the year Clayton died. While a law student, Clayton had been a clerk in the Legislature. His wife's death left him no bride but the law and a mild, though shrewd, ambition. Had she survived, he could hardly have been more useful, but his days would have been lengthened by regular habits of eating and sleeping, and tempered and widened by female society. Yet a gentleman, inborn to the son and cultured in the husband, sweetened his widower's estate, deepened his religious feelings, and put the crown of human nature on a life of politics and debate.

He bred his sons, who grew to be men at his side, and one of them was nearly his equal in intellect. In after years they married in gossip to the widow of President Polk and other ladies of the Senatorial Court, and his talents, position and person were so inviting that he was courted by women of wealth. His affections were in the grave with the bride of his youth, and he lived only with men, measures and books.

His social position was now among the best. The Fishers were an old family in the State, and Clayton married his sister to one of his brothers-in-law. Another married Judge Kellum, of the Eastern Shore of Virginia. His mother lived until 1829, the year he was sent to the Senate.

The Chew Mansion, Dover Green, c. 1880. *Courtesy General Collection: Houses, Delaware State Archives.*

WALKING UP.

He bought the old Chew or Sykes mansion on the Green in Dover, in one end of which he opened his law office, and his practice was described by Mr. Cullen in Congress, as follows:

"I must say to this House and to the nation that never have I witnessed the display of such quickness of apprehension, such memory, such a grasping intellect, such learning, such zeal and ingenuity as were displayed by the deceased on every occasion in which he found it necessary to exert his great mind in the progress of a cause. As a lawyer he was profound and industrious, and of untiring patience. He viewed his cases in every point of light in which they could be seen, and he could see every point in them at a glance. But he was not satisfied with a glance. He investigated every position, and was prepared for every Question which could arise in the case. I have seen gentlemen whose legal minds I thought were equal to his, but when he prepared himself never has there been known in the State of Delaware a man who could be said to be his equal. It is confidently everywhere asserted that he never saw his equal, especially as an advocate before a jury. As an advocate he excelled any member of the bar whose career has been witnessed by any person now living. I have known him to be successful in cases which any other lawyer would have despaired of: and so keen was his perception of the ludicrous that if the case of his opponent presented any features of which advantage could be taken by turning them into ridicule he was sure to succeed. I have known him to gain causes certainly against law and the evidence and the facts of the case by his superior ingenuity and his deep knowledge of human nature. As a special pleader, he was not surpassed by any gentleman at that profession. His talents as a lawyer, even when he had been but a few years at the bar in the practice of his profession, soon became known throughout his native State; and before he was at the bar three years he was sought after and engaged in every important cause in the State. Every litigant was anxious to procure his services, thinking his aid sufficient to procure certain success.

AGAINST KIDNAPERS.

To get office in Delaware requires intimacy with the people and the power of combination among the leaders. In that State it is not usual for the Governor to be a man of law or letters. He is oftener selected from the farmer or mercantile class, and the Secretary of State is expected to write his messages. The Senate and Assembly generally contain a majority of farmers, who look with suspicion upon an ambitious lawyer. Clayton united the good fellow and the good politician with the great lawyer and courted popular causes. For this reason much of his early fame is attached to what were called kidnapping cases.

By the laws of Delaware slavery was wholly a domestic institution, no traffic in human liberty being legal across the State line. The value of a Delaware slave was, therefore, much impaired, as he was not legitimately marketable for foreign export, and this discrimination led to the existence of a worthless and desperate class of abductors, who sometimes stole a slave, sometimes a free negro, and occasionally a dark white, and carried him over the Chesapeake, to the indiscriminate markets of Alexandria and Norfolk. On the other hand, the demi-neutrality of Delaware fostered among the Quakers the spirit of succoring fugitives from Maryland and Virginia, and John Hunn, Thomas Garrett, Ezekiel Jenkins and others were station-keepers on the Underground Railroad, Jenkins inhabiting the Town of Camden, where Mrs. Clayton had been wooed. Chief-Justice Taney, at Newcastle, fined and imprisoned Hunn and Garrett, and the anti-slavery sentiment of the North hastened to engage Clayton in a series of counter-kidnapping cases. He drove one Joe Johnson, of Sussex, to the pillory and banished him from the State, and argued the right of a kidnaped boy, William Clarkson, to give testimony in the case of his injury, although white persons participated in the kidnaping. This was an important point to make, and Chief-Justice Richard H. Bayard heard the case. It is in Harrington's Reports: The State against James Whitaker. Upon the admission of this testimony Clayton took them up, man by man, following the trail of individual human nature, and as the night drew on, and the Court-house at Dover looked lurid in the light of tallow-candles, he saw the tears run down the cheeks of the most obstinate juryman. "I've got him," said Clayton in a whisper, and so it proved; for, when the jury retired, the kidnapers' principal friend remarked: "I'm a-going to sleep. When you all agree upon a conviction, wake me up for that's my only way to decide and save my soul!" He made kidnaping a terror to the Peninsula people, and in 1820 the State Assembly passed an act protesting against the extension of slavery to the Territories of the Union. The Congressional delegation, led by the ambitious Louis McLane and Nicholas Vandyke, declined to accept these sturdy instructions.

AS A JURY LAWYER.

Some years later Mr. Clayton was employed in a celebrated murder case at Elkton, Maryland, an old settlement just over the Delaware line and people by a mixture of races, Dutch, Swedish and English, much like the northern counties of Delaware. A Democratic politician, in an endeavor to chastise a Whig editor who had exposed his private character, had been shot with all the contents of a revolving pistol, charge after charge, being delivered in his body, and the trial of the accused assumed all the importance of a political cause celebre. As a Whig no less than an advocate, the case was committed to Mr. Clayton and he acquitted the defendant.

During these years he spent his time in the little office of the Chew, now the Jump Mansion, next door to the State Capitol, playing the fiddle to his crew, walking up and down before the spittoon, deep in thought and tobacco, and the mantel is worn nearly through where he propped back his head to doze, or play, or listen. Napoleon's Marshal, Grouchy, came to Dover to shoot in the marshes, and old residents speak of the thorough interviewing Clayton gave him, who was a juvenile admirer of the exiled Emperor.

Clayton appeared in partisan politics about 1824, as a John Quincy Adams Federalist. He not only took example from his cousin, Senator Tom Clayton, in this affiliation, but from the State of Delaware, which, with unimportant exceptions, has voted for Federalist candidates and measures with hardly less pertinacity than Massachusetts and Connecticut. Delaware first of any State ratified the Constitution, and voted to place the Capital on the Potomac. Her delegates voted for John Adams twice for Vice-President, and her leading Anti-Federalist, Caesar A. Rodney, reached Congress in 1802 for one term, and reached the Senate in 1822—a lapse of twenty years. Delaware voted in 1801 for Aaron Burr for President; in 1805 and 1809 for C. C. Pinckney; in 1813, after the Republicans had turned Federalists, for Monroe; but even then stood out against D.D. Tompkins for Vice-President, and cast four votes for Daniel Rodney, of Dover. The Delaware United States Senators, headed by the first Bayard, voted against the embargo and only Delaware and Kentucky in 1820 voted with the North for the protective policy. In 1825 Delaware divided its vote between Crawford and J.Q. Adams and voted for a second term for Adams against Jackson, and again for Clay against Jackson's second term. Delaware voted for Harrison against Van Buren at two elections, for Clay against Polk and for Taylor. Thus for sixty-four years the smallest of the States supported the highest exercise of the Federal authority. Never, until the extinction of the Whig party, did it begin to grope among the "sovereignties."

FAMILY.

It was Clayton's grand-uncle who governed the State at the adoption of the Constitution, and died a United States Senator the same year with Washington. The Governor's kinsman, his preceptor, spent seventeen years in Congress and the Senate, and John M. Clayton was four times a Senator at Washington. The Clayton family, aided by the earlier Bayards, had a great influence in molding the State Federalist and Whig, and when Louis McLane took office under Jackson his political career closed in Delaware, and he removed to Maryland. Delawareans thus had scant Executive patronage, being constantly in the minority.

The protective policy was abetted by Delaware disinterestedly at the time Mr. J. Q. Adams affirmed, to the contrary of Mr. Monroe, that Congress possessed constitutional power to protect manufacturers and prosecute internal improvements. Large States, like New York, and Virginia, might be jealous of their nation; not so the little States, and the ideas of J.Q. Adams awoke the Delawarean farmers' unselfish approval. Clayton, particularly, admired the work and policy of that lonely and persecuted, if pugnacious and wayward, ruler, and made it the example of a future opportunity. Mr. Adams had married a Maryland lady. Adams abetted an Inter-Republican Congress at Panama; the Clayton-Bulwer treaty was, perhaps, its sequel. Adams was hooted for suggesting a National Observatory; Clayton, twenty years afterward, would have sent the first expedition to the Pole. Adams wanted a University at Washington; Clayton's last great speech was for humane institutions there. Mr. Adams spent $14,000,000 on national works, a sum unexampled at that period. Clayton believed in such expenditures, and preferred them to the cost of war. He disliked Jackson, and took his place with Clay, and spent his life in the great legislative debate where all the leaders but himself and Crittenden had grievances.

PARTY.

About the time Mr. Clayton appeared in the Senate there was a general reformation of parties. Henry Clay, who had been acting with the Madisonian Republicans, was forced over the National Republicans, as the Whigs were then called, by the resentment of the body of his party for his coalition with Adams to beat Jackson for the Presidency. Adams nominated Clay, Secretary of State, and Jackson, Hayne, John Randolph and twelve other Senators voted against him. Randolph became so abusive that Clay challenged him to fight a duel. The two Delaware Senators, Thomas Clayton and Nicholas Vandyke, voted for Clay; and when John M. Clayton went to the Senate, in the first year of Jackson's first term, he was ready to accept Mr. Clay as the leader of the party which at the next Presidential election adopted the name of Whig.

Clayton took his seat in a Senate of forty-eight, among them Webster, Levi Woodbury, Edward Livingston, Thomas Benton, W. R. King, Robert Y. Hayne, John Tyler and Theodore Frelinghuysen. Louis McLane, who had preceded Mr. Clayton in the Senate from Delaware, soon after became Jackson's Secretary of the Treasury, recalled from the British Mission for that purpose. He was the son of Allen McLane, a Revolutionary officer, who once kept a tavern north of Dover. Clayton disliked him as much as he disliked any body, regarding him as a bad counsellor of Mr. Clay, and afterward renegade to him. McLane died on the Bohemia River, and a few miles distant the Revolutionary Governor, Clayton, is interred, at Bethel Methodist Meeting.

HIS WASHINGTON LIFE.

Mr. Clayton took the same quarters at Washington which his cousin Thomas had just vacated, in the house of James Young, a merchant. His mess companions were Asher Robbins, of Rhode Island; John Holmes, of Maine, and S.A. Foot, of Connecticut. Foot soon afterward offered the resolutions which brought on the Webster-Hayne debate. Clayton played euchre at nights with Dr. Broadhead and Mr. Jones of the Treasury Department (the latter a Delawarean, to whom General Dix addressed the "shoot him on the spot" dispatch), and with Mr. Beale, some time Sergeant-at-Arms. It is related that while in this residence he never escorted a lady to any place except once, when Mrs. Young desired to hear a speech, and he took her to the Senate.

He displayed the growing indolence of body, activity of mind and irregularity of eating which, perhaps, deprived him of his full meed of honors. He never showed the effect of drink but once slightly, when he returned from one of Mr. Van Buren's dinners in good humor. On another occasion, when Mr. Pendleton, of Virginia, passed the proprieties of debate, Clayton sent Mr. Crittenden to call him to account. His courage at that period was undoubted, but he was said to have become so indolent at one time that he let his servant Henry carry his watch to tell him the time, and substituted shoes for boots to avoid the difficulty of putting them on. Mr. Young was an Irishman who had landed in Delaware, and the two Claytons called him a Delawarean. Dr. Noble Young, son of his host, grew up an intimate friend of Clayton, and attended him in his last illness. He related to me that Clayton sometimes forgot to eat for days when mentally absorbed, and then, feeling the pangs of hunger, would order Lou, his servant, to make chicken soup at midnight and indulge in heavy suppers voraciously. He was always shy of women, liked men's company, his fiddle, information and plenty of food, with periods of complete privacy and steady work. He was hasty in his promises of getting public office for applicants, and suffered a world of timidity and dunning thereabout. I made much unnecessary efforts to find what his drink was, but it appeared to change with different men. One said he kept a little gin on the mantel and sipped of it at long intervals as he walked up and down. Another disavowed the gin and said it was a very little brandy. A third knew where he bought his whisky, and a fourth was positive that his stock was Madeira. He probably liked a little good liquor of any kind now and then, but he was respectable in his habits and dress always. He seldom walked off Capitol Hill, and during the four terms he sat in the Senate lived around and about that airy but unfashionable quarter, many of his lodgments now being razed for the extension of the Capitol grounds. He chewed or rather ate tobacco, keeping an immense spittoon, and he was popular with every Senator, such loquacious amiability as his being overwhelming. But his power in debate was chaste and vigorous, his speech addressed to high motives, and his partisanship unflinching. His life appears to have had

TWO AMBITIONS.

First, to fasten his head and heart into the statutes and monuments of Delaware, and survive there as the greatest of her public men. His tomb and the tombs of his parents attest this, besides his relinquishing the Senate to become the head of the Delaware judiciary, and also the various establishments he built or bought on Delaware soil. Next he had that impassioned, nervous love of country and its increase and the spread of liberty abroad from it, natural to the inhabitant of a small State, and a disposition to keep out of foreign war, or local feud. He was a Whig, therefore, in the fullest sense. During his third term in the Senate he said, after the victorious Mexican war: "For one I never have been and am not now willing to acquire one acre of ground from Mexico or any other nation under heaven by conquest or robbery. I hold—and however old-fashioned the notion may be, I shall maintain it as long as I have a seat here—that character is as valuable to a nation as it is to an individual, and inasmuch as I would scorn as a private citizen to despoil my neighbor of his property, so as a public man I can never sanction such a course of conduct on the part of the Government of the country."

Clayton took his seat in the Senate December 7, 1829, and made his first considerable speech on the 4th of March following, on Foot's resolution, that small proposition to suspend the sale of public lands, which plunged the Senate into one of the greatest of its debates. Calhoun was presiding in the chair, the uneasy author of such an issue. In his defense, Hayne spoke, anticipating the future, and the corruption to result from a division of a possible surplus in the Treasury. Webster replied with the argument that the danger of the future was not consolidation but disunion. These great speeches have passed into the school-books and traditions of the nation. Clayton's speech has passed out of notice, but it was one of the best of that series, and thus dexterously divided Jackson and Calhoun:

"Sir, when I witnessed the manly and candid manner in which the honorable Senator from South Carolina on my right (Mr. Smith) spoke of the grievances of his constituents, when I saw him evidently soaring above mere party feeling, menacing none, denouncing none, and touching with all the delicacy which characterizes him the subjects in difference between us, the reflection forced itself irresistibly on my mind how different might have been the reception of these complaints had they always come thus recommended. South Carolina, though erring in a controversy with her sisters, would by all have been believed to have been honestly wrong; and if, under such circumstances, she should ever throw herself out of the pal of the Union in consequence of such a misconception of the Constitution as we have endeavored to prevent, I would rather see my own constituents stripped of their property acquired under the protection furnished by the Government to their honest industry, than compelled by any vote of mine here to drive the steel with which we should arm our citizens into the bosoms of that gallant people. And I will now say, without meaning to express any further opinion on this delicate subject, that, for myself, whenever pounds, shillings and pence alone shall be arrayed against the infinite blessings of the Union, I shall unhesitatingly prefer the latter, for the simple reason that I can never learn how to calculate its value."

He said further: "I would recommend to a State groaning under the operation of a law which she deems unconstitutional to apply first to the Federal judiciary, where she will generally obtain relief if her complaint be not hypochondriac or imaginary ill.... That tribunal has decided a hundred such cases, and many under the most menacing circumstances. Several States have occasionally made great opposition to it. Indeed, it would seem that in their turn most of the sisters of this great family have fretted for a time, sometimes threatening to break the connection and form others, but in the end nearly all have been restored by the dignified and impartial conduct of our common umpire to perfect good humor. Should that umpire ever lose its high character for justice and impartiality, we have a corrective in the form of our Government."

CLAYTON SAVED CALHOUN FROM JACKSON

His reputation was made almost as soon as he appeared at Washington, and this may have been a reason why he apparently wearied of Federal politics so soon.

Mr. Clayton's first notable achievement in "managing politics" was to prepare the compromise of 1832 between President Jackson and the Nullifiers of South Carolina. That struggle Clayton regarded as a Democratic family quarrel, a trial of rival obstinacies, with a substantial difference on the tariff. Jackson had sworn to hang "the traitors" at their own door-posts, and to try them by Court-martial. The Whigs, who had begun by regarding Jackson as a military madman, were confused by the vigor of his Administration and its tendency toward a stiffer Federalism than they had ever asserted. For party reasons they desired a settlement, so that the Democratic Executive should not annihilate their *quasi* ally, Calhoun, and win .....*(word illegible)* honors as the champion of the Union. Besides, pacificators like Clayton deprecated hostilities which seemed inevitable where duelists like Jackson and Benton, each of whom had killed his man, were arrayed against highstrung provincials like Hayne, James Hamilton and McDuffie. Clayton, at thirty-six years of age, was equally shrewd as a partisan and eclectic as a lover of human nature.

He saw that Calhoun was already the personal sacrifice of the gamesters in his constituency and of the people around the President, too able to be lost, yet doomed if bloodshed should arise through his incautious tuitions. General Jackson was remorseless about taking life under color of martial law. He had been triumphantly re-elected, and designed to take steps immediately after his inauguration to terrify Calhoun, of whom there is no record that he was a person of physical prowess.

The incidents of Clayton's mediation are fully related in the eighty-fifth chapter of Benton's first volume. Clayton and Dallas represented the immense manufacturing interests of Philadelphia and Calhoun, following the political economy of Dr. Cooper and the College of South Carolina, was an enforced free-trader, although once a Protectionist. Jackson's re-election had apparently doomed the protective system, and Clayton made use of the terrors of the nullifiers to force Calhoun to vote for a tariff compromise for eight years and for a home valuation on imports. The Protectionists alleged that with protection until 1842 they could place the manufactures upon a self-preserving basis. Clayton used Robert Letcher, of Kentucky, to bring Calhoun and Clay together, who did not speak. Letcher also plied between Jackson and McDuffie and heard the President's oath to try Calhoun for high treason.

FINIS.

"To help Mr. Clay with the manufacturers, Clayton put the amendments into his hands to be offered in the Senate, notifying Mr. Calhoun and Mr. Clay that unless they were adopted, and that by the Southern vote, every Nullifier inclusively, the bill should not pass, and he himself would move to lay it on the table. Behind these ostensible leaders of parties Clayton secretly organized his allies, and stood guard over the compromising chiefs. Calhoun voted for every protective feature except a home valuation, when Clayton moved to lay this bill on the table. Clay then expostulated with Clayton in vain, but a night was suffered to pass, and Calhoun employed it seeking to be personally released from recording his vote against his principles. The principle at stake—the constitutionality of discriminating duties—was that against which at the moment South Carolina was levying troops. When Calhoun, therefore, voted for the whole bill, yeas and nays, under Clayton's rod, the war of nullification had no statesman left, and South Carolina slunk back to her allegiance. "And thus," says Mr. Benton, "the question of mastery in this famous compromise, afterward mooted in the Senate by Mr. Clay and Mr. Calhoun as a problem between themselves, is shown by the inside view of this bit of history to belong to neither of them, but to Mr. John M. Clayton, under the instrumentality of General Jackson, who, in the Presidential election, had unhorsed Mr. Clay and all his systems, and, in his determination to execute the laws upon Mr. Calhoun, had left him without remedy, except in the recourse of his compromise."

Whatever may be our economical theory it is the historical fact that Clayton was the achiever of protection during the opposition terms of Jackson and Van Buren, and it became the settled policy of the country. He had, perhaps, derived some of his tariff ideas from his connections, the iron-making Douglases, but he was also a bank man and presented a petition of 1,650 citizens of Delaware—"the largest meeting ever held at Newcastle"—for the restoration of the public deposits. In short, he was a Whig through life seeking to put sectional questions at rest and unite the country on a National polity.

HIS FIRST BIG FEE

About 1834 Mr. Clayton appeared at Newcastle in a civil cause which procured him the largest fee he ever received, and he recovered, perhaps, the largest damages ever awarded in the State. A contractor by the name of Randall had a suit against the Chesapeake and Delaware Canal Company for violating the terms of a large contract. His case seemed so hopeless that he could find no counsel to give him any encouragement, and Mr. Clayton also replied that he didn't want the case.

"It's too hard," said Randall, much downcast. "I've as good a case as any poor man ever had against a rich company, and it's because I am poor that no lawyer will assist me."

"Stop!" said Clayton. "I'll take your case. Come in and let me look at it."

His opponents were James A. Bayard, James Rogers and Robert Frame, all able advocates, and Frame was as much of a genius and a truant in his way as Luther Martin, of Maryland. The argument of these men occupied nine days. Clayton did not take a note, but answered their points *seriatim*, overthrowing each and speaking three days. His cumulative, arousing, interesting, style threw the jury into such a state that they gave Randall the full amount, above $220,000 damages, which represented Clayton's argument and not the plaintiff's injuries, as he offered to compromise the suit for $10,000. Of this immense award Mr. Clayton took only $30,000, which he was obliged to attach on the tolls of the canal. That fee was a fortune in Delaware in those times, and is an independence now. Before such prowess the bar of the whole State shrank dismayed, but no jealousy attended the exhibitions of such transcendent intellect; none undertook to explain away his power; it was universally recognized, and he was known to be neither vain nor avaricious. His mere arguments obtained among the people the respect which attends judicial decisions.

FIRST LEAVING THE SENATE.

There were signs from the beginning that he did not like Washington life, and as early as 1831 the National Intelligencer announced that he desired to resign on account of bad health. "Distinguished as the present Senate is for men of pre-eminent abilities, the withdrawal of scarcely any member of the body would be more regretted." He did resign in his second term in favor of Thomas Clayton, his preceptor, and became Chief-Justice of the State. His decisions were never reversed, if ever appealed from, and he gave such copious authorities for all his rulings that he overcame criticism and exception. Men say he gave many a sly point to young practitioners who had not observed them. But, as in the Senate, Clayton succeeded too easily on the bench, and wearied less of the labor than the possession of the honor. He resigned the Chief-Justiceship in the summer of 1838 at the age of forty-three, and betook himself to practice, to rest, and to farming.

A FARMER.

He had been living in Dover about a quarter of a century when, after his resignation of the Chief-Justiceship, he indulged the dream of rural felicity. His sons were now young men and needed better habits than a small Courthouse and political village would afford. The flat, bilious, summer climate of Kent no longer agreed with him, and the upper country of Newcastle, tilled like a Belgian prospect, rolling picturesquely and with a more animated society, attracted his eye. He was exceedingly fond of sitting at a window or on an open veranda and watching the sails of vessels, and had once carried this taste so far as to buy the great old Nicholson mansion, near the Washington Navy-yard, that he might look off on the Potomac. In that house he never lived, but his estate in Newcastle was situated only a mile from the

Delaware, and the artist who would represent him in retirement must make the broad gray river and its shipping a feature of the picture. He bought 325 acres of land from the old Bennett Downs estate, as old as any on the Delaware, and expended about $25,000 on a new mansion, which was placed nearly half a mile back from the State road, and between it and the Frenchtown Railroad. He was about four miles from Newcastle, and ten from the City of Wilmington at the narrowest part of the State, where it was but ten miles wide. The house is still seen from the Delaware Railroad—a broad, red brick, with double-chimneyed gables and large back buildings, surrounded with cedars and forest shade, flanked by barns and cattle-houses, and environed by one of the noblest apple-orchards in the country. Clayton paid little attention to the fickle peach, but the great growers of that fruit, Major Raybold and his sons and Colonel Rothwell, were his most constant visitors. This industry in 1876 produced nearly nine million baskets of peaches a year on the Peninsula.

From his bedroom windows he could see the blue line of Iron and Chestnut Hills, and the ridge beyond the White Clay and Brandywine. The Pea Patch Island, and its fort and willow trees, seemed to close the vista of the bay, and the low Jersey shores to float upon the horizon line. Here Mr. Clayton gave fine dinner parties to the best people in the State, and equals and clients from Washington, New York and Philadelphia. Mr. Clay paid him a short visit. The national politics of the Whig party was to a great extent plotted and debated in this mansion, and had Mr. Clayton been placed on the ticket with Mr. Clay in 1844, his friends claim that the sectarian expressions of Mr. Frelinghuysen would not have been thrown in the scale against it to incite the Plaquemine frauds in Louisiana.

He proceeded to conduct his agriculture with the same stability and thoroughness he had shown in the law. Farming was the staple interest of Delaware, and he wanted to make his money useful to that industry where example would do the widest good. So he introduced fine stock and set out choice apple and pear plants, thinking there were peaches enough. For a part of the time he lived in Newcastle Town, in the great Read mansion, where the boys saw him pitching quoits in the grounds or heard the strains of his fiddle through the half-open windows and the roar which attended his anecdotes. Next door to the Read mansion was a Swedish house still on the spot, bearing the date of 1685. He lost his boys while living at "Buena Vista," as he called his farm, in honor of Taylor's victory, and was left alone with a satiated ambition and without a family, so he returned to the United States Senate, having neutralized the jealousy of him in the upper county by adopting it for his home.

FAT MAN ANECDOTES.

The politics of Delaware has been smooth-sailing, and to Clayton's management was owing to its good temper. He thought enemies inconvenient, and kept a high level of public combat, and never bore malice nor nursed revenge. In the arena he was a gladiator. Some have said that his private relations with men were too ostentatiously warm, and that at times they amounted to insincerity, but he lived in a State where the middle classes are at once the more peaceable and the most exacting of consideration. Strangers are bowed to on the streets; a gentleman used to ask permission in Delaware to drive past another on the roads; hospitality was hardly a virtue, because it was a delight. The public man sat down in the cot of the forester and asked for a piece of pie or potato bread, and went away with the diploma of a "clever man." Clever in Delaware does not mean "peart," it means highly considerate and obliging. John M. Clayton loved the people and mixed with them, and he probably made a good many promises he could not fulfill. He told an anecdote which afterward gave the name to a faction called "The Polly MacNotts," which illustrates his way of electioneering. Stopping one day at a roadside farm-house and asking for a baked potato, he said, as if incidentally:

"Mrs. MacNott, your husband's all right this year, ain't he?"

"I don't know, Mr. Clayton, he's a mighty uncertain."

"Jimmy's a good Whig or ....?"

"Well, when he's with the Whigs, he's a Whig, with the Democrats he's a ...., and at home he's a derned rascal."

As years and flesh and sedentary habits crept over his warmly nervous temperament, he grew more like slave in his affability, and took too much pains to please mere intruders, at whose exit he would show petulancy. The Hon. Benjamin Biggs states that once at his Newcastle farm, where Clayton was seated among some political cronies, a large, countrified Pennsylvanian came in and said:

"Mr. Clayton, I am not one of your constituents. We don't particularly like the United States Senators from our State; but your reputation is very high, and I drove over here to ask your co-operation on an honest, if a private, matter."

Clayton, weighing two hundred and forty pounds, arose, and overwhelmed the man with his reception.

"Take my chair," he said. "That's my chair. You sit in it. Tell me all about your troubles now, neighbor."

The man took Clayton at his word, narrated a long grievance, and was heard with cordiality until he went away after several hours. As the door closed upon him, Clayton exclaimed: "Look there! See how my time is taken up. That long-legged, cantankerous Dutchman crosses the line to make use of my time," &c.

No doubt this and other stories are true; there is a nervous spirit put in check by the obligations of good nature which breaks out in some great natures too much ridden. Mr. Webster had this great voluptuous personality, but he put the finish of a fine bombast upon it. Clayton substituted butter for the bombast, but he was careful of his professional credit as Mr. Webster was not. No man nor *coterie* paid his expenses; he paid his way, lived within his means and supporting many others, left a handsome fortune when he died. Yet he was liberal to a fault. One day his nephew, Douglass, was seated with him at the farm when two Philadelphians appeared to ask Clayton's opinion about a matter of business on jurisdiction, and he gave them all the facts and relations on their subject with lucid and copious powers. As they rose to go they asked:

"What is your charge, Mr. Clayton?"

"Nothing at all."

They bowed their way out, protesting their willingness and means to compensate him. After they were gone Douglass said: "Uncle, I think you ought to have taken a few from those gentlemen." "Why, James, do you want any money? If you do I'll give it to you." "No, sir; but you ought to take pay for your counsel." The fat old man put his hand on the nephew's head and said: "My boy, those gentlemen will be friends of mine as long as I live, and perhaps of yours after I am dead. What can we do with more money than we want?"

His nephew's daughter is still living on the farm, a well-considered lady, Miss Douglas.

Mr. Biggs relates a scene which happened at Clayton's residence in Dover. A countryman entered with a cowhide whip in his hand. Says the countryman to the statesman:

"Mr. Clayton, I have got a load of wood here which I want to sell. Can I do any thing with you to-day?"

"Yes, old friend," says Clayton: "just have my gate opened, and drive it into the back yard."

When the countryman was gone a person present said: "Mr. Clayton, did you want that wood?" "Want it," said Clayton. "No; there are about three hundred cords of wood in my back yard, and all the farmers in this region know that if nobody else will buy their cord-wood they can sell it to me. I take it because I am too indolent to say no; and, beside, I get half an hour's talk out of every farmer, which is all good for votes."

HIS PUBLIC WORK.

Clayton was the principal agent of Pennsylvania to achieve her tariff legislation. On July 27, 1846, Mr. Clayton passed through the Senate his resolution "to remove the new duties imposed by the pending Tariff Bill in all cases where any foreign raw material is taxed to the prejudice of any mechanic or manufacturer," so as to reduce the tariff on raw material to the schedule of 1842.

In 1848 Mr. Clayton anticipated Mr. Clay by two years with a compromise bill on the subject of slavery extension. Clay's compromise was a nosegay of measures, as Mr. Benton called it, a Fugitive Slave Bill among them; Clayton's remanked the question of slavery in the Territories to the Courts of law, so that the Supreme Court of the United States could settle the status of a slave taken to California, New Mexico or Oregon. He called it "a Non-intervention Bill," by which the parties in a controversy relating to personal freedom would be necessarily driven into the Courts." It passed the Senate after a session of twenty-two hours, and was beaten in the House by 112 votes to 97. In lieu of this, Clayton would have proposed to extend the Missouri compromise line to the Pacific, as he estimated that this would give freedom, without a battle, 1,600,000 square miles of land, and to slavery only 262,000, chiefly barren, desert and mountain. He was weary and worn out with agitation on the subject, and took a lawyer's view of the way to its solution. He was not a member of the Senate when the Fugitive Slave Bill passed.

The defeat of Mr. Clayton for Vice-President, at Baltimore, by the obscurer Frelinhuysen, whose nomination had neither alliteration nor celebrity, was wholly a matter of State power. Delaware might not have produced a Clay, but a greater scion would have arisen from her soil in vain at that time to expect the suffrages of a Presidential Convention. Clayton said to his friend, Comegys:

"We *must* make a new State or be added to another. We will never have influence, small as we are, and no heed is paid to us at Washington or any where else. If we could get the eastern shore of Maryland to unite with us, there might be some chance."

Clayton liked Marylanders of the Peninsular side of the bay. Senator Jas. Alfred Pearce was at Chestertown nearby, and they met and conversed frequently. Clayton had tried a law case at Chestertown earlier, and exchanged high words with Ezekiel Chambers, another of the four Senators bred at that little riverside town. Pearce survived him to ride to the Capital beside President Lincoln on the latter's first inauguration. By an agreement, if not a law, every alternate United States Senator was to be selected at

Annapolis from the Eastern side of the bay. Clayton had often been invited to follow the example of Governors McKean and Dickinson, who moved to Pennsylvania, and were elected Governors there also; for he was popular in that Commonwealth, and no man of his period was his equal in the Keystone State, not excepting Mr. Buchanan. The Pennsylvania manufacturers took his advice, and relied upon him chiefly, but he was peninsular in his tastes and affections, and yet too indolent to agitate sufficiently for the proposed union.

A BIG WHALE FENCED IN

The peninsula of which Delaware is a part is about one hundred and eighty miles long by from ten to seventy miles wide, and is the most populous of our peninsulas, with above three hundred thousand people, contained in fourteen counties, three State Governments and six thousand square miles. Less than half the population and only one-third of the territory is Delawarean. Two-ninths of the whole tract is subject to Virginia, though with less than sixteen thousand Virginian citizens. The various elements of old settlers are well mixed, and there is yet variety of occupation enough to make of the whole one versatile Commonwealth. The deep, broad rivers are all in Maryland, though within a morning's walk of the arbitrary boundary line, Delaware has navigable creeks, but no seaports, yet claims to the Jersey shore by some obsolete and whimsical law, and fights the Jerseyman for the oysters of Maurice Cove while the other two States have an annual oyster war, which compels both Virginia and Baltimore to keep armed police navies. On the Maryland side, at St. Michaels, the swift Baltimore clippers were built, which ran all the blockades of Europe; on the Delaware side are powder and cotton manufacturies. The peninsula is full of water power, and has hematite ore, and coal on descending grades could run from the anthracite mines the length of the region to Hampton Roads. With nearly four hundred square miles of oysterbeds, ten millions of baskets of peaches grown *per annum*, with marl and peat, lime and timber, five hundred miles of sea and bay coast and the isthmus open to the North the State of New Sweden might have supported the second city of the Chesapeake, nearer the sea than Baltimore and on a healthier site than Norfolk. Such a State could have paid the expenses of respectable institutions and built a Penitentiary to dispense with the whipping-posts. Avoiding the wide rivers west of the Chesapeake, its stem railroad would have passed the Southern tourist in one night from New York to a ferry-ship below the latitude of Richmond. Nearly twenty years after Clayton's dream Virginia was broken in half, and a Maryland railroad man was allowed to define the extent of the sundered part. By that definition Maryland might have been compensated for the loss of the peninsula—a region once so homogenous that the historian relates how, at the commencement of the Revolutionary war, it had sixty parish churches of the English faith. Such a State would have had both credit and revenue, with a concentrated political relation adapted to its topography to build and run its railroads, instead of parting with their control; for Boston is now the tollkeeper of the Peninsula. Louis McLane, of Delaware, Clayton's old competitor, had quit politics to take the Presidency of the Baltimore and Ohio Railroad, and at that moment was building it to the coal regions. The material concord of the Peninsular State would have been secured by an illustrious personal galaxy: John Smith and William Penn, Commodores Decatur and MacDonough and Admirals Goldsborough and Dupont, Rodney and McKean, Luther Martin and Samuel Chase, the painter Peele and the designer Darley, the Bayards and Dickinson. In Washington's day, his favorite route to Mount Vernon was down the Peninsula to Rock Hall: he wrote after the British, under Clinton, passed down the coast for the Chesapeake: "We have heard nothing of them since they passed our watch at Sinepuxcut." It was from Tangier Isle at the foot of the Eastern Shore that the British descended upon Washington and Baltimore in 1814; from the Elk, at its head, they marched on Philadelphia in 1777; and at Lewes, Alexander Hamilton boarded the French fleet which came to our relief. The agitation for a Peninsular State was most ardent in 1831, and Secretary Cameron proposed it as a war measure in 1862, extending Western Maryland to the Ohio, to make a new State. The Maryland people favored the plan, but the Delawareans, from usage, and, perhaps, from jealousy, gave indifferent support. It is noteworthy that the Maryland part of the peninsula has the superior race, if its quality be not also finer than that of Marylanders of the Western Shore. Clayton's mother was of Annapolis.

Filling now his third term in the Senate, Clayton in 1817 prepared for Executive honors by abetting one of the two Whig Generals who had conquered Mexico for the Presidency. It was the only way to evade the Whig opposition to that war.

NOMINATING TAYLOR.

The nomination of General Taylor is said to have been contrived between John Crittenden and Clayton. The former had taken Clay's seat in the Senate on the occasion of Clay's voluntary retirement in 1842, when he made a formal farewell speech, the only performance of its kind in our history. Clay was now about to return again to "get even," as some said, and Crittenden and other Kentucky Whigs were a little weary of the veteran's superfluous lagging on the stage. Five times Senator, seven times Speaker of Congress, and thrice Presidential candidate, Mr. Clay had led the Whig party to defeat repeatedly only to reassert his domination over his delegation and party associates the more after each calamity. His imperious will and fine arrogance were the terror of his Whig peers. It is related on one occasion he heard some of them were in council against him at Washington, and proceeding to the place knocked at the door and announced his name, whereat they all escaped through a window. At another time he overheard two of them talking against him at a place where there was no such escape, and he waited till one emerged, and proceeded to lecture him; the other, not daring to appear, was kept captive for an hour. He went into Tom Corwin's lodgings late in life to tell him what he must do, looking Corwin in the eye like a mind-reader. Corwin rebelled, saying; "Mr. Clay, I'm of lawful age, and I have made up my mind to act for myself in this case."

Clay looked at him a minute in silent choler and then threw his long cloak over his shoulder, stalked out without a word, and cut Corwin for the rest of his life. Such is the story.

General Taylor was of kindred self-will, as it appeared by Mr. Clay's statement in Colton's Life Biography. He addressed Mr. Clay before the campaign of 1848, and told him that he should run for the Presidency if the Whigs nominated him, and should probably run in any event. The Convention met in Philadelphia, and Mr. Clay was unable to hold his own delegation. Seven out of the twelve Kentuckians voted for Taylor on the first ballot. Taylor had 111 votes, Clay 97, General Scott 43. Mr. Webster 22, John M. Clayton 4, and Judge McLean, 2. Taylor was nominated on the third ballot, and Mr. Clay never gave him even that support during the campaign which he had grimly given to General Harrison eight years before. He attacked Clayton incidentally in the Senate, July 3, 1850, as a man much praised in McMichael's North American. As early as 1833 Mr. Clayton wrote to Mr. Clay that it would promote the latter's ambition if he should declare in the Senate that he was not a candidate for the office. Clay also accused James Alfred Pearce, Clayton's neighbor and Senator from Maryland, as the author of the failure of his compromise resolutions. He was old and soured and intolerant of opposition. "I'll just take him down here to the Potomac," said Clayton, "and say, old horse, I don't like to put you in the water, but it's a very little suffering for you and a great deal with us."

Clayton went by general consent out of the Senate.

INTO TAYLOR'S CABINET.

Three nights before the inauguration of Taylor he gave a fine dinner to which Clayton, already recognized as the incoming Secretary of State, was present with President and Mrs. Polk—soon to be a widow—Vice-President and Mrs. Dallas, Millard Fillmore, General Cass, Jeff Davis, Mr. and Mrs.

R.J. Walker and Mr. and Mrs. Marcy and a dozen more. When Mr. Clayton took this honorary place in the Cabinet the Senate (of sixty members) contained the leading spirits of the old and the new schools of opinion: Webster, Calhoun, Clay, Corwin, John Bell, James Alfred Pearce, Dayton Hale, Chase Seward, Jas. M. Mason and Hunter Benton and Douglas, John Davis and Jefferson Davis, Cass, Sam Houston, Dickinson and Hamilton. Millard Fillmore presided. In the House over two hundred and thirty members, and among them Robert C. Winthrop and Horace Mann, Taddeus Stevens and... A. Seddon, Jas. L. Orr, A.H. Stevens, Robert Toombs, Howell Cobb, Chas. M. Conrad, Joshua R. Giddings, R.C. Schenck, Andrew Johnson, Edw. D. Baker. The slavery question gave the controlling character to affairs, and three weeks were consumed choosing a Speaker. Howell Cobb finally receiving a plurality of three votes. The compromise measures were introduced by Mr. Clay, and Mr. Calhoun made his last speech and died at Washington during the life of General Taylor.

HIS DEPARTMENT.

Mr. Clayton's appointments were not numerous, considering that he had sixteen months of power. They were in the quiet line of Whig family and Whig service. His old friend, "Honest John Davis," who was his senior in years, but not in the Senate, and who died two years before Clayton, had a son, John C. Bancroft Davis, whom Mr. Clayton sent to Great Britain as Secretary of Legation under Abbott Lawrence, also of Massachusetts. This young man lived to be the presentor of the American case against England in the matter of the Alabama claims and Minister to the German Empire, and is now Assistant Secretary. Wm. C. Rives was sent to France, with Henry S. Sanford as Secretary: James Watson Webb to Austria, Geo. P. Marsh to Turkey, Walter Forward to Denmark, Mr. Clay's son James to Portugal, and even the son of Lewis Cass, against whose father General Taylor had been matched, was sent to the Papal States. Bailie Peyton went to Chili, Gales Seaton as Secretary to North Germany, and Robert P. Letcher to Mexico. At that time Hungary was in the throttle of Austria, and Mr. Clayton shared the public indignation on the subject to such a degree that he sent Dudley A. Mann to Hungary as a special agent, with large treaty powers among the minor States of the Continent. He sent Ephraim G. Squiers, of Ohio, whose articles have frequently enlivened Harper's Monthly, to Central America, where the principal act of Mr. Clayton's policy was meditated.

THE CLAYTON-BULWER TREATY.

Sir Henry Bulwer was at this time forty-five years of age, and had been married little more than a year to the niece of the Duke of Wellington. His diplomatic success had been equal to that of his younger brother, Edward, in literature. Entering diplomatic life about the time Clayton first entered the Senate, Bulwer had been in the British Legations of five countries, and Minister to Spain, and was a man of sincerely liberal sympathies, who had been recently ordered out of Spain for assisting the Republicans. He was a good speaker, and a man of democratic spirit, and very fond of Clayton. He weighed about one hundred and thirty pounds, was hardly more than five feet seven inches in height, and not very prepossessing, as he was pitted with the small-pox, and had the address and peculiarities of a London swell.

Clayton's residence was then on F street, Washington, opposite the present Ebbitt Hotel, only a block distant from the old State Department. There, in the second-story, George P. Fisher drew the *projet* of the treaty; Bulwer and Clayton signed it in the second story of the dwelling, nearly at midnight, and a fire broke out a few minutes afterward close by, to which Bulwer and Fisher ran and passed up buckets of water to save a widow's house. The district firemen worked so slowly that Bulwer, who was excited after his wont, stamped his foot and cried: "By damme! I do hate slavery."

The treaty was a plain, brief document in nine articles. The Queen and the United States were declared to be desirous of consolidating their relations of amity, and to this end mutually abandoned separate pretensions to a canal between the Atlantic and Pacific by way of the rivers of Nicaragua and Managua; nor were they to fortify, occupy, colonize or treat for rival advantages there, nor either accept privileges over the other in such a canal any-where in Central America. Two free ports were to be established at the ends of the canal, with the consent of the native Government possessing the jurisdiction. America and England were to supervise and protect the construction of the work and to guarantee its perpetual neutrality even if they should engage in war with each other. In war or peace, it was to be a peaceful channel, and the seas in its vicinity were to be equally water sanctuaries like a neutral harbor. Neither blockade, detention nor capture were to be permitted there, and this artificial strait was also to be protected from interruption, seizure or unjust confiscation. The only occasion of withdrawing such protection, after six months' fair notice, would be exactions or partiality by the persons or Company operating the canal. Whatever association or incorporators had already obtained a concession for such a canal should be first patronized, and the work was to be done by the first comers of whatever country. England and America invited the co-operation and aid of any State with which either was friendly "to maintain ship communication between the two oceans for the benefit of mankind on equal terms to all.".... "Not only to accomplish a particular object, but to establish a general principle." And the two nations extended their protection to any similar railroad or canal on Tehuantepec or Panama.

. . . .

The editors have here omitted seven pages of text, referencing matters of historical but not biographical interest. They skip to the final chapter of the article.

THE OLD MAN'S LAST LONG REST.

His fourth election was a concession rather than a struggle. His party had a majority in one branch of the Legislature: the other branch was Democratic and refused to come into joint ballot, hopeful of unhorsing the old Cid who had routed them so often. In this emergency Clayton was befriended by a State Senator whom he had cleared for the crime of kidnaping—a boyish lark of thirty years before. This man Sorden, a Democrat, who owed his reputation to Clayton's eloquence, broke from the caucus, saying that he would not have Cass and Douglas attacking "the old man" behind his back. Therefore, on the 4th of March, Clayton was in his place to reply to the solicitors of the Irish vote.

I heard Mr. Clayton make two speeches. The first was immediately following the nomination of Winfield Scott, in 1852. An immense man, a perfect Daniel Lambert, as it appeared to me, stood on the doorstep of a dwelling at Delaware City; his hair white and fine, his necktie of white, his clothes black, and low shoes on his feet. A great stomach, which seemed to be an exaggerated copy of his double chin, was suspended between hips powerful enough but for such weight, and yet there was an easy expression on his face, so great and gracious that I should have thought it treason to smile at his fat. He carried a large silk handkerchief in his hand to wipe away the copious perspiration which flowed as he proceeded, although his skin was of a clear color, and his general neatness exceptional among the two hundred or more listeners. The speech was a talk, full of persuasion, observation, humor and vigor. He addressed himself to calm the arousing fear of negro equality, which was the more timorous in a community of many free blacks, and styled it "the negrophobia." He said the blacks of Delaware were a good natured, inoffensive class of dependents, in whom only demagoguery could see evil purposes. There was such a mass of agreeable and new information in the speech that he might have talked a whole day and kept his audience. He was then in physical pain and heaviness, and flesh, as I have observed, is the plague of most of the Claytons. The day had already passed when he could cross the border to Lancaster, at the Buchanans' home, and assemble and inspirit thousands of Whigs.

I heard him again at the endowment services of Delaware College, the only collegiate institution the State possessed, and incidentally the parent school of the University of Pennsylvania, and a godfather of Princeton and Dickinson. Francis Allison, an Irish graduate of Glasgow University, arrived in Delaware about 1735, and was employed as private tutor in John Dickinson's family, near Dover. He started several Academies, of which the Delaware Academy was the principal, and although its charter from the Penns dates only to 1768, its nucleus goes back to 1749. Princeton and Dickinson, the former long presided over by Samuel Davis, of Delaware, and the latter founded by the author of the Farmers' Letters, anticipated the raising of a College on Newark Academy, which was postponed until 1821, when a transit tax was imposed on strangers through Delaware for the purpose. The College had been dragging along for nearly twenty years, when Clayton and others came to its rescue in 1851. His speech at that time was pleasant to listen to. Money was raised, and the old Academy, which was a shoe factory in the Revolution, has kept open its doors for upward of a century, having been attended by seventy-one pupils as long ago as 1771.

The last general works of Mr. Clayton were to vindicate his treaty from aspersions, and to second philanthropic legislation at Washington. The Government Insane Asylum, with six hundred patients, is one of his benefactions. It was opened in 1855, after the usual opposition on the constitutionality of helping the sick or any body. Clayton delivered a long and emotional speech on the subject and led the bill.   GATH

Recollections and Reflections.

PUBLISHED IN

LIPPINCOTT'S
MONTHLY MAGAZINE.

NOVEMBER, 1886.

by
George Alfred Townsend.

George Alfred Townsend in middle age.
Courtesy University of Delaware Library, Newark, Delaware.

RECOLLECTIONS AND REFLECTIONS

NEARLY twenty-seven years of correspondence and literary and general composition embarrass the selection of the experiences you desire me to send you. As there is no royal road to learning, there is hardly any other road than the common street to the newspaper. The writer's vocation is a perpetually exhausting one, and replenishment is the first law of his being.

The newspaper of our day has passed beyond the duty of reporting public events and commenting upon them, and has invaded general life: so that fiction itself is left barren, and fails to seize the imagination, when the newspaper is laid down.

The decline of literature, as of oratory, has undoubtedly been effected by the enterprise of the press and by the intrusion of the reporter into household narrative: besides, intercourse has brought with it almost universal adventure and episode. The village incidents which made the long talk of our grandmothers are now the regular staple of the journal: the young woman who became infatuated with the clairvoyant was a household topic for twenty years when she lived abreast of my childhood, but she had the felicity to keep out of print; whereas at the present day she appears in print before her own relatives have found out her mutiny. Yet this enlarged and superabundant newspaper has only been the creation of about fifteen or twenty years.

No one has ever estimated sufficiently the influence of a single worldly journal in the family. It has been the great revolutionary power to many a humble son whose father, by some accident, finally subscribed for a daily newspaper. When I first used to see a secular paper in my father's house it was either a weekly publication or a borrowed daily paper: indeed, borrowing the newspaper was a very general thing in the plainer parts of Philadelphia while I was going to school there. Money, before the war, did not abide long in ordinary families, and when the carrier came for his weekly bills he was decidedly a more formidable visitor than at present: so the newspaper passed from house to house, and a family well informed on all matters of the day was considered to be over-intelligent and restless.

About seven or eight years before the civil war there was a multiplication of weekly and story papers through the country, which were served by carriers to the country hamlets; and they, according to my notice, had more influence to draw boys away from home and make travellers and observers of them than such average daily papers as existed prior to the great battle-events of 1861 and 1862. Patriotic stories, such as created the fortune of Robert Bonner, also gave lads a tendency towards public life and exploit. It was from some of these papers that I derived a disposition to see something of mankind, especially in conflict, in Congress, and in pageants and movements. I began to write a tale at the age of thirteen, and from that time onward never for a whole day have been out of sight of the writing purpose and occupation. No doubt there must be a strong original propensity in that direction to give a lad precocity and development in the art; and I well recollect that when, for a few months, I was in a city store making a feeble effort to be a merchant's clerk, some neighboring apprentices would stroll in to enjoy my confusion when they said, "Where is that boy who is going to write a book?" It took many years to produce a book, but in the mean time I was going, through an unconscious apprenticeship to whatever appertained to public occurrences and the relating of them.

My father was a clergyman, and had few secular books in his library; but even the religious books assisted me towards analysis and perception. My holidays were spent wandering to places which had historic associations, and the battle-fields of Germantown, Brandywine, and Red Bank were familiar to me by the aid of Lossing's old Field-Book, which I carried with me on these excursions. I also owed to the much-denounced system of free transportation accorded to reporters the only opportunity I had for years of looking at places and people. While at High School, at the age of sixteen I published a little magazine for an advertising personage; and a brother of Stephen Foster, the song writer, who was vice-president of a railroad, gave me on that behalf tickets to Pittsburgh and return,—a longer journey than I had made in all my preceding days. I walked across the Allegheny Mountains, and formed a certain instinct for nature at that time which might otherwise have been left out of my composition. The writing of compositions became my only ambitious endeavor at school; and, while in many departments I was slovenly and "marked" down, in this one department I was always at the top without much trouble. At fifteen years of age I could write verses at will when a subject was given out for composition to be prepared during the hour and in the master's sight.

Competition in declamations, wherein I was not the cleverest by any means, generally gave me the advantage of appearing with an original piece; and I recall one instance where the real orator of the class—indeed, the orator of the whole school—lost what justly belonged to him because the composition I delivered was pertinent to things upon the spot. My first publication was in a public school journal, and I think I read it over a hundred times. From that time onward I made appearances in inferior literary journals or sometimes a miscellaneous Sunday paper; but a want of confidence to press in among crowds and through policeman and worldly folks made me feel indescribably fresh and bashful in a newspaper office. I saw no way at last of getting into the newspapers at all: their employees all had an off-hand way and a cool draught about them which put me back. About the time I graduated—at nineteen years of age—I had not the least idea of what profession I should adopt or how I should get along in this world.

It happened in this case, as in all other cases of attempt or enterprise in life, that my juvenile performances had not been unobserved. The night before I made my speech as a Bachelor of Arts, a person stepped up to me and asked if I had any definite purpose, saying that he had been reading after me when he was a pupil at the school, and was empowered to offer me a situation also on a newspaper. The gates of heaven opening on golden hinges could not have turned more melodiously than this newspaper wicket seemed to me to sound.

But at the beginning it was a rough enough life, and I had little tractability in it. My blushing appearance was still against me. I found myself in an editorial room, surrounded by men who appreciated each other and themselves and greatly valued the editorial privilege. For a time I wrote editorials; but somebody was always brought into the paper who looked important and felt important, and who monopolized the editorial control, and in the courage of time appeared as a very important person at the clubs and public meetings; while, generally speaking, he had no longevity in his nature. I have passed on the road at least a score of these men who used to lord it over the newspaper, many of them trying to get a living in practical situations, and hardly one of them keeping up his newspaper confidence to the present time. The reason is, I think, that the editorial room gives the mind more dogmatism than air, more confidence than experience; and without perpetually freshening up the nature all writing sinks to be perfunctory, and the oxygen is out of it.

I wanted to be a correspondent, or what was called at that time a "special" correspondent, of which there were very few in the whole land. But the journals where I happened to be had no pecuniary enterprise, and a man was never sent anywhere to report. He was furnished with a free ticket, and was more than half expected to get his meals and lodging at the expense of the publicans.

So I became a reporter about the city, never having a chance to get far beyond its environs; but in this small occupation I had enterprise according to my opportunity, and became in request, so that in a little while I was what is now called the city editor.

It became apparent to me that I must find in some other city a career which, after two years of experiment in Philadelphia, had come very far short of my own expectations. Living at home, I spent all the little money I earned in seeing and acquiring information. My salary was fifteen dollars a week, I think, and I could pick up about ten dollar more a week in the same city by fugitive operations. The leading newspaper in New York got in the habit of sending for me to do up the local events when occasionally they happened. In that way I passed the whole of the first year of the civil war, and meantime took something of a literary position in addition to my regular duties, receiving, it is needless to say, no compensation for the literary work, though it required double the labor of the editing and reporting pursuits. I was what is called the dramatic critic of a newspaper of considerable standing, as well as the city editor of that paper and its travelling correspondent. We published no issue on Sunday, and therefore had to work on that day and break the Sabbath, whereas on Saturday we were as devout as the Jews who keep that day.

The events in the first year of the war were of a very taking nature, not only as to men, but as to means and organizations. The eye was kept continually in use, and readers as well as writers were educated upon the high fevers of battle and excitement.

I never gave any time to getting the intimate confidence of any of my employers beyond doing my work in my own way, and thus individuals more watchful of the small proprieties of life seemed to be ahead of me; though I found, in the long run, that leaning upon personal friendship in any career is a staff of straw. It took me a good many years in the press to earn the privilege of saying what I thought and believed; and I think that much of the cowardice which retards the newspaper in its influence is due not to real care, but to real jealousy and smallness in the conduct of the columns of the journal. A man who is on the outside looking at things should have a clearer idea of what is taking place than he who is cooped up in such editorial rooms as we formerly had, which were hardly fit for a dog to occupy. The reporters of twenty and twenty five years ago had no quarters at all worth being considered so, and had to do their writing at night among the printers, up at the end of some alley where a little cage was set aside for them. No wonder that the writing talent has increased in the country, when we see the spacious accommodations at present, in which men can both read and think deliberately.

There were no newspaper libraries in general use when I began, and the books which the publishers sent to the editors were considered the perquisite of whoever had the most audacity or was first making his demands. Those books should have been used for the common benefit, and in the course of time they would have made notable libraries for their purpose.

Nevertheless, the two years I spent on the daily papers of Philadelphia were not so filled with drudgery but that I could collect a small library and do a good deal of reading; and during all my occupation on the press I have been an habitual reader as well as a periodical looker-on. I generally combine the two vocations, and if I have a distant place to see I take the books along, reading as I go; and when I get there I need not stand like a fool, asking silly questions, but can go on to conclusive things.

Books on local history, American biography, the comprehensive works of the organizers of the republic, and lexicons, guides, and almanacs, are all important to the journalist. These books are in many cases expensive; but *Americana* has also greatly appreciated in value during the past ten years, and much of it is due to the consultation of local history by the newspaper writers.

Indeed, I often think that the great failure of the newspaper of our day is in its complete success. It disturbs the mind and possibly hinders progress by its universal explicitness.

The telegraph wires have become in our day things of vulgar access, whereas I was a good while on a newspaper before I ever had occasion to use the wires at all. When Abraham Lincoln made his celebrated speech at Trenton, where he affirmed for the first time that be would resist the disunionists, I took it to the telegraph office and felt almost like a culprit when I sent it over the wires, though it was hardly five minutes long. At the present time I often send eight thousand to twelve thousand words over distances of one thousand to four thousand miles,—say from Chicago to Boston, New York, Cincinnati, and California,—and the matter gives no more concern than when, in 1861, some real battle would come into the editorial room and you would hear the editor exclaim that there would be the devil to pay next morning down-stairs; meaning when the publishers got the bills. I have known men of enterprise, at the commencement of my experience, to be turned off the newspapers, not for sending too little matter, but for sending too much; whereas, in our time, to send too little is an offence nobody will overlook.

About March or April, 1862, I took newspaper service in New York and went to the war. The press at that time was far beneath a true sense of self-respect, and a good deal of the war was described in such a careless way as to embroil the correspondents with the commanders and disguise the true issues to the people. I wrote up the six days' battles on the Peninsula for the paper which then had the largest circulation in the country; but we were not allowed to have the use of our names, and I might as well have thrown the account into the James River as to expect any good from it to myself. About 1865, when I returned from a long absence in Europe, the newspapers had entered into more distinctive competition, and were compelled, in special cases, to accord men the use of their names. I have found the latter provision, which I made when I last went to the war, to make all the difference between notoriety and obscurity: besides, it put one upon his mettle, and he would exert extraordinary means to achieve success. The battle of Five Forks was the only battle of the war which I ever had a good chance at. I obtained my account from General Sheridan himself, and rode alone all that night, through a somewhat hostile country, to get to a railroad in the morning, and thence I went straight to New York, writing as I went along.

The events at the close of the war were so widely read, and gave me such unexampled opportunities, that in a few weeks I found my box filled with letters of application to write and to lecture, and there began my connection with the newspapers of the West, which have had such an important influence to change the status of the newspapers in the East.

The news itself in our time is more likely to come from the West than from the East. I recollect that the first distinguished embassy I ever saw came to America in 1860 from Japan. The Chinese soon followed. No settlement in the land has done more to give literary and newspaper stimulation than San Francisco. Its journals were expensive, and therefore, even upon a limited circulation, they could afford to pay well for contributions. The nature of the life and mixing there brought out some of our best humorous and story writers. At the conclusion of the war we found a new West, while the East relatively remains what it was previously. Therefore the vigorous and aggressive work on the press has come from the Western men, those who were either raised in the West or who derived considerable knowledge of it. Such men as Richardson the correspondent and Stanley the African traveller were of Western newspaper breeding. The rise of large cities in the West made reporting there a more stimulating employment than in the reposeful parts of the East.

For two years after the close of the Rebellion I made journeys to Europe in pursuit of the events then considered important,—such as the war between Austria and Prussia and the chief Paris Exhibition; but I speedily found that Europe is not a place for newspaper enterprise, but for newspaper idling. So about 1867 I concluded to go to Washington City and study the government, of which at the time I had the flimsiest knowledge: I did not know how business was formed and advanced from bills to committees, and from committees to reports, and from reports to legislation. Seven years in Washington gave me a certain satiety and an appetite to go to New York and see how many men became rich and what were the financial laws which decoyed so many Senators over to New York on Friday nights. Since that time I have resided in New York and kept one hand on Washington, moving to and fro. When I first went to Washington in 1861, while troops were quartered in the Capitol, we had a single line of rail and a single track, and it was a matter of a long day to make the journey. Now there are some nine trains a day in each direction, the journey is reduced to five or six hours, there are competing lines of rail, and bridges at every river, and all the cities have been flanked, while newspaper rates, which were five or six cents a word between the capital and New York, have been so reduced that matter can be sent from Washington and Boston, or the West, for something like a quarter of a cent a word.

Twenty-five years ago the most successful newspaper writer, not a proprietor, in the city of Philadelphia received a thousand dollars a year, or twenty dollars a week. He was a man of diligent research, and wielded a trenchant pen.

Twenty years ago came the first improvements in salaries. About 1865 I could make a hundred dollars a week; but much of the work required of me at that time was discouraging. Instead of taking comprehensive matter, there was an itching for local sensation. In the course of time correspondence bore down mere reporting by the superiority of its themes and broader capacity of treatment; and it is my belief that this special correspondence has been the great revolutionary agent in the newspaper,—for certainly the editorial writing does not greatly differ from what it was at the commencement of our century, and the reporting of events never had much significance so long as it was confined to the particular city in which the journal was published. Intrepid, original, well-informed men, who have seen life in many States and countries, pushing to a distant point of interest, rapidly assemble their story, and as rapidly drive it home through the telegraph to the minds of the readers while yet the events are alive and startling. The writer therefore receives the same stimulation of enactment which the readers obtained.

Another thing of note about the press is its positive wealth compared to its condition twenty-five years ago. Newspapers which made twenty-five thousand dollars a year were thought to be great properties before the war. Their conductors depended so much upon official patronage and party support that the politics of a mere boy was a thing of moment when he was to be employed. The newspaper offices were generally hired buildings until after the civil war, when even New York *Herald* bought Barnum's Museum, having previously been on a side-street. Some of the journals have become real-estate partnerships, and expect to derive a large portion of their receipts from rents; but this kind of income seldom has other than a depressing effect on the newspaper itself, making it, as in the old political days, somewhat dependent upon tenants and petty prejudices. The wealth of the press, extending to some of its employees, has enabled them to surround themselves with the instrumentalities which increase productiveness and substantiate the news of the present with the biography and example of the past. I think, too, that with this wealth has come an increase in the truth-telling power of the journal.

Wherever there seems to be habitual misrepresentation in the news it can be charged to the want of agreeable or easy communication between the seat of news and the purveyors of it. The older newspapers had but a slight sense of responsibility, because they could not afford to employ persons who were not periodically endeavoring to eke out subsistence at something else. One of the most respectable of these old papers which I knew had for its editor a man would come into the office late at night and give his whole day to speculation. In another case the editor was a job printer, being obliged to take care of his family somehow.

The wealth of the journals has made them intolerant of each other by increasing their greed. There is nothing so greedy as a shark with half a meal; and a newspaper which is on the eve of making one hundred thousand dollars goes partly crazy, and wants two hundred thousand dollars or somebody's life.

You see the same scene in mercantile life or among speculators. Savage instincts are always strongest when the prey is nearest at hand, and journals which make more money than is good for them hate nothing so much as journals which are cruising abreast of them. It is sad to consider that the highest offence a man in our business can commit is not murder, not incendiarism, not any of the lower order of crimes: his greatest crime is to publish another newspaper where there was one before, or to assist a rival newspaper to get the wind of its opponent.

As to the future of the press, that is uncertain. Some kind of change must come upon it through the exigencies of change itself, if nothing else. I apprehend that with the increase of competition the profits of the newspapers will be reduced. The first step of progress ought to be improvement in quality rather than exuberance of themes. Public news only deserves reporting. The passion to get advertisements is one cause of the enormous size of daily sheets which are attempting to paralyze each other by a show of prosperity, while really, perhaps, an aching heart is underneath the audacious mask of the exploiter. Signs of feeling this pressure are to be seen in the avidity with which inventions are taken up which will reduce the cost of type-setting or roll off more newspapers.

The people themselves need not be governed by the newspaper beyond what they are willing to concede; for in our age it is often good medicine to lay aside the daily news for a week or a month. When one returns to life; so to speak, it then seems quite healthy pabulum; but taken in great quantities and for a long periods the news is like any other form of stimulation, and must be left off for a time.

Writing for the press involves something of that demoralization I speak of which the reader feels. If it is wearing to read the newspaper every day in the week and read it all through, it must also be injurious to write all the time and increase rather than diminish the amount of one's contributions. There are times when the healthiest brain will feel the satiety of conflict, of competition, and of misrepresentation; yet nothing in the newspaper world wears a man down like his own injustice. The quarrel where he has given the provocation and insists on staying wrong makes him more tired of his business than any other method or errantry.

Newspaper writing ought to have its reliefs; and there is no relief equal to journeying backward rather than forwards,—as to some historical shrine instead of towards the scene of to-morrow's tumult. The library also affords a pleasant rest; and there are times when one's bed, after he has written almost gluttonously, is a very heaven of delight. After coming home from some large convention or scene of great disorder which has overtaxed my pulses, I like to close the chamber door and read and bathe and sleep until, finally rested, I think of some unexplored scene of sylvan repose, and go there and change entirely the regimen of life. On coming back again to the world the curiosity is alert, and everything seems healthy and normal again.

One of the saddest thoughts in connection with our daily press is its unindexed publication. There are few papers in the world which make indexes to themselves; but most of our American journals avow their mortality when they employ, with all their present facilities, no drudge to keep their contents for purposes of consultation. So I will close this flitting paper with a few lines which I once addressed to the New York Press Association when I was called upon for a poem:

> We, too, are doomed, like poles that hold the wires,
> To be supplanted when our use expires-
> Our names to perish from the vaults of sound
> And all we writ unindexed and unfound:
> In unconsulted dust the mirror page
> Where came and went the image of our age.
> Debarred from fame, we, in our little hour,
> Should feel that nothing lasts but moral power;
> Ceasing to shine with strong and separate ray,
> Yet, in yon silver-gleaming nebulae,
> The good, the brave, the gracious we have done
> Will belt the heavens as with glory sown.
> Then may we know immortal is our craft,
> And every idle word photographed,-
> Cast in the ether, kept till time is done,
> And caged in framing tissues of the sun.

George Alfred Townsend

An Interviewer Interviewed.
A TALK WITH "GATH."

PUBLISHED IN

LIPPINCOTT'S
Monthly Magazine.

NOVEMBER, 1891

THE DUKE AND THE COMMONER.

One of the Lowery Gang, Illustration from the *Swamp Outlaws*.

AN INTERVIEWER INTERVIEWED.

Mr. George Alfred Townsend is a large man, weighing two hundred and twenty pounds in his clothes, about five feet ten inches in height, with a smooth, sanguine complexion, high cheek-bones, and broad face, and the general appearance of a portly man of business with neither the natural nor the affected signs of his vocation. The opportunity was made use of at the seaside to obtain fragments of his experience, as an experiment of the interview sort for a literary magazine.

"You must be, Mr. Townsend, among the oldest special correspondents, as they used to be called?"

"I think I am the oldest continuous special correspondent on the stage: three are still living who preceded me a little while, and two of these, Messrs. Edward House and Stephen Fiske, enticed me by their style of work into the newspaper, or this department of it. In the Crimean war, Mr. William H. Russell, who is still living, almost created this species of demi-literature. Of course, travellers, like Lamartine, had gone out before, to Greece and other countries where something was occurring, and had written for the reviews, and possibly for the newspapers, something which they saw; but Russell, an Irishman in English employ, showed the possibilities of special correspondence,—that is to say, correspondence from a man sent to see a particular thing, to look all around it, and to describe it quickly, so as to anticipate the official reports. The Mexican war had ended eight years before the Crimean war, and the Americans had done a good deal to bring news of their battles home. I suspect that James Watson Webb, of New York, was as much a pioneer in this business as anybody: he lived to a great age, and left an effective family of children successfully following various professions. The impending conflict in the United States accompanied railroad development, and the Prince of Wales, the Chinese, and the Japanese all came to this country just before the civil war, and furnished occasions to send out special correspondents. Reading some of these reports in the four New York newspapers, my emulation was aroused. I graduated at the Philadelphia High School at the commencement of 1860, and public speeches and writings I had made for three years previously brought me employment at once. A newspaper in the second city of the country was to be altered in form and matter and made like the New York papers. I had to go through some bureau employment, such as news editor and editorial writer, reporter, and city editor, but all the time my bent was towards special correspondence, and I took eight years at least, if not twelve, out of my life, and invested it in experience, saving nothing, but going many a thousand miles that I might learn how to see; for the eye is to the writer what the hand is to the mechanic."

"You say you had written and published in boyhood?"

"I commenced at eleven years of age, unconsciously, to be a seer and writer for the public. My father was a clergyman in a country town not too remote from a large city. In that city I one day saw a woman sitting in a market-house with a basket full of books with water-color illustrations. Nothing had ever affected me so much before, except a painted picture I had seen on the side of an omnibus as I came into the same city at the age of six. I bought some of the books at a penny or two apiece, and a box of water-colors, and began to paint drawings which I made from life. In the course of three years it seemed to everybody that I was to become an artist, for I copied and imitated hundreds of drawings. At fourteen I undertook to write a story or romance. At sixteen I published both story and poem, or rhyme, in a juvenile newspaper. From the time the first piece appeared in print, I was captive completely to the writing propensity. And though I could have continued to hold the place at school, which I once easily won, at the head of the class, I paid but little attention to most of the studies for the two last years of my schooling, but read a great variety of books,—generally took other books to school than the text-books, and read them under or on the desk, and had a wandering turn on holidays, to go out into the country and see something and find what had taken place there. In that way I wandered, with Lossing's 'Field-Book of the Revolution,' over the battle-fields like Brandywine, Valley Forge, Germantown, and Red Bank. For a long time the poetic form, which does a good deal to strengthen style and teach etymology, was a favorite with me. I had a dread of the daily papers, for the men about them seemed to be off-hand, practical, and I have never in my life been a worldly person. The blush I had in childhood comes readily to my face now. The principal literary effort I ever made at school was a poem called 'The pleasures of Timidity.' In fact, I was finding my way into the newspaper by a process I knew not of. As soon as I got there, the other reporters thought I must be plagiarizing; and I heard the editorial factotum cry out one night, 'Who is this boy who is publishing editorials in the reporters' column?' But for the great civil war soon coming on, I might have retired from the newspaper in disgust; but the country at that time was passing out of its provincial condition, and the uneasiness in the air was indicative of some great transformation. My intention had been to be a literary man. Time has taught me that there is no such profession in the United States as literature; but indeed the news has always been close behind real literature. The Crusaders made Tasso and Cervantes; the rounding of the Cape of Good Hope made Camoens; and

Dickens would never have become famous had he not been a press reporter, who saw with his own eyes another world than Scott had seen. When he named his son for Henry Fielding, the police magistrate, who also was an author, you could see that the realistic occurrences of modern life had guided both those men in their novels. De Foe, and even Shakespeare, obtained inspiration from large contemporary occurrences, like the planting of America and the Protestant Revolution in England. I bade adieu to literature when Fort Sumter was fired on, and went to the civil war, seeing McClellan pass through Philadelphia on his way to take command of the Army of the Potomac, and seeing his army embattled in Virginia. I reported the seven days' battles for the New York *Herald* in July, 1862, but, that concern suppressing its correspondents' names, I got no other assistance from the work than a Sunday newspaper in New York gave me by having me write the events over again, for in that day only one of the dailies had a Sunday edition. During Pope's campaign I gratified a desire I had entertained, of visiting Europe, and there I stayed almost two years, and had hardly stepped ashore when I began to write, still in the line of the war news. If you will look at the *Cornhill Magazine* at the close of 1862, you will see my articles there, called 'Campaigning with General Pope,' and 'Richmond and Washington during the War.' When I came back from Europe I went to the army again, and saw Grant and Sheridan close out the war; and by this time the government had compelled the newspapers to print their correspondents' names, so that in a few weeks I had the reputation I should have had in 1862. There began my bias for the government, as better than any of the institutions which berate it."

"How much do you suppose you have written and published?"

"I have not written less than two columns a day for thirty-five years, or four thousand words a day, making a total of more than fifty millions of words. This is considerably under the aggregate."

"You do not mean to say you did all this with your own hand?"

"Oh, no. After I removed to Washington City, to write personal and political correspondence, toward 1867, when I had exhausted lecturing, I found that the attempt to supply four or five different papers at once with hand-written manuscript was destroying my nervous organization. Then came to my assistance another little experiment of my school-days, when I had founded a literary and debating society. I found that I could dictate, at first to long-hand and afterwards to short-hand writers; and for about twenty-three years I have talked nearly the whole of my correspondence, though I find it a rest now and then to pick up the pen and write three thousand to four thousand words. In transferring the strain from the eye and hand to the head, another species of oppression comes: my relief from that has always been to make a journey into some open country, and in forty-eight hours I come back completely refreshed."

"Do you find that reading assists your newspaper work?"

"That is just as important as seeing well. The great mass of newspaper writers never read, and hence the superficiality of the press. When I went to Washington City it was not to make money by writing, but to discover for myself how the government transacted its business. I passed through the skeptical and scornful stage and become a constructive writer, holding that what the county did was, on the whole, wise."

"Who was the first great man you ever saw?"

"I saw Stephen A. Douglas, in the campaign of 1860, at the Girard House, Philadelphia, with his coat off, his boots off, his feet upon a marble-top table, and a decanter of—probably—brandy at his side, and realized his bitter disappointment, from his conversation, at finding the apparently obscure Lincoln coming into sudden and wide prominence. I have often been merely lucky in striking an event at the climax. For instance, I ran up to Trenton when Lincoln was coming towards Philadelphia, and heard him in the State-House of New Jersey make the speech which presaged his official resistance to secession. Greater than his speech was the fierce applause which attended his words, 'It may be necessary to put the foot down firm.' I realized that the North was ready for war and rather desired it. In the course of seven or eight years, I saw James Buchanan lying in his coffin in the hall of his residence at Wheatlands, and saw in the same town, hardly a year from that time, old Thaddeus Stevens dead, with his Pennsylvania Dutch constituents swarming into Lancaster. As soon as I was established in Washington, at about the commencement of the impeachment trial of President Johnson, I began to visit the homes of the Presidents and principal public men, and I am still doing that thing, so that I can distinctly see men who went before me when their names rise up. I gave great attention to local history, and almost invariably bought a book instead of borrowing it, if the subject interested me, so that at fifty years of age I have a working library by which I can test and prove almost everything, personal and otherwise. Of course this has led back to collecting books upon the races which have settled America, and the languages those races spoke, etc. 'How do you find so much to write about?' is often asked of me. I never write as much as I would like to tell. This business, like others, is cumulative, and, having been upon the daily papers nearly a third of a century, almost every event gets light from things gone before; yet I never reprinted a paragraph. It would be harder to hunt up the paragraph which I wished to reprint than to make another one."

"How many times have you been abroad?"

"I have been six times in Europe; I saw Meyerbeer buried, and saw the Prince of Wales and his bride and her sister, now the Empress of Russia, enter London: a room-mate of mine, Mr. Billings, did much of the illustrating of that event for the *London News,* whilst I was writing a book in the next room on the American war. I also saw the closing scenes in the war between Prussia and Austria in 1867, and on my way to Germany I stopped at Chalons, where there was a camp of one hundred thousand men, and studied their *morale,* believing that the next war would be between France and Prussia. At the close of the war I saw many of the beaten leaders of the Confederacy in Europe, such as Breckenridge and George Sanders."

"I suppose you never saw Clay, Calhoun, or Webster?"

"No; but when at school in Delaware I saw the funeral train of Webster go past, and I remember being rebuked the morning Henry Clay died for crying on the green, 'Hurrah for Henry Clay!' A good many of the curious characters of the past I have seen or conversed with, such as Mrs. Eaton and Amos Kendall. Many a man of former station I have seen hanging around the vestibule of a newspaper office, trying to sell his wares among us lads, who had seemed so lowly to him: the face of William B. Reed, of Philadelphia, arises to my mind. I remember going to see George M. Dallas when he had returned from London as minister and was in his house on Walnut Street; and I think the world would have been no worse if the interview system had then been current and I could have put down what he said."

"Are you the inventor of the interview?"

"By no means. The first interviews I saw with public men made me shudder at their audacity: they looked like breaches of confidence. But a curious incident lifted the fear from my mind. A newspaper publisher in Philadelphia bantered me to go and interview Alexander H. Stephens. I did not like that method of newspaper work, but my mettle was aroused, and I went to the house of his publisher, taking a witness along, and on the way it occurred to me to ask Mr. Stephens for some advance sheets of his book, upon the ground that the public were mightily curious. The strange little gentleman responded to that suggestion with much volubility. I wrote out what he said, and thought next morning I would go out of town, lest he might denounce me as a miscreant. On the contrary, he sent down to the newspaper office for several hundred copies of the paper; and I thought I saw that I would make enemies among the public men if I made no record of what they said. This did happen in the civil war. A prominent general, who afterwards ran for President of the United States, said to me when I went to his camp that he did not wish any personal laudation made of things there; and I strictly obeyed him, for I was but twenty years old. In the course of time I found I was not getting on well at that head-quarters, and after I had changed my residence one of his officers said to me, 'He was piqued because you left him out in your correspondence.'"

"Did you ever talk with Abraham Lincoln?"

"Alas! no; I had not the hardihood. When he died, however, I was in the East Room whilst they were preparing his body and funeral, and about that time I said to Colonel Hay, his secretary, that he ought to write the Life of Mr. Lincoln. He replied that he and Mr. Nicolay had already conferred on the subject; and as I went home I thought I would write a novel on the subject of Mr. Lincoln's taking off. I did not do it for nearly twenty years, but I never gave up the intention. Indeed, I find that whatever you heartily wish you can realize."

"Did you ever come in contact with any of the great editors?"

"Oh, yes. At Michie's farm-house, some seven miles from Richmond, just before the great battle there commenced, Henry J. Raymond, who had probably worn out his welcome at McClellan's headquarters by his newspaper letters, came to solicit a bed, and he slept in my bed. Night and morning I would sound him upon his contemporaries: he liked none of them; Greeley, Bennett, Webb, were all, he thought, men of mean, selfish motives. My feat at that time was to meet the Richmond newspapers at the picket-line and ride back with them to our base, so that they could be published in New York in advance of other papers. Mr. Raymond chafed under seeing these papers in my hands going to another concern, and he offered me a place on his paper, which I think I should have accepted if I had had a more worldly experience at that time, for he was never jealous of his contributors. It is rather strange that in the course of time I wrote for nearly every paper except Raymond's paper; but on one occasion a gentleman who was supposed to have a large foreign experience, and had been solicited to give it, came to me and paid me liberally to put his matter into shape, so that I was in fact a considerable contributor to that paper. I have been employed by almost every solvent newspaper in the United States."

"Did you see any of the great ladies of that period?"

"I have never been a society character; but I have seen a good many of the important women of our history. I once went to the Washington Navy-Yard, just after Ellsworth's body had been brought over from Alexandria, and it was embalmed in a little engine-house at the navy-yard; Mrs. Lincoln came down in her carriage with friends, and I stood by the carriage and heard her conversation. It is not always well to rush into the company of great personages and thus be misplaced socially. Only a year or two ago a friend of mine said to me, 'I am going to give you a place next to the Prince of Wales and his family at Buffalo Bill's show. I could sell that place for fifteen hundred francs to a big newspaper publisher, but I prefer that you shall have it for nothing.' So there I sat during the whole show, and heard the prince, his son, his wife, and three daughters, with two maids of honor, chatter very much like other people. Recently I took Lady Macdonald, of Canada, to see Edison at Menlo Park."

"You spoke of pieces of luck, but did not give me an instance."

"Well, I went alone of newspaper writers with Jefferson Davis and his wife from Fortress Monroe to Richmond when he was released after his captivity, and I saw his bail-bond signed by Horace Greeley. Up to that time I had never spoken to Mr. Greeley, though he had sent me appreciative messages, through General Halpine, for some little tales I had printed in the New York *Citizen*, which I edited with Halpine. Following Greeley out of the court as he was going down the street with John Minor Botts, I sat with those two gentlemen at their lunch at the hotel in the private room, and I exerted myself to set Greeley's act in its philanthropic relation to the public; but when I came to see the story in the newspaper, the publisher and his minions had reduced it to such a miserable piece of neutrality that for a long time I was afraid to speak to Greeley any more. I think he relied upon that account to break the shock of his partisan apostasy to the country. I recollect Jefferson Davis on his way up the river getting up upon the railing at the forward part of the boat and calling to a man ashore, 'Hey, Mr. King! howdy? howdy?' After Davis had been bailed out I went to his room, and saw two beautiful little girls climbing upon his knees, as he stood up, and he and they were weeping, in full Southern exuberance. The last time I saw Jefferson Davis was in the depot at Jersey City, upon his return from Europe, not long before he died. I went up and spoke to him. He looked dazed and old, as if he did not recollect much of anything."

"I suppose you have seen many of the Presidential candidates at effective times?"

"I was sent by Elihu Washburn to Covington, Kentucky, just after Grant had been nominated for President, to keep another correspondent from bearing rough partisan testimony against him. There I met the two old men Dent and Jesse Grant, and General Fred Dent assured me that General Grant could take care of himself, adding, 'He is going to run like wildfire.' Finding my errand superfluous, I wheeled about, and struck Horatio Seymour just as he returned from the nominating convention in New York; he made a speech at the doorsteps of Baggs's Hotel. He was an Indian-looking man, with something discomposed in his countenance; and it occurred to me then that a civilian of that infirmity of eye would not beat Grant. I went to Mentor before Garfield's house was finished, just after he was nominated, and talked with his old mother and with his wife, whom I had known well before. I took my daughter into Guiteau's cell, and talked with him about an hour in the presence of General Crocker, the warden of the prison. Guiteau said that he had been on the point of giving me his speech once in a New York hotel. I also saw Garfield just before he was shot, when he was at Long Branch and was about returning to bring his wife on in an invalid car. Garfield seemed to me to be about as unhappy as any man I had ever seen holding such a dignified place: having spent his life in purely legislative work, the Executive office, with its social oppressions, sat hard upon his boyish nature. I have always been of the opinion, since, that if he had continued President he would not have added to his fame. As for Arthur, his successor, I once stayed up with him until about two o'clock in the morning, and was surprised to see a comparatively great man drinking cocktails at that time of day. Of course his mixing with city politicians required him to be around at night, when those night-hawks are best consulted. When Mr. Tilden died, I went to Greystone the day after his friends had been allowed to see the body; but Mr. Smith, his executor, took me to the lonely room where the old man lay in the undertaker's frame, and as I was getting ready to say something serious, as might have been expected in the presence of death, I looked around, and found that Mr. Smith was gone, and there, left with that old bachelor who had so narrowly missed the Presidency, I recalled the two long conversations I had had with him at Saratoga, of two or three hours each, where he went over with me the comparative records and merits of Van Buren, Silas Wright, Marcy, and Seward. I took my son to see where Booth had hidden in the woods, and we were guided by the man who had fed him."

"Did you ever undertake anything adventurous in your newspaper career?"

"I went down among the Lowery band, in North Carolina, and wrote up their various assassinations and wrongs, and my letters had such an effect upon a young gentleman in a country town that he was tempted into the newspaper profession and made a second trip into that region and almost lost his life. A few years afterwards I found him editing a newspaper in San Francisco, and he told me that a man, subsequently assassinated, had loaded his gun to kill my successor, in revenge for my own sincerity, but that before he could execute his work the Lowerys intercepted the poor fool and shot him.

I afterwards went to a similar vendetta in Arkansas; and the London *Times* published an editorial upon these letters, stating that the American correspondents had great advantage over those in Europe in such a romantic variety of themes."

"How are you able to blend literature with so much newspaper writing?"

"By the effort of hard purpose and industry. I had designed to write a series of American historical novels, quite early in my life; I found my fortieth birthday approaching and nothing achieved; nearly in despair, I sat down and wrote 'The Entailed Hat,' which consumed a considerable part of two years: it had to be cut down by the publishers to get it within commercial paying space. I then wrote, in the next two years, 'Katy of Catoctin,' the novel I had designed twenty years before: this was published entire. I began to feel, when I concluded that book, the first symptoms of old age, for meantime I had carried on a correspondence of tremendous extent. The third novel I wrote, on Alexander Hamilton and Mrs. Reynolds, had to be cut down, and I went in the dead of winter to my country place at Gapland and cut one hundred and ten thousand words out of it, possibly to its improvement as a story, though the sacrifice of portions of the work affected me almost like the death of my children."

"Do you find that you can write when you are not in the mood for writing?"

"The newspaper man must learn, as his first task, to write against his moods. Not until the will and application defy your indisposition to write are you fully fit for your work. Still, the hardest work I ever did was to come back to newspaper offices, after large events, wearied with hearing and seeing and tramping, and there to produce three or four columns of matter, by hot gaslight, in contemptible newspaper rooms. When the assassins of President Lincoln had been killed or captured in Virginia, I went to Washington, by the slow trains of that day, sitting up all night, and the next day talked to Lafayette Baker and nearly all the personages present at the killing, and wrote four or five columns to be telegraphed that night, which Croly, the managing editor of my paper, once said, in a speech, was the most extraordinary instance of pure literary triumph over fatigue he had ever known. But no man should be a newspaper writer who cannot write finally with freedom: to follow this business, if you have to stimulate or fight *ennui* to achieve results, is suicide. I once buried from my house a superb newspaper writer who had worn himself out by straining his temperament in order to stand high in his profession. A great deal consists in natural fitness for whatever vocation you take up. One day an old fellow-reporter took to John W. Forney, one of my earliest employers, a whole page of newspaper matter that I had written under immediate spur. By this time Mr. Forney was discouraged and worn out, and he was publishing a little weekly paper. He looked over the matter, uttered a sigh, and said, 'Well, here is a man who manifestly loves his occupation.'"

"How have you been able to get leisure and keep in good health?"

"By system. When I want a week off, I do two weeks' work in advance. If I am to go anywhere, as to Europe, I lay out where I shall go, inform myself upon the subjects in hand, and sometimes prepare anecdotes, studies, etc., which may be interpolated. I have seen it somewhere stated that I keep copious scrap-books to inform me, and I wrote to the editor of a juvenile paper telling him that it was false, and he answered, making apology, and asked permission not to make the correction, lest it might disparage his publication: so I let it go, as of not much consequence. Indeed, the public is both magnanimous and forgetful: no man can ever write you out of the business, but you can trip yourself up by a single mistake. You have to go through years of disparagement with your compeers, if you are pushing them hard, and unless you realize that disparagement you may suspect that you are not succeeding well. The American people are wonderfully kind and charitable to newspaper writers. Many a time has some strong public man whom I had underrated and belittled taken the pains to treat me as a son and inform me fully; and, looking back from this stand-point, my heart is full of gratitude to these and to the public. Instead of the newspaper vocation having destroyed my faith in public men and public affairs, I believe that all men who are successful have both merit and justification. I won the confidence of John Morrissey, the prize-fighter, when I used to go to Saratoga. Upon one occasion he resolved to attack John Kelly, his former ally, and he sent for me; in a little room at his club-house he made his points, and made them well, but he drew out a piece of paper whereon he had put down elegant sentences, as he thought, which were nonsense. I was not on good terms with the paper that wanted this matter, and, finding that I was to get nothing for it, Morrissey sent me a hundred dollars to pay for my time.

A man who does his work according to the best light he has, without fear, but without insolence, can have a constituency before he gets to middle age that will be worth almost as much as a lawyer's of no more capacity than himself. I once had a book to publish which did not go down with the publishers; a friend of mine, who observed my interest in the subject, paid all the publishing bills, sending me his check for a thousand dollars. He never asked me to do anything, and has never since made the least suggestion of any kind to me. Again, I often find the best employers those who have no affectation for literary composition themselves; a genuine business-man, unless he be a mean man, is the best critic of the news which he buys, and such a man generally discovers that if he 'doctors' a writer's copy and keeps him under restraint he is merely taking the soul out of that man and employing his hand, whereas it is the *soul* that he wants."

"Do you recall any examples of your work which had a controlling political influence?"

"I gave the newspaper aid and comfort in 1868 which defeated the impeachment scheme at Washington; and when the Potter committee was created in 1877 to reopen the Presidential dispute, I interviewed President Hayes, against his will, and almost against his knowledge, and that interview caused the opposition Congress to pass a resolution that his title and term were not to be molested: so we went on to specie payments and fourteen years of prosperity."

Hearing My Requiem
[Journalist Series]

PUBLISHED IN

Lippincott's
Monthly Magazine.

OCTOBER, 1892.

"I never heard anything of the sort," said T. "Nevertheless, it was true. When I followed you into that country I went to a woman's cabin, was entertained by her, and after the usual fashion of those women, she told me this secret. Of course, all those people around there knew where I had gone.. He followed you to kill you before you could leave that region and publish the tale in which he supposed his private scandal would appear. When I came to that country he resolved to kill me, lest he might be published in the same role.. In either case he thought he would be burying an unpleasant secret. Fortunately, I did not go back to Shoe Heel, but took another course, and escaped, for I was warned that I was doomed to die that night. Concluded my friend, "Well, you know what happened. That white man made an appointment, of a treacherous sort, with the remaining Lowery brothers and their cousins, the Strongs. He meant to betray them. They understood it.. As he went to the rendezvous they waylaid him from behind one of the old "log blinds" they were so deadly at manufacturing, and they filled him full of buckshot, and he died with the unforgiven thirst for murder in his heart. Another train waited for by you would have altered your fates."

Hearing this, my mind went back to the night at Shoe Heel, when there seemed to be something ghostly and ghastly in the moan of the pines, and we could not sleep.

George Alfred Townsend

Corrections to final page of article *Hearing My Requiem* in Townsend's own handwriting. *Courtesy of University of Delaware Library, Newark, Delaware.*

HEARING MY REQUIEM.
[Journalist Series]

Twenty years ago, a rich newspaper, through the eruption of a new managing editor, heaped tasks upon me, paying me by the column, and though I was not a member of the staff, so called, under any obligation to be sent hither and thither at the editor's behest, an affectation of feudal authority in the paper caused its instructions to me to be couched in peremptory tones, such as, "Proceed immediately to Russell County, Virginia; go to Forsytheville and interview Judge Stam; find out all about the homicides!—SNORKEY."

Consulting my map, I found no such localities in the State; but I was so well aware of the hap-hazard way of sending forth commands from that place that I started for Virginia, and telegraphed for more instructions to meet me upon the train. The Richmond agent of the paper also missed me, but forwarded a letter which I received in North Carolina. Some private inquiries had rendered it probable that the scene of my investigations was to be the latter State, and the key to explore that region was the city of Wilmington. It was, I think, the year 1872.

An occasional correspondent of the newspaper at Wilmington set me in order. He took me to the president of the railroad which skirted the South Carolina boundary, proceeding westward toward Charlotte, but at that day this railroad, since completed, terminated in air, in the midst of the swamp and forest lands about the sources of the Pedee River. The president had been a Northern man, and had a cool head. He told me that a conflict between the authorities of one of the interior counties and certain free mulattoes had been going on since the middle of the civil war, and had become worse by bloodshed until within a recent period some twenty startling assassinations had taken place. The whites for the moment were cowed, and unable to capture the ringleaders of the mulattoes, who were known as the Lowery band or family. The president said, with the habitual caution of white men in the minority at that time, that he thought I would find wrong on both sides, and not all the wrong on the part of the mulattoes. "But," said he, "there can be no question that they will have to be exterminated. You can take sides or you can occupy middle ground, but you had better proceed cautiously, as much ignorance pervades that sequestered community, and I advise you not to publish your conclusions until you have left the region."

I spent a day in Wilmington, as only one train proceeded to the seat of disturbance every twenty-four hours, and visited the jail, where some of the mulattoes had been brought for safe-keeping until the court at Lumberton should begin its sessions, which would be the next day but one. Though I was very quiet and private in my researches, it was soon apparent, when I took the train the next day, that my business was understood, for the conductor, to assist my sketching the different localities, would hold the train up until I was finished. In the train was a sheriff, or deputy sheriff, taking cousins of the Lowerys, persons by the name of Oxendine, I think, to Lumberton: they were heavily ironed, but their appearance was generic; they were nearly white mulattoes, of a Highland Scotch admixture, relics, probably, of the Jacobite emigration to the province after the defeat of the Young Pretender, whose particular guide, Florence Macdonald, had married her cousin, a leading man of the clan Macdonald, and both had settled in North Carolina a little previous to the Revolutionary War, where, not intending to figure into two rebellions against the king, they organized his loyal subjects, and Macdonald was captured and taken to Pennsylvania, where he was kept a prisoner during much of the war. Upon the train was a strange, sporadic judge, a native of the State, I think, who had been reconstructed under what was called the Scallawag dominion and commissioned to try offenders. He seemed to know very little about these homicides in that extensive State, and somewhat muddled the thread of the sheriff's conversation with me by his asseverations that if he found thus and so when he got to the seat of justice he would in person go out among those outlaws and summon them in the name of the court to come in and be punished. "Yes, sah! I'll do that to-morry or nex' day, sah!"

We were a long time reaching Lumberton, and I marvelled at the primitive character of the country and its petty hamlets, as we steamed along at a little more than a trotting horse's pace. My head was bruised with reminiscences and my pocket-book full of notes when finally we arrived at Lumberton, some time in the afternoon, and found a scattered town of wooden houses, weather-blackened by time and want of paint, and at the principal hotel I had given me the bang-up room, next to the judge, which was a sort of attic, with low, flat windows. Nearly everybody in that place had a Sottish name, blacks as well as whites. The court-house was a large building, like a two-storied church, as I now remember it, with an open area or field before it, in which I think was an old pole well. The town seemed to be crowded with persons who had come to attend the court, and among them were a good many exceedingly handsome mulatto girls. It seemed to me that if I had been in some distant province of Asiatic Turkey I could have hardly found a general society so unaware of any greater world and so disconnected from its methods and understandings. Little booths of groceries were the centres of public concentration, and the trade seemed to be of that character which one might encounter in the oases of the sandy Sahara Desert at the times of caravans and fairs.

As I must either take a buggy and drive out to the locality of the outlaws, twelve miles or more distant, which bore the name of Scuffletown, or await the next day's train, which would carry me to a station called Shoe Heel, somewhat nearer the trail of blood, I took advice from the better townsmen, and particularly from the merchants and those politicians who were in sympathy with the political *status quo*. All told me not to venture into Scuffletown with a horse or buggy, or if I went there in such fashion to be sure to go alone or take no one with me who could be identified as of the white majority. In any event it seemed to be the notion that I would have trouble, or, if not trouble, at least privations, as Scuffletown was not a place, in the usual conception of an instituted hamlet. Neither hotel nor stores would I find, they said, but merely little cabins in the woods along sandy streams and swamps, and if benighted out there I might never again be heard of. In short, the population was a good deal scared, for as they described it, several of their "best people" had been put to death, and the temper and hardihood of the mulattoes were increasingly wicked.

A weekly newspaper was published in Lumberton, of which I procured a file from the editor, running back several years, and sitting in my twilighted room I annotated all the paragraphs I could find there about the crimes, threatenings, and escapes of these mysterious people. These paragraphs were seldom more than a few hundred words in length, but after working several hours I came to some intelligent comprehension of the task before me.

The next morning the court opened, with more *éclat* than we ever see in the populated North. A crier would come either to a door or an upper window in the gable of the court-house, and cry aloud, "Neil McNeil! Donald Macdonald! Angus Macpherson! Come into court, as you are this day ordered, to render testimony as to the things on which you will be questioned." At these Scotchy summonses I would frequently see, not white men walk forward, but mulattoes, of the type I have described, and in some cases I noticed that these had bushy red hair, showing that the Highland progenitors of these partial Africans had been able to dye their posterity's wool down to the third and fourth generations.

I was about thirty years old, and had been a correspondent in the civil war, and had generally managed to cut out some plan of campaign, but this particular job was something of a foretaste of what my old contemporary warcorrespondent Stanley was about that time doing in the wilds of Africa. He had something of an expedition, and could command an audience of the wild tribes among whom he went. Nor was there any war to impede Mr. Stanley's advice toward the hidden camp of Dr. Livingstone. Here in North Carolina was a race of Africans as old as the oldest whites by descent, and for a long period of time, how long nobody seemed to know, they had been free, possibly manumitted in the early portion of our century, when, through the influence of Benjamin Lundy, "Emancipation Societies" had been formed in many of the Southern States, and these had been nowhere more numerous and effective than in North Carolina, where Quakers and other peaceable sects listened with docility to the mild teachings of liberty which preceded Garrison's rougher hectorings and more uncompromising propositions. Probably the white owners of such slaves had moved westward beyond the Blue Ridge or into Tennessee and even Indiana and Illinois. Thus made free, a light mulatto generation had arisen, at the brink of the civil war, which had the audacity of free people, the revengefulness of their Highland antetypes, and the looseness of the Africans.

Nothing had happened in the Old North State after the Revolutionary War to excite or ferment its population until the great Rebellion or Confederacy came to be organized, after the election of Mr. Lincoln. Then, as State after State met in convention and seceded from the Federal Union, North Carolina also took the stand that the Union without slavery must be resisted. From the bottom up came the spirit of war, the poor men having it perhaps even more resolvedly than the planters and politicians.

Among these volunteers were the young free mulattoes of the Scuffletown district.

It was not thought meet, however, that these should stand in the ranks of race slavery. They were not considered to have military rights, but only laborers' duties, and they were conscripted to go down below Wilmington and throw sand out of the ditches upon the fortifications. At this they rebelled, and some were ill used and others ran away, and in their absence from their native districts the whites, it was said, had outraged their households.

In course of time graver subjects of quarrel arose. There was a prison-pen at Florence, in South Carolina, nearly south of the Scuffletown district, at a considerable distance, from which at times Northern soldiers escaped, and, working their way up through the swamps and untrackable parts, came to a settlement almost exclusively of negroes, in the Scuffletown region. The fugitives were gladly entertained by the mulattoes, and to provide enough food for these numerous and unexpected guests some raids were made upon the hogs of the nearest whites, and these hogs, being all marked for identification, were traced to the house of an old man named Lowery, who had sons and daughters. The story was told to me, but whether true or not I refrain from passing judgement, that old Lowery in punishment of his hog-stealing and disloyalty was made to dig his grave and stand beside it to be shot dead.

He had a young son, who had passed into local history as Henry Berry Lowery, who made the further complaint that some of his young companions were killed because they had threatened white men of the conscription corps who had made nameless trespasses upon their households.

Whatever the circumstances, the younger mulattoes who grew to manhood after the war found deadly arms, and proceeded to kill such whites as they disliked or feared, and after every white man's assassination a raid was made upon the outlaws of their kin, who continued to be treacherously peaceable, and thus by the unreasonableness of a vendetta the strife had gone on, until it now attracted the attention of the external world, and a managing editor desirous to serve up something red and spicy for his columns had taken the initial step of sending me in to make the ragged narrative tangible.

I took the train the next day for Shoe Heel, still making sketches, as I went along, of the different stations, at each of which some murder had been done. These were published in *Harper's Weekly*. At one place the chief outlaw had waylaid constables as they were carrying off his wife and family for hostages, and had shot the former to death and delivered the latter. As near a race insurrection as has taken place in the South at any time was probably there, and there seemed to be an idea that the United States would come to the deliverance of the State authorities, after I should have developed the facts.

Shoe Heel was a good, large country store and a few sheds, and in a grove of pines near by was a frame house, newly constructed, which, for a consideration, entertained passengers. Here I conducted my investigations as people came in from the Scuffletown district.

I found the whites there suspicious of every new-comer, and several scamps in the guise of detectives had come among them who were suspected of having sold arms and ammunition to the Lowerys. I did not know until afterward that my own errand was regarded askance. The idea of a newspaper in New York sending all that distance to describe a quarrel with negroes seemed absurd.

A poor old colored woman at one end of the store served my dinner, and, being alone with her, who was possibly a connection of the Lowerys, I questioned her closely, and found that she was the best witness in all that country. She alone seemed to grasp the idea that a newspaper had some connection with public opinion and might prevent crime or justify the resentments of an inferior race. I fear that the old woman suffered for some of her disclosures afterwards. My purpose, however, was to disclose a disconnected series of murders, lasting from 1863 down to the time of my visit, and numbering twenty-two.

As long as daylight lasted I kept cramming and analyzing upon this topic. Finally the shades of night descended, and I went over to the house in the pine grove to sleep.

It was the house of a Major — , who appeared to be looked up to in that district as the type of public spirit who would finally bring the Lowerys to bay.

He was not at home, but his wife was there, with a very young baby upon her knee, sitting before a pine-wood fire, and having nothing to say.

A mysterious gloom, almost like foreboding, came upon me, in this residence so far from any town, and so near Scuffletown, with its ever-lurking and now incarnadined fiends.

There was a drummer from Charleston, selling phosphates, in the house, and he had learned but a part of the story, and after we went to bed together we talked a long time about the Lowery episode.

It was nearly midnight when I attempted to go to sleep, and then the pine-trees moaned deep and sad, and now and then we could hear the baby crying down-stairs. I found it impossible to sleep, and at last I spoke to my companion, and said he, "This bloody story has made me feel so queer that, though I was in the war, in many a battle, I feel afraid in this house, as if something was going to happen to us!"

We did sleep, however, at last, and next morning I took the train for the all-day journey back to Wilmington. I did not commence to write anything on the subject of the Lowery band and its mysterious "queen" and "king," as they were called, until I was on the waters of the Chesapeake.

The accounts, being published in a series of four or five long letters, were widely read, and a young man living in Pennsylvania, among others, was so affected by them that he offered to keep up the sensation by going into Scuffletown, and interviewing the bandit "queen," who was the wife of Lowery.

He confirmed what I had intimated, that the principal outlaw was already dead, having shot himself accidentally. Neither element upon the spot was particularly pleased with my descriptions: the whites thought all the blame ought to have been thrown on the negroes, and the negroes considered that every victim on the other side had been a persecutor. A play was presented at one of the Bowery theatres, called "The Swamp Angels," which was the colored head-line put over my letters in the newspaper by the intellectual or office department, and the hero of the play was made to be a reporter.

In the course of some seventeen years I was taken, in San Francisco, to the office of a daily newspaper, and introduced to its managing editor, whose name I at once identified as that of the young man who had embarked in our profession by the opportunity my Lowery disclosures had opened for him. In the mean time, after the usual mutations of an out-of-door writer, and figuring the Cuban insurrection, he had arisen to be a managing editor.

Said he to me, "Do you know how close both you and I were to meeting our death at Shoe Heel?"

"No."

"Well, after you wrote your descriptions, the man who lived in that house where you slept read them, and he suspected that you had some knowledge of a criminal intimacy of his."

"I never heard anything of a sort."

"Nevertheless, it was true. When I followed you into that country I went to a woman's cabin, was entertained by her, and, after the usual fashion of those women, she told me this secret. Of course, all those people around there knew where I had gone. The instinctive wrong-doer followed you to kill you before you could leave that region and publish the tale in which he supposed his private scandal would appear. When I came to that country he resolved to kill me, lest he might be published in the same *role*. In either case he thought he would be burying an unpleasant secret. Fortunately, I did not go back to Shoe Heel, but took another course, and escaped, for I was warned that I was doomed to die that night.

"Well," concluded my friend, "you know what happened? That white man made an appointment, of a treacherous sort, with the remaining Lowery brothers and their cousins the Strongs. He meant to betray them, and they understood it. As he went to the rendezvous they waylaid him from behind one of the old log 'blinds' they were so deadly at manufacturing, and they filled him full of buckshot, and he died with the unforgiven thirst for murder in his heart. Another train waited for by you would have altered both your fates."

Hearing this, my mind went back to the night at Shoe Heel, when there seemed to be something ghostly and ghastly in the moan of the pines, and we could not sleep.

George Alfred Townsend

MONTICELLO:—THE WESTERN FRONT.

Monticello

and

Its Preservation,

Since Jefferson's Death, 1826-1902.

CORRESPONDENCE OF
GEORGE ALFRED TOWNSEND,
"Gath."

Thomas Jefferson.

PREFACE

The letters which follow were written by the veteran special correspondent, "Gath," for the *Boston Globe, Kansas City Star,* etc., at the time of the Good Roads Convention at Charlottesville, in April, 1902. Mr. Townsend, their author, had been twice at Monticello when it was empty and unowned, following the civil war, and was now surprised to see how furniture, ornaments and modernization, brought out the old mansion's sociality.

His inquiries were, like a newsman, close to the subject of Monticello's *preservation,* which had not been treated by any other writer with carefulness.

In the almost three-quarters of a century since Commodore Levy and his heirs have possessed Monticello, they have made no publication of their almonry, desiring to have Mr. Jefferson's great benignity ever at the front. His toleration and humanity were, and are, the inspiration of their long connection with his shrine.

Late frivolous biographies, however, treat Monticello as if it were but incidentally or recently held; not in the possession of an uncle and his nephew longer than of the original proprietors.

Almost a generation before Mt. Vernon was bought for preservation by a society, Monticello was quietly bought by a commissioned officer of the United States Navy at a time when race and religious prejudices were making their last sullen resistance to Jefferson's justice.

The need of some short account of the preservation of Monticello, to answer the inquiries of its numerous visitors, is at last enforced by the swift railroads which put Monticello in the suburbs of Washington. "Gath's letters come near enough to the events to supply a *souvenir* and relieve the owner of Monticello from daily interrogations.

GATH'S MONTICELLO LETTERS.

I.
SLEEPING IN MONTICELLO.

MONTICELLO, VA., *April* 12, 1902.

After passing the night at Monticello I was escorted by a pair of greyhounds to a red granite cenotaph on the lawn, before breakfast, and read the very recent inscription:

> Thomas Jefferson
> Citizen, Statesman, Patriot.
> The greatest
> Advocate of Human Liberty.
> Opposing Special Privileges
> He lived and trusted
> The People.
>
> To Commemorate his
> Purchase of Louisiana.
> Erected by the Jefferson Club
> Of St. Louis, MO.
> On their Pilgrimage Oct. 12, 1901.
> To Express their
> Devotion to his principles.

I stopped at the word "Pilgrimage," and reflected that perhaps Jefferson came the nearest to founding a national religion or dispensation, of any American, from his projection of modern popular institutions and confidence in the multitude.

The most inconsonant races, such as the Irish, French and Italians, revere the lawgiver who broke up the support of the parish churches, and put on his tomb for his three beatitudes, Independence, Toleration and University.

If liberty is the shibboleth of modern times, stimulated from American example, Jefferson is the author of the sect.

He seized the occasion of being first alternate upon the Congressional Committee, to incorporate in the Declaration of Independence a philosophical idea—"Men are endowed with inherent and inalienable rights. * * * All men are created equal." He also denounced slavery.

This much pruned document, therefore, made of a colonial revolt, a universal pronunciamento, and probably no other man in that Congress would have wandered so wide to argue Democracy at large in a paper of Occidental independence.

He was then thirty-three years old, one generation old; had never been but once, before the Continental Congress, out of his native State, and was nine years at the bar. He must have been, by nature and the times, the most advanced radical in the world. Robespierre, who was of Irish blood, as Jefferson of Welsh—both, therefore, of Celtic base—was then only eighteen years old, and it was to be thirteen years before Robespierre incurred Mirabean's prediction, "That young man believes what he says; he will go far."

Jefferson, therefore, was an inspiration *to* and not *from* the French Revolution. He was eleven years younger than Washington, whom he resembled in most circumstances, both surveyors and topographers, wedded to wealthy widows, fellows in the legislature. The old are generally the doctrinal and the young the military men. In this case the rustic David promulgated before Saul.

His very next effort was to abolish family and clerical influence in Virginia, the same things as the French nobility and clergy, which dissolved themselves later.

At that time Jefferson was in one of the newest and most western towns in America—Charlottesville is almost on the longitude of Altoona, Pa., and Niagara Falls.

The first of his name to be educated, it fell upon Monticello's red clay strength of soil.

An electrical receiver, a Leyden jar, he stored up sparks and shocks. He was red haired, of a freckling skin and hazel spotted eyes. The wonder is that he held out so unchangeably to the age of 83. His ideas had drawn the son of Adams to Jefferson's party and succession, Adams and he dying the same day, the Fourth of July, but Adams was 91, his son, the President, only 24 years Jefferson's junior.

Upon that Fourth of July when both of the old men died, President John Quincy Adams attended services in the Capitol to raise money for Jefferson. Only four or five persons subscribed.

The next day, but one, news was received of Jefferson's death.

Henry Lee, half-brother of Robert E. Lee, had been waiting around Monticello to get some papers till convinced that Jefferson was dying.

It was not till the ninth of July that J.Q. Adams heard of his father's decease at Quincy. While the President-son was breakfasting at a roadside tavern he was informed by the tavern-keeper, near Baltimore, that his father had been five days dead and he recorded: "The time, the manner, the coincidence with the decease of Jefferson, are visible and palpable marks of divine favor."

The influence of Jefferson upon mankind appeared in large relief sums voted to his daughter by legislatures and in other donations, which kept his family in means. Louisiana and South Carolina each voted her ten thousand dollars and she lived to 1836.

Jefferson endorsing for Governor Nicholas, a family connection, is said to have precipitated his own ruin.

The estate divided up, that portion of it containing Monticello went into the hands of a person who was hostile to Jefferson's liberality of belief, and this person's despoiling of the park, etc., led to the publication that he did not wish to leave one brick of the house upon another.

This statement met the attention of Lieutenant Uriah Phillips Levy, of the United States Navy, a bachelor of means, who had been fifteen years in the Navy and at sea nearly all his life. He said to President Jackson: "I have been thinking about buying Monticello in honor of Mr. Jefferson, whom I love." General Jackson replied with vigor: "I order you, sir, to buy it."

"I always obey the orders, Mr. President, of my superior," said Lieutenant Levy, who was thirty-eight years old.

He did buy the place, and Martin's Gazetteer, of Virginia, published at Charlottesville in 1835, said:

"The late proprietor (Barkley) injured the appearance of Monticello very much by cutting down the beautiful shade and ornamental trees for the purpose of cultivation; but it is believed that the deep veneration entertained by the present owner, Lieutenant Levy, for the character of Mr. Jefferson, and the respect he entertains even for the inanimate objects associated with his memory, will lead him to restore it, as far as possible, to the condition in which he left it, and attend carefully to the preservation of every object which could be supposed to have occupied his attention or added beauty to the residence."

For over two generations the Levys, uncle and nephew, have worked at this property, to regain its land and restore its Jeffersonian reality.

Jefferson's 30,000 acres had dwindled to 640 when Commodore Levy bought 223 acres; his nephew has extended it to 900 acres, keeps a herd of wool sheep, has milch cows, and took the prize in Albermarle for the best pair of carriage horses in the Union.

At this time, seventy-six years after Jefferson's death, the Library is being restored. Jefferson began it about 1764, before his mother's home, at Shadwell, in plain sight of Monticello, was burned. Here, just after New Year's, 1772, he brought his bride, Mrs. Skelton, in a gale of snow. The house was then half of that one wing of the present house, which was afterwards Jefferson's study, bedroom and living room, and could be fairly warmed by the local fire-places.

This year (1902) a steam apparatus was put in which sometimes consumes four tons of coal a week.

The character of Washington conveys awe and form; that of Jefferson intimacy and fraternity. So Mount Vernon was rigidly held by Washington's nephew and great-great-nephew, till they could support it no longer, and with pains and labor a few acres around the mansion were bought by a formal body of female "regents." No one can sleep there and it is not deemed healthy to spend a night there. You must enter there between close hours and keep out on Sunday.

But Jefferson's mould in the grave was still perfect when a lover of his public work and thoughts took his home into his pious care, and its healthy elevation and majestic scenery have kept it habitable for 138 years. Never probably as comfortable and adorned as now, Monticello is occupied every summer to October, by the relatives of the owner, Mr. Jefferson Monroe Levy, late member of Congress of New York city, where he was born, although his mother, wife of Captain James P. Levy, of the United States ship *America* in the Mexican war, lived previously at Monticello.

Each of the Virginia Presidents' homes is now in opulent stranger ownership. The new proprietor of Montpelier is said to be spending $100,000 upon it, and Oak Hill, Monroe's porticoed mansion, is in the hands of Henry Fairfax, a rich ex-contractor, who breeds city hackneys and British ponies.

Commodore Levy, however, was 60 years ahead of all others in that respect for a personal shrine which has now become so general a trait. Each of the Virginia Presidents had become land-poor. But Monticello has had a reinforced succession until the Levys have had it many years longer than the Jefferson-Randolphs. The burial enclosure of the Levys is below the lawn.

When the bachelor proprietor is at home the American flag flies over Monticello. Then the college students, young ladies, and strangers come up the almost 500 feet from Charlottesville, three miles below, and walk freely over the grounds, and with informal precautions enter the house and find almost the cordiality of Jefferson from the young public man who comes so far to maintain his patron uncle's wish.

Mr. Levy is a lawyer of New York City, where there is a record of his family since 1665. Part of them removed to Philadelphia, where Benjamin Levy was one of the five signers of our Revolutionary currency, and prominent as a signer of the Non-Importation agreement before that war. Michael Levy, father of the Commodore, married a beautiful Miss Phillips, and had a dozen sons. Perhaps from the Holland descent of the Levys a passion for the sea has often marked them.

Uriah Phillips Levy was on the brig *Argus* which took W. H. Crawford, in 1813, as Minister to France, landed him at L'Orient, and then returned up the British channel to repeat Paul Jones' feats and burn two and a half millions dollars' worth of British shipping. She was finally taken after a terrific battle, by the *Pelican*, to whose crew medals were given. The memory of the *Argus* and of the insurance rates she caused British vessel owners, operated down to the Alabama Claims treaty. Young Uriah P. Levy was put part of two years in Dartmoor prison pen.

Although he became an officer of exacting discipline, the humane or Jeffersonian side of his character made him initiate the movement to abolish flogging in the Navy. This was not abolished in the British navy till 1881, and had been immemorial in both navies; as many as one thousand lashes had been administered to one sailor.

Commodore Levy bought cats-o'-nine-tails in quantity and supplied them to members of Congress, to illustrate upon the stamp the heartless punishment, till the issue passed over the heads of the naval board to the people and the law-making power, just as slavery afterward was beaten by novels and biographies. Over thirty years before the British abolition of flogging, the American Navy threw out the barbarity.

The portrait of Commodore Levy in the hall at Monticello represents above his shoulder the combat between the *Argus* and *Pelican*; in his hand is a scroll saying: "Author of the Abolition of Flogging in the Navy of the United States." A proud motto for the landlord succeeding Jefferson.

In the balcony semi-circling this hall, is the *Macedonian* full-rigged, with all her guns out, in the sailor's model work of ninety years ago. He also left Monticello pictures of sea-fights, shipwrecks, etc. The Navy vindicated the declaration of war in 1812.

Both Uriah and Jonas Levy, in the sailor spirit of that time, ran away from home to go to sea, and thus felt sailors' wrongs when they became sailors' masters.

Jefferson disputed the constitutionality of the Navy, but Monticello illustrates it in paintings of naval actions, the full uniformed Commodore Levy, and the large model of the *Macedonian* over Jefferson's head.

The satisfaction of sleeping at Monticello, free to wander at will by night or before breakfast, alone, through the idiosyncratic and artistic villa, till its variety becomes an entity on the mind, was complete. I went there Sunday, had nobody but Mr. Levy and one of his neighbors to talk with, and at ten o'clock at night took two hours and a half to discuss the dwelling.

I took the whole of the next forenoon alone, or till two o'clock dinner, and then was driven till six P.M. around the mountain and Charlottesville.

I had previously visited Monticello in 1869, and in 1872 when it was stripped, desolate and apparently doomed to ruin.

This interval of and after the civil war had a strange romance.

In his old age, Commodore Levy married, and then left Monticello by will to the United States, or to the State of Virginia, for a naval orphan asylum. As he had derived his money from never needy ancestors, the will was disputed by his kin, and Clarkson N. Potter, the law preceptor of Commodore Levy's nephew, broke the will.

The Commodore had previously offered Mr. Lincoln his *fortune* with his sword.

He died March 22, 1862, at his house in St. Mark's Place, New York. The Confederacy was not able to confiscate Monticello till 1864, through the resistance of the Albermarle people, who liked the Levys. But finally the Commodore's slaves were sold, and the dismantling of the furniture began, the losses amounting to several hundred thousand dollars. Soldiery broke off the carved sculpture of the many mantels. Other people peddled the bust of Voltaire by Houdon and similar treasures to rich men in New York. Captain Jonas P. Levy, when he visited the place to save it from confiscation, was held as a hostage, but he told the people that the revolt would end and that they would have to restore the property. Virginia courts declared the bequest of Monticello void. Therefore it was returned to the Levy heirs, and to straighten up the title they had a suit among themselves, and Jefferson M. Levy, who previously inherited five-sixths of the place, bought the remaining sixth from his relatives.

In this partition suit was the one and only competition for Monticello, said to have been the thought of Mr. Thomas Jefferson Coolidge, of Boston, whose father, Joseph Coolidge, had married one of Jefferson's granddaughters.

A late book on Jefferson says that T. J. Coolidge spoke of buying Monticello to Commodore Levy, who forthwith took a train to the spot and bid it in.

At that time T. J. Coolidge was an infant, and his father had not the fortune to shoulder such an expensive luxury, and there were no railroads whatever "to take" in 1829. Such is the new history.

Equally baseless is the statement that Commodore Levy tried to present Monticello to societies and institutions. He willed it with an endowment to his Government, or to Virginia only, and his own family recovered it at law and resumed their residence in it.

It has been said in Charlottesville that the cost of Monticello to keep it up is as much as $40,000 a year. It stands nearly half-way between Washington and Richmond, about three hours from each, on two excellent railroads, the Southern and the Chesapeake and Ohio.

Hardly any view in the United States equals that from Monticello, of river, plain, sea-horizon, city, University, and different and enormous mountains overhanging Charlottesville. A second chain, the Ragged Mountain is to the south; a third twin mountain is a distant apparition, and the Blue Ridge stalks through the sky like a broken blue world collided with ours or stranded on our rim.

The only suggestion of scenery like this is at Reading, Pa., or at Mt. McGregor, where General Grant died, or the Catskills and Hudson, as seen from Livingston's manor. Jefferson said of it, "How sublime to look down into the workhouse of nature, to see her clouds, hail, snow, rain, thunder, all fabricated at our feet."

I was reminded of my visit to Newstead Abbey as nobly maintained by another, unrelated to Lord Byron, since 1818, at a cost of $500,000 in repairs, when I looked over the works of art at Monticello.

Here are Sichel's lovely portrait of Queen Louise, of Prussia, a gold-brown Vandyke of Miosa, the Spanish Minister to the Court of Charles I, formerly in King Joseph Bonaparte's collection; a portrait of a fine lady (Lady Noel), by Sir Joshua Reynolds, a gorgeous portrait of Marshal McDonald, the well-known portrait of Jefferson, in a fur collar, by Dick, Power's bust of Franklin, Cerrachi's busts of Washington, Hamilton and Jefferson, and a large bronze statuette of Henry Clay.

Alexander Hamilton's pure marble bust, with head upright, is hospitably housed on a bracket opposite Washington's; Jefferson's stands upon a capital of one of the corn and tobacco columns he devised.

The furniture of Monticello was scattered before the purchase of the residence by Commodore Levy, and the house abandoned at Jefferson's death, and in the civil war, Commodore Levy's providence ceased. Yet many things were recovered and some were found in secret ceiling closets, which Jefferson, with his memory of Tarleton's visit, built in the partitions. Tarleton's horse's hoofs are said to be some impressions within the hall.

Other furniture was traced to houses under Monticello in the landscape, and replevined after the war.

Now, the contents of Monticello are rather of Jefferson's preferential love of the French, than heirlooms. The drawing-room is furnished with sofas and chairs of the style of the last three Louis of France, whose conclusion Jefferson witnessed—gilt and white with upholstery of white and rose. The twenty pieces in this room are two hundred years old, bought out of the royal furniture of Paris. One firm hand, like Commodore Levy's, held upon the contents of Monticello, is worth a hundred assumptions. His nephew is mild, constant, patient, but of discrimination. It is difficult to see how a property like this could have been conserved in one family seventy years, under only two possessors, with no mistakes.

Monticello is still progressive, still conservative. It is deliberated to refurnish it, like Mount Vernon, in the verisimilitude of Jefferson's day, and restore the Library.

An idea has been spread abroad by some sectarians that Commodore Levy was persecuted on old ismatic scores. This is repudiated by his posterity. He was antagonized somewhat because he was a naval martinet—one of the old Decatur school who kept his ship in order, that small, floating republic which required a Jefferson in command, stiff amidst his liberality.

Commodore Levy killed a man in a duel after standing up for six shots and firing into the air. His first shot, the seventh, brought the bloodthirsty man to the dust. In Brazil he interposed his hand in a cutlass fight against his officers and sailors and suffered a gash in the fingers; the Emperor offered him a ship to command. The New York *Herald*, at Commodore Levy's death, published two columns of strong incidents like the above, saying:

"To-day we have to record the demise of Commodore Uriah P. Levy, whose long service in the Navy, and devotion to the Union in the hour of trial, have given him an enviable prominence in the annals of the United States Navy. Deceased was a native of Pennsylvania, and first entered the Navy on the 29th of March, 1812, in which he remained up to the hour of his death, being a period of forty-eight years and two months, of which he spent fourteen years and eight months in active sea duty, one year and six months doing shore service, and the remainder waiting orders. In his last active sea-service he was in command of the Mediterranean squadron, his flagship being the sloop of war *Macedonian*. Deceased was a man of good personal appearance, refined education, and was distinguished for many acts of personal bravery. In both public and private life he was highly esteemed for his gentlemanly deportment and strict discipline.

"A large full-length portrait of the Commodore was seen above his corpse upon the walls. None could help feeling, as they gazed upon that splendid portrait of the dead, what a brilliant ornament to society and sterling American patriot had been swept away. The high forehead, open countenance and flashing eye bespoke unmistakably the heroic man and noble officer."

It is not uncommon for the tourist to be told that Monticello passed into the Levy family within a late period, so wanting in precision are hearsay and instinct. An educated Northerner observed to me that, probably, as little was known and said about Jefferson in Charlottesville as anywhere. If Monticello had been inhabited as early as 1764, it would be 65 years in the Jefferson family and 73 years in the Levy family. But it was not lived in till 1770, and therefore the Jeffersons possessed it only 59 years.

Notwithstanding Jefferson's original and popular traits, he was thought by the Randolphs to be of minor family importance to them. Grigston says the ancestor of the Randolphs was a prosperous barn-builder.

Peter Jefferson was a pioneer surveyor from south of Richmond, and his wife, a native of Shadwell parish, London, gave name to their new house under Monticello in 1738.

In the map of Virginia by Jefferson's father, printed in 1775, which I now possess, Shadwell and Edge Hill are marked, while Monticello is only named "The Green Mountains."

Having more inclination for the fertile plains than the "Little Mountain," the Randolphs removed to Edge Hill right after Jefferson's decease in 1826.

The majestic panorama from Monticello is due to its height, apparently raising up the opposite mountains and extending the horizons. The Randolphs never wished to return to the summit, farming their lands below. As there were many of them, the souvenirs they removed left the mansion bare.

Jefferson was not a financial failure. Poplar forest, three counties beyond, was sold for a large sum, which supported the Eppes family.

Maria Jefferson, Mrs. Eppes, died in 1804, while her husband was in Congress.

Thomas Jefferson Randolph lived to 1875, and married in 1824 the daughter of Governor Nicholas, for whom Jefferson, unfortunately, indorsed.

President Jefferson made of himself and for himself, few mistakes. The so-called lottery, much made of, was a proposition rather than a fact.

Mr. J. M. Levy said to me with considerate feeling: "I hope you will not dwell on Mr. Jefferson's lottery or poverty, for he was a great man and ought to be treated from the large and not the little points of view. He was the providence of his household, and his estate almost came out right; after he went his loss was manifest. Monticello was the seat of political power more than fifty years. In retirement he was less disputed than in office. He combined the natures of Franklin, the philosopher, with Washington, the explorer and executive.

General Miles, Senator Hanna, many public men, and all the fine girls of Charlottesville were at Monticello as Mr. Levy's guests this week.
The place might be a care but for the proprietor's interest in it and his bachelor freedom.

II.
THE SHADES OF JEFFERSON.

MONTICELLO, VA., *April* 13, 1902.

The beautiful houses our time throws up with a wealth of machinery and materials, still draw their components from models like Thomas Jefferson's Monticello. Its models were the Greek and Roman houses in France with their English appendages, preceding the Revolution.

The tastes of Louis XV, subdued by Louis XVI, Italianized by the Directory, classicized by the Consulate, may all be traced in the early American mansions, of which there were almost none before our independence.

William Bingham built one of the first in Philadelphia, after he and his fine wife had explored France. The porticoes followed our Revolution. Jefferson sent from Roman Nismes, in France, the columned Augustinian model for the State Capitol of Virginia in 1786. That was the popularizing of porticoes.

It is difficult to reconcile at Monticello the recorded progression of the house, over a period of thirty or more years, with its unity as it now stands.

It appears to have advanced northward from the original plantation wing, in which is the least perspicuity.

That south end was Jefferson's study, library, bed, domesticity and seclusion, some four rooms in a *suite,* with a private hall.

The opposite wing somewhat resembles the first, as if built to be its complement.

But the center of the house appears to have been built last, perhaps rebuilt, and consists of three lofty rooms, the hall, the drawing-room and the dining-room. These break through the attic floor which everywhere else makes a subdivision.

The great hall has a wide entrance into the drawing-room and each is faced outside by a portico, the width between their outer steps near 110 feet. As Monticello is 115 feet long I supposed its habitable width to be some 70 feet.

An architect would find a bright induction here, to trace the life of the building from the dissimilarities, and tell its development in dates. Traditional statements are next to worthless. Family Bibles are not reliable on births, marriages and deaths. Spacious intelligence is the only measure of evolutionary architecture.

The central parts of Monticello show the European traveller, who returned to his Virginia lodge and grew a calyx into it, a noble and lofty centre, cool and inspiring. At each step of the house's career you can see the mind of the man unfolding from little to large. All the men can live in the Hall; all the women and their pursuers in the Drawing-room; the Dining-room is the alternative from both, not as expansive as either, but high, tasteful, refined. Here is where John Trumbull, the artist, flinched at Jefferson's modern theology.

At Mt. Vernon Washington built *ends* to his old square house, for banquet hall and library.

Jefferson had to put his state rooms in the middle of a house already built.

There seemed to be a reason for every feature, nevertheless.

He had Italian artificers with whom, like Louis XIV, he conjectured and drafted.

But only now, when the decoration is up to the design, do we feel a happiness in Monticello. We can sit in the hall of thirty feet square with the pretty winding landing above, and be in the "living room."

He took the stairway out, as the camel's nose, which would soon want all the space. You can see such an ugly stairway coming down like a geological snake in Carroll of Carrollton's house in Baltimore.

Jefferson also wanted to closet the bedsteads; those sprawling furniture things we still are seeking to make modest by folding beds and lounges. He only effectuated wardrobes instead of bed alcoves, but the bed problem is still active in sleeping cars and hospitals.

The real front of Monticello is not that which you see rounding the knob, because you wind under its top-shaped lawn and enter in the rear. This lawn is now in fine grass sown with daisies, and through the woods below is the real Scotch broom, delight of Mr. Smith, the Scotch gardener of Congress.

The lawn is some six hundred feet square, and has few trees but some cedars, till near the house. It is there flanked by two small brick offices with porches. The house between hardly seems a mansion, rather a Trianon or villa, so low is it; one visible story with a white dome above it upon an attic octagon.

The red brick story with its central portico of white columns and pediment shows above it only the red-cone roof. A white baluster runs along the eaves; a white railing is on the roof ridge. From the ends of this tasteful garden temple, a low stone wall extends across the lawn, with square return wings along the ramparts of the plateau to the two offices.

Monticello is a neat, classical villa, bevelled off at the ends into bays. The chief feature under the West portico is the tall pedimented middle door. On this side the steps are overgrown with grass like an inclined plane.

At the ends of the house are low flights of steps which enter covered and closed verandahs with tall arched windows. One of these was just outside Jefferson's study; another adjoined the tea room.

The villa recedes from the portico by four off-sets, and the cornice and baluster of white go clear around, making a beautiful flowing line which adds to the lightness and grace of the house.

Upon the opposite side the other portico is a little less imposing, but more sylvan, deeply recessed into the red edifice and cut into white blocks around the three fine arched windows there, which come down to the platform. These blocks seemed to me to be of stone. By using wax or enamel in painting them, the effect of the magnolian white against the large sized deep red bricks is in better contrast than ever before. The white woodwork of Monticello is a fairy composition with the red walls.

The dome or ball room is only over the true front, or least visited, portico.

Under the quieter portico are many easy chairs of rattan. This porch seems to add a third room to the width. The straight lines and thoroughly habilitated interior promise to keep Monticello up some hundreds of years.

On the east side are some small sharp dormers almost hidden behind the coping. Five chimneys are seen, two of which in the conical roof are ventilation shafts.

Here the two small windows on each side of the portico support two smaller ones in the visible attic above them. Rich ivy covers the south wing.

Beech trees on the lawn had been grafted upon poplars, etc. The oaks, tulips, pines, are still rugged and protecting.

Sometimes the winds here are solemn as a storm playing an orchestra.

The descent of night upon the lofty mountain leaves the soul above the earth, and then comes a security of height, a peace of intercourse delightfully mutual.

The many white marble friezes in the mantel pieces disclose their faces in the gloaming. They are supernumerary now, whilst steam, as upon a steamship, fills all the former chilliness.

The present proprietor is a reminder of Jefferson's figure, slender and tall, as he talks with unvarying support, of the maker of Monticello.

I did not notice till morning how I had forgotten our helplessness at that woody eyrie. Something social took off the lonely and superstitious. Jefferson left no ghosts.

I lay in bed by a bright small lamp and read of the housebuilder till I fell asleep as in some age without violence.

My coffee brought to me at morn, I looked about my room—the Adams room.

It had grown in the night from its unobtrusive sufficiency. It was eighteen feet square with a protruding chimney, mantel and fireplace six feet wide, and a recessed bed alcove, seven feet by five, formerly slatted, so as to dispense with bedsteads.

The present stairways are two sky-lighted wells, six feet by seven, up which the stairs go steeply, the steps not two feet wide, and are balustered in square segments with frequent turns and landings.

My bedroom had three square marble tiles before the fire-place; the floor was hard pine boards; the mantel a board; the bed recess now a wardrobe; the vestibule entrance between the alcove and the angle, carpentered over the two recesses and the cornice around the room deeply rimmed. The two windows, about four feet high, were set a few inches from the floor, with wide sills in the brick wall, and leaving room above for maps or pictures. One window opened under the ceiling of the east porch.

As the room was studied, it appeared that it had a charming art as to the effects of opposites. As at present furnished, it is a French bed-chamber, with a dark red velvet *portière* drawn across the bed alcove, to match the red door, and a silken red screen covers the fire-place. The red window *portières* ride on brass rods, the floor is stained brown, the walls tapestried in ribbed cloth of drab and ecru, with the bedstead covered with the same. Bedstead and bureau are lace-canopied. The treatment is French, abreast of Jefferson's administration.

Outside the vestibule is a closed hall, 25 feet by 6, at the far end of which is the toilet, a triumph over Jefferson's age in its beautiful plumbing. The bedrooms in this house seldom have door transoms.

Each half hall, above, opens through a wide door upon the great central room and the beautiful balcony, which is pentagonal. The two halls face each other across the 30 feet span, which is the balcony's width, its sides 18 feet long, squared opposite the doors, and balustered fairly and airily.

The moulding around this square vestibule is a yard wide with a Greco-Assyrian frieze. A model of Commodore Levy's war vessel, the *Macedonian,* is up in the balcony, full-rigged. Opposite to it, over the central of three high glass doors, is Jefferson's celebrated square clock with a pediment, connected by cords with pulleys in the corners and ball weights near the floor. On one side are calendar strips to show the dates, on the other a fox and geese ladder which folds up into a pole and opens to be the ascent to wind the clock. On one side of the door is Cerrachi's bust of Hamilton in marble; on the other side, Washington. Jefferson, by the same regicide sculptor, is on a pedestal nearer Washington. Franklin, by Powers, is near Jefferson. Henry Clay is between Jefferson and Washington—a handsome bronze statuette. A full suit of armor with lance and shield in hand is here. A large flying eagle flattened into the ceiling suspends the chandelier.

Visitors to Monticello multiply rather than diminish. The bed rooms are named for Lafayette, Madison, Adams, Monroe, etc., and are about 15 in number. The extensive cellar was said to have been divided into rooms to house the commoner constituents who considered their vote to have been worth a tavern bill.

This cellar is said to have had tunnels from it to convey the sewerage out to pits, by earth cars, and two air shafts still run up from cellar to vent chimneys in the wings. Of the five visible chimneys above the cone roof, two are air shafts.

Modern plumbing has come to the rescue of those old *cul de sac* air toilets. The large cisterns on the lawn are supplemented by an engine which drives up soft sandstone water 300 feet from a spring.

Trap rock under the mountain is supplying broken stone for an experimental road up from Charlottesville, which starts and keeps a high grade. Mr. Jefferson Monroe Levy had previously graded Jefferson's old road at large expense, ramparting the embankments with red stone walls.

In addition to his relative, John Randolph, Daniel Webster in 1824, and nearly all of the Southern school of public men, William H. Seward drove here from Auburn with his wife via the Natural Bridge several years before the war. George H. Pendleton, grandson of Hamilton's second in that fatal duel, I heard address the University of Virginia in 1869-70.

Since Mr. Jefferson Monroe Levy has reoccupied Monticello, almost all the statesmen have been here: Vice President Stevenson and the whole Senate, Samuel J. Randall and Grover Cleveland, and McKinley was booked to come the week after he died. Tom Reed was given a garden party on the lawn: "This is my joy," he exclaimed, "pretty girls!" Blaine slept here and said, going away: "I want you, Mr. Levy, to know that, though a Republican, I am a follower of Jefferson."

"He ought to have been President," said Mr. Levy to me. "He was the ablest of the Republicans."

William J. Bryan came to Monticello while a member of Congress, and Mr. Levy predicted to him that he would be nominated for President, but believed he would lead the party astray and lose it. Bryan said he would bolt the party if it negatived silver. "That would justify others in doing the same," said Mr. Levy.

Jefferson stopped the coinage of silver.

When I was here in 1869, an employee of the University told me he had seen Jefferson, Madison, and Monroe walking together across the college campus.

The college now has 600 pupils, and a new facade of temples to the south made of stone. The old part is the most purely academic quadrangle to be seen anywhere. It had suggestions from the famous school of Montpellier in France, whence Madison named his villa.

The alcove beds, which were all over Monticello, have been removed, as to the slats, which were fixed from hooks in them, but the alcoves remain.

To ascend to the ball room in the dome by these eighteen-inch stairs must have been awkward for ladies.

Jefferson's bed alcove, a deep, square opening which had entry to the bed from both the study and the bedroom, still remains, but in the bedroom are now twin French bedsteads of blue and gold. His secretary table is new. The old brackets for his globes are there.

The floors of this house are filled in with brick, the drawing-room is in squares of hard wood.

Monticello is not an extensive mansion, but an artistic one.

The lawn is six acres—a truncation or razeeing of the mountain.

An enthusiastic amateur with books, Jefferson's admiration for architecture was tried upon this house, afterward upon the Capitol at Washington and the University of Virginia. Jefferson was only a hold-over governor when the legislature met at Charlottesville and his term had expired three days when Tarleton's troopers simultaneously seized the villa and the town.

To me, Monticello looks as if Jefferson completed it after he had been to France. As he is said to have been thirty years building it, and as he had ordered window sash for it in London as the Revolution broke out, I judge that the Nineteenth Century had arrived before he was done building it.

He left Virginia in 1784, left the Cabinet in 1794, and Parton says that in the latter year "the house was unfinished, and its incompleteness made conspicuous by the rude way in which it was covered up." He was building till 1797-98, endeavoring to improve upon his original designs from what he had seen in Europe.

Indeed, while Secretary of State, he had been transported by the model of the Philadelphia Library, which had a central pediment, pilasters, and upon the roof, a balustrade.

While sitting in Monticello, Mr. Lyman, formerly of Buffalo, New York, said to me: "The best houses in Virginia are *not* in the tide-water counties, and were built after the Revolution, generally in the first quarter of the Nineteenth Century; they are to be found in Albemarle, Fluvanna, Greene, Nelson, and a few other western counties. The statesmen of the period were so abstracted in making a government and institutions that they let their private affairs go to pieces."

Mrs. Jefferson died in the fall of 1782, leaving three children.

The condition of the White House, when President Adams occupied it, was probably not different from Monticello at the same time—space unfinished, ideas still half executed.

But the sequel was triumphant—a home like Olympus, where the political Jove for a quarter of a century fulminated from the clouds. He cut his timber on the mountain top, baked his bricks there from the basic red clay, and made his nails in the nailery which still rears its chimney and forge fire place, luxuriant in English ivy, on the precipitous approach.

Jefferson made his house as he made his Government, which he worked out for a quarter of a century. The one is the unit or model of the other.

Jefferson resigned from Washington's cabinet a year after the execution of Louis XVI. In two years he was elected Vice-President. When he left the Presidency he owed $8,000 in Washington and had to make a loan in a Richmond bank. He then built a house at Poplar Forest, Bedford county, to be rid of the slavery of entertaining summer constituents.

He lived seventeen years in declining prosperity, partly caused by his own Embargo and other measures.

As Washington located the Capital at Alexandria, Jefferson, a quarter of a century later, put the University of Virginia at Charlottesville, at a State cost of $320,000; it was opened the year before he died.

Meantime Jefferson had sold his library to Congress for $23,000. His endorsement was protested for $20,000. About $17,000 was raised for him as a gift by New York, Philadelphia and Baltimore.

"This is the Fourth!" were said to be nearly his last words. With $20,000 contributed to his daughter, his debts were paid, making about $60,000 contributed to the family in money.

Monticello was sold to perhaps the only man in the country who had both the means and devotion to keep it up.

Commodore Levy invited all the posterity of Jefferson he could reach to come and dine with him, and at dinner, rising, said: "I leave the table to you. Your bedchambers will be found ready for you as when you lived here."

This was the last reunion of the family, some seventy years ago.

In the concentrated privacy of Monticello, looking from its height upon the whole associations of Jefferson's birth and youth—upon Shadwell, Edge Hill, Tufton—I began to perceive the man, whose many ideas and excursions had given him before to me, a chameleon, spectrum variability.

At Williamsburg, in Philadelphia, in Paris, at Washington, he had flitted, to my conception, like a satellite of three different Revolutions—the American, the French, and the Democratic.

Now, like the bones of the Mastodon which he took in his carriage when going to be Vice-President at Philadelphia, he reassembled his disjointed parts.

He seemed a continuation of General Washington, not the passive, derivative vestryman but the urgent, scintillating spirit, projecting into the future society.

And there is no doubt that Jefferson's influence in the present is from his scientific liberality, the very thing he was attacked for from the orthodox point of view.

He welcomed the innovations which carry liberty, trust and materialism onward, and that is his pedestal, rearing him like Monticello's height, to grander panoramas and the continental scope.

He also explored the West through his secretary, Lewis, who was the landscape beneath him.

The West was Physics, while the East was Dogma.

As Gibbon wrote to Dr. Priestly, the theologically perverted scientist: "Give me leave to convey to your ear the almost unanimous and not offensive wish of the philosophic world, that you would confine your talents and industry to those sciences in which real and useful improvements can be made."

So Jefferson helped the material sciences.

He was as mathematical as Hamilton, but upon the physical side. He followed Copernicus instead of Calvin. In his study still stand the brackets which held two globes.

He preceded the Signal Service with meteorological observations and records, almost a hundred years.

The superiority of Hamilton to Jefferson was in scientific book-keeping; of Jefferson to Hamilton in the study of the Arcana, including Man.

Commercial exactness, natural experiment, make the great United States; Hamilton and Jefferson were the two pillars of Hercules.

I walked back to the graveyard, some seven or eight hundred feet from the house, on the decline toward the higher mountain, in the natural woods.

Without much order the Randolphs are buried here under slabs flat on the ground or standing dispersed, the obeliskish, gray granite monument of Jefferson near the gate corner.

The new gate is already lock-broken; a little gate with a spring would have been wise.

As the spring birds sang, I comprehended the juvenility of life.

This often-shrinking man, without the speech-making confidence, retiring many times from the storms of state, still loved Nature only as associated with Man.

The compass of his imagination was exploring the unknown West.

After acquiring Louisiana he sent off Lewis, Clarke, and Pike, and encouraged Astor to commercialize the vast interior.

It seemed to me that his eagle spirit deserved as much recognition as his toleration and his University.

Commodore Levy not only saved Jefferson's home but his form and lineaments.

John Quincy Adams writes:

"March 25, 1834, the Speaker (John Bell) laid before the House a letter from Lieutenant Uriah P. Levy, of the Navy of the United States, offering as a present a colossal bronze statue of Thomas Jefferson, executed at Paris by the celebrated David and (by) Honoré Ganon, which communication was referred to the Committee on the Library."

Lafayette superintended the modelling of this statue.

David was then professor of Art in Paris.

The statue was not rejected, as many books, like Ben: Perley Poore's, say, but was placed before the White House, and is now in the Capitol, and is the best of Jefferson's portraits, so pronounced by Brown, the sculptor, as well as the best piece of art in Washington.

GATH.

NOTES UPON THE SALE OF MONTICELLO.

Commodore Levy travelled to Monticello from Washington in his own coach with postilions. The picture of the gold box presented to him by the Councils of New York indicates his respect and popularity in the city of his fathers from the middle of the Seventeenth Century.

"If I remember aright, the deed from Barclay to my uncle was about 1832. I remember that there was a legal controversy between Barclay and Commodore Levy as to the number of acres in the property, and the courts at that time gave possession to the Commodore on payment of the purchase price, and the deed was held in abeyance until the question of acreage was settled. Therefore the deed was not delivered until one or two years after the actual purchase and possession. It may have been 1833 instead of 1832, but it was somewhere about that date."— *Memorandum of Hon. J. M. Levy,* 1902.

The Virginia *Advocate,* published at Charlottesville, attacked in the fall of 1827 "the disagreeable intrusions and impertinent investigations of prying visitors to Monticello who seem to regard the domicil and its contents as though it was an inn—to rummage everything from garret to cellar, run their noses into every corner that was open or could be opened, and to intrude upon the privacy of the family without ever asking permission."

Mr. Thomas Jefferson Coolidge was born August 26, 1831, yet is said in a late book called "The True Jefferson" to have intended to purchase Monticello in 1832.

Hardly a dissenting vote was given to the resolutions of South Carolina voting $10,000 to the legal representatives of Mr. Jefferson for the benefit of his right heirs, in December, 1826.

There was no competitor of public spirit to Commodore Levy in the purchase of Monticello.

Henry Lee, half brother and elder of Robert E. Lee, was at Monticello a few days before Jefferson's death and wrote:

"You remember the alcove in which he slept? There he was extended, feeble, prostrate, but the fine and clear expression of his countenance not all obscured. At one time he became so cheerful as to smile, even to laughing, at a remark I made. He alluded to the probability of his death as a man would to the prospect of being caught in a shower—as an event not to be desired, but not to be feared. I observed that he kept the flies off himself, and he seemed to decline assistance from his attendants. He was exceedingly averse to giving trouble."

General Jacob Brown, the hero of Lundy's Lane, and John A. Dix, of New York, visited Monticello several years before Jefferson's death. General Dix sketched the house on paper, as a faultless specimen of Italian architecture, and Jefferson, looking over young Dix's shoulder, said, "Very exact."—*Life of John A. Dix, by his son.*

NOTE UPON COMMODORE LEVY AND W.H. CRAWFORD

The fact that Commodore Levy, when under age, was on the *Argus*, which delivered Minister Crawford to France, becomes interesting at Monticello from the fact that Mr. Crawford was the last Jeffersonian regular candidate for the Presidency, and was Mr. Jefferson's choice in 1824. "He gave me at Monticello," said Governor Edward Coles, of Illinois, "the decided preference to Mr. Crawford, and said it was greatly to be regretted that he should have lost his health and, with it, the election."

NOTES ON FLOGGING IN THE NAVY.

The personal example in his fleet and upon his ship of Commodore Levy laying flogging aside, long before it was abolished by law, started the agitation which was only efficacious in 1850, and white men were flogged to within twelve years of the abolition of slavery. Commodore Stockton's celebrated speech in the Senate refers to flogging as having been for some time a subject of indignation.

Commodore Stockton entered the Navy 1811, Commodore Levy 1812.

The life of Stockton, published when he was a candidate for President, 1856, said: "His speech on flogging in the Navy absolutely *terminated* all controversy on the subject. The abolition of flogging *had other able champions*, but the *testimony* of Commodore Stockton in favor of the abandonment of the practice settled the question.

Mr. Jefferson had been dead some months before the city of Baltimore and State of Maryland assented to the citizenizing of Hebrews, and till that time females were imprisoned for debt in the State which enacted the first toleration.

The agitators, Lundy and Garrison, soon followed with their *abolition* newspaper in Baltimore, which was continued elsewhere till slavery ceased. Thus *abolition* of all the forms of unequal laws and laws of severity had a sequential relationship, and probably the beginning of the end of all of them was Commodore Levy's denunciation of the lash for American sailors. So says the scroll he holds in his hand in the portrait at Monticello, "Author of the Abolition."

The Thirtieth Congress in 1848, required by law that the Secretary of the Navy give them "the number of persons in the naval service flogged in each of the years 1846 and 1847, specifying the name of the ship, the offence, the sentence, and the number of lashes inflicted; and it shall be his duty to make a similar report for each year thereafter." This act let in the light upon the relative brutality of commanders.

The *Cyane*, Commander Dupont, had eight whippings in two months of 1847—57 lashes of the cat. On the ship *Warren* were whipped 22 men; on the *Jamestown*, 48 men; on the *Germantown*, 37 men; on the *Plymouth*, 19 men; on the *Decatur*, 5; *Brandywine*, 5; *Ohio*, 44; *Marion*, 43; *Preble*, 10; *Cumberland*, 70; *Congress*, 23; *Dale* 10; *United States* 77; nearly all the maximum 12 lashes.

The Thirty-first Congress in 1850 put a proviso to a mail subsidy bill—"provided, that flogging in the Navy and on board vessels of commerce be, and the same is hereby, abolished from and after the passage of this act."

NOTE ON COMMODORE LEVY'S GIFT OF A STATUE OF JEFFERSON.

The civil war threw the fame of Jefferson temporarily in the background, and it was kept alive by such private efforts as have been here recorded. Northern pilgrims to Monticello gave liberally to extend and support the University of Virginia, in which is one of the very few statues of Mr. Jefferson, whose likenesses are of a variable standard. Hiram Powers, in 1863, executed a marble Jefferson for the wings of the American Capitol, which has not often been exploited. Its exaggerated prettiness was the other extreme from the heaviness, perhaps clumsiness, of the statue in the University. But when his statue of General Winfield Scott was being placed in position in Washington City, after the civil war, Henry K. Brown, the sculptor of that fine Washington on horseback, at Union Square, New York, was strolling, around the public grounds and came upon a statue of Jefferson he had never heard of. He rubbed into the verdigris which encoated it and saw the name of David of Angers, the graceful sculptor of Anjou, who made the figures for the Pantheon's pediment in Paris and Marco Bozzaris for Greece. "Here," said Mr. Brown, "is your best piece of sculpture at the Capitol City and by the best master of the art. Why do you banish it to a garden? Put it in your Capitol!" This statue had been presented by Commodore Uriah P. Levy to Congress nearly forty years before. It never was rejected, as has been said, but its artistic quality was undiscovered till the bold native sculptor spoke. Since that time the statue has been cleaned and placed in the Areopagus of statuary in the old Hall of Representatives, of which it is the dean, following only Hondon's Washington. It puts Commodore Levy's devotion to Jefferson in the story of the Arts.

Wm. H. Seward's letters say: "The subject of our visit to Monticello was mentioned to President Jackson. You are to know, by the way, that Lieutenant Levy, the present proprietor of Monticello (1835), has procured a bronze statue of Mr. Jefferson, to be made at Paris and presented to Congress. The House of Representatives voted to accept it; the Senate has not yet acted on the subject. * * * 'It is an excellent likeness, sir,' said General Jackson."

Thus Seward, the Northern Jefferson, nine years after Jefferson's death, leaves a trace of the condition of Monticello under its New York preserver, saying in his domestic letters: "The estate, after passing through the hands of an intermediate owner, came to be the property of Mr. Levy, of New York, a lieutenant in the navy. From Monticello is one of the most glorious prospects I ever looked upon. The annual expense of keeping the edifice and its appurtenances in repair must have been very great. Although neglected it is still a magnificent place."

Jefferson's dining-room, in its blind pantry and dumb-waiter arrangements, its wine closet and bottle lift, is artfully contrived. Just outside the dining-room, behind glass, is the tea room. He was frugal, but loved wines. Three opportunities established the influence of Jefferson: writing the Declaration, studying France and Europe with the eye, and becoming the head of Washington's cabinet.

CREDITS

Cover graphic from Civil War Stationery, Special Collections, University of Delaware Library, Newark, Delaware 19716.

Frontispiece portrait: George Alfred Townsend, Historical Society of Delaware, 505 Market Street, Wilmington, DE 19801

(Page opposite frontispiece) Anonymous Quote: From a loose newspaper clipping, Special Collections, George Alfred Townsend Collection, Maryland State Archives, MSA SC 684.

(Introduction) Cigar wrapper Graphic from the Townsend Papers, Special Collection, Maryland State Archives, MSA SC 684.

(Opposite page 1) The Reverend and Mrs. Stephen Townsend, Photocopy from the Townsend Papers, University of Delaware Library, Newark, Delaware 19716.

Page 3. Newark Academy, late 1800s. Purnell Collection, Delaware State Archives, Dover, Delaware 19903.

Page 21. *Lt. Gen. U. S. Grant and His Generals*, John Durand & Company, New York, 1865.

Page 34. Political Rally in Georgetown, Delaware, from the Purnell Collection, Delaware State Archives, Dover, Delaware 19903.

Page 39. Memorial to Civil War Correspondents in Gathland State Park, Maryland. Copy of a newspaper photograph, Townsend Papers, Special Collections, University of Delaware Library, Newark, Delaware 19716.

Page 45. Graphic of the Rev. George Foot of Old Drawyers Church, Odessa, Delaware, whose address "embracing the Early History of Delaware" was delivered in the Church on May 10, 1842. From Townsend papers, University of Delaware Library, Newark, Delaware, 19716.

Page 51. Notice of Lecture delivered while GAT was a student at Central High School in Philadelphia. From Special Collections, Townsend Collection, Maryland State Archives, Annapolis, Maryland, 21401, MSA SC 684.

Page 57. Political Cartoon from Special Collections, the Townsend Collection, "Posters & Prospectuses on books and lectures," Maryland State Archives, Annapolis, Maryland 21401, MSA SC 684.

Page 71. President Rutherford B. Hayes. *The Life of Rutherford B. Hayes, 19th President of the United States*, Volume 1, Charles Richard Williams, Houghton Mifflin Company, Boston, 1914.

Page 78. This genealogy was copied from the work of Ruthanna Hindes, in her 1946 biography of George Alfred Townsend, *George Alfred Townsend: One of Delaware's Greatest Writers*, Hambleton Printing & Publishing Co., Wilmington 99, Delaware.

Page 84. Chief Justice Roger Taney. (Chicago Historical Society, Negative ICHi. 12644) as printed in *The Civil War: Brother Against Brother, The War Begins*. William C. Davis, Time-Life Books, Alexandria, VA, 1983.

Page 89. Frontispiece, *The Life of Charles A. Dana*, James Harrison Wilson, LL.D, Harper and Brothers, New York, 1908.

Page 101. President James Abrams Garfield, from General Collection: Portraits, Delaware State Archives.

Page 118. Gaines's Mill Battlefield, Map drawn by Donald Wildham in August, 1929, to accompany a study by Colonel H.K. Landers, Historical Section, Army War College, Map Division, Library of Congress. From *Civil War Times Illustrated*, Volume III, Cowles Magazine, Harrisburg, PA 1964-1965.

Page 121. Battle of the Chickahominy, *Pictorial Battles of the Civil War*, Volume I, Sherman Publishing Company, New York, 1885.

Page 130. From the Pierce Family Papers, Special Collections, University of Delaware Library, Newark, Delaware 19716

Page 144. Civil War Stationery Graphic, Fulton Letters. University of Delaware Library, Newark, Delaware 19716.

Page 146. Illustration of John Wilkes Booth and
Page 148. graphic of Ford's Theatre from *The Life, Crime, and Capture of John Wilkes Booth*, GAT, Dick and Fitzgerald, Publishers, New York, 1865.

Page 188. Civil War graphic with poem from Stationery, Special Collections, University of Delaware Library, Newark, Delaware, 19716.

Page 190. *Guiseppe Garibaldi and the Making of Italy*, George Macaulay Trevelyan, O.M., Longmans, Green and Company, London, 1948.

Page 191. Drawing of Garibaldi's home on Staten Island, from *Century*, 1907. Reprinted in *American Heritage*, Volume XXVI, No. 6, October 1975, American Heritage Publishing Company, a subsidiary of McGraw-Hill, Inc.

Page 228. Abraham Lincoln. General Collection: Portraits, Delaware State Archives, deValinger, Jr. Hall of Records, Dover, DE 19903.

Page 242. Brigham Young. Copyright by the Latter Day Saints Church. Latter Day Saints Visual Resource Library, 50 E.N. Temple, Salt Lake City, Utah 84150.

Page 274. From Civil War Stationery, D. Lilley letters, Special Collections, University of Delaware Library, Newark, Delaware 19716.

Page 276. John M. Clayton, General Collections: Portraits, Delaware State Archives, Dover, Delaware 19903.

Page 283. Parson Thorne Mansion in Milford, Delaware. (Photograph by Daugherty) Purnell Collection, Delaware State Archives, Dover, Delaware 19903.

Page 286. Walnut Street (South from Front) in Milford, Delaware, late 1800s, as it might have looked when Clayton visited his mother. (Photograph by Daugherty) Purnell Collection, Delaware State Archives, Dover, Delaware, 19903.

Page 291. Chew mansion on the Green in Dover. Purnell Collection, Delaware State Archives, Dover, Delaware 19903.

Page 314. Photograph of George Alfred Townsend from the Townsend Collection, University of Delaware Library, Newark, DE 19716

Page 326. A drawing of one of the Lowery Bandits of North Carolina, from *The Swamp Outlaws*, by George Alfred Townsend, Robert M. DeWitt, Publisher, New York, 1872.

Page 340. Entire edited manuscript of "The Last Requiem" in Special Collections, the Townsend Collection, University of Delaware, Newark, Delaware 19716.

Page 348. The Western Front, *The Domestic Life of Thomas Jefferson*. Compiled from Family Letters and Reminiscences, by his great-granddaughter Sarah N. Randolph. Harper & Brothers, Publishers, New York, 1872.

Page 350. Frontispiece, *The Life and Letters of Thomas Jefferson*, Francis W. Hirst, The Macmillan Company, New York, 1926.